INFAMY

Books by John Toland

INFAMY: PEARL HARBOR AND ITS AFTERMATH

NO MAN'S LAND

HITLER: THE PICTORIAL DOCUMENTARY OF HIS LIFE

ADOLF HITLER

THE RISING SUN

THE LAST 100 DAYS

THE DILLINGER DAYS

BUT NOT IN SHAME

BATTLE: THE STORY OF THE BULGE

SHIPS IN THE SKY

INFAMY

Pearl Harbor
and Its Aftermath

JOHN TOLAND

METHUEN

Maps by Rafael Palacios

Memoirs of Admiral Thomas C. Hart, Admiral H. Kent Hewitt and Frances Perkins at the Oral History Research Office, Columbia University by permission of the Trustees of Columbia University in the City of New York, 1972.

No copyright is claimed on material used from U. S. Navy Department records.

First published in Great Britain 1982 by
Methuen London Ltd
11 New Fetter Lane, London EC4P 4EE

Copyright © 1982 John Toland

ISBN 0 413 49820 4

Printed in Great Britain by
Richard Clay (The Chaucer Press) Ltd,
Bungay, Suffolk

To the Victims of Pearl Harbor

Contents

Part 3   Congress Dances

Part 4   The Tenth Investigation

Cast of Principal Characters

BEFORE PEARL HARBOR

Washington
Franklin Delano Roosevelt, President of the United States
Cordell Hull, Secretary of State
Henry L. Stimson, Secretary of War
Frank Knox, Secretary of the Navy
Harry Hopkins, the President's adviser and confidant
Harold L. Ickes, Secretary of the Interior
Frances Perkins, Secretary of Labor
Admiral Kichisaburo Nomura, Japanese ambassador
Saburo Kurusu, Japanese special envoy
Captain Johan E. M. Ranneft, Netherlands naval attaché
Colonel F. G. L. Weijerman, Netherlands military attaché
Dr. Alexander Loudon, Netherlands minister

U. S. Navy Department
Admiral Harold R. Stark, Chief of Naval Operations
Rear Admiral Royal E. Ingersoll, Assistant Chief, Naval Operations
Rear Admiral Richmond Kelly Turner, Chief, War Plans Division
Rear Admiral Leigh Noyes, Chief, Communications Division
Commander Laurance Safford, Chief, Security Intelligence Communications (Op-20-G)
Rear Admiral Theodore Stark Wilkinson, Chief, Intelligence Division, Office of Naval Intelligence (O.N.I.)

Lieutenant Commander Alwin Kramer, Chief, Translation Section, O.N.I. (attached to Op-20-G)
Commander Arthur H. McCollum, Chief, Far Eastern Section, O.N.I.
Captain John Beardall, White House naval aide
Lieutenant Lester Robert Schulz, assistant to Beardall as White House communications duty officer

War Department
General George Catlett Marshall, Chief of Staff
Major General H. H. Arnold, Deputy Chief of Staff for Air
Colonel Walter Bedell Smith, Secretary, General Staff
Brigadier General Leonard T. Gerow, Chief, War Plans Division
Brigadier General Sherman Miles, Chief of Intelligence (G-2)
Colonel Rufus S. Bratton, head, Far Eastern Section (G-2)
Colonel Otis K. Sadtler, Signal Corps, operations officer
William F. Friedman, chief cryptographer, Signal Intelligence Service (S.I.S.)

Honolulu
Robert L. Shivers, agent in charge, F.B.I.
Lieutenant John A. Burns, head, Honolulu Police Espionage Bureau
Nagao Kita, Japanese consul general
Ensign Takeo Yoshikawa, Japanese naval spy

Hawaiian Department
Lieutenant General Walter C. Short, Commanding General

United States Pacific Fleet
Admiral Husband E. Kimmel, Commander in Chief
Lieutenant Commander Edwin T. Layton, fleet intelligence officer

Fourteenth Naval District (Pearl Harbor)
Rear Admiral Claude C. Bloch, Commandant
Lieutenant Commander Joseph J. Rochefort, Communications Security Unit

San Francisco
Captain Richard T. McCollough, Chief, Intelligence, Twelfth Naval District
Lieutenant Ellsworth A. Hosner, an assistant
Seaman First Class Z, Hosner's assistant

Station M: The U. S. Navy's East Coast Intercept Installation
Ralph T. Briggs, one of the qualified operators assigned to monitor Japanese intercepts
Chief Radioman DW, his superior

Java
General Hein Ter Poorten, Commander in Chief, Netherlands East Indies Army
Dr. Walter Foote, U.S. consul general
Brigadier General Elliott Thorpe, U.S. military observer

Others
Admiral James O. Richardson, Kimmel's predecessor
Dusko Popov, British double agent, code-named "Tricycle"
Kilsoo Haan, agent for the Sino-Korean People's League
Major Warren J. Clear, U. S. Army intelligence agent in the Far East
Captain and Mrs. Harold D. Krick, close friends of Admiral Stark
Tyler Gatewood Kent, code clerk at the U. S. Embassy, London
Dr. Henry Field, special assistant to President Roosevelt
C. A. Berndtson, Commodore of the Matson Fleet and commander of the S.S. *Lurline*
Rudy Asplund, chief radio operator, *Lurline*
Leslie E. Grogan, first assistant radio operator, *Lurline*

AFTER PEARL HARBOR
Admiral Ernest J. King, Stark's successor and Commander in Chief of the U. S. Fleets
Admiral Chester W. Nimitz, Kimmel's successor
James V. Forrestal, Knox's successor

Harry S. Truman, Roosevelt's successor
Thomas K. Kimmel, Kimmel's son
Edward Kimmel, Kimmel's son
Manning Kimmel, Kimmel's son
Charles B. Rugg, Kimmel's chief counsel
Lieutenant Edward B. Hanify, USNR, Kimmel's assistant counsel
Captain Robert A. Lavender, U. S. Navy, Retired, Kimmel's assist-
    ant counsel
Admiral Thomas Hart, U. S. Navy, Retired, Stark's counsel
Lieutenant David W. Richmond, USNR, Stark's assistant counsel
Captain Robert Diggs, Marshall's counsel
Percy L. Greaves, Jr., chief of minority staff during Joint Com-
    mittee hearings

The Nine Investigations
1. Knox personal inquiry   December 11–12, 1941
2. Roberts Commission   December 18, 1941,
                                        to January 23, 1942
    Associate Justice Owen J. Roberts, U. S. Supreme Court,
        Chairman
    Admiral William H. Standley, U. S. Navy, Retired, member
    Rear Admiral Joseph M. Reeves, U. S. Navy, Retired, member
    Major General Frank R. McCoy, U. S. Army, Retired, mem-
        ber
    Brigadier General Joseph T. McNarney, U. S. Army, member
3. Hart Inquiry   February 22 to June 15, 1944
    Conducted by Admiral Thomas C. Hart, U. S. Navy, Retired
4. Navy Court of Inquiry   July 24 to
                                        September 27, 1944
    Admiral Orin G. Murfin, U. S. Navy, Retired, President
    Admiral Edward C. Kalbfus, U. S. Navy, Retired, member
    Vice Admiral Adolphus Andrews, U. S. Navy, Retired,
        member
    Commander Harold Biesemeier, judge advocate
5. Army Pearl Harbor Board   August 7 to October 6, 1944
    Lieutenant General George Grunert, President
    Major General Henry D. Russell, member
    Major General Walter H. Frank, member

6. Clarke Investigation   September 20, 1944
                                            to August 4, 1945
      Conducted by Colonel Carter W. Clarke, U. S. Army
7. Clausen Investigation   January 24
                                            to September 12, 1945
      Conducted by Major (later Lieutenant Colonel) Henry C.
      Clausen, JAGD
8. Hewitt Inquiry   May 14 to July 11, 1945
      Conducted by Admiral H. Kent Hewitt, U. S. Navy
      Counsel: John F. Sonnett
      Assistant Counsel: Lieutenant John Ford Baecher, USNR
9. Joint Congressional Committee on the Investigation of the
      Pearl Harbor Attack   November 15, 1945
                                            to May 31, 1946
      Alben Barkley, senator from Kentucky, Chairman (D)
      Jere Cooper, representative from Tennessee, Vice Chairman
         (D)
      Walter F. George, senator from Georgia (D)
      Scott W. Lucas, senator from Illinois (D)
      Owen Brewster, senator from Maine (R)
      Homer Ferguson, senator from Michigan (R)
      J. Bayard Clark, representative from North Carolina (D)
      John W. Murphy, representative from Pennsylvania (D)
      Bertrand W. Gearhart, representative from California (R)
      Frank B. Keefe, representative from Wisconsin (R)
      William D. Mitchell, general counsel (through January 14,
         1946)
      Gerhard A. Gesell, chief assistant counsel (through January
         14, 1946)
      Seth W. Richardson, general counsel (after January 14,
         1946)
      Samuel H. Kaufman, associate general counsel (after January
         14, 1946)

Foreword

In *But Not in Shame* I concluded that every American would have to accept a share of the blame for the disastrous attack on Pearl Harbor, and that it had been a largely unprovoked act of Japanese aggression. Nine years later, after considerable research in Japan, I came to the startling conclusion in *The Rising Sun* that Pearl Harbor had been the result of American as well as Japanese miscalculations and mistakes. "A war that need not have been fought was about to be fought because of mutual misunderstanding, language difficulties, and mistranslations as well as Japanese opportunism, *gekokujo*, irrationality, honor, pride and fear—and American racial prejudice, distrust, ignorance of the Orient, rigidity, self-righteousness, honor, national pride and fear." At that time I saw no villains or heroes on either side and could not, above all, believe that President Roosevelt knew ahead of time that a Japanese striking force was approaching Pearl Harbor.

Even so, many aspects of Pearl Harbor had troubled me. The various investigations left too many crucial questions in doubt and in limbo. Was it possible that Roosevelt had engineered a conspiracy to get America into the war with Hitler by the back door? Had some of our military and civilian leaders lied under oath? Had some good men been persuaded or threatened into perjuring themselves? Had there truly been a "winds" execute message in early December 1941? Had the nine investigations, in short, been an elaborate cover-up to place the blame primarily on Admiral Kimmel and General Short while whitewashing those in Washington?

Forty years after the "date which will live in infamy," I have attempted to answer these and other questions that have been nagging Americans and Japanese all these years. Upon embarking on this quest I was warned that the recent wholesale release of controversial Pearl Harbor material under the Freedom of Information Act was a smoke screen and that the cover-up of Pearl Harbor was still in force. On the contrary I found the U. S. Navy and the National Security Agency not only open but helpful; they made only a few deletions of the highly controversial material submitted to them, and these only for security purposes.

And now into the murky depths of Pearl Harbor.

Part 1

TANGLED WEB

"Oh, what a tangled web we weave,
When first we practise to deceive!"

Sir Walter Scott

Chapter One

"HOW DID THEY CATCH US WITH OUR PANTS DOWN, MR. PRESIDENT?" DECEMBER 6–7, 1941

1.

On Saturday morning, December 6, 1941, one of the translators at Op-20-G, the Security Intelligence Section of U. S. Naval Communications, in Washington, D.C., began skimming through a pile of intercepted Japanese messages in the consular code. She came across one sent three days earlier from Consul General Kita in Honolulu to Tokyo, transmitting a scheme of signals regarding the movement and exact position of warships and carriers in Pearl Harbor. The translator, Mrs. Dorothy Edgers, had been on the job only a month but at first glance she thought it was important enough to be completed immediately. She asked the senior translator, Fred Woodrough—her brother—if she should remain after the noon closing time to finish the message. He thought it was "a crank deal" but of sufficient import to stay over. As she translated the details she became excited, for the message told about giving signals from the window of a certain house on Oahu to Japanese ships hiding offshore. Fascinated, she showed what she had written to the yeoman presiding over the six translators. It was "interesting," he said, but didn't warrant attention on a weekend.

Even so, Mrs. Edgers stayed at her desk and by 3 P.M. was finishing the message just as Lieutenant Commander Alwin Kramer, chief of the Translation Section, walked in. He had studied Japanese assiduously but Mrs. Edgers, like her brother, had been brought up near Tokyo and her command of the language was far superior. She waited expectantly while he read the entire telegram standing up. He seemed more annoyed than electrified even though the last paragraph read:

> If the above signals and wireless messages cannot be made from Oahu, then on Maui Island, 6 miles north to the northward of Kula Sanatorium . . . at a point halfway between Lower Kula Road and Haleskala Road (latitude 20°40′ N., longitude 156°19′ W., visible from seaward to the southeast and southwest of Maui Island) the following bonfires will be made daily until your EXEX signal is received; from 7 to 8, Signal 3 or 6, from 8 to 9, Signal 4 or 7, from 9 to 10, Signal 5 or 8.

Nicknamed "The Shadow," after the radio character, Kramer was tall and slender with a pencil mustache. He combined the traits of a dreamer with extreme punctiliousness. Every message that passed through his hands had to be meticulously, painstakingly corrected and recorrected. He told Mrs. Edgers the intercept needed a lot of work and she should run along home. They could finish editing it sometime next week. She protested but he politely insisted she leave.

Kramer himself was busy supervising the decryption of a long message in the Japanese code known as Purple. This was the most secret system used to transmit information between Tokyo and foreign embassies. First had arrived a pilot message from Tokyo alerting Ambassador Nomura to make ready to receive a crucial message—the answer to America's reply to Japan's final offer in the long negotiations between the two countries in an attempt to end their difficulties in peace, not war. Thirteen parts of a fourteen-part message that was in English were decrypted by dark and these made it obvious the Japanese were completely dissatisfied with the American reply, which was a repudiation of their offer.

As soon as President Franklin D. Roosevelt read these thirteen parts that evening, he turned to Harry Hopkins, his chief adviser, and said, "This means war."

Even so no warning was sent to Hawaii where the Pacific Fleet was based at Pearl Harbor. In fact, no Purple intercepts had been sent to the fleet's commander, Admiral Husband Kimmel, for months. Nor did he have a Purple machine which would have enabled his intelligence officers to read the series of disturbing messages being exchanged between Tokyo and Washington.

The message in the consular code that attracted Mrs. Edgers' interest had been intercepted in Hawaii by MS-5, a special Army monitoring station at Fort Shafter. But General Walter Short, the Army commander in Hawaii, had not been cleared for any of the decrypted Japanese messages known as Magic. Short did not even know of MS-5's existence. Nor had the Army major in charge of the station been given decrypting facilities. His orders were merely to ship the intercepts air mail to Washington in their original form.

The consul's message was by no means the only one that morning which indicated the Japanese might be planning a surprise attack on Pearl Harbor. Two months earlier S.I.S., the U. S. Army Signal Intelligence Service, had decrypted a message from Tokyo to Consul Kita dividing the waters of Pearl Harbor into five areas and asking for the exact locations of Kimmel's warships and carriers. Both Army and Navy intelligence officers in Washington guessed this could be a grid system for a bombing attack. Several of these men urged that Kimmel and Short be warned but for some reason their superiors would not allow this. Three other messages between Tokyo and Kita also indicated unusual Japanese interest in Pearl Harbor. One instructed Ensign Takeo Yoshikawa, a naval spy posing as one of Kita's assistants, to report all ship movements in Pearl Harbor "twice a week"; another ordered Yoshikawa to subject the fleet air bases on Oahu to special scrutiny; and a third, on November 8, requested information about strategic points around Honolulu. None of these messages was sent to Kimmel or Short. And there were eight other revealing telegrams which the overworked Americans had not yet had time to decrypt, including two sent December 6 by Yoshikawa. One listed ships presently anchored in Pearl Harbor, noting that it appeared no air reconnaissance was being conducted by the fleet air arm. The other reported that the battleships probably did not have torpedo nets, and also stated, "At the present time there are no signs of barrage balloon equipment. In addition, it is difficult to imagine that they have actually any. However, even though they have actually made preparations, because they must control the air over the water and lava runways of the airports in the vicinity of Pearl Harbor, Hickam, Ford, and Ewa, there are limits to the balloon defense of Pearl Harbor. I imagine that in all probability there is considerable opportunity left to take advantage for a surprise attack against these places."

These two messages were immediately monitored by MS-5 at Fort Shafter and started off on the erratic air route to Washington. Twice a subordinate naval intelligence officer in Washington had urged his superiors to allow Kimmel's intelligence officer to decrypt these consular messages upon reception at MS-5. Both times permisson had been refused on the grounds that such information was no business of Kimmel's.

What did Kimmel and Short know on December 6? For months they had been aware that war with Japan was not only a probability but undoubtedly a certainty, and both had been preparing their forces for battle. On November 27, the day after Secretary of State Cordell Hull sent his reply to Tokyo refusing to bow to Japan's unacceptable conditions, warnings from the two heads of the Army and Navy, General George Marshall and Admiral Harold R. "Betty" Stark, were sent to their commanders in the Philippines, the Panama Canal and Hawaii.[1]

General Douglas MacArthur in Manila got this message:
NEGOTIATIONS WITH THE JAPANESE APPEAR TO BE TERMINATED TO ALL PRACTICAL PURPOSES WITH ONLY THE BAREST POSSIBILITIES THAT THE JAPANESE GOVERNMENT MIGHT COME BACK AND OFFER TO CONTINUE PERIOD JAPANESE FUTURE ACTION UNPREDICTABLE BUT HOSTILE ACTION POSSIBLE AT ANY MOMENT PERIOD IF HOSTILI-

[1] Although the Army message bore Marshall's name, he was out of town and it was dispatched by Secretary of War Henry L. Stimson.

TIES CANNOT, REPEAT CANNOT, BE AVOIDED THE UNITED STATES DESIRES THAT JAPAN COMMIT THE FIRST OVERT ACT PERIOD THIS POLICY SHOULD NOT, REPEAT NOT, BE CONSTRUED AS RESTRICTING YOU TO A COURSE OF ACTION THAT MIGHT JEOPARDIZE YOUR DEFENSE. . . .

A similar message was sent to General Short but it also ordered him to do nothing "to alarm civil population or disclose intent." Short took all this to mean he should institute only a sabotage alert. He informed Washington of this but apparently nobody there read his reply carefully. He was never told he had missed the import of the instructions.

Stark dispatched to Kimmel and Admiral Thomas C. Hart, commander of the Asiatic Fleet in the Philippines, the same message:

THIS DISPATCH IS TO BE CONSIDERED A WAR WARNING X NEGOTIATIONS WITH JAPAN LOOKING TOWARD STABILIZATION OF CONDITIONS IN THE PACIFIC HAVE CEASED AND AN AGGRESSIVE MOVE BY JAPAN IS EXPECTED IN THE NEXT FEW DAYS X THE NUMBER AND EQUIPMENT OF JAPANESE TROOPS AND THE ORGANIZATION OF NAVAL TASK FORCES INDICATES AN AMPHIBIOUS EXPEDITION AGAINST EITHER THE PHILIPPINES THAI OR KRA PENINSULA OR POSSIBLY BORNEO X EXECUTE AN APPROPRIATE DEFENSIVE DEPLOYMENT PREPARATORY TO CARRYING OUT THE TASKS ASSIGNED IN WPL [WAR PLAN] 46 X. . . .

No other warning had been sent either Kimmel or Short and, on December 6, both assumed the negotiations were continuing.

Short, like Marshall, a graduate of V.M.I., was noted for his efficiency, and he had brought his troops to a high point of effectiveness. In his supervision of the Civilian Defense Force, he had shown his diplomatic ability to deal equably with local leaders while getting results.

Roosevelt had selected Kimmel over the heads of men who outranked him. Promoted to the temporary rank of full admiral, he was now one of the few four-star admirals in the Navy. Kimmel was known for his ability to get the best out of his subordinates. Brilliant, energetic and hard-boiled, he was a work horse who drove himself as hard as he did others. Curt, authoritative and

crusty, he had never strived to be loved by his men. But they respected him, for he was easy to get along with as long as they produced; and they knew he never demanded more of them than he
did of himself. He had left his wife in California upon taking over
command of the fleet in early 1941 so that he could dedicate all
his time and energy to whipping his forces into war readiness.
Kimmel had accomplished this by December 6. His fleet was
primed and eager to fight.

It was Short's responsibility to protect Oahu against enemy air
and sea attack and to provide short-range air reconnaissance while
Kimmel took care of long-range reconnaissance. By December 6
men and machines of both air arms were in poor shape after so
many missions. Both Kimmel and Short had been complaining for
months of shortages of personnel, planes and radar but Washington's main attention had gone to the Atlantic where American war
materials were being convoyed to England in the desperate fight
against Hitler. To make matters worse, most of the Flying
Fortresses which were to assist Kimmel in long-range reconnaissance had been sent on to the Philippines.

Kimmel and Short knew that the main Japanese carrier force
had left home waters only to disappear in late November. It was
assumed it was probably with the invasion force heading south
toward the Philippines, Thailand or the Kra Peninsula. On December 2 Kimmel was informed by his intelligence officer that the
carriers were still missing. If this disturbed Kimmel he didn't show
it; in fact, he facetiously asked, "Do you mean to say that they
could be rounding Diamond Head this minute and you wouldn't
know?"

"I hope they would be sighted by now, sir."

But no one in Hawaii seriously considered an attack on Pearl
Harbor; the Japs weren't that stupid. Marshall and Stark agreed.
So did their staffs.

Six carriers, along with fast battleships, two heavy cruisers, a
light cruiser, eight destroyers, and a train of three oilers and a supply ship were bound for Hawaii. This formidable striking force,
Kido Butai, was scheduled to hit Army and Navy airfields and
Pearl Harbor at dawn, December 8, Tokyo time. On December 3

Kido Butai received a message in a new code: "Climb Mount Niitaka 1208." This meant: "Attack as planned on December 8." In Hawaii it would be Sunday, December 7.

Kido Butai was cruising eastward at a modest 14 knots to conserve fuel, advancing in ring formation with three submarines ahead scouting for neutral merchant ships which, if found, were to be boarded and seized. A chance encounter with the U. S. Pacific Fleet, however, could not be handled so easily. Admiral Chuichi Nagumo ordered all ship captains to start traveling with no lights and to inform their entire crews of the Pearl Harbor attack. That night a spirit of intense, subdued excitement swept from ship to ship. By late morning of the next day the final major reservicing point was reached—42 degrees north and 170 degrees east—and all ships were refueled.

On December 6 *Kido Butai* was still undiscovered, so it seemed, as it sped southeast at 20 knots through gales and high seas. Several of the exhausted lookouts had already been swept overboard and the fog was so thick it was often impossible to see the ship ahead.

That night the thirteen parts of the vital Japanese message were delivered not only to Roosevelt but to Admiral Theodore Wilkinson, Chief of Naval Intelligence, who happened to have as a dinner guest General Sherman Miles, Chief of Army Intelligence. Marshall and Stark could not be located.

In Hawaii, Short spent the evening at the Officers Club in Schofield Barracks; Kimmel left a party at Honolulu's House Without a Key, at 9:30 P.M. He wanted to get to bed. He had a date to play golf with Short in the morning.

Kido Butai was racing full steam at 24 knots toward the launching point, two hundred miles north of Pearl Harbor. The pilots and crew were routed from their bunks at 3:30 A.M., December 7, Hawaiian time. They put on clean *mawashi* (loincloths) and "thousand-stitch" belts, then ate a breakfast of red rice and tai, a red snapper eaten at times of celebration.

In Washington it was 9 A.M. The fourteenth part of the Japanese message had come in and was already decrypted. It stated

that it was "impossible to reach an agreement through further negotiations." Admiral Wilkinson took the entire message to Admiral Stark. While they were discussing what action should be taken
another intercept was brought in instructing Nomura to submit
the fourteen-point message to Hull "at 1 P.M. on the 7th, your
time."

"Why don't you pick up the telephone and call Admiral Kimmel?" asked Wilkinson.

Stark did pick up the phone at about ten forty-five. It was an un-
godly hour to call Kimmel in his sleep, especially since the November 27 "war warning" to him was enough to keep the Pacific Fleet
on its toes. Besides, an attack on Pearl Harbor was unthinkable.
Stark decided instead to call the President but his line was busy.

In the meantime Colonel Rufus Bratton, an Army intelligence
officer, had been frantically trying to find Marshall, who had
dropped out of sight since early Saturday evening. The 1 P.M. note
had sent Bratton into "frenzied" action. Convinced that "the Japanese were going to attack an American installation," he literally
ran to the office of his chief, General Miles. But he was at home.
Bratton phoned Marshall's quarters at nearby Fort Myer. An orderly said the general had just left for his Sunday morning horseback ride.

By the time Marshall is said to have finally reached his office it
was 11:25 A.M. At that moment *Kido Butai* was at the launching
point. The first faint light of dawn glimmered in the east. Forty-
three fighter planes began leaving the six carriers. Then would
come forty-nine high-level and fifty-one dive bombers; and finally
forty torpedo planes.

After reading the long message and the 1 P.M. note, Marshall
hastily jotted down a dispatch to his Pacific commanders: "The
Japanese are presenting at 1 P.M. Eastern Standard Time today
what amounts to an ultimatum. Also they are under orders to destroy their code machine immediately. Just what significance the
hour set may have we do not know, but be on the alert accordingly." He telephoned Stark, who offered to send the warning
through the Navy's rapid transmission facilities.

"No, thanks, Betty, I feel I can get it through quickly enough," said Marshall, and marked the message "First Priority—Secret." It was sent by Western Union.

At 1:23 P.M. Zeros were approaching Pearl Harbor where it was 7:53 A.M. At that moment the flight commander radioed Admiral Nagumo TORA, TORA, TORA! The repeated code word, meaning, "tiger," stood for "We have succeeded in surprise attack." Two minutes later torpedo bombers began diving on Battleship Row.

2.

Admiral Kimmel was putting on his white uniform, for he had been informed that the destroyer *Ward* had sighted and sunk an unidentified submarine. Hearing the sound of distant explosions, he rushed outside.

Planes were darting overhead, the Rising Sun on their wings visible. They circled and began diving on the ships in the harbor. "There goes the *Arizona!*" exclaimed Kimmel's next-door neighbor, Mrs. Grace Earle. He said not a word but she would never forget that "he looked stricken, and was as white as his uniform."

A car pulled up. Kimmel jumped in and shortly reached his temporary shore headquarters at the submarine base. Even as he rushed inside he noticed a sailor on a tied-up tug pumping away at a 50-caliber machine gun "as fast as he could get the thing going."

Inside Kimmel joined several of his officers at an open window. As he watched the attacks on Battleship Row, Kimmel could not help but admire the planning that must have preceded the Japanese attack. All at once a spent 50-caliber bullet struck the left breast of his white uniform. It smacked into his glasses case and fell to the floor. He picked it up, put it in his pocket and said, "I wish it had killed me." His career was over; he should somehow have prevented what was happening. Still looking cool, the austere Kimmel strode into an inner room. When he emerged a few minutes later, Chief Yeoman Ken Murray, his writer, noticed his four-star shoulder boards had been replaced with two-star boards. He had demoted himself from his temporary rank of full admiral to his permanent rank of rear admiral.

"Oh no, Admiral," a young aide said.

"Hell, yes, son."

It had been a warm December in Washington but today was brisk. At 1:50 P.M. the following message arrived from Kimmel's headquarters:

AIR RAID ON PEARL HARBOR THIS IS NOT A DRILL.

Soon the message was relayed to Admiral Stark. Secretary of the Navy Frank Knox was about to order lunch when Stark burst into his office. "My God," said Knox, "this can't be true! This must mean the Philippines!" He telephoned the President, who was in his study lunching from a tray with Harry Hopkins.

"No!" said Roosevelt incredulously. Hopkins said there must be some mistake. Surely the Japanese would not attack Honolulu "The President discussed at some length," recalled Hopkins, "his efforts to keep the country out of the war and his earnest desire to complete his administration without war, but that if this action of Japan's were true it would take the matter entirely out of his own hands, because the Japanese had made the decision for him."

At 2:05 P.M. Roosevelt called Hull, who was about to receive the two Japanese diplomats, Saburo Kurusu and Nomura. They were obviously bringing a declaration of war but Hull was not to let on that he knew the attack had already been launched "but to receive their reply formally and coolly and bow them out."

But Hull had a temper and gave the two Japanese strong Tennessee mountain language. "In all my fifty years of public service," he told them, in the official expurgated version, "I have never seen a document that was more crowded with infamous falsehoods and distortions—infamous falsehoods and distortions on a scale so huge that I never imagined until today that any Government on this planet was capable of uttering them."

Secretary of War Henry L. Stimson was lunching at his nearby estate, Woodley, when Roosevelt called to ask excitedly, "Have you heard the news?" Stimson said he knew about the Japanese advances in the Gulf of Siam. "Oh, no, I don't mean that. They have attacked Hawaii. They are now bombing Hawaii!"

Throughout America radio programs were interrupted with brief announcements of the Hawaii and somewhat later Manila bombings. In Chicago the New York Philharmonic concert was broken up by an announcer so excited he twice pronounced the program as "Philharminic." Most people were stunned but there were no scenes of panic. Strangers in the street began to look at each other with a new awareness. Personal problems were overshadowed by national catastrophe; and the bitter wrangles between the interventionists and America Firsters suddenly had no meaning. With few exceptions 130,000,000 Americans accepted total war with determination and unity.

The Washington correspondent of the Domei News Agency, Clark Kawakami, felt not only shock but shame. An American citizen, he wrote his newspaper colleagues at the Department of State, "I cannot tell you how deeply I was shocked by Japan's action. . . . That shameful double-dealing coupled with the equally shameful manner in which she launched her attacks on Sunday, without warning, indicates how completely the militarists in Tokyo have gone over to the methods of Hitler and the Nazis. Not only I but my father, too, feel that these acts constitute the blackest and most shameful page in Japanese history."

Another Japanese newsman named Hatanaka was apologizing to C. L. Sulzberger at the Grand Hotel in Moscow. Bowing and smiling, he said, "So sorry, we sank your fleet this morning. Supposing we are at war."

At 8:20 P.M. that evening members of the Cabinet began arriving at the White House. As they were assembling in a semicircle around the President's desk in the Oval Office, Knox, his face white, whispered to Stimson that they had lost seven battleships.[2]

"The President was deeply shaken," recalled Attorney General Francis Biddle, "graver than I had ever seen him." Roosevelt told what he knew and answered a few questions; then a group of congressional leaders arrived and he repeated his story. There was silence for a tense moment. Finally Senator Tom Connally, his face purple, sprang to his feet, banged the desk and shouted, "How did they catch us with our pants down, Mr. President?"

[2] Eighteen ships had been sunk or seriously damaged, including eight battleships. All but two of the battleships—*Arizona* and *Oklahoma*—were later salvaged. At the airfields 188 planes were destroyed—96 Army and 92 Navy. Of the 2,403 killed, 2,008 were Navy, 109 Marines, 218 Army, and 68 civilian. Nearly one half died on the *Arizona*.

With head bowed, the President muttered, "I don't know, Tom. I just don't know." But everyone in the room including Roosevelt knew they had to find out who was at fault—and fast. Once the shock of the attack wore off, the public would begin demanding to know who was to blame: Washington, Hawaii, or both?

Secretary Morgenthau returned to the Treasury Department and told his intimates, "It is just unexplainable. And they caught us as unprepared as the others—just the same." The battleships were a perfect target: and all the Army planes were crowded together to prevent sabotage. "That's what Stimson kept saying," said Morgenthau. "He kept mumbling that all the planes were in one place. They have the whole Fleet in one place—the whole Fleet was in this little Pearl Harbor. The whole Fleet was there. . . ." He was stunned, puzzled. "They can never explain this. They never will be able to explain it."

All over America people were wondering who was to blame. To the hard-core isolationists the answer was simple: Roosevelt. But to most people it was: Kimmel and Short.

Army cryptanalyst William F. Friedman, whose team had solved the Purple code, found it difficult to believe what had happened. All he could do was pace back and forth, so his wife recalled, and mutter to himself repeatedly, "But they knew, they knew, they knew."

Aboard a tramp steamer three days' sailing from New York, Dusko Popov, a British double agent, code-named "Tricycle," heard the captain announce in a funereal voice the attack on Pearl Harbor. Popov was triumphant. That fall he had personally passed on to the F.B.I. a detailed plan of the Japanese air raid which he had obtained from the Germans. "It was the news I had been awaiting. I couldn't say anything to relieve the tension of my fellow passengers, but I was sure the American Fleet had scored a great victory over the Japanese. I was very, very proud that I had been able to give the warning to the Americans four months in advance. What a reception the Japanese must have had! I paced the deck, no, not paced it, I floated about it exultantly."

Chapter Two

MR. KNOX GOES WEST
DECEMBER 8–16, 1941

1.

The next morning two adjacent buildings on Constitution Avenue were the center of activity. These were the outmoded barracks-like Munitions and Navy Buildings, which had housed military and naval headquarters during World War I. Stimson walked from his office on the second floor of the Munitions Building along the corridor to the connecting bridge to the Navy Building and on to Knox's office. He did so "just to show that I was not going to be one of those who attack the Navy when it is down. I took as an excuse a paper that I wanted him to sign but he appreciated my call very much." Secretly Stimson was seething at the unconscionable neglect and inefficiency of Admiral Kimmel, whom he blamed primarily for the disaster.

Yesterday scarcely a uniform was in sight but today any serviceman who possessed one wore it with pride. Tailors all over the city were busy making uniforms for officers who had been borrowing a friend's for special occasions.

Tin Pan Alley was also in operation and patriotic songs such as "You're a Sap, Mister Jap," were being prepared for popular consumption. By dawn Max Lerner had composed a more thoughtful one, "The Sun Will Soon Be Setting on the Land of the Rising Sun."

Behind the nation's bravado was a nagging question: How could tiny, backward Japan with pilots who wore glasses and flew inferior planes bring such a crushing defeat? Why were the Army and Navy caught napping? Who were to blame? Public officials as well as private citizens were asking the same questions. That morning it was reported in the New York *Times* that Senator Tom Connally, a Democrat, apparently had already given Knox "uncharted hell" for Pearl Harbor. Connally made no comment, except to wonder where American planes and patrols had been during the attack.

The White House had a new look that morning, with military police and sentry boxes set up at intervals inside and outside the picket fence. The White House police were already being reinforced by the metropolitan police, and the Secret Service was rushing extra men from field stations. On both the office and house blackout curtains were being put up.

By late morning the last changes had been made on the President's speech to Congress. He delivered it to a joint session of Congress in the chamber of the House of Representatives at 12:30 P.M., beginning with words that would be long remembered: "Yesterday, December 7, 1941, a date which will live in infamy, the United States of America was suddenly and deliberately attacked. . . ." Then he called for a declaration of war for this "unprovoked and dastardly attack." Ordinarily plaudits for the President at such appearances came only from the Democrats but not today. "The applause, the spirit of cooperation," recalled Samuel Rosenman, who helped write Roosevelt's speeches, "came equally from both sides of the chamber."

Thirty-three minutes later Congress passed a resolution declaring that a state of war existed between the United States and Japan.

Roosevelt cabled the news to Churchill:

. . . TODAY ALL OF US ARE IN THE SAME BOAT WITH YOU AND THE PEOPLE OF THE EMPIRE AND IT IS A SHIP WHICH WILL NOT AND CANNOT BE SUNK.

The night before Churchill had gone to bed "and slept the sleep of the saved and thankful." Today when someone at the War Cabinet meeting suggested continuing the same gentle approach to

America used before Pearl Harbor, he replied, "Oh! that is the way we talked to her while we were wooing her; now that she is in the harem, we talk to her quite differently." After all, the Americans were amateurs of war and had to be shown how to wage it.

Rumors were multiplying in Hawaii. Paratroopers had landed and twenty-one Japanese transports were offshore, waiting to sneak in. Many Navy officers were still in shock. When Admiral Raymond Spruance, commander of a division of five cruisers, entered Pearl Harbor that Monday morning to see the shattered wrecks of beloved battleships he was stunned. Years of study had not prepared him for such a sight. He found Kimmel's staff unshaven, still wearing their mud-splattered white Sunday uniforms. He was heartbroken to see Kimmel, a man he had always admired, dazed and disheveled. Others sat numbed and stunned.

Noted for his own coolness, Spruance's self-control collapsed by the time he reached home. Choked with emotion, tears running down his cheeks, he tried to tell his shocked wife and daughter what he had seen and felt. It was the most shattering experience of his life.

In his office Kimmel was telling two of his staff, "If I were in charge in Washington I would relieve Kimmel at once. It doesn't make any difference why a man fails in the Navy, he has failed." The two captains protested; nothing like that would happen. But Kimmel knew he was right.

2.

On the West Coast there was understandable panic because of the large Japanese-American population. False rumors of enemy air attacks were followed by widespread fear of a Japanese landing although it would have taken a force many times the size and strength of the Imperial Navy to land a single division on the American mainland.

In Washington, Knox had already asked the President for permission to leave Washington. Where was he going? "Pearl Harbor," said Knox, "with your permission." Somewhat reluctant to let him go, Roosevelt wondered what he thought he would accomplish. "I can find out a great deal more than here." Knox was deeply concerned by the rumors of dereliction of duty at Pearl Harbor and feared the thought of "a nasty congressional investigation."

By Tuesday evening the Knox party was in El Paso in time to hear the President's fireside chat. "The sudden criminal attacks perpetrated by the Japanese in the Pacific," Roosevelt began, "provide the climax of a decade of international immorality. Powerful and resourceful gangsters have banded together to make war on the whole human race." Every single man, woman and child in America was now a partner in the most tremendous undertaking of its history. "We must share together the bad news and the good news, the defeats and the victories—the changing fortunes of war. So far, the news has been bad. We have suffered a serious setback in Hawaii." The Philippines were being attacked and it seemed likely that Guam, Wake and Midway islands would be seized. He urged the people to ignore rumors, and the newspapers and radio stations to cease dealing out "unconfirmed reports in such a way as to make people believe they are gospel truth."

The road ahead, he said, was going to be difficult. "We must be set to face a long war against crafty and powerful bandits." But America "can accept no result save victory final and complete. Not only must the shame of Japanese treachery be wiped out, but the sources of international brutality, wherever they exist, must be absolutely and finally broken."

Despite the favorable public reception to Roosevelt's speech, there were stirrings of discontent in Congress. The next day a Republican representative complained that the President gave no details of the losses at Pearl Harbor and then quoted a damning dispatch from news correspondent Leland Stowe in Chungking:

> . . . It seems incomprehensible here how the Japs were able to get the Army's big airfields in Oahu, losing a few planes, and without large numbers of American fighters getting in the air promptly. . . . On Sunday evening [Chungking time], at least one hour before the Jap blitz on Hawaii, an official of the United States gunboat *Tulitz* [*Tutuila*] warned your correspondent: "It is going to happen tonight."

Before dawn of December 11, battle stations were sounded aboard the Knox plane, a Navy flying boat, as it neared the Hawaiian Islands. The passengers donned life preservers and parachutes. Machine guns were manned. They were prepared for the worst. They broke radio silence, got a fix and soon were landing at Kaneohe Bay. Knox was appalled. The air station hangars were hulks and wreckage of seaplanes could be seen on the ramps and in the water. The party was driven to the Royal Hawaiian, a grim contrast to the holiday hotel of peacetime. Kimmel met them there and escorted them to his headquarters.

From the submarine base Knox got his first view of what was once Battleship Row. It was a shambles. Smoke was still pouring from the wreckage of the *Arizona.* "Did you receive our dispatch the night before the attack?" Knox asked. Kimmel had not. "Well, we sent you one. . . ."

That day Adolf Hitler solved another of Roosevelt's problems by declaring war on America. If the President had been forced to act first, he would have risked opposition from a substantial segment of the country.

On Capitol Hill, the debate in Congress over responsibility for Pearl Harbor resumed. Republican Senator Charles Tobey of New Hampshire expressed disappointment at the President's failure in his speech to make "a definite statement as to the losses suffered in the debacle at Pearl Harbor."

A Democrat instantly came to the Administration's defense. The Japanese undoubtedly still didn't know how much damage they had done. The public should be told the truth "but I think as this struggle proceeds we must all realize that sometimes it is better Americanism not to withhold the truth when it can be told, but to withhold it when it aids our enemies more than it serves our own people." There was a burst of applause from the galleries.

Unabashed, Tobey then began attacking Knox and quoted an article in the *Christian Science Monitor* entitled "Why, Mr. Secretary—why?" criticizing Knox for not taking proper precautions. Where were the patrols that were supposed to protect the fleet?

It was obvious that the unity brought by Pearl Harbor had abruptly ended in Congress and the battle between interventionists and isolationists, however subterranean, would be resumed.

"Now, all that I feared would happen has happened," wrote isolationist leader Charles Lindbergh in his diary. "We are at war all over the world, and we are unprepared for it from either a spiritual or a material standpoint." It probably would be the bloodiest and most devastating war of all history. "And then what? We haven't even a clear idea of what we are fighting to attain."

During the day Stimson held his first press conference since the disaster. With Marshall's help he jotted down brief notes and then talked effectively to the newsmen. "Altogether," Stimson wrote in his diary, "much is brewing. We are doing our best to keep from having a row with the Navy. There is bitterness on both sides over the failure at Hawaii and the younger and less responsible—and some of the irresponsible older men—are all trying to throw the burden off on the other Department."

On his own initiative, Stimson had already sent two of his own people to Hawaii to investigate the Army side of the attack, a major general and a colonel, the former to relieve General Short. On the afternoon of the twelfth their B-18 took off from Phoenix, Arizona, destination Hamilton Field, California. It crashed into the snow and ice of the high Sierras.[1]

Unaware that Army investigators had been sent to join Knox in Hawaii, the President was dodging questions about the attack at his own press conference. There was no need to be uneasy about being scooped, he assured the White House press corps. He told them that Knox had arrived in Hawaii the night before and warned those who planned to "tell all, and publish all" they had better wait until the Secretary of the Navy made his report.

3.

On Sunday, December 14, Stimson finally had time for his first relaxation in a week. But after a good horseback ride with his military aide he found a new crisis: two urgent telegrams from MacArthur in the Philippines asking for help. "He was instigated to do so

[1] The wreckage was not found until early May 1942, two miles northwest of Burch Mountain at an altitude of 11,000 feet.

by a conference he had had with Admiral Hart who took the usual Navy defeatist position and had virtually told MacArthur that the Philippines were doomed, instead of doing his best to keep MacArthur's lifeline open."

That afternoon he showed the President the two telegrams. "He read them most carefully with tremendous interest, if not excitement. To my great joy he took the position which Marshall and I took and against the Navy." Stimson had brought along a memorandum of his plans for reinforcing MacArthur. "I read this to the President and it all fitted into the same plan so that by the end he had fully made up his mind to side with us against the Navy." Stimson was delighted at his success in "upsetting the Navy's defeatist plan." That evening he exulted on having apparently gotten the President firmly on his side: ". . . and so tonight I went to bed with a feeling we had probably gotten over the hump, so to speak, and were going to embark on an aggressive constructive policy which will bring the end of the war just that much nearer."

He did not know that Knox was already at the White House. He had returned from Hawaii and at ten o'clock personally delivered a typed report to Roosevelt. The Japanese attack, he said, came as a complete surprise to both Kimmel and Short. "Its initial success, which included almost all the damage done, was due to a lack of a state of readiness against such an air attack, by both branches of the service."

Knox did not accuse either Kimmel or Short of dereliction of duty and pointed out that neither had been privy to the Magic intercepts. He also reported that Kimmel and his staff had been convinced that the principal danger to the fleet was a submarine attack for which they had taken the necessary precautions. As for Short, he feared sabotage and bunched his planes so they could be more easily protected; but this, of course, made them easy air targets for the Japanese. Knox also pointed out that several factors were beyond the responsibility of the two commanders: Japanese fifth columnists and inadequate fighter planes and anti-aircraft guns.

Clearly displeased with a report practically exonerating Kimmel and Short, Roosevelt next morning summoned Knox, Stimson,

Hull and other high officials. He instructed the War and Navy secretaries to hold separate press conferences and cover *only* the parts listed on a piece of paper he handed Knox. Nothing else, Roosevelt said, repeat, nothing else in the Knox report was to be made public at this time. It was to be admitted that neither military nor naval forces had been prepared for the air attack but that, once engaged, the defense was heroic. The burden of blame, by inference, was to fall on Kimmel and Short.

At the press conference later that day, Knox held his audience spellbound as he graphically revealed the story of the gallant actions after the sneak attack. "You could have heard a tiny pin drop on the carpet of the room," recalled a Navy public relations officer. "Hardened veteran war correspondents present were visibly moved."

Knox's formal statement was almost a verbatim version of the President's notes. "The United States services were not on the alert against the surprise air attack on Hawaii. This fact calls for a formal investigation which will be initiated immediately by the President. Further action is, of course, dependent on the facts and recommendations made by this investigating board. We are entitled to know if (a) there was any error of judgment which contributed to the surprise, (b) if there was any dereliction of duty prior to the attack." He then read off Roosevelt's list of those ships lost: the battleship *Arizona*; the target ship *Utah*; an old minelayer; and three destroyers.

The reaction to the drastically revised Knox report was enthusiastic. The *Nation* called it "as fairly extensive and unvarnished" as was possible until after the war. The New York *Times*, satisfied that some information about the attack had been disclosed, noted that "it was almost possible to hear the immense sigh of relief that arose yesterday when news of [Knox's] statement reached the American public." The sigh of relief would not have been so immense if Knox had revealed that the actual losses were far greater than those on Roosevelt's list.

The most important difference between the original Knox report and the one released was the omission of the fact that Kimmel and Short had not been privy to the decoded Japanese message indicating a surprise move was imminent. If it had been made public, the Japanese would have known the United States was decrypting their top secret diplomatic code. This necessary suppression, however, misled the American people into placing the burden of blame on the two local commanders; nor was the public informed that there were insufficient fighter planes, anti-aircraft artillery and radar on Oahu. And so the truth about Pearl Harbor was kept from the public. The question was how long could the cover-up last.

Late in the afternoon Knox called Stimson. He had just seen the President, who wanted to appoint a commission of two Army and two Navy officers and one civilian to investigate the responsibility for the losses at Pearl Harbor and to make recommendations. The Secretary of the Navy was going to recommend two former commanders of the fleet, Admirals Joseph Reeves and William Standley—and a federal judge in Chicago named Sullivan. What did Stimson think of these choices?

"I'll get right busy on it and let you know later," he said, and took the problem home to Woodley. That evening he queried friends about Judge Sullivan but no one knew him well. The Assistant Secretary of War, John J. McCloy, suggested Supreme Court Justice Owen Roberts. McCloy had been active in the Black Tom explosion case which had been tried before Justice Roberts. Stimson also had been impressed by Roberts' investigation of the Teapot Dome scandal and he was inclined to recommend him.

That evening Mrs. Charles Hamlin dined with the Roosevelts. "Our pièce de résistance were two pheasants from Hyde Park," she recalled, and the President, looking well and in fine spirits, carved them. He said he was going to appoint Owen Roberts to head the Pearl Harbor inquiry. The justice, he remarked, "seemed very friendly lately." As Roosevelt was being wheeled off to his study he said with a twinkle, his cigarette tipped at its usual angle, "Hungary, Roumania and Czecho-Slovakia have all declared war against us. I told Cordell to take no notice of them and I will not inform Congress."

Later Knox arrived. At the press conference he had assured the reporters that there would be no reassignments until after the investigation. But now he felt Kimmel should be relieved immediately since his name was inescapably associated with disaster.

Roosevelt concurred, and they both agreed that Admiral Ernest J. King should be appointed to a new, independent post as head of the Navy. They would sleep on who should replace Kimmel.

4.

By early morning Stimson had made up his mind on the military members of the commission. Before 8 A.M. he telephoned Marshall to say he had definitely decided on Frank McCoy, a trusted friend for thirty years,[2] and they should pick an airman for the second. Marshall agreed and returned his call a little later. Joseph McNarney, he thought, was the best man. Recently promoted to brigadier general, he was Marshall's trustworthy right hand.

Stimson now telephoned Knox at his apartment just as he was getting up. How about Justice Roberts for the civilian? he asked. Knox agreed and said he would back Roberts.

Stimson immediately wrote the President his suggestions, adding a paragraph which was the first disclosure outside the War Department that the Hawaiian top commanders were to be fired *before* the investigation. "Most confidentially we are sending to Hawaii two men to relieve Short and [F. L.] Martin, the present Army Commander and Air Commander and I think nothing should be said about it until they arrive to take command."

In a rather informal postscript Stimson wrote, "My opinion is that the housecleaning which I describe in the last paragraph should be synchronised with a similar housecleaning in the Naval Command, and all announced at the same time."

Knox was already at the White House discussing Kimmel's replacement. It took little time for them to agree on Rear Admiral Chester W. Nimitz, Chief of the Bureau of Navigation. "Tell Nimitz to get the hell out to Pearl and stay there till the war is won," said Roosevelt.

Nimitz was startled to be selected. Upon learning that he was

---

[2] As Secretary of State in Hoover's administration, Stimson had been unable to bring the President around to his anti-Japanese views. So he persuaded the League of Nations to appoint General McCoy to the committee investigating Japanese actions in Manchuria. McCoy was so successful in pressing Stimson's ideas that Japan withdrew from the League.

going to be the new commander in the Pacific, his wife said, "You always wanted the Pacific Fleet. You always thought that would be the height of glory."

"Darling, the fleet's at the bottom of the sea. Nobody must know that here, but I've got to tell you."

That afternoon the President summoned Knox and Stimson. After a long wait, they were informed that their recommendations for Army and Navy members of the investigating commission had been accepted. Then Supreme Court Justice Roberts was brought in. He agreed to head the commission and promised to turn up at Stimson's office next morning for instructions.

The two secretaries were pleased. All their selections had been accepted and the crucial investigation was now in hand. With the wrong members the unity of the nation might have been jeopardized. Both Knox and Stimson were Republicans, appointed for their agreement with Roosevelt's interventionist policy. Both were men of positive views, confident that theirs was the right way.

But of the two Stimson was the stronger. He was now convinced that both Short and Kimmel had been derelict in their duties and he resented any suggestion that they had not. The fault was in Hawaii, not in Washington. He was particularly unsympathetic to Kimmel, who he felt was most to blame. In fact, Stimson was suspicious of admirals in general. Most of them were defeatists like Hart.

A graduate of Yale University, Henry L. Stimson still took seriously its motto, "For God, for country, and for Yale." He carried this messianic message through life, staunchly convinced that the principles of his class and country were best for all the world. An ardent believer in exercise, he rode horseback, chopped wood and participated in active games, particularly deck tennis, played by tossing a quoit over the net. Only close friends knew he was blind in one eye; and his aide was careful to pick opponents. Vice-President Henry Wallace, for instance, was never invited after an aggressive first match. His idol was Theodore Roosevelt, whose motto he also took seriously: "Speak softly and carry a big stick." Stimson had carried his big stick in service to Taft as Secretary of War, to Coolidge as governor of the Philippines, and to

Hoover as Secretary of State. Despite all these titles, the one he chose for personal use was "Colonel." He had earned this in the Great War and still sentimentalized over his Army service. To him the greatest virtues were soldierly. He had never looked upon war as evil but as a necessary fact of international life.

His firm lips and set jaw were indicative of a one-track mind, and once he had made it up would stick tenaciously to his decision. This was proven in his persistent hatred and fear of Japan. It had begun, while he was Hoover's Secretary of State, with the Japanese conquest of Manchuria in 1932. Stimson took this as a personal affront, and the bombings of Shanghai further ignited his hot temper. His solution was to apply against the Japanese drastic economic pressure and, if necessary, military and naval force. Hoover was equally offended by Japan's aggression but with him it was a moral and legal protest. He would not tolerate force.

In 1940 Stimson found a President more to his taste, albeit a Democratic one. He agreed to serve as Roosevelt's Secretary of War, and in the next months consistently pressed him to get tougher with both Nazi Germany and Japan. It was Stimson, above all, who convinced the President to freeze Japanese assets in July 1941. Since America had been Japan's major source of oil imports, this left Japan in an untenable position. To the New York *Times* it was "the most drastic blow short of war." To Japan's leaders it was even more. This freezing was the last step in the encirclement of their empire by the ABCD (American, British, Chinese, Dutch) powers, a challenge to their nation's very existence.

Throughout the fall of 1941 Stimson kept pressure on Roosevelt to take a stronger stand against the Japanese. The President was reluctant to provoke a war in the East when the real danger was in Europe. But Stimson, seething with moral indignation at Japanese depredations, persisted. For a while Roosevelt was tempted to make a compromise reply to the final Japanese offer of settlement in late November since Stark and Marshall had urged conciliation, both arguing that America would not be ready for war until the following spring. But Stimson and his adherents won out, and on November 26 Hull sent the strong reply to Tokyo that had resulted in Pearl Harbor.

Now Stimson's task was to beat both the Nazis and Japanese

and save the world. To do this the Pearl Harbor controversy had to be quelled. If the Administration and George Marshall could not be completely exonerated of all culpability, the war effort would be seriously impeded. And, in his opinion, this was unthinkable to any true patriot. Therefore, Kimmel and Short had to take the blame.

Chapter Three

"SOME ADMIRAL OR SOME GENERAL IN THE PACIFIC MAY BE MADE A GOAT"

Herbert Hoover

DECEMBER 17, 1941– JANUARY 29, 1942

1.

The Roberts Commission, with the exception of Admiral Standley, met next morning before ten o'clock in Stimson's office. The Secretary said that the Army and Navy wanted to cooperate fully with the commission, adding that he felt it was not a question of Army versus Navy or Navy versus the Army. Then he turned to Knox. "How about that, Frank?"

"That is absolutely right."

Praise was already coming to Roosevelt for securing such a prestigious commission. The selection of Justice Roberts was particularly applauded, for it guaranteed, as one eminent judge wrote, "that the whole truth concerning the unhappy eventualities of December 7th will be revealed in an irrefutable and satisfactory manner." Unmentioned was that Justice Roberts had been an active member of William Allen White's aid-to-Britain organization.

Herbert Hoover sent his congratulations to his old friend, General Frank McCoy, on his appointment. Then, with apologies, added a warning:

> When Hull's ultimatum was delivered to the Japanese on the 26th of November [1941] I and many others of some experience knew that sooner or later it meant war, and said so. . . . My point is: Did the State Department apprise the Army and Navy of the ultimatum and its serious import? If so, did the Washington heads of these departments transmit it to the forces in the field? Now the only reason why I write this is the feeling that some Admiral or some General in the Pacific may be made a goat for action or lack of action higher up, and thus a great injustice done.

At about 10 A.M. the membership, still without Standley, convened down the hallway at the Board Room, 2309. After preliminaries, General Marshall, assisted by the Chief of the War Plans Division, General Leonard T. Gerow, outlined a number of warning messages sent to General Short.

Standley was just landing at the Washington airport. Retired in 1938 after four years as Chief of Naval Operations, he had been ordered to proceed immediately from San Diego and report to the Secretary of the Navy. He was blunt, outspoken and inclined to be crusty to those he regarded as fools. "Well, Admiral," greeted Knox, "we're in a mess and, as always, we need your help." Standley had no idea what he meant until the Secretary explained about the commission. "That's your first job, Admiral."

Standley found Justice Roberts sitting at the head of a table flanked by three men, obviously his three colleagues. But what was General McNarney doing there? What right had a member of the Army General Staff to be a member? How could he possibly have an objective view of Washington's responsibilities in the case? In fact, he himself was somewhat prejudiced. "I knew from first-hand experience the shortcomings of our base at Pearl Harbor, for which Short and Kimmel were in no way responsible."

"Hello, Betty," said Standley to Stark, present as a witness, and they shook hands. He was presented to Justice Roberts and spoke to the other members.

Once the questioning of Stark was finished Standley was determined to discover what he had gotten into. Was this, he asked, an

Army or Navy board or a joint commission or what? Would they go by Army, Navy or civil procedure? Could they summon witnesses, administer oaths and take testimony? "The answers I got were not at all reassuring." It was a mixed commission with no precedent. The recorder had little or no court-martial experience; and a Marine Corps colonel was provost marshal. Most astounding was that none of the witnesses had been sworn in.[1] Shocked at such irregularity, Standley protested so vigorously that his colleagues agreed to have Congress pass a joint resolution giving them the authority to subpoena witnesses and administer oaths. Why this hadn't been done earlier, particularly by a body headed by a Supreme Court justice, puzzled Standley. Had this strangely constituted body been purposely set up informally so as to whitewash the Washington authorities for their failures and place the blame primarily on Short and Kimmel? Standley feared that if it came to a vote he could only count on McCoy.

In the House that day the commission was discussed and praised by a Democratic representative from Michigan. "There is no question but that under the chairmanship of Mr. Justice Roberts the testimony will be fair and fearless and that the findings of the Board will be equally fair and fearless. Such facts as cannot, because of military necessity, be revealed, can be passed over by the people without uneasiness when they are assured by this Board that concealment of such facts is necessary."

Next day the commission again met at 10 A.M. in Room 2309. They listened to the Army and Navy intelligence chiefs and to the officer in charge of communications for the War Department. And so by the time of adjournment soon after noon, the commission had been provided by the Army and Navy with "every document that could have bearing on the situation at Pearl Harbor."

So Justice Roberts thought. But except for the fourteen-point message of December 6–7 none of the other numerous Magic intercepts was produced and, without these messages, it would be impossible for the commission to determine how much Washing-

---

[1] A transcript of the witnesses' testimony was not taken. The only known minutes of this and the next day's testimony are brief and unrevealing summaries by the recorder.

ton knew in advance of the attack and how much had been sent on to Kimmel and Short.

Based on these two days of unsworn and unrecorded testimony, the commission formulated its plans and by the time the members left the Washington airport at 4:17 P.M. bound for Hawaii the general feeling was that they had been thoroughly prepared to proceed with the investigation.

After a long, tedious trip they arrived in Honolulu at 7:20 A.M. on the twenty-second. The day was spent in preparations at Fort Shafter and it was not until nine the next morning that the first Army witness, General Short, was interrogated. He said he regarded Marshall's warning of November 27 as an order to prevent sabotage uprisings and subversive action among the many Japanese living on the islands. While he had been warned "hostile action possible at any moment," he was cautioned to let "Japan commit the first overt act . . ." and that reconnaissance and any other measures he deemed necessary "should be carried out so as not to alarm civil population or disclose intent." He had replied the same day, "Department alerted to prevent sabotage. Liaison with Navy." Two days later he sent another wire giving details of the full precautions he was taking against subversive activities and was never told he had misunderstood instructions.

No meeting of the commission was scheduled for Christmas. Early that morning Nimitz arrived from Washington by flying boat. It came to a halt on the choppy waters of Pearl Harbor. As the door was thrown open he was met by an appalling stink of black oil, charred wood and burned and rotting bodies. On the launch trip to shore through steady rain, an escorting officer explained that the boats moving in the harbor were fishing out bodies. They were grotesquely bloated, still rising to the surface.

"This is a terrible sight," murmured Nimitz, "seeing all these ships down." After breakfast he was joined by Kimmel. Ordinarily of imperious presence, Kimmel seemed stooped and deflated. "You have my sympathy," said the shocked Nimitz. "The same thing could have happened to anybody."

There was still a grim spirit in Washington. Churchill, arrived three days earlier for conferences, went with the President to a service at the Foundry Methodist Church. General Marshall and his wife were eating Christmas dinner at home alone. But the Starks were entertaining friends, including four children, in the festive aura of a brightly decorated Christmas tree in the hall surrounded by presents. Stimson had risen early for a horseback ride before driving to his office.

The next day Churchill told Congress how thankful Great Britain was for all the help America had sent. These were indeed dismal days but there were some good tidings from across the Atlantic. Hitler was suffering in Libya and the lifeline of supplies from America was flowing steadily and freely. "If the United States has been found at a disadvantage at various points in the Pacific Ocean, we know well that it is to no small extent because of the aid which you have been giving to us in munitions for the defense of the British Isles and for the Libyan campaign, and, above all, because of your help in the battle of the Atlantic, upon which all depends, and which has in consequence been successfully and prosperously maintained."

On the twenty-seventh the Roberts Commission moved to Pearl Harbor where the day was spent in the wardroom lounge of the submarine base interrogating Kimmel. The admiral brought with him an old friend, Rear Admiral Robert Theobald, to help locate papers pertinent to his testimony. Roberts told Theobald with a smile, "Of course, you are not here in the capacity of a defense counsel because you and Admiral Kimmel both understand that no charges have been preferred against him; he is not in the status of a defendant." Theobald bowed silently but thought Roberts' statement was incomprehensible. How could any investigation of the Commander in Chief of the United States Fleet be conducted without regarding him as a defendant—and without counsel?

Late that afternoon Roberts began questioning Kimmel "in a loud tone of voice; in fact, in a manner more to be expected of a trial lawyer in a lower court." Kimmel felt he was being treated not as a witness but as a guilty defendant, and that Roberts was not a judge but a prosecutor. Admiral Standley also was unhappy. It seemed as if Roberts was angry at Kimmel because his statement to the commission was not as orderly as Short's. The justice should have realized that most of the admiral's staff had gone to

sea after the attack and he had been unable to draft a comprehensive report by himself. Moreover Kimmel, not having been allowed to be present at the inquiry previously held at Fort Shafter,
had no idea what testimony or documentary material had been
presented.

After adjournment Roberts, Reeves and Standley visited the
basement headquarters of Commander Joseph Rochefort, chief of
the Communications Security Unit. While the two admirals were
in close conference with Rochefort, Roberts asked Commander
Jasper Holmes, an intelligence officer, to see the charts and logs
kept during the attack. Holmes also mentioned some of the
relevant information they had discovered since the attack by
decrypting Japanese consular messages. If only they had had access
to consular messages before the attack, they might have stopped
the Japanese, lamented Holmes, who did not know that many of
those messages had been decrypted in Washington before the attack.

The following day Roberts must have had some feeling of dissatisfaction with his own harsh conduct and half apologized to
Kimmel. Although inwardly seething Kimmel replied "that he
desired to offer no objection to the treatment he had received
from the Commission up to that time."

As the inquiry continued it became evident to Standley that the
sixty-nine-year-old Admiral Reeves, a veteran of naval aviation's
most formative years, shared Roberts' conviction that the two Hawaiian commanders, and particularly Kimmel, were entirely at
fault. Standley could not subscribe to this view. "I felt that, with all
the information available to them in Washington, Admiral Stark
and General Marshall were equally culpable."

Kimmel was frustrated that he had no opportunity to confront
the other witnesses or to submit evidence on subjects they
discussed. He had no idea what the others had testified or what
material had been placed in evidence since each witness had been
ordered to keep his testimony secret.

When the commission resumed its inquiries after the New Year
holiday Standley asked Lieutenant Commander Edwin Layton,
Kimmel's intelligence officer: "Has the Naval Intelligence in

Washington all the information for making the estimates of the
situation and drawing conclusions?" Yes. "If that is true,
wouldn't they be in a better position to estimate the whole situation than you are here?"

"That is the way the system is laid."

This line of questioning would inevitably lead to criticism of
Washington and Roberts took over. "If you are an intelligence
officer for the Commander of the Fleet of the United States, you
do not expect that anything of value to you as to any important
situation would be withheld from you by the authorities in Washington, do you?"

"No, sir," said Layton.

On January 5 the commission convened at Suite 300 of the
Royal Hawaiian Hotel. Yeoman Ken Murray accompanied Kimmel to the hotel that morning with a large box of correspondence
relating to the admiral's efforts throughout ten months to improve
the defenses of Pearl Harbor. Murray was not permitted inside the
hearing room and sat outside for two days without being summoned. Finally he was instructed to take the papers back to headquarters and file them.

Adding to the problems of both Kimmel and Short was the
inefficient recording by the two stenographers brought from Washington by Roberts. One, an adult, had little or no experience in
court reporting, and the other was a teen-age young man who at
times could not even read his own notes and omitted considerable
material. Kimmel found the transcript of his first days of testimony so muddled that it took him a day and a half to correct it.
Omitted was his entire main statement. Theobald protested to the
recorder, who reported that Roberts was opposed to any extensive
correction. Theobald tried to explain that Kimmel had no desire
to modify his testimony in any respect, only to bring it in accord
with what he had originally said before the commission. The answer was that Roberts was "opposed to any correction of the testimony other than by numbering the errors and placing the correct
statements in an addendum to the Commission's report." But
what reader would bother to turn to an addendum every few
words?

Although Theobald appealed to Standley, he confirmed that

Roberts would not permit the original transcript to be altered. "But Mr. Roberts is only one member of the Commission," protested Theobald, "and there are four military men on that Commission who must know how this matter is handled in case of testimony before a military court." Did Roberts' wishes control the actions of the entire commission?

"Theobald," said Standley, "you and Kimmel fully understand what Kimmel is up against in this inquiry, don't you?"

"Of course we do."

Next morning Kimmel renewed his request to Roberts himself in the presence of Standley. "Admiral," said Roberts, "you are not on trial."

"Words don't alter facts," replied Kimmel. "In the eyes of the American people I am on trial and nothing you can say will alter that."

On January 10 the commission left Honolulu, arriving in San Francisco the next day. En route to Washington by train the group began to draft their findings. On the evening they arrived Standley reported to Knox. "Mr. Secretary," he said, "under the circumstances, Admiral Kimmel and General Short had to be relieved of their commands. Yet, I can't help regretting that Admiral Kimmel had to go. I have never seen the Fleet in a higher state of efficiency than was evidenced during the course of our investigations at Pearl Harbor."

2.

It took three days for the commission to finish the draft of their findings. Then on the nineteenth, they spent much of the day in Room 2905 of the Navy Building, interrogating General Marshall. Unlike Short and Kimmel, he was treated with extreme consideration. He was asked few penetrating questions and no embarrassing ones concerning the alert sent to Stark on November 7 and the warning of December which did not reach the recipient until long after the Japanese attack. His explanation of why this second message was sent by commercial cable and not by radio or telephone was accepted at face value. Nor was he asked why it had taken the Chief of Staff until 11:25 A.M. to get to his office that fateful day.

The next morning, the twentieth, the commission went into executive session to draw up its report. That evening the chairman dined at the home of a fellow justice of the Supreme Court, Felix Frankfurter. Present also was Stimson, who as a district attorney in 1906 in southern New York State had launched Frankfurter, just out of Harvard Law School, on his career as his assistant in several trust-busting cases. "We sat up until twelve o'clock," Stimson wrote in his diary, "talking over with Roberts the view he had formed on the general situation in Hawaii as distinguished from his decision which is not yet ready for announcement. He has been impressed in the same way that I have with the defensive spirit of the Navy and he has been impressed as I have with the fact that Hawaii is no longer a safe advance base for the Navy under the conditions of modern sea and air warfare." Stimson was pleased that Roberts thoroughly approved of sending more troops to Hawaii. "We sat until midnight and it was a fruitful evening."

The board room in the Navy Building became an arena of battle during the next few days, Reeves insisting that Kimmel was completely at fault, while Standley maintained that the burden of blame belonged in Washington. The conflict between the two men was open, their enmity dating back to when Standley, as Chief of Naval Operations, refused to recommend Reeves's reappointment as commander of the Pacific Fleet. As a result, deduced Standley, Reeves's animosity "apparently persisted long after we both had retired and seemed to motivate his actions during our service on the Roberts Commission."

Standley was so shocked by the prejudicial attitude of his colleagues that he warned Knox that if Kimmel was ever court-martialed he would take his case and see that he was acquitted. But Knox was so successful in persuading him to work with the group that Standley agreed not to submit a minority report lest it divide the country and harm the war effort. On the twenty-third he reluctantly signed Roberts' report, though he later wrote that "it did not present the whole, true picture. The findings as to sins of commission presented true enough statements, but the many sins of omission in the picture were omitted from our findings because the President in his executive order setting up the Commission had specifically limited its jurisdiction."

Roberts wanted to release his report directly to the newspapers but Roosevelt insisted on seeing it first. It took two hours for the President to study the document in full and ask Roberts a few questions. Then, pleased by what he had read, he said, "Is there any reason why this report should not be given to the public in its entirety?" There was not. Roosevelt tossed the document across his desk to one of his secretaries. "Give that in full to the papers for their Sunday editions."

Stimson spent the next morning poring over newspaper accounts of the report. He was as pleased as Roosevelt. "It is an admirable report, candid and fair, and thorough in its study of the facts. It points out with merciless thoroughness the faults in the defense of Hawaii on December 7." The commission, thought Stimson, had done its work well. In the conclusions it found that Hull and Knox had fulfilled all their obligations by keeping the Army and Navy Departments informed of the course and significance of negotiations with Japan. And Marshall and Stark had fulfilled theirs by consulting with each other and their superiors. Moreover, both had fulfilled their command responsibilities by warning Short and Kimmel of probable hostilities and ordering them to take appropriate measures.

The lack of readiness in Hawaii, concluded the report, was laid to the failure of Kimmel and Short "to consult and cooperate as to the necessary action based upon the warnings and to adopt measures enjoined by the orders given them by the chiefs of the Army and Navy commands in Washington."

Although unnamed officers in the War Department were scolded for leading Short to believe that sabotage was the only danger, the great burden of blame fell on Short and Kimmel. "The Japanese attack was a complete surprise to the commanders, and they failed to make suitable dispositions to meet such an attack. Each failed properly to evaluate the seriousness of the situation. These errors of judgment were the effective causes for the success of the attack."

Asked for a comment, Senate Majority Leader Alben Barkley declared that the report was a "comprehensive and admirable view of the facts and the people are justified in believing that nothing will be kept from them." This should end all suspicion, he added, "now that everybody knows what happened."

The majority of Americans agreed with this verdict. Letters poured into the White House calling for prompt disciplinary action. "I am hopeful," wrote Mrs. Herman Groth of Oak Park, Illinois, "that Kimmel and Short will put an end to their lives even before you make your decision as to their punishment. In this way they would at least apply the same lack of consideration for their own lives as they did for the lives of those fine American boys who perished as the result of their negligence."

This apparently ended the Pearl Harbor dispute for most Americans. But there remained many who regarded the report as prejudicial and one-sided. Vice Admiral Joseph Taussig wrote Kimmel that he knew he was "not guilty of anything either in the way of dereliction of duty or in your judgment" despite the findings of the Roberts board. "I, probably as much, if not more, than any high ranking officer have studied the Hawaiian Defense—and the Pacific situation in general, having spent 8 years at our War College—been Chief of Staff of the Fleet, and Assistant Chief of operations. . . . I have always felt that the entire blame for this whole affair lies right in Washington—but, of course there is no way that I can see to get at the culprits. So they have to find a goat and the mantle falls on you, who through circumstances happen to be the CinC."

Support for Kimmel and Short also came from the Congress. Senator David Walsh, a Democrat, pointed out that there were important facts which the Roberts report had omitted and that "the public will demand to be informed."

Senator Robert La Follette, Jr., charged that some of the blame lay in Washington. Even Felix Frankfurter, who had suggested the private meeting between Roberts and the President, was concerned. That day he told Roberts, "Naturally it stirs many reflections from what I think I can fairly read between the lines. . . ." There was, he said, "an inert and unimaginative mentality in command at Pearl Harbor" which still remained in the Army General Staff and the Office of Naval Operations.

Upon reading the report that morning in Oklahoma City Short

was completely dumfounded. "To be accused of dereliction of duty after almost forty years of loyal and competent service was beyond my comprehension." He immediately telephoned Marshall, an old and trusted friend for thirty-nine years. The Chief of Staff said he had not yet seen the report. He'd been in New York.

"What should I do?" asked Short. Having the country and the war in mind, should he retire?

"Stand pat," said his old friend, "but if it becomes necessary I will use this conversation as authority."

Short replied that he was placing himself entirely in Marshall's hands, having faith in his judgment and loyalty. "After I hung up I decided it wasn't fair to him to have to use the conversation as authority, so I wrote out a formal application which I enclosed in a personal letter to him."

> Dear General Marshall:
> I appreciate very much your advice not to submit my request for retirement at the present time. Naturally, under existing conditions I very much prefer to remain on the active list and take whatever assignment you think it necessary to give me. However, I am enclosing application so that you may use it should you consider it desirable to submit it at any time in the future.

Short then pointed out that the Roberts report did not mention that twelve B-17s had arrived from the mainland in the midst of the attack with skeleton crews, without ammunition, and with guns packed in heavy grease for preservation.

> From my point of view this is a strong argument that the War Department agreed with me that sabotage was the most dangerous thing to the Hawaiian Department and for that reason did not direct me to take action against an air attack although it had known since November 28th of the precautions taken by me. . . . I shall appreciate very greatly anything you may be able to do in my case.

On Monday morning Stimson talked over with Marshall what they should do in respect to Short since the President had left it in their hands. Marshall pointed out that Short had already telephoned him making an application for retirement, and that Stark was hoping Kimmel would do likewise. Stimson warned of the danger of acting too hastily "as I feared it might give the impression that we were trying to let off these people without punishment because we felt guilty ourselves. Of course this would be a wholly false inference on both sides, for the retirement would not legally affect a court martial which could still be had, and on the other side I pointed out to Marshall that the Roberts Report seemed to me to be such an accurate analysis of the facts that our consciences could rest clear on its statements. Congress and the press are showing signs of going through a ghost hunt for victims and the isolationists are beginning to take up that cry in Congress, but it seems to me that the report virtually met all such trials."

To Stimson's dismay a ground swell of protest came from the press and Congress for further investigation. "The Roberts Report has left the FBI, Naval Intelligence and Military Intelligence under a cloud," commented a columnist in that day's Washington *Times-Herald*. "Congress should penetrate that cloud and fix due guilt for negligence where it belongs." In New York City both the major papers agreed. The *Times* objected that the Roberts conclusions "seemed too sweeping in exculpating their superiors in Washington from blame and in too easily finding that each of these 'fulfilled his obligations.'" And the *Tribune* charged, "The want of foresight at Pearl Harbor was paralleled higher up."

In Congress Democratic stalwarts, led by Barkley, were predictably supportive and the Administration critics predictably skeptical. Senator Dewey Short felt the guilt extended to Washington. "It's high time we were getting rid of these incompetents. We've got a lot of gold-braiders around here who haven't had an idea in twenty years. They should be court-martialed." Another isolationist senator went further, demanding an investigation of Stimson and Knox.

On Tuesday the attack on the Administration spread. In the House Naval Affairs Committee momentum was growing for a "thorough study" of Pearl Harbor. A similar uprising in the Senate so concerned Harry Hopkins that the President's chief adviser, in a confidential memorandum, accused Senator Walsh, chairman of the Naval Affairs Committee, of hating "the British more than he cares for our country." He also charged that another senator was "a Nazi-minded person."

Despite these rumblings, Stimson still expressed faith in the commission's findings. "This is just a hasty line," he wrote to Roberts, "to tell you what an admirable job I think that you and your colleagues have done in your difficult task of drawing the report on the disaster at Pearl Harbor. I think it is a masterpiece of candid and accurate statement based upon most careful study and analysis of a difficult factual situation."

Two days later, on Thursday the twenty-ninth, the Democrats in Congress counterattacked. In the House Naval Affairs Committee meeting the motion for an investigation was defeated 14 to 6. "I think it is regrettable that the committee voted as it did," countered a Republican congressman from Minnesota. "The Roberts report settled nothing fundamental. It fixed the local blame, but not the real cause of Pearl Harbor. . . ."

Roosevelt had been kept informed of the course of this debate by House Majority Leader John W. McCormack, who warned that the second-ranking minority member of the Naval Affairs Committee, James W. Mott, was now requesting that the stenographic report and documents of the Roberts Commission be brought before the committee. Roosevelt reacted aggressively. "If you think it would be a good thing to have me send for Mott and give him a fatherly talk about how a war has to be run, I will do so," he wrote McCormack. But the scolding was not necessary. The House majority leader stifled the attempt by having Mott's request tabled. In the Senate a similar move for an investigation was choked off.

All seemed under control and Stimson wrote that evening that the Pearl Harbor business which came up at his press conference "went off very well." But the criticism had by no means ended. In a week the magazine comments began coming in. David Lawrence of *U. S. News* flatly charged that Roosevelt was responsible for the failure to coordinate defense operations and his Chief of Staff and Chief of Naval Operations should have made sure Kimmel and Short had taken the necessary precautions. Lawrence hoped that the two local commanders would not be made scapegoats for "the negligence in Washington"; and in the next issue openly accused the Administration of suppressing a congressional inquiry.

By now it was obvious that the Roberts report had only opened

the door to a wider investigation. It could not come in the foreseeable future but it was bound to take place, for too much discontent, suspicion and bitterness had been raised in both civilian and
military circles. "I cannot conceive of any honorable man being
able to recall his service as a member of that commission without
great regret and the deepest shame." These words came from the
man who had turned over command of the Pacific Fleet to Kimmel, Admiral J. O. Richardson. "A more disgraceful spectacle has
never been presented to this country during my lifetime than the
failure of the civilian officials of the Government to show any will-
ingness to take their share of responsibility for the Japanese success
at Pearl Harbor. . . .

"It is my firm belief that, when the President realized the extent
of the damage done by the attack at Pearl Harbor, he lost his
nerve and lost his head, and ordered the convening of the Roberts
Commission, believing that he could best protect his own position
by focusing public attention on Pearl Harbor."

Richardson's indignation was shared by leading admirals on active duty. The new head of the Navy, Admiral King, later wrote, "It
seems to me that this committee did not get into the real meat of
the matter but merely selected a 'scapegoat' to satisfy the popular
demand for fixing the responsibility for the Pearl Harbor debacle.
For instance, Admiral Kimmel was not asked the important questions nor was he given the proper chance to speak for himself. In
fact, he and General Short were 'sold down the river' as a political
expedient." The continuation of the Pearl Harbor cover-up had
been done with the approval of the President on the grounds that
revelation of the whole truth would impede the war effort. But
there was another possible motive: did Roosevelt have something
to hide?

Chapter Four

"SETTLE YOURSELF IN A QUIET NOOK SOMEWHERE AND LET OLD FATHER TIME HELP THIS ENTIRE SITUATION"

Stark to Kimmel

JANUARY 25, 1942–FEBRUARY 1944

1.

Kimmel had already joined his wife in Long Beach, California, when he was informed on January 25 that General Short had submitted a request for retirement. Until then the admiral had not even thought of submitting a similar request. But he "took this as a suggestion" that he do likewise and submitted his own resignation the next day as a patriotic act, declaring himself in readiness "to perform any duty to which I may be assigned."

Several days later he received a personal letter from Stark. "I showed the Secretary and the President your splendid letter stating that you were not to be considered and that only the country should be considered." The general feeling in Washington, Stark added, was that, until definite action was taken regarding Kimmel's future orders, it was "better for you not to return to any temporary duty."

Kimmel was puzzled. Nor was he reassured by Stark's next words:

> I do want you to know that we will try and solve the problem on the basis of your letter—whatever is best for the country; that is about all I can say.
>
> That you are sitting on a question mark hoping for something definite at the earliest possible moment, we realize and I can assure you you are very much in our thoughts.

Even so, Kimmel promptly informed Secretary Knox on the twenty-eighth, "I desire my request for retirement to stand, subject only to determination by the Department as to what course of action will best serve the interests of the country and the good of the service."

That afternoon, at a private conference with Stimson, the President was personally directing the method of handling the Kimmel and Short requests for retirement. He ordered the Army and Navy to act in concert. "Wait about a week," he instructed, "and then announce that both officers have applied for this immediate retirement and that this is under consideration." Then, about a week later, it should be announced that the applications had been accepted with the condition that acceptance did not bar subsequent court-martial proceedings.

Courts-martial of Kimmel and Short, of course, would have revealed the inequities of the Roberts report and had to be avoided at all costs; and so such proceedings were to be described as impossible "without the disclosure of military secrets."

Stimson agreed so completely with the Roosevelt plan of action that he regarded it as his own; and it was he who put it into operation. He brought Knox into the picture. "I told him the way in which I had arranged with the President we should treat the problem of Kimmel and Short and he agreed to it."

While everyone concurred that courts-martial were out of the question, the Administration wanted to avoid public criticism for barring them. On the other hand, it did not wish to stimulate the public or Kimmel and Short to expect or demand such proceedings. The wording of the condition in the acceptance of the requests for retirement was the most troublesome matter. All concerned labored over the language, finally agreeing that the phrase to be used in acceptance was "without condonation of any offense or prejudice to future disciplinary action."

Kimmel and Short were each retired by letter. The latter's was handed to him personally at Oklahoma City on February 18. Kimmel got his the next morning at eleven-five. He was stunned, and birthday greetings from Stark three days later did not help: "I wish for you, amid the clouds of uncertainty, COURAGE—courage that will enable you to think bravely, act wisely, and endure. . . . Make over your own world. Let your courage be its architect. May God give you strength, wisdom, balance, courage, and hope." This advice was followed by more later in the day: "Pending something definite, there is no reason why you should not settle yourself in a quiet nook somewhere and let Old Father Time help this entire situation, which I feel he will—if for no other reason than that he always has."

Kimmel replied in words indicating he was not yet ready to settle in his quiet nook. He protested the wording of his retirement:

> I stand ready at any time to accept the consequences of my acts. I do not wish to embarrass the government in the conduct of the war. I do feel, however, that my crucifixion before the public has about reached the limit. I am in daily receipt of letters from irresponsible people over the country taking me to task and even threatening to kill me. . . . I have kept my mouth shut and propose to do so so long as it is humanly possible. . . . But I do think that in all justice the department should do nothing further to inflame the public against me. I am entitled to some consideration even though you may consider I erred grievously.

Before this letter was received Stark wrote another, this one addressed to "Dear Mustapha," Kimmel's nickname. They all had a tough year ahead and would need courage to think bravely and act wisely. "I do not have to tell you that my faith in one Husband Kimmel and in the fine fiber in his innermost makeup is such that I know it will carry him through, regardless of how rough the going."

Ignoring Kimmel's request, the disclosure of the retirement ap-

plications was about to be made public when the President, who
had been kept in bed several days with bronchitis, summoned
Stimson and Knox to the White House on February 25. The President said that, after sizing up the situation, he had concluded that
"the temper of the people" required courts-martial for Kimmel
and Short, and he preferred they request them. Then they could
be delayed until a time "commensurate with the public interest."
Why punish the two Hawaiian commanders severely? They
should merely be reprimanded enough to placate the public.

Stimson was astonished that the President had completely
changed his position but could do nothing but follow orders. He
summoned Marshall, who was also shocked. The Chief of Staff
sought advice from his Judge Advocate General, who advised
against issuing a statement that Kimmel and Short were going to
be tried by courts-martial. There was no law that authorized those
two officers to request courts-martial; such trials had to originate
from sworn charges and specifications. Armed with this information, Stimson pried a compromise from the President: the retirement disclosure would also announce that charges were being
prepared against Kimmel and Short for trials by courts-martial, al-
leging dereliction of duty. These trials would not be held "until
such time as the public interest and safety would permit."

Announcements were made by the Army and Navy on the last
day of February. But the compromise between Roosevelt and
Stimson, designed to defuse the Pearl Harbor controversy, loosed a
flood of indignation and hatred upon Kimmel and Short from all
over the country. "Why," a New Jerseyite asked the President, "do
you protect or shield for one solitary minute your Messrs. Kimmel
and Short from the punishment of death and ignominy which in
my candid judgment and that of countless but probably inarticulate
fellow-citizens, these two individuals have so completely and indubitably earned?" Thousands protested the granting of pensions of
six thousand dollars a year to commanders guilty of dereliction of
duty. Hadn't Representative Andrew May, chairman of the House
Military Affairs Committee, urged in a speech at Pikesville, Ken-
tucky, that these two men should be shot? One man named Mix,
a Yale graduate and a former circuit judge, advised Kimmel to

show that he was a real man "by using a pistol and ending your existence, as you are certainly of no use to yourself nor the American people."

The families of the two officers were subjected to hate mail. How dare the three Kimmel sons serve in the Navy when their father was an infamous traitor! As the months went on there were increased demands to punish the guilty men. At the same time a growing minority was looking upon the two men as scapegoats created by the Administration to cover up its own dereliction.

Even so the Pearl Harbor controversy was far overshadowed throughout the nation by events in the Pacific. Late that February the Japanese Navy inflicted a crushing defeat on a combined Anglo-American-Dutch fleet in the Java Sea. This resulted, a few days later, in the fall of Java itself. The Southwest Pacific area was now in Japanese hands except for two bastions in the Philippines, Bataan and Corregidor.

By the beginning of April the Japanese had driven the American-Filipino defenders of Bataan to the end of that peninsula, forcing the surrender of over 76,000 defenders, including 12,000 Americans. It was the greatest capitulation in U.S. military history. This humiliation had been preceded by the forced flight of MacArthur from Corregidor to Australia. Then came the long, tragic Bataan Death March of prisoners of war to internment camps, and the fall, on May 6, of Corregidor itself.

From despair came a sudden, shocking victory less than a month later. Thanks to a group of cryptanalysts at Pearl Harbor, Admiral Nimitz was able to learn that the target of Japan's next major naval assault would be Midway Island. On June 4 gallant Navy and Marine pilots sank four Japanese carriers in one of the greatest sea battles of history. It signaled the turn of the tide in the Pacific.

2.

That June General Short journeyed to West Point for the graduation of his son. At a garden party given by the superintendent of the Academy, General Marshall came across the lawn to speak to the Shorts. They talked for five minutes about their early service together but not a word was said of Pearl Harbor or Short's retirement.

Kimmel was now living in Bronxville, New York, working in New York City for the shipbuilding firm of an old friend, Admiral Frederic R. Harris. Kimmel was involved in drawing up drydock blueprints for areas in the Pacific where docks were unheard of. In his spare time he began planning for an eventual court-martial. He asked the Secretary of the Navy for access to the files on the attack. Knox gave him permission to study the files and get copies of whatever he needed.

Two of his sons, Manning and Tom, were submarine officers on duty in the Pacific. The latter, now a lieutenant, was in Australia. His submarine, the *S-40*, had escaped, after harrowing adventures, to Perth. While his boat was maneuvering in the harbor, a Dutch liner, one of the few ships that survived the exodus from Java, approached. Aboard was Nancy Cookson, who had met young Kimmel on a ship bound for China, the *President Adams*, several years earlier. The daughter of a consultant on a Malayan rubber plantation, she was escorting four children out of the battle zone. "I know that man on that submarine," she told a friend. "That's Tom Kimmel."

That afternoon she went to the Perth Post Office to send word to her parents that she was safe. By chance Kimmel was also there sending a three-word message to his family: "Well and thinner." Three months later they were married and in late August 1942 they left for America on a Danish ship. When the young couple arrived in Bronxville Tom was amazed by the strange welcome he received. His parents thought he was not supporting his father since he had written nothing about the Pearl Harbor controversy. Knowing only that his father had been relieved of command, he was astounded to learn about the Roberts report, the hate campaign launched against the family and how Stark had let down his father.

Later in the year Kimmel's third son, Ned, also a Navy officer, chanced to meet Stark, now commander of naval forces in Europe, on the *Ranger*, which was anchored at Scapa Flow. Having no idea there was bad feeling between his father and Stark, Ned expected Stark, who had known him since he was a boy, to embrace him warmly. But the admiral was very cool. "Oh, how are you?" he said, and ended the conversation.

3.

Allied joy over the Midway triumph had been followed a few weeks later by dismay at the fall of Tobruk to Rommel. Then came news on the second of July that Sevastopol in the Crimea had fallen to Hitler's troops. On the same day the British Eighth Army was compelled to retreat to the gates of Alexandria. What if the German forces in Russia broke through to the Caucasus and linked up with Rommel? Then it would be only a question of time before an even more ominous link-up with the Japanese.

On the other side of the world, however, an American assault on the island of Guadalcanal in the Solomons, Japan's southernmost outpost, was already under way. In the first week of August, 11,000 Marines landed on Guadalcanal. Despite vigorous attempts to dislodge the invaders by ground assaults and sea bombardments, the Americans enlarged their gains.

That fall the raging ground and sea battles in the Solomons along with the German assault on Stalingrad so occupied the minds of politicians and public alike that the Pearl Harbor controversy did not become a major issue in the congressional elections. There were attempts by the Administration to purge the most outspoken prewar isolationists but these efforts failed and the Republicans emerged with forty-four additional seats in the House and nine in the Senate, giving them a total of thirty-seven, enough to block a two-thirds vote. And in the House the Democratic majority had dwindled to two. These gains, at the expense of liberals and New Deal supporters, furthered the coalition between Republicans and Southern Democrats which had begun some four years earlier.

The period of November 1942 to the summer of 1943 was one of significant victories for the Allies. In the Pacific, the bloody Battle of Guadalcanal had ended in a desperate escape of the surviving Japanese troops; and MacArthur was driving across New Guinea toward Lae.

Hitler's successes in North Africa and Stalingrad had turned into catastrophic defeats; and Field Marshal von Manstein's mass tank assault near Kursk was stopped so decisively that the initiative on the Eastern Front now belonged to the Soviets. A fourth blow came fifteen days after an Anglo-American force landed in Sicily on July 10, 1943: Mussolini, forced to resign, was placed under arrest.

4.

By the fall of 1943 Admiral Kimmel was convinced that he would have to spend full time defending himself. He submitted his resignation to Admiral Harris and prepared to leave for Washington. Harris strongly urged him to reconsider. The people in Washington would destroy him.

"That is the chance I will have to take. But I have to live with myself and my mind is made up." Knox had agreed to let him examine all records in the Navy Department bearing on Pearl Harbor.

The problem now was to get a good lawyer. Already several had offered their services. "I had a feeling they were planted by the administration in an effort to sabotage any effort I might make."

At "my wit's end," Kimmel finally sought out a retired Navy captain, Robert A. Lavender, a patent lawyer familiar with court proceedings. He refused to act as Kimmel's chief counsel since he didn't have enough experience. But he knew a man who had: Charles B. Rugg, of the Boston law firm of Ropes, Gray, Best, Coolidge and Rugg.

Ropes, Gray was one of the most prestigious firms in New England and Charles Rugg one of the most respected counselors in the country. Son of a chief justice of the Supreme Judicial Court of Massachusetts, he was a graduate of Amherst and Harvard Law School. In 1930 Herbert Hoover appointed him Assistant Attorney General of the United States. His individual participation in litigation was characteristic of his prodigious energy and capacity. In three years on this assignment he personally argued more than seventy-five cases before the Court of Claims, and thirty-five cases involving separate and distinct issues before the Supreme Court. Nor did he argue from a brief written by others but took an active part in the draftsmanship of each brief, its arrangement, its selection of cases and its style. He earned the respect of the justices of the Supreme Court and one, Justice Butler, commented that he had "the soul of an advocate."

Since 1933 Rugg had returned to private practice where his skill in presenting evidence and his powers of persuasion won scores of cases. His speech was picturesque, his laughter contagious, and he dominated a courtroom with his wit and carefully laid plan of attack. He was, in short, just the kind of fighter that Kimmel needed. He carried his brief case into the courtroom as if it were a weapon, and his "I object" crackled like a rifle shot.

Early in 1944 Kimmel was invited to Boston and, upon entering Rugg's office, was disconcerted to see a signed photograph of Roberts hanging on the wall. For two hours Kimmel gave a history of what had happened to him since Pearl Harbor. "I did not spare the Roberts Commission nor Mr. Roberts himself but castigated the Commission and Mr. Roberts in particular with every invective at my command." These invectives brought a frown to Rugg's face.

Kimmel was not intimidated. "If you believe what I have told you," he said, "I would like to have you act as my counsel. If you don't believe me, I don't want you." Rugg did not hesitate. "I will take your case," he said, then added, "I shall have to ask some embarrassing questions." "Go ahead," said Kimmel. "I hold nothing back. No question can embarrass me."

"We are going to get along fine together." A moment later Kimmel described Roberts as "that son of a bitch."

"Admiral," protested Rugg, "please don't call him such names. He is an old friend of mine."

"I won't call him any names," Kimmel promised, "until I hear you doing it."

On the train ride back to New York, both Kimmel and Lavender read most of the way. As the admiral was getting off at 125th Street he said, "Lavender, this will be the first night since Pearl Harbor that I can go home and sleep."

By the time the three men next met, Rugg had read the transcript of the Roberts Commission proceedings. "You were right about Roberts," the lawyer said.

A few days later the chance Kimmel had long been awaiting suddenly came. On February 12 Knox wrote Admiral Hart ordering him to examine witnesses and take testimony under oath pertinent to the Japanese attack on Pearl Harbor. In view of the fact that Admiral Kimmel had an interest in the matter, Hart was instructed to "notify him of the times and places of the meetings to be had and that he has the right to be present, to have counsel, to introduce, examine, and cross-examine witnesses, to introduce matter pertinent to the examination and to testify or declare in his own behalf at his own request." Although not a court-martial, this was the first step in allowing Kimmel to tell his story—and with the aid of counsel.

Kimmel's good fortune continued nine days later with the appearance in his New York office of Captain Laurance Safford, head of Op-20-G, the Navy's cryptologic organization. Years earlier Safford had served briefly as a gunnery officer on a ship commanded by Kimmel. The admiral had observed, "He couldn't shoot a gun worth a damn," and told him, "Safford, you're not cut out for this, so I'm going to see that you're transferred." Since then Safford had not only founded the Navy's communications-intelligence organization but constructed a new cipher machine which greatly surpassed any known at the time. Brilliant and innovative, he was recognized as the Navy's foremost cryptanalyst.

Safford revealed that, when Congress was demanding the admiral's court-martial, he had expected to be called as a witness. To prepare his testimony and to refresh his memory he examined the secret files of the intercepted Japanese messages which had come through his office. To his amazement, he said, he discovered for the first time that none of these messages had been transmitted to Kimmel. Until then Safford had condemned Kimmel for dereliction of duty. Now he was outraged that all this vital information had been denied the admiral.

Kimmel's excitement can be imagined. He scribbled on a pad as Safford told of the messages from Tokyo indicating that war was inevitable and imminent. But his elation was mixed with a surge of resentment, particularly when he learned about the fourteen-point message received on December 6 and 7. Why had Washington deprived him of this knowledge? How had they dared to accuse him of dereliction![1] For three hours Safford talked but finally had to excuse himself. He was in the city, he explained, to attend an exhibition of his wife's paintings and had to get back to the gallery. His wife, a talented artist, was a domineering woman with a temper. Safford himself was a professional, a quiet man fanatically dedicated to his work. He was slightly stooped, an unforgettable sight as he hurried down the corridors of the Navy Building in short, rapid steps, his diminutive secretary, Miss Feathers, scurrying at his heels, pad in hand, jotting down his latest inspiration. He was now willing to jeopardize his career by revealing the truth.

Kimmel took his penciled notes to Rugg, who agreed that the Safford testimony would be of the greatest importance. The lawyer was faced with an unusual responsibility. His first duty was to preserve and record this new material in the best interest of his client. Yet he had to protect Safford's career from destruction, and the captain himself from possible punishment or liability. Further, there was the transcendent consideration of the national interest. Nothing could be done in defense of his client to disclose to the Japanese that their codes were still being read.

Since the Hart Inquiry would be conducted in secrecy, Rugg advised Safford "to make a complete disclosure of the existence and substance of the intercepted messages. Then, in any future proceedings, counsel for Kimmel could request access to this record and have it available for further legitimate inquiry."

At last Kimmel would have his day in court, his fate dependent on a canny lawyer from New England and a quixotic Navy captain.

---

[1] Ned Kimmel recalled that these revelations by Safford "got father's dander up" and, "by God, he turned into a tiger."

Part 2

PANDORA'S BOX

Chapter Five

MUTINY ON THE SECOND DECK

1.

Among the many ironies surrounding Pearl Harbor was the fact, unknown to the public, that the Roosevelt Administration had freely given to the British throughout 1941 much secret information denied Kimmel and Short. The most secure Japanese code, the one used by Tokyo to communicate with their embassies abroad, had been solved by a team of code breakers led by William F. Friedman, chief cryptanalyst of the Army Signal Corps. Eight machines were constructed to duplicate the original Japanese machine. There were four in Washington, two for the Army and two for the Navy; one in the Philippines at Cavite; and three in London. But none went to Hawaii. It was in this code, known to Americans as Purple, that the controversial fourteen-part message to Admiral Nomura in Washington was sent on December 6. If Kimmel or Short had been informed of its contents even a few hours before the Japanese attack, the American losses could have been reduced and perhaps the attack been seriously blunted.

When Kimmel's intelligence officer had learned that Cavite had the Purple machine, he asked Washington for another. On April 22, 1941, Commander Arthur H. McCollum, head of the Far Eastern Section of O.N.I. (the Office of Naval Intelligence), refused. "I thoroughly appreciate that you would probably be much helped in your daily estimates if you had at your disposal the DIP [the diplomatic code]. This, however, brings up matters of security, et cetera, which would be very difficult to solve. . . . The material you mentioned can necessarily have but passing and transient interest as action in the political sphere is determined by the Government as a whole and not by the forces afloat. . . . In other words, while you and the Fleet may be highly interested in politics, there is nothing that you can do about it."

Once the British learned the Purple code had been solved they requested the Joint Army-Navy Board in Washington for a machine. In return the British Chiefs of Staff agreed to reciprocate with a German Enigma cipher machine. After much haggling, two Purple machines had been sent to London in January 1941; whereupon the British refused to turn over the Enigma on the grounds that British intelligence was under the Foreign Office and any agreement made by the British Chiefs of Staff was null and void.

Once this was reported to Rear Admiral Leigh Noyes, director of Naval Communications, he exploded, accusing Rear Admiral Richmond Kelly Turner, chief of War Plans, of involvement in the double cross. Although slender, Turner was a forbidding sight with lantern jaw and heavy, black eyebrows. He was a feisty Irishman known as "Terrible Turner" because of his sulphuric temper. He retorted with vitriol. Thus began a feud on the second floor of the Navy Building that reached a climax early that fall. While Noyes was a gentle soul, a fine tennis player, and a favorite of ladies in Navy society, he surprised observers by opposing the abrasive Turner. Well known as a "fusser" in his Academy days, Noyes also had a habit of hoarding dispatches and then permitting the recipients only a glance at them. Even as recipients were initialing such messages, Noyes would snatch them away in his overzealous protection of secret material. Such behavior further infuriated Turner. "That Noyes!" he would rage in open contempt. "He and his goddamn secrets!"

His conflict with Noyes was aggravated by an even more critical one with Captain Alan Kirk, the new chief of O.N.I. Kirk, once naval attaché in London, was one of the few men junior to Turner who dared stand up to him. Turner resented this and was extremely irritated to learn that Kirk felt it was his responsibility to keep Kimmel informed concerning Japanese diplomatic moves and had actually sent him an occasional Purple intercept. Regarding this as intolerable interference, Turner complained to Stark that he was being impeded by O.N.I. His own mission was to prepare the estimate of enemy intentions, interpret, evaluate and disseminate all information on possible enemy nations. O.N.I. was simply a collection agency. "Betty" Stark greatly esteemed Turner and, some whispered, was dominated by him. In this case, at any rate, the chief of Naval Operations, an affable and accommodating man, sided with Turner.

Despite Turner's coup, Kirk felt obliged to keep Kimmel informed and during July 1941 sent him information from ten more important Purple intercepts. General Marshall, fearing this might tip off the Japanese that their top code had been solved, pressured Stark into cutting off any more such information.

To make matters worse, Kimmel was given no explanation and thenceforth labored under the delusion that the cessation of messages was only because there was nothing of importance to report. Even more important, he was also denied a look at the steady flow of messages to and from Honolulu and Tokyo via the Japanese consular code.

On September 24 a Mackay cable was delivered to the Japanese Consulate at Nuuanu Avenue in Honolulu. It was addressed to Nagao Kita, the consul general. Although the radiogram was signed Toyoda, for Foreign Minister Teijiro Toyoda, Kita knew it was from Captain Ogawa of Naval Intelligence. It was marked "very urgent" and when decoded read:

HENCEFORTH PLEASE MAKE YOUR REPORTS CONCERNING VESSELS ALONG THE FOLLOWING LINES INSOFAR AS POSSIBLE:

1. THE WATERS (OF PEARL HARBOR) ARE TO BE DIVIDED ROUGHLY INTO FIVE SUB-AREAS. (WE HAVE NO OBJECTIONS TO YOUR ABBREVIATING AS MUCH AS YOU LIKE.)

AREA A. WATERS BETWEEN FORD ISLAND AND THE ARSENAL.

AREA B. WATERS ADJACENT TO THE ISLAND SOUTH AND WEST OF FORD ISLAND. (THIS AREA IS ON THE OPPOSITE SIDE OF THE ISLAND FROM AREA A.)

AREA C. EAST LOCH.

AREA D. MIDDLE LOCH.

AREA E. WEST LOCH AND THE COMMUNICATING WATER ROUTES.

2. WITH REGARD TO WARSHIPS AND AIRCRAFT CARRIERS, WE
WOULD LIKE TO HAVE YOU REPORT ON THOSE AT ANCHOR, (THESE
ARE NOT SO IMPORTANT) TIED UP AT WHARVES, BUOYS AND IN THE
DOCKS. (DESIGNATE TYPES AND CLASSES BRIEFLY. IF POSSIBLE WE
WOULD LIKE TO HAVE YOU MAKE MENTION OF THE FACT WHEN
THERE ARE TWO OR MORE VESSELS ALONG THE SAME SIDE OF SAME
WHARF.)

Kita summoned Ensign Takeo Yoshikawa, who was posing as a
consular official but was in reality the sole Japanese Navy spy in
Hawaii. The ensign explained that Ogawa was setting up a grid
system for Pearl Harbor and wanted the exact locations of ships
pinpointed for the benefit of bombardiers and torpedo pilots.

This message was intercepted that day by MS-5, the monitoring
station the U. S. Army had set up recently at Fort Shafter, but
General Short had not been cleared for any of the Magic messages
and did not even know of MS-5's existence. Nor had the major in
charge of the station been given decrypting facilities. His orders
were merely to ship the intercepts air mail to Washington in their
original form. The next Pan American Clipper flight, scheduled
to leave in two days, was canceled by bad weather and so the important message was sent by ship. It arrived in Washington on
October 6 and was decrypted by S.I.S. (the Army's Signal Intelligence Service) three days later.

That same day the message was transmitted to the Navy. Realizing it could be a bomb plot for an air attack on Pearl Harbor, Kirk
urged it be sent to Kimmel. As had happened so often in the past
months, Turner objected. Nor did he relent when Captain H. D.
Bode, head of Foreign Intelligence, sided with Kirk. Turner appealed to Stark and once again the chief of Naval Operations
backed him. The intercept, which would become known as the
Bomb Plot message, was never sent to Kimmel; and a few days
later both Kirk and Bode were "detached" from intelligence and
reassigned.

Captain Kirk was replaced by Theodore "Ping" Wilkinson, the
fourth chief of O.N.I. that year. Top of his class at Annapolis in

1909, he was a tall, handsome man who had won the Medal of Honor in 1914 at Vera Cruz during the Mexican campaign for "leading his men with skill and courage." Scholarly, bright and intelligent, he was completely inexperienced in intelligence. Any hope that he and Turner could work harmoniously was dispelled immediately. The chief of War Plans was openly antagonistic. Perhaps Turner, still bitter that he had been fifth in the class of '08, could not abide the fact that Wilkinson had been first the following year. He bullied the newcomer relentlessly in an overt effort to dominate O.N.I. Taking advantage of Wilkinson's lack of experience, Turner began assuming some of his responsibilities. All decryptions from O.N.I. and Communications directed to Stark's office now had to be cleared through Turner, which made him, in effect, the ultimate censor. At the same time this gave him the option to release to Wilkinson and Noyes only that information he chose.[1]

The problems of those on a lower level at O.N.I. were compounded by their own differences with the Communications chief, Noyes. Commander Safford was as concerned as Kirk and Bode about the Bomb Plot message. It was obvious to him that Lieutenant Commander Joseph J. Rochefort, head of the Communications Security Unit of the Fourteenth Naval District located at Pearl Harbor, should have the message as well as the keys to the consular code so future intercepts could be solved on the spot. He drafted a message of instructions to Rochefort but this was disapproved summarily by Admiral Noyes, who remarked irately, "I'm not going to tell any district commandant how to run his job!"

A few weeks later Rochefort's monthly report for October ar-

[1] The feud on the Second Deck (the second floor of the Navy Building) was continued during the Battle of Savo Island off Guadalcanal in 1942. It was perhaps America's most humiliating naval defeat and is still bitterly debated and recollected with rancor and shame by men of the U. S. Navy. At the beginning of the battle, Admiral Turner, in command of the amphibious force, sent out a desperate call for help. His old adversary, Admiral Noyes, now in charge of the air support group, refused three times to send his carrier and destroyers to Turner's aid. "Both officers were good haters," Safford later commented. "Turner had his little victories in Washington: and now Noyes had his revenge." The latter was relieved of command for incompetence after losing his carrier, *Wasp*, several weeks later.

Captain Bode also was ruined by the Savo Island battle. In temporary command of *Chicago*, he inadvertently steamed away from the main battle. He committed suicide.

rived with its last paragraph requesting instructions. Safford made
a second attempt to comply but again Noyes dissented.

Despite the confusion on the Second Deck caused by rivalries
and cross-purposes remarkable progress was being made because of
a talented group of junior officers. "It was a strange madhouse,"
one of them recalled, "with sane inmates ruled over by madmen."
This dedicated group included Safford, Lieutenant Francis Raven,
Ensign Prescott Currier, Lieutenant George Linn and Commander Arthur McCollum. The last was chief of the Far Eastern
Intelligence Section. Born in Nagasaki, he understood the Japanese and their language. He was not embroiled in the Bomb Plot
message argument only because he was in England at the time and
on his way home was one of two survivors in an air crash. But he,
like Safford and others, agreed that the commanders in the Pacific
were not getting sufficient information. On December 1 he warned
both Turner and Stark that in his opinion "war or rupture of
diplomatic relations is imminent." Had Admiral Hart in the Philippines, he asked, been "adequately alerted"? Given categorical assurance that this had been done, he still worried. What with
Turner's bullish antagonism and Noyes's secretive nature, there
was no telling what had actually been sent out to the Pacific. On
December 4, McCollum was so convinced war with Japan was imminent that he drafted a brief, condensed dispatch warning all
commanders from the Caribbean to the Philippines. He took it to
Wilkinson, well knowing that he would only be shunted on to
Turner, and once the War Plans chief saw the dispatch he began
revising it. With a scowl Turner showed McCollum the war warning
message sent to Kimmel on November 27.

"Good gosh," said McCollum. "You put in the words 'war
warning.' I do not know what could be plainer than that, but nevertheless I would like to see mine go too."

"Well, if you want to send it, you either send it the way I corrected it, or take it back to Wilkinson, and we will argue about it."

McCollum scanned the diluted dispatch and, deflated, took it
back to Wilkinson, who said, "Leave it here with me for a while."

The emasculated warning was never sent. Noyes chanced to see
it and remarked characteristically, "I think it is an insult to the intelligence of the Commander in Chief." He was referring to Kim-

mel who, having received no warnings since November 27, had the feeling the alert was over.

2.

On the first of January, 1942, Safford was promoted to the rank of captain. But two weeks later, on the day the Roberts Commission arrived in Washington, he was called to Noyes's office to be informed that his professional career was virtually ended. Noyes explained that Admiral King felt his job was too big for a single officer to handle and that it would be split into its component parts. Safford would retain the smallest part, cryptographic research. He had performed this duty eighteen years ago with the rank of lieutenant. "No other reason was given by Noyes," Safford wrote in an unpublished memorandum, "and there was no criticism of Safford's performance of duty." What Noyes said was at variance with a written directive of the previous day ordering Commander John R. Redman to set up and head a Radio Intelligence and Deception Section. This directive blandly ignored the fact that such an organization had been set up under Safford, seventeen years previously, and that it numbered about a thousand people on January 15, 1942.

Safford was appalled "but there was nothing to do but bow to fate. There was a war on and the United States was taking a terrible beating from the nation which our Top Brass had badly underestimated and had refused to take seriously." Wilkinson's assistant commiserated with Safford. "You have been capsized," he said, "just as we have been capsized."

Perhaps Safford was unaware that his downfall had been plotted by Captain Joseph Reasor Redman, Noyes's assistant, who became chief of Communications that February. A shrewd bureaucrat, he had always disliked Safford's informal, disorganized working style, regardless of his accomplishments. Safford's erratic management had gone unnoticed by high quarters before Pearl Harbor but, with America now flung into a two-ocean war, Redman reasoned that it was essential Op-20-G have a tighter organization to intercept and break the German U-boat codes and thus protect the vast convoys that would soon be crossing the Atlantic. And so Captain

Redman, an efficiency expert, maneuvered his younger brother into taking over the major part of Safford's job.

The entire operation expanded under the efficient Captain Redman and Op-20-G, with allied agencies, moved from the old building on Constitution Avenue into the red brick structures of a former girls' school near the intersection of Nebraska and Massachusetts avenues.[2] Here, Safford was shoved aside into an office where he was supposed to be primarily "tinkering with gadgets."

"Although in the official doghouse, Safford managed to contribute essentially to the War in the Atlantic," he later wrote, "and to mitigate in some degree one of Admiral King's worst blunders." Safford was far too modest. His contribution would rank high among the unsung feats of the war. He not only uncovered a blunder that was costing America numerous ships and lives but ended that unnecessary destruction. Since early 1941 he had suspected the security of the code being used for high-level communications between the British and the United States, Naval Cipher No. 3. It was exactly like the Japanese Fleet code, JN 25, "except that it was lacking in the protection afforded by the complexity and ambiguity of written Japanese." While "tinkering" at his little office in the former girls' school, Safford confirmed his suspicions that the Germans had broken Naval Cipher No. 3, which was still in use. He was positive that the appalling toll of Allied shipping in the Atlantic by German submarines was because the enemy was now "reading solid" all the U.S.-British communications pertaining to convoy-and-routing as well as anti-submarine warfare.

He warned his superiors but they did not take him seriously. Neither did a British technical expert whom he alerted that summer. In desperation Safford took action. In all haste he succeeded in designing a system that would thwart the Germans by "'marrying' the British-Type-X cipher machine with the American ECM [the Electronic Countermeasure device created by the S.I.S. cryptographer Friedman]. . . . By working from each machine towards a common meeting-point, Safford succeeded in developing a third type of cryptographic principle which would enable the two radically different machines to inter-communicate." Within

2 Today the Naval Security Command Headquarters at the same address faces the new Japanese Embassy.

eight months he had designed and built working models of the necessary adapter units for both machines. Simple and comparatively inexpensive, they could be installed and removed without tools in seconds. "Most important, when removed the two machines operated in their original, unique cryptographic principles."

Before placing a production contract for his Combined Cipher Machine, that November Safford urged temporary use of the ECM devised by Friedman. The suggestion was forwarded to the U. S. Joint Chiefs of Staff, who rejected it.

Even so the stubborn Safford, spurred on by the appalling losses in the Atlantic, began building his own machine from scrounged material. In the next four months almost two million gross tons of shipping were sunk at the cost of but fifty U-boats. It was evident that if Doenitz's wolf packs were not rendered harmless Germany would win the Battle of the Atlantic. Still Safford's new system, although now completed, was not put into use. In mid-October of 1943 one of the leading cipher experts on the British Military Mission in Washington visited Safford privately. "You were right about Naval Cipher No. 3," he said. "It is no good and the Germans have been reading it all along as you predicted. Our faces are very red and your stock is very high in London."

Several days later Friedman also made a private visit. "General Marshall has just learned that a British troop ship was sunk and 900 U.S. soldiers drowned because the Germans had broken the Naval codes. He is boiling mad and ready to raise hell over it. He has instructed me to make a personal investigation as to the circumstances, find out who is to blame, and what emergency measures should be taken to prevent recurrence of such losses."

Safford unraveled the whole story: How Admiral Robert Ghormley had accepted the British proposal to use Naval Cipher No. 3 for "possible" combined U.S.-British naval communications as one of his first official acts in November 1940 after assuming office as special naval observer in London. How Stark had approved of this decision before conferring with Noyes. How Noyes would not ask Stark to reconsider the matter or even permit Safford to talk to Stark about it. How Safford's efforts to alert his superiors had failed. "I further informed Friedman that the three men to blame [Admirals Ghormley, Noyes and Stark] had subsequently been relieved of command for incompetence, and that nothing would be gained by raising hell."

The conversation with Friedman ended Safford's frustration. In December 1943 his Combined Cipher Machine at last came into use in the North Atlantic, and the effectiveness of Doenitz's wolf packs was terminated.

3.

Several months earlier Safford also had had time to gather material on Pearl Harbor for what he believed would be the impending court-martial of Kimmel. "I realized I would be one of the important witnesses, that my memory was vague, and I began looking around to get everything that I could to prepare a written statement which I could follow as testimony. That was the time when I studied the Roberts Report carefully for the first time and noted no reference to the 'winds' message or to the message which McCollum had written and which I had seen and I thought had been sent."

Up to this time he had been convinced that Kimmel, derelict in his duty, deserved his harsh fate. But now he began to suspect that perhaps the admiral had *not* been given all the information about Japanese intentions that Safford had been led to believe. The "winds" message referred to one of the most important Japanese intercepts. On November 19, 1941, the Japanese Foreign Office advised its representatives abroad in the consular code that, in case diplomatic relations were about to be severed with the United States, Great Britain or Russia, a signal in the form of a false weather report sent in the clear would be broadcast and all code papers were then to be destroyed. If the signal was *"Higashi no kaze ame* [East wind, rain]" that meant a break with America; *"Kitano kaze kumori* [North wind, cloudy]" a break with Russia; and *"Nishi no kaze hare* [West wind, clear]" a break with Britain.

After this message was decoded and translated in Safford's office on November 28, everyone on the Second Deck was alerted to watch for the crucial execute of the "winds" code. All interception stations were instructed to forward all such weather reports. Safford distinctly remembered seeing a message reading "East

wind, rain" about the third or fourth of December. He had assumed the warning had been transmitted to Kimmel but failure to
find the so-called "winds" execute in the files aroused his suspicions. Moreover, further study of the Roberts report convinced
him Kimmel had been made a scapegoat. Realizing he himself had
done the admiral an injustice, Safford threw himself into further
investigation with the same intensity and fervor he had exerted on
ridding the Navy of Cipher No. 3. He went through files and queried many colleagues. By mid-November 1943 he began to suspect
that Kimmel had been deliberately deprived of this information;
that he was not only a scapegoat but the victim of a complex
frame-up. In December he uncovered more material which practically confirmed his suspicions and on the twenty-second he wrote
for additional information to Lieutenant Commander Alwin
Kramer. Before Pearl Harbor, O.N.I. had loaned Kramer to
Op-20-G as head of the Translation Section. Since Safford could
not understand Japanese, he had relied heavily on Kramer, who
had studied the language.

Kramer was currently stationed at Pearl Harbor and Safford's
greeting, "My dear Kramer-san," was followed by the announcement that he was "preparing a secret paper" covering
events taking place in early December 1941.

> I realize that your reply will have to be censored and therefore
> you must be guarded as to what you state. Also, I am phrasing
> my questions very carefully, in the event that my letter might
> fall into unauthorized hands. I am saving a copy of my letter
> so it will be merely necessary to give the *question number* and
> a brief answer, which should not disclose anything to an out-
> sider.

He then asked what time on December 6 Kramer had brought
the Japanese intercept to the President, whom he referred to as
"Mr. R." Was Hull ("Mr. H.") with him? When were Admirals
S. (Stark) and W. (Wilkinson) informed of the message? He
also asked what time Kramer reached the Navy Building on the
morning of the seventh. And were Mr. K. and Mr. S. (Kimmel
and Short) telephoned or notified in any way? He also asked what
happened to "the original Weather Report." It had disappeared

from the files. He was referring, of course, to the "winds" execute, "East wind, rain."

Safford continued his assiduous research. Clearing Kimmel had become a crusade. The days passed but there was still no answer from Kramer. Finally on January 17, 1944, he received a memorandum from Hawaii. Kramer revealed he had taken the fourteenth part of the Japanese message to Stark at about nine o'clock on the morning of December 7. This indicated to Safford that there had been plenty of time, about three and a half hours, to send Kimmel the warning he never received until after the attack. Convinced that he had "absolute proof" that Kimmel had been framed, Safford sent Kramer an excerpt from a *Saturday Evening Post* article on Admiral William F. Halsey, commander of the Third Fleet, in the December 25, 1943, issue by J. Bryan III. "Halsey's devotion to Kimmel, an Annapolis classmate, is almost religious," wrote Bryan. "He was shocked to see him cast as a scapegoat. When the Roberts Committee of Investigation asked Halsey how he, almost alone, happened to be ready for the Japanese attack, his answer was, 'Because of one man—Admiral Kimmel.' It would surprise none of Halsey's friends if, on retirement, he applied himself to Kimmel's exoneration." The clipping was pertinent since Kramer had just been ordered to Halsey's staff. On a blank space in the article, Safford had typed:

> My dear Kramer:
> When the proper time comes, show the above to Admiral Halsey as a sort of letter-of-introduction. Assure him that his ambition will come true. And it will not be necessary for him to wait until his retirement to see Admiral Kimmel completely exonerated. But we will need Admiral Halsey's help. Do not hesitate to tell him *everything*.

Three days later, on January 22, 1944, Safford wrote Kramer at length. "What a break for you, as well as the cause, to be ordered to Admiral Halsey's staff. I can see the hand of Providence in it. . . . With regard to taking Admiral Halsey into confidence, wait patiently for the proper moment, and then shoot the works. Tell him everything he will listen to and show him whatever documentary proof you may have. Use your own judgment and don't force the issue." Kramer was to be prudent and patient. "I am just beginning to get things lined up on this end. No one in Opnav [Navy Operations] can be trusted. Premature action would only tip off the people who framed Adm. Kimmel and Gen. Short, and will also get Kramer and Safford in very serious trouble. Yet we must have backing, the rank, and the prestige afforded by Adm. Halsey." Kramer was to tell Halsey that Safford "has overwhelming proof of the guilt of Opnav and Gen. Staff, plus a list of about fifteen reliable witnesses."

Fearing their correspondence might be "tapped" by those trying to hide the truth, Safford also sent a condensation code for future correspondence. It was like something out of a spy novel. No. 1 meant Roosevelt. 2 was Hull, 3 was Stark. He himself was 8 and Kramer was 10. The Son of Heaven (The Emperor) was 109. There were numbers for every department, for codes, for messages, for cities (Pearl Harbor was 92) and even for dates (December 6, 1941, was 136, December 7 was 137, and 1325 Eastern Standard Time, December 7, was 138).

Prepared to go the limit to reveal the truth, Safford journeyed to Kimmel's office on February 21, 1944. First he was screened by Admiral Harris, who asked "Were you ever on his staff?" He wasn't. "Are you a close personal friend?"

"No, sir, just a casual acquaintance."

"Then why do you wish to see Admiral Kimmel?"

"Because Admiral Kimmel is the victim of the dirtiest frame-up in the history of the Navy. And I have the proof of it."

"In that case," said Harris, "you can see him."

On February 1, 1944, Nimitz island-hopped from Tarawa all the way to Kwajalein in the center of the Marshalls. His next goal was another bold leap all the way to the Marianas from whence the new B-29 Superfortresses could bomb Japan.

Chapter Six

THE HART INQUIRY
FEBRUARY–JUNE 1944

1.

Soon after sending Rugg the notes on Safford's revelations, Admiral Kimmel had second thoughts about the Hart Inquiry. Was this really the best way to bring his case before the public? After all it would hardly be a free and open trial, merely a taking of testimony, and it might prevent him from getting a proper hearing later. Lavender and Rugg agreed and it was concluded that the admiral should not participate. Safford's testimony alone should provide grounds for a genuine trial. "I feel that I am entitled to a speedy and public trial and to be informed of the nature and cause of any accusation against me," he wrote Knox. "To date I have been offered neither." The Hart Inquiry, he added, will be restricted in scope, "will not be free and open and will not be of the character to which I am entitled."

Knox replied, "It must be well known to you that the public interests make a speedy and public trial impossible at this time. Similarly Admiral Hart's examination cannot be 'free and open' since matters of a very secret nature will be dealt with and their disclosures would be inimical to the war effort." In any case the Hart Inquiry would proceed and he hoped Kimmel would participate.

With the help of Rugg, Kimmel replied at length why this was impossible. The simple recording of testimony was "entirely inadequate." Also the absence of formal charges made it impossible for him "to prepare and intelligently to cross-examine witnesses who may testify before Admiral Hart and to enable me to present evidence in my own behalf. . . ." Limiting witnesses to members of the naval forces was also unfair. "In the nature of the case, it is apparent that personnel of the Army as well as civilians are intimately concerned in the events pertinent to the Pearl Harbor attack." He and Rugg of course were thinking of such key witnesses as Knox himself, Stimson and Marshall.

On February 22 the Hart Inquiry began. During the next four months he recorded the testimony of forty naval officers, most of them admirals, in Washington, San Francisco and the Pacific area. One whose testimony turned out to be particularly unfavorable to Kimmel was Admiral Turner. He met with Hart at Pearl Harbor on April 7. Since coming to the Pacific as commander of amphibious forces of the Pacific Fleet he had lived up to his reputation as a man difficult to deal with and shared the title of Most Hated Man in the Navy with King. But he was a brilliant tactician and had been promoted to vice admiral. What many did not realize was that his drinking problem was getting out of hand, although so far he had been able to bound back from hangovers and operate at his usual high efficiency.

He stated that he was "not in the least" surprised by the attack on Pearl Harbor. He and Stark and other senior assistants all considered a surprise air attack "a strong possibility." Moreover, he had sufficiently warned Kimmel. "The letters and dispatches on that subject initiated by my office are not many because we felt, and it was the Chief of Naval Operations policy, not to nag on matters of that sort. The problem was put where it belonged, in the hands of the Commander-in-Chief." That is, Kimmel. The "war warning" message of November 27 was all that Kimmel needed to be on the alert for any surprise attack. Turner's testimony, an indictment of Kimmel, went in the face of sworn statements to Hart made by Kimmel's staff.

Back home there was increasing pressure for a public trial of Kimmel and Short. During his April 11 press conference, Secretary

Knox was questioned in connection with Congress' extension of the time for Kimmel's trial. As a former newspaperman, Knox was accustomed to speaking freely and replied spontaneously that he was going to seek the Judge Advocate General's legal opinion since he was "confused." That officer must have shuddered; fearing the Navy might lose the initiative in the case, he quickly drafted a press release in Knox's name stating that he had received a memorandum from Admiral King officially declaring that "certain officers in the Navy now serving on battle fronts in various parts of the world, could not be withdrawn from their military duties in order to participate in court-martial proceedings in connection with Pearl Harbor." The release pointed out that Kimmel had long since signed a waiver "and there is now no necessity to construe any acts of Congress on this subject."

Kimmel regarded this latest announcement as another trick to deny him a trial. "I presume you have noted the recent maneuvers in Washington by Mr. Knox," he wrote his oldest son, Manning, "and his contradictory statements issued in regard to the court-martial. From this mass of confusion I think it is becoming quite clear that the Administration has absolutely no intention of bringing General Short and me to trial."

2.

Kimmel now had additional counsel. Edward Hanify, formerly of Rugg's law office but now a Navy lieutenant j.g., was permitted by the chief of the Bureau of Naval Personnel to assist Rugg. Hanify had come to Ropes, Gray in 1936 after Holy Cross and Harvard Law School, and greatly admired Rugg, with whom he had often worked. On his way to see Kimmel in Bronxville, he read the Roberts report. It was so damning, he felt there would be difficulty defending Kimmel but a few minutes with the admiral changed Hanify's mind. He was impressed by the decisiveness of the admiral's actions and the profound look of deep sadness in his eyes. "I said to myself, 'There's something the matter with the Roberts Report because this is not the type of man who could be guilty of any carelessness.'"

While digging up background on the case, Hanify interviewed

Admiral Richardson. The admiral said he was going to tell a story that the lieutenant could regard as a parable. "Assume," Richardson said, "you were the leader of the greatest nation in the world, and assume that you saw, in another hemisphere, the development of a power which you regarded, and with reasonable support, as a total threat to Western civilization as you knew it. Supposing, however, that for various reasons, your conception of the danger was not shared by your constituents, your own people. And you saw the total destruction of Western civilization in the hands of this adversary, and you detected in your own people, at the time, on the basis of everything they knew, a lack of appreciation of the problem. Assume that you saw that the only salvation of Western civilization was to repel this particular power but that that required you to enter a foreign war for which your people were not psychologically or militarily prepared. Assume that what was needed to galvanize your own people for a unified approach towards this basic danger to civilization was an incident in which your posture was clearly of passive non-aggression, and apparent unpreparedness; and the incident in question was a direct act of aggression which had no excuse or justification. Assume that you saw this potentiality developing on the horizon and it was the solution to the dilemma, as you saw it, of saving civilization and galvanizing your own people. It is conceivable, is it not, that you might be less disposed to create a situation in which there might be doubt as to who struck the first blow. You'd want to be sure that whatever the incident, it happened under circumstances where it was perfectly clear that you were not the aggressor, and the resulting incident galvanized your own people to a realization of the terrible threat which they faced from this totalitarian force. Now just think about that. I don't say it's an hypothesis even. It's a fable. You just think about that fable as you study some of this material. And it's conceivable that it might have some enlightening factors."

In the meantime Hart's investigation continued. Admiral Halsey staunchly defended his friend Kimmel. "I did not feel that we were well informed on what the Japs were doing and I felt we were operating in the dark. I had the personal feeling, entirely per-

sonal, that they knew a lot more in Washington than we knew out
there and that we should have been informed." Had he discussed
this with Kimmel? "I recall, vaguely, discussions along that line
and damning them for not letting us in on the information."

On April 17 Hart finished his examinations in Hawaii and
started back to Washington. On the twenty-ninth the most important witness, Captain Safford, reported to Admiral Hart at the
Navy Building. First they talked off the record. When Safford told
of the "winds" execute and how all copies had been destroyed, the
admiral sternly observed that such remarks should not be entered
as evidence. "I have just come from the front office, and I have
seen your 'winds' message. Now don't make statements that you
can't verify."

Heartened by confirmation that someone else had seen the
"winds" execute, Safford agreed to withdraw from his testimony
any mention of destroyed messages. But he insisted on testifying
under oath how, on December 3, he had prepared a dispatch warning Kimmel of imminent danger. "Before drafting my message, I
called Commander McCollum on the telephone and asked him,
'Are you people in Naval Intelligence doing *anything* to get a
warning out to the Pacific Fleet?' And McCollum replied, 'We
are doing everything *we* can to get the news out to the Fleet.'
McCollum emphasized both 'we's.' In sending this information I
was overstepping the bounds as established by approved war plans
and joint agreement between Naval Communications and Naval
Intelligence, but I did it because I thought McCollum had been
unable to get his message released."

Hart asked if the units at Pearl Harbor had any material from
which they could have gained this information through their own
efforts. "No, sir, they did not have the material and they could not
possibly have gained this information."

Hart had no wish to continue this line of questioning but
Safford insisted on telling in detail about "winds." He revealed
how, on December 4, McCollum drafted a long message quoting
the "winds" execute, ending with the positive warning that war
was imminent. Captain Wilkinson approved this message and
then discussed it with Admiral Noyes in Safford's presence. Wilkinson had then asked, "What do you think of the message?" "I

think it is an insult to the intelligence of the Commander-in-Chief," observed Noyes.

"I do not agree with you," Wilkinson had replied. "Admiral Kimmel is a very busy man, with a lot of things on his mind, and he may not see the picture as clearly as you and I do. I think it only fair to the Commander-in-Chief that he be given this warning and intend to send it if I can get it released by the front office."

Safford explained that at the time of Pearl Harbor he had assumed the warning was sent. He hadn't realized until two years later, after studying the Roberts report carefully, that it had never gone out. As he recalled it, the "winds" execute was received during the evening of December 3 but Safford did not see it until the next day. "Lieutenant A. A. Murray, U.S.N.R., came into my office with a big smile on his face and a piece of paper in his hand and said, 'Here it is!' as he handed me the 'Winds Message.' As I remember, it was the original yellow teletype sheet with the significant 'Winds' underscored and the meaning in Kramer's handwriting at the bottom." He gave a list of those who must have read the "winds" execute; those who had heard about it by hearsay; and those who should have some recollection of it.

"The 'Winds Message' was last seen by myself about December 14, 1941, when the papers which had been distributed in early December were assembled by Kramer, checked by myself, and then turned over to the Director of Naval Communications for use as evidence before the Roberts Commission, according to my understanding at the time."

Although there was no way all this information could be made public, it had at last been put on the record, despite Hart's reluctance; and it would greatly assist Kimmel once he got his day in court.

The findings of the Hart Inquiry were not to be revealed to the public until after the war and its significance could only be guessed at by those outside of top naval and Administration circles. Hart filed no report but he did write Admiral Stark in London that what he had learned threw some suspicion on the Navy Department's role in the Pearl Harbor debacle.

Something the President told him would also concern Hart for the rest of his life. "I happened to remark to him," he later revealed in a taped interview, "that perhaps it was unfortunate that the Japanese heard too much about the date of 1 April [1942] being given as the date on which General MacArthur and his forces would be ready for war. The President replied that he had been assured by General Marshall in November [1941] that the Army's forces in the Philippines were ready then! Now I understand that at that date Secretary Knox was assuring the world that our fleets were entirely ready for the Japanese, but I still wonder if General Marshall really did say that. Anyhow, the President said, and I'm quoting his words, 'If I had known the true situation, I could have babied the Japanese along quite a while longer.'"

By the beginning of June 1944 Italy had surrendered and the Allies ruled the Mediterranean. On the Eastern Front it was only a question of how long the Wehrmacht could hold back the resurgent Red Army. Attacks by American daylight bombers on fuel plants in central and eastern Germany had already seriously endangered Hitler's entire armament program. And the Allies were making final preparations for a massive landing in France.

In the Pacific an armada of 535 ships was approaching Saipan. It carried 127,571 troops, most of them Marines.

Chapter Seven

THE ARMY AND NAVY CLUB
JUNE–OCTOBER 1944

1.

Even before the Hart Inquiry closed, Rugg realized that it was time to attack "to prevent the whole story from being shelved and buried." The statute of limitations for prosecuting Kimmel and Short was nearing its deadline. If it were not extended the two men might never get the open hearing they both wanted. It was, thought Rugg, an anomalous situation. His client, the accused, was anxious to confront his accusers while the powers that be were obviously hoping that the matter would die. There were legal reasons to wonder whether a congressional extension of the statute would withstand attack. "Kimmel's waiver of its provisions might be treated as incapable of curing a jurisdictional defect," commented Hanify later. "No others but Kimmel and Short had waived the statute." Hence, Rugg decided it was essential that Congress not only extend the statute further "but combine the extension with a mandate to the Secretaries of the Army and Navy severally to investigate the Pearl Harbor disaster."

"Admiral, this is the crossroads," Rugg told Kimmel. "If I go down to Washington and have this statute passed, we're going to be in for a tempestuous time. The other course may be that they will drop this business and you will be free from any more public discussion."

Kimmel was a fighter. "I am determined that the American people know this story, and you are authorized to go all out and see that it is done. I am prepared to face the consequences, embarrassment, misunderstanding, time, anything. Go to it."

And so in mid-April Rugg and Hanify went to the capital. Rugg himself drew up the substance of the statute; the next day Hanify dressed up the preamble and put on the formal, finishing touches. Hanify took the draft to the Supreme Court Library where he studied it before rewriting the final draft by hand. Having no typewriter, he took the draft to the office of Senator Walsh of Massachusetts. Walsh was chairman of the Naval Affairs Committee. "To my great consternation," recalled Hanify, "when the thing was finished and was to be delivered to Congressman [Dewey] Short's office, Walsh called in a Navy yeoman assigned to his committee to make the delivery. And I thought to myself, 'If this youngster ever happens to divert the document and the Secretary of the Navy and the Secretary of the Army discover that a lieutenant j.g. is getting laws prepared on this delicate subject, you will end up on some atoll very soon.'" But the messenger reported straight to Congressman Short, who publicly demanded a further extension of the statute of limitations and courts-martial for the two commanders.

On May 24 a senator telegraphed Kimmel asking what his position was regarding extension of the statute. He replied that he wanted a trial by court-martial as soon as possible. "I have wanted it since Pearl Harbor and have said so in letters to the Secretary of the Navy. I want a free, open and public hearing. I am ready now." For two and a half years he had waited for the Navy Department to bring him to trial. "In the critical years following Pearl Harbor I understood why I had to bear, in silence, the burden of shame heaped upon me by the report of the Roberts Commission and by published interpretations of that report. Now, with our armed forces on the offensive on all fronts, I owe it to my family, to my friends and to the public to make it clear that I want a trial by Court-Martial at the earliest practicable date." He had been accused of dereliction of duty by Roberts. "I want to answer that accusation in a formal and public way. . . . To be held under a shadow of blame for an additional prolonged and indefinite period is intolerable. The public has a right to know what happened. I have an American's right to my day in court."

The following day he got a telegram from Senator Homer Ferguson, a Republican from Michigan, asking the same question. Kimmel gave a similar reply. The senator's response was to introduce a bill to extend the statute beyond its June deadline. This, he hoped, would force an immediate trial before the fall. Debate over the proposed extension might give the Republicans, and anti-New Deal Democrats, the opportunity to link the White House with the Pearl Harbor debacle. And it would come at the best possible time—the months preceding the presidential election.

The debate on Congressman Short's resolution in the House on June 5 turned out to be promising. When a Democrat from North Carolina opposed any wartime inquiry he was greeted with a loud chorus of boos and shouts of "Shame! Shame!" "Mr. Chairman," proclaimed a Republican from Illinois, "why is it necessary, after two and a half years, to continue to insist upon keeping the truth about Pearl Harbor a secret? Can it be that the court-martial of Admiral Kimmel and General Short will reveal that our military and naval commands were not negligent but rather the negligence was on the part of the civil heads of the Government? . . . The administration fears an adverse public reaction to what the court-martial would reveal on the manner in which the 'affairs of state' were handled prior to the war and, with an election approaching, the administration is determined to keep the true facts about Pearl Harbor hidden."

The debate spilled over to the next day, the sixth, and some Democrats tried to whip up a patriotic counteroffensive by exploiting the D-Day invasion which was thrilling the nation. "It would be a splendid contribution on the part of the Members of the House," said Emanuel Celler of New York, ". . . if we would no longer continue deliberations on this bill and discard it. That would be a fitting tribute to the brave and intrepid commanders of our armed forces and the boys under them." But the Republicans and their anti-New Deal colleagues would have none of such rhetoric. Even supporters of the Administration realized it was a losing battle and Dewey Short's provision for immediate courts-martial and a three-month extension was passed overwhelmingly, 305 to 35.

A week later both houses passed a joint resolution directing the Secretaries of War and the Navy to proceed forthwith with an investigation into the facts surrounding the catastrophe of December 7. At last Kimmel and Short would have their day in court; that is, if the President did not veto the bill. Franklin Roosevelt, reading the temper of Congress, again proved what a master politician he was. He was confident, he said in a formal statement, that Congress "did not intend that the investigation should be conducted in a manner which would interfere with the war effort. On the strength of this confidence I have approved the resolution." This implied that it was Stimson and James V. Forrestal (successor to Knox as Secretary of the Navy after the latter's death by heart attack five weeks earlier) who were attempting to impede trials for Kimmel and Short and not he. He undoubtedly had in mind the coming presidential campaign during which the Republicans would be likely to make Pearl Harbor a major issue.

2.

On July 8 the Army Pearl Harbor Board was appointed with Lieutenant General George Grunert as president. But the Navy had not selected their members by the thirteenth when Kimmel wrote Rugg that he still felt such an inquiry was inadequate to investigate the case fully. "Nothing short of an impartial investigation of the Executive and the War and Navy Departments will ever set forth the facts clearly. . . . Just how far a Naval Court of Inquiry can go in an investigation of the War and Navy Departments will depend upon the character of the members and the pressure that will be brought to bear on them by these and other agencies. It is conceivable that a Naval Court of Inquiry might be stopped if they pursue certain phases too tenaciously."

That same day the Navy Court of Inquiry was finally selected. Admiral Orin G. Murfin, formerly judge advocate general and commander of the Asiatic Fleet, was the chairman. The two other members were also well-known retired admirals. Adolphus Andrews, a former aide to three Presidents, had commanded the Eastern Sea Frontier, responsible for protecting the East Coast in the early years of the war. Edward C. Kalbfus, president of the Naval War College for all but one year from 1934 to 1942, was the most sympathetic to Kimmel, being already convinced that he should not be held solely responsible for Pearl Harbor.

The three members of the Army Board were still on active duty. Grunert, once a private, was a close friend of Marshall and very well thought of by the War Department. Convinced that Short had been derelict, he desired to vindicate the War Department. The Army Air Force representative, Major General Walter H. Frank, was the only West Pointer on the board. He too was convinced that Short must suffer the consequences since he surely had enough information before the attack. The third member, Major General Henry D. Russell, was an odd choice. He had commanded a National Guard division until his relief in May 1942. He disliked Marshall intensely, blaming him for the anti-National Guard policy held during the war. He admired Short but had been reluctant to serve on the board. Wincing at the thought of getting involved in a controversy over the Army's role in the disaster, he accepted for the sake of giving Short a fairer hearing.

On July 17 the Navy members began preparations for the inquiry. A week later they were sworn in. They would be ready to start procedures on the last day of July.

Admiral Kimmel was already in Washington making last-minute preparations with Rugg, Lavender and Hanify. So far he only had Safford's unsupported word that there were incriminating intercepted Japanese messages in the secret Navy files. Now was the time to produce such messages, if they did exist. He went to Secretary of the Navy Forrestal's office. By lucky chance Admiral King happened to be Acting Secretary that day, and after Kimmel asked permission to have an aide search the files, King readily complied. "Mr. Knox promised you access to all the files so I can see no reason to refuse."

That same afternoon Kimmel sent Lavender to unearth the missing messages. "I knew pretty well the general subject of them," Lavender recalled, "but I was astounded when I was shown into a room and there was a stack of papers two and a half feet high of intercepted messages." He had a limited time for search but Safford had given him the numbers of the most important intercepts. Also very helpful was the man in charge, a former junior member of Kimmel's staff. Lavender extracted some forty-three messages typical of what he thought should have gone to Kimmel. "As I sat back in my chair and looked over the selected messages and then at the piles of other messages I became nauseated when I realized what the information in my hands would have meant to Kimmel and the men of the Fleet who died."

That evening Rugg and Hanify dined with Lavender at the Willard Hotel. "I found the messages and many more," he told them but was still so sickened by what he had uncovered that he could not eat.

The messages had the same effect on Hanify. "I cannot now describe the revulsion I felt as the war and its carnage continued and I pondered why the highest leaders of the government of the United States reading the most secret designs of their potential enemy would keep this material from trusting and loyal commanders at the distant, lonely, and inadequately protected bastions of defense with the lives of my fellow citizens in the armed forces at risk. Was this an incredible, fantastic, gargantuan series of mistakes or was there operating some sinister design?"

The following day Marshall's deputy telephoned the director of Naval Communications to vigorously protest Lavender's visit to the secret files. Orders, he said, forbade such an inspection. When the director said he had received no such orders, the deputy hastily explained he merely meant that orders *should* forbid such inspection.

Even though the messages had been segregated and authenticated, the copies were not delivered to Lavender but kept in the custody of Naval Communications. There was nothing for Rugg to do but wait until the court of inquiry began. Then his demand for the intercepts would be a matter of record.

Admiral Stark was also preparing his defense. After his dismissal as chief of Naval Operations, he had been sent to England as commander of the United States naval forces in Europe. "It appeared that this assignment had been made originally because the President wished, for political reasons, to have Stark out of Washington."[1] So wrote Admiral King in his biography. But Stark was convinced King himself was involved in his being "kicked upstairs." Ordinarily a man of remarkably even temper, Stark was not one to hold a grudge. But in this case he could not forgive King, whom he had personally selected as commander of the Atlantic Fleet. Although his new position in Europe was an important one, Stark felt he was being rushed out of the country in semi-disgrace. As he said good-by to his former aide, Commander Harold Krick, he was downcast. The Kricks were close personal friends of the admiral and he treated their children as his own grandchildren. "He was hurt and disappointed and crushed," recalled Mrs. Krick, who had often played golf with him.

In England, Stark was in charge of the logistical planning for the Normandy invasion and its success was due in part to him. News of the Navy inquiry came as a surprise to him and he had made no preparations for his defense by the time he arrived in Washington with Lieutenant David Richmond, a law school graduate who had little court experience. Richmond was to assist Admiral Hart, who had offered to act as Stark's counsel. The Judge Advocate General sent several lawyers to assist but they did not appear very enthusiastic and Stark dismissed them. "I'm not really very excited about having a lawyer," he told Hart and Richmond. "That looks as though I have something to hide. I haven't. I may not remember all this but I've nothing to hide."

Both inquiries began on the morning of August 7 within a few hundred yards of each other in the elongated connected headquarters of the Army and the Navy. Someone observed it was like an annex of the Army and Navy Club. The Army Pearl Harbor Board convened an hour later than their Navy colleagues, and their first witness was George Catlett Marshall, the most revered and admired military leader in the country.

Marshall admitted his recollection was "very hazy" about the controversial "war warning" message to Short on November 27,

[1] "I have never been able to understand," wrote King after the war, "how or why FDR could fire Admiral Stark without doing the same to General Marshall. In my opinion one could not possibly be more suspect than the other."

1941, since he was in North Carolina at maneuvers that day and didn't return until that night. He was also hazy about Short's reply that he was only preparing for sabotage. When General Frank asked if the Hawaiian reply was satisfactory, he said, "In the first place, as I told you, I have no very distinct recollection of the matter. The first definite reaction I have on it would be confused with the 'backsight' state of mind."

A few minutes later General Russell, his old antagonist, began putting pressure on him. Was he rather well acquainted with the foreign policy of the United States as related to Japan? "Yes, sir." Did he regard that policy as a rather definite and firm policy? "I don't believe I could comment on that. In the first place, I don't quite understand the question, and in the next place I would rather not be involved, as a military official, in expressing myself on the foreign policy of the United States." After a few more questions he abruptly announced, "I have got to go. I have got something that just won't wait."

It was incredible that the Chief of Staff should have been called away from his office in the Pentagon while more than a million Allied troops were attempting to smash their way across France.[2] It was also a pity that other military and naval officers found themselves involved in two lengthy inquiries at such a critical moment. The blame for this expenditure of time and energy was being placed upon the Republicans by the Democrats whereas it was the latter's Administration that had caused it. There need have been no wasteful investigations of Pearl Harbor if Roosevelt had called upon the people in 1941 to await all judgments in the national interest until victory was won. But the Administration had felt it necessary to fix blame and made scapegoats of two good men. This had aroused such indignation, not only among private citizens but within the Army and Navy, that further investigations could not be avoided.

Four days later Short took the stand. His answer to Marshall's warning, he said, had simply been that his command had been alerted by Washington to prevent sabotage. During the long ses-

[2] Construction on the Pentagon began August 11, 1941. Immediately after its completion on January 15, 1943, Army personnel moved in but it was not until seven years later that Navy top-level officials left the Munitions Building for the Pentagon.

sion Short repeated himself and spoke without eloquence. But his feeling of frustration and indignation was so eloquent that Russell was swayed if not his two colleagues.

The Navy inquiry was far more charged with emotion. Kimmel, outwardly cool to Stark, had broken off their personal correspondence since he felt Betty had walked away unscathed to let him shoulder all the blame. Although hurt, Stark was careful to say nothing in his testimony that would reflect on his old friend. He still admired Kimmel and on his last fitness report for the period ending 17 December 1941 had written: "I have always considered Admiral Kimmel an outstanding officer in ability, integrity and character. I still do."

At every session Rugg had requested to no avail that the authenticated copies of the intercepts be introduced into evidence. On August 11 Rugg added a new twist. He had Kimmel read a statement that he had been informed that the judge advocate had received a letter from the Acting Secretary of the Navy denying to this court certain data on file at the Navy Department. If this material was of such a highly secret nature that it could not be presented to this court, Kimmel suggested, why not request that the members of the court alone inspect it?

Kimmel conferred with Rugg. "I don't wish to be insistent in this matter," said Kimmel, "and I don't want to be in any sense disrespectful, but I think I must emphasize the fact that this data which I have requested is essential for proper examination of the witness now on the stand, Admiral Stark, that what I have requested is to show affirmatively in the record that I have exhausted every means at my command to accomplish the introduction of this data at this time."

Admiral Murfin called for a resumption of testimony but Kimmel interrupted. "Just a suggestion—that the decision made by the Secretary is now an accomplished fact. It has been decided that this data is denied the court."

"Denied *you*, sir," cut in Commander Harold Biesemeier, the judge advocate.

Kimmel insisted on his wording. "Denial to me and the judge advocate is not nearly as important in my mind as denial to this court, in order to arrive at a proper verdict; and that is the burden of every statement I have made on this subject. I would respectfully like to be informed of the decision of the court as to how they will proceed in this matter."

Biesemeier was just as persistent. "The judge advocate would like to advise the court, in his capacity as legal adviser to them, that, in response to Admiral Kimmel's request that they view this evidence themselves in the files of the Navy Department, it would be highly irregular and illegal for the reason that it does not permit of usual cross-examination by other interested parties or the judge advocate, and the court would be receiving the information from a source not set forth in the record."

"I admit that extraordinary conditions require extraordinary procedures," said Kimmel.

Admiral Murfin had had enough of this and ordered the inquiry to proceed with Stark's testimony. He couldn't remember anything about December 6. "Do you recall what time you left the office after the routine day, the time in the afternoon or evening?"

"No, I do not."

"Do you recall what you were doing Saturday evening, 6 December?"

"No, I couldn't say what I was doing that evening. My remembrance is—I think I was home but I couldn't say. I don't recall clearly."

"Do you recall receiving at your home, or wherever you were, between 9 and 10 P.M., Washington time, important intelligence information brought by an officer messenger?" This was in reference to the fourteen-point message from Tokyo, of which thirteen points were delivered to a number of officers that night.

"No, I haven't the slightest recollection of anything of that sort on that evening."

Admiral Adolphus Andrews was not a sympathetic listener. There was a rumor that Andrews blamed Stark for his not being promoted.

The drama continued with the next witness, Rear Admiral R. E. Schuirmann, formerly Stark's liaison officer with the State Department. Upon being asked if November 25, 1941, was regarded as the deadline for all negotiations between the Japanese and the

United States, he refused to answer on the grounds that it would disclose information detrimental to the public interest. He claimed his privilege against revealing state secrets.

After the court honored Schuirmann's claim, Rugg tried another line. "Do you recall whether you had information from Naval Intelligence that the deadline originally determined or fixed, was extended at some later date?"

"This is the same line of questioning and the same objection to it," said Schuirmann, and the court said he need not answer the question. But Rugg pressed the attack. Now was the time to get the Japanese intercepts. "I feel that Admiral Kimmel is entitled to have indicated on this record the fact that he seeks information from this witness, not once but as to the several items of information; that the cross-examination of this witness is being precluded to Admiral Kimmel on that ground and I see no way of accomplishing that other than asking several questions on different lines of information more or less on the line that I asked Admiral Stark yesterday afternoon."

The court repeated that this line of questioning could not be continued on the ground of security.

Rugg asked the same question in slightly different words. Again Schuirmann claimed his privilege against revealing state secrets. And again the court told him he need not answer. Now Rugg made a veiled reference to the "winds" message. "Do you recall whether on or about November 26 you received information from the Office of Naval Intelligence that it had specific evidence of Japan's intention to wage an offensive war against both Britain and the United States?"

Once more Schuirmann protested. If this line of questioning continued, he threatened to leave the courtroom. Murfin again upheld him.

As Rugg calmly, doggedly proceeded with the cross-examination, it was becoming apparent that the Boston lawyer was trying to get so much on the record that the intercepts would have to be released. "During the early part of December, December 3rd or December 4th, do you recall receiving information from the Office of Naval Intelligence that Japan would wage an offensive war against both the United States and Britain?"

This was a direct reference to the "winds" message, and now Judge Advocate Biesemeier himself realized what Rugg was doing. "I must object to the question," he said, "on the ground that counsel is getting into the record the specific sort of information that he is trying to get, although he knows that it is objectionable on two grounds, one of them being national security, and the other being that it is beyond the scope of the direct examination." The harried Biesemeier requested that the court be cleared. Young Richmond, unaware of Magic, asked Hart what the fuss was about. "You'd better stay and see what goes on," said Hart, and left the room.

A few minutes later the court was reopened with the announcement that the judge advocate's objection was not sustained but Schuirmann need not answer the last question.

Rugg insisted on continuing his line of questioning on the ground that this was essential to the interests of his client. "On December 4th or 5th," he asked Schuirmann, "do you recall receiving information from the Office of Naval Intelligence that the Japanese consul in Hawaii was furnishing Tokyo with intelligence as to the number of United States warships in Pearl Harbor, and their location in the harbor?"

The judge advocate again objected on the same ground as before. Objection not sustained. Again Schuirmann claimed his privilege. And again the court told him he need not answer. It seemed like a standoff but Rugg had cleverly managed to get a good deal of information on the record. His persistent line of questioning had also given Admirals Murfin, Kalbfus and Andrews much pause for thought.

When the Navy Department still refused to release the vital forty-three intercepts that had not been forwarded to Kimmel, Rugg suggested that the admiral write a letter to Secretary Forrestal requesting that, since the intercepts could not be submitted in evidence, they should be sealed in the presence of Captain Lavender until the time they could be divulged. Kimmel personally delivered the letter to the assistant chief of Naval Operations.

In the meantime the inquiry continued. After Vice Admiral William Pye, Kimmel's chief of staff, had completed his testimony on August 19 he came to Kimmel's temporary office where he was handed a copy of Captain Safford's testimony at the Hart investigation.

The usually calm Pye became excited as he read. "Here it is! Here it is!" he exclaimed.

"What do you mean?" asked Kimmel.

"Why, here is what you told me last April. I thought you were crazy. I believed this thing had preyed on your mind so much that you had gone nuts." That all this information had been withheld from the commanders in Hawaii was so incredible to Pye that he could not believe it. "Here was a man," wrote Kimmel, "whom I had known all my adult life who concluded I was crazy when I told him of the evidence I had discovered. What chance had I to convince the public of these incredible facts except by indisputable evidence." Both he and Rugg concluded that they must break loose the intercepts at all cost.

At this time word came to the Navy Department that the U.S. submarine *Robalo* had hit a mine off Palawan Island in the Philippines. Its commander, Captain Manning Kimmel, had gone down with his boat. King instructed Rear Admiral Walter DeLany, a close friend of Kimmel's, to inform the admiral. He arrived at Kimmel's office while he was discussing a statement with Hanify. DeLany said he had some bad news. "Manning?" asked Kimmel, and, after DeLany nodded, simply said with little show of emotion, "Those things happen." But later he told his son Ned, "That son of a bitch"—he meant Roosevelt—"has now killed my son!"

He hastened to Bronxville to console his wife but after a few days returned to Washington to testify before the Army Board.

3.

Little of import had happened at the Munitions Building since Short's testimony. There was talk of the "war warning" of November 27 that was not clearly understood; and of the radar report on the morning of the seventh which was not heeded. But nothing new had been revealed.

There was a stir of excitement when Kimmel appeared on August 25. He told the Army Board how well, despite false reports, he and Short had cooperated. At the end of his testimony, General

Grunert asked if there was anything else he wanted to say. Lieutenant Hanify, who had accompanied Kimmel, suspected that the Army Board knew nothing of the intercepts and was operating in the dark. And so he and Kimmel had prepared a statement which Kimmel now read. Vital information in the hands of the War and Navy Departments, he said, had not been supplied to Short and himself. In Washington they knew the Japanese had set a deadline of November 25; that a day later an ultimatum had been sent to Japan. As Kimmel read of other secret messages he noticed that one could have heard a pin drop. "All this information was denied to General Short and me." On December 7 the precise time of the attack was known. "Had we been furnished this information as little as two or three hours before the attack, which was easily feasible and possible, much could have been done."

Grunert thanked the admiral. The Board had had some intimation that this kind of material existed, he said, but thus far had not gotten it. Russell had paid little attention to Kimmel's previous testimony but the statement brought him to sharp attention. He put his head in his hand, then looked up and asked, Could the admiral supply the Board with the source of this information?

"I will cooperate to the best of my ability, in conformity with the restrictions which have been imposed upon me." Kimmel was thinking: "They all know where to get it . . . every Goddamn one of them."

Since there had been no answer to his last letter to Forrestal, Kimmel inquired when he would receive an answer. He was told his letter had been misplaced. Would the admiral kindly submit another? He wrote again repeating his request for the forty-three messages, delivering it in person, as he had the first letter, to King's assistant, Vice Admiral Richard Edwards. "Dicky," he said this time, "it won't do you a Goddamn bit of good, and you can tell those SOB's in the Secretary's office it won't do any good to lose my letters, because from this day forth I am going to send a letter here every day until I get my answer." His voice carried well, and Kimmel was sure everyone within fifty yards heard it. Very soon a clerk came running. "Here, Admiral, here's your letter." The original, by a remarkable coincidence, had just been located.

A day later Kimmel was informed that the forty-three messages would be sealed in the presence of Captain Lavender as requested. Since this satisfied neither Kimmel nor Rugg, the latter suggested they resort to dramatics. After the session at the Navy Inquiry on August 27, Kimmel began speaking to Lavender as they walked into the corridor. In a booming voice that could be heard by everyone in the room, he remarked that since it was apparent the messages would not be released he would have to hold a press conference and reveal that vital information essential to the case was being withheld.

The ruse succeeded. The next morning the judge advocate announced that he had certain documents he would like to introduce into evidence. Lavender would never forget the reactions of Admirals Murfin, Kalbfus and Andrews as the intercepts were read into the record. "Well, I never saw three officers, who were able officers, just simply blanch as they did when they heard these things read out. . . . Admiral Murfin threw his pencil down on his desk so hard that it bounced about ten feet. Admiral Kalbfus simply shrunk and Admiral Andrews—I never saw anybody look so terrible. From then on we got our stuff in." Hanify recalled that Murfin, a slight, wiry man, said, "Jesus Christ, we'll adjourn!" and flung his pencil down. "He couldn't believe it."

Kimmel had never told Short about the intercepts because he suspected his counsel, Brigadier General Thomas Green, was a Marshall man. But as soon as he left the courtroom the admiral telephoned Green, only to learn that Short was in Texas. "Why in the hell isn't he up here looking after his interests? Send him a telegram and tell him I have something for him."

Upon Short's return to Washington, Kimmel told him about the intercepts. "Short," he then said, "Marshall is your enemy. Haven't you found that out yet? He is doing everything he can to doublecross you and has been right from the very beginning. I know from what I have heard and from what I have seen that this is so and if you stick with him you will be in a hell of a fix. I can tell you that."

On the twenty-ninth the drama at the Navy Building reached its crisis. Captain Laurance Safford, looking professorial and inoffensive as he peered through horn-rim glasses, took the stand.

After appearing before Hart, Safford had scoured the files for the intercepts but could not even locate the fourteen-part message. He asked a reserve officer on duty in the Code Section where the Pearl Harbor intercepts were now kept. The answer was that Kramer had turned over the packet with a request that they be placed in the safe. Safford promptly searched Kramer's files and found all but one, the "winds" execute. After making copies for his own convenience, Safford returned the originals to their proper file.

Safford told the Navy Board in detail about the "winds" execute. He was extremely tense, and as he spoke in a rather high-pitched voice his eyes searched from side to side. "It was an alert apprehensiveness which I think was a mannerism," recalled Hanify, who guessed such wariness had come from years of dealing with codes and ciphers.

The following day Stark was asked why he had not telephoned Kimmel on the morning of December 7 as a subordinate had suggested. "The telephone is purely hind sight with me as to wherein I was wrong that I didn't do more to alert them." A remarkable admission, he then underlined it. ". . . and I regret that I did not pick up the telephone, regardless of secrecy, as things have turned out, and notified them." This regret was all post-Pearl Harbor? "Yes, it is all hind sight, and it is in search of my own conscience as to what I might have done."

He weakened his position even more a minute later when asked if he had considered it advisable to keep Kimmel informed in detail of the progress of events in relation to Japan. "I didn't consider it. I endeavored to keep him informed of what I thought would be useful to him in the main trend."

Then Stark admitted he knew nothing about the original "winds" message which had caused such a stir in Naval Intelligence and Communications; and that he couldn't even recall the important note Hull sent to the Japanese on November 26.

After the session, Stark confided to Hart that he wished he had just gone in and expressed his thoughts. "Perhaps I was tired," he added. "Perhaps part of the trouble was my fondness and loyalty to Kimmel, my actual desire to share the burden and protect him so far as I could, and trying too hard to be so one-hundred-percent-plus honest, so that in spots I may have made more or less a mess of it."

Three days later George Marshall walked down the long corridor from the Munitions Building to the Navy courtroom. There was subdued excitement as he entered. David Richmond for one was apprehensive. "I don't know how Marshall's going to take questions by a lieutenant," he told Hart.

"Well, I've got four stars here. Just go ahead and ask him any questions you want. If there's any trouble, I'll stand up. But you go ahead." After an early clash with the judge advocate, Hart had no wish to interrogate and instructed Richmond to take over.

Rugg realized he would have to be very cautious in his handling of Marshall since this was not in a civil court. If he too aggressively pressed a man surrounded by the aura of the Army's highest rank before a body composed of officers, he would run the risk of endangering Kimmel's case. At the same time, to dig out the truth he had to be incisive and exhaustive.

With patience he kept probing Marshall about the events of December 6 and 7 but he would only say he didn't recall where he was on the night of the sixth and was hazy about the seventh. And to Rugg's penetrating questions about the Hull note of November 26 and the November 27 warnings to Hawaii, the Chief of Staff three times could not recollect. He also replied once with "No, I don't know about that," thrice with "I don't recall," and five times with "I don't recall that."

What a cool and calculating witness! thought Hanify. There was no animus in the long exchange. Marshall and Rugg were obviously sparring and there was no apparent victor. But in so deftly evading the questions the general had not enhanced his credibility.

4.

The Army Board had been taking testimony at the Presidio in San Francisco since August 29 about the possible connection of Colonel Theodore Wyman, Jr., with a suspected German spy, Hans Wilhelm Rohl. Wyman, district engineer in Honolulu in 1940–41, had been in charge of many activities including construction of hangars, landing strips and the aircraft warning system. The testimony had been conflicting, inconclusive and boring. The Army Board postponed this tedious line of questioning on September 5 and made plans to transfer their activities to Fort Shafter on Oahu.

The Navy Inquiry, after concluding the Marshall testimony, also was making plans to go to Hawaii. Rugg would stay in Washington while Lavender and Hanify would accompany Admiral Kimmel. On the flight to Hawaii in a Navy flying boat, there was camaraderie among the group. After most of the members had gone to sleep, Hanify chatted at length with Admiral Andrews, who finally asked what the lieutenant thought of Roosevelt's unconditional surrender formula. "To give you an honest answer, Admiral, I think it's a tragic mistake." To his surprise, Andrews said, "I couldn't agree with you more. I think it is a disastrous policy." Here, obviously, was a man of independent mind, thought Hanify. It boded well for Kimmel's case.

The Navy interrogators began work at the Navy Yard in Pearl Harbor the following day. Rugg had instructed Hanify to interview Kramer informally before he had been confused or intimidated by the court, the advocate general or the counsel for Stark. Rugg wanted fresh testimony and Hanify was entitled to interrogate him informally since there were no property rights in witnesses. On the morning Kramer was scheduled to testify Hanify and Lavender waited in the corridor. As the commander got off the elevator, the two lawyers introduced themselves. "We don't know what else you'll be asked at this inquiry," said Hanify. "We have these questions for you."

Kramer was willing to talk.

"Did you ever see, or do you recall, an execute of the Winds Code?"

"Yes," he said decisively without hesitation.

"What is your best memory of the words used in the Execute?"

Without pause he said, "*Higashi no kaze ame*. East wind, rain." Both Hanify and Lavender were convinced Kramer was telling the truth. He had just arrived from the war zone, no one had prompted or harried him, and he had spoken freely.

A few minutes later, on the stand, Kramer testified how he had seen the "winds" execute about the third or fourth of December. He had taken it to his superior "and from that point Captain Safford took the ball. I believe Captain Safford went directly to Admiral Noyes' office at that time."

Could he recall what the Japanese-language words were? "*Higashi no kaze ame,* I am quite certain. The literal meaning of *Higashi no kaze ame* is East wind, rain. That is plain Japanese language. The sense of that, however, meant strained relations or a break in relations, possibly even implying war with a nation to the eastward, the United States." Lavender and Hanify were delighted. His testimony here was as straight as in the corridor.

Kramer believed the message was typewritten on teletype paper. This would indicate it came from a U.S. intercept station. He added that he had received the execute from the watch officer who received information coming from the teletype.

Was Kramer the one who went to the communications officer and said, "Here it is"?

This time Kramer gave Safford his former rank. "I believe I used that expression when I accompanied the watch officer to Commander Safford's office. . . . I left Commander Safford's office as soon as I knew he had the picture and knew what the message was, and I believe he at once went to Admiral Noyes' office. I knew that Admiral Noyes was highly interested in that particular plain language code [the "winds" code] because of his previous instructions to me to make out these cards so that he could leave it with certain high officers and the Secretary [Knox], all with the view of getting the word to those people promptly, whether it was any time of the day or night."

"When the original Winds message was received, was that to your knowledge sent to the Office of the Chief of Naval Operations?"

"I'm sure it was, yes, sir." This was the message Stark claimed to have no knowledge of. It was, explained Kramer, "a message which we had been looking for many days and that we had made special provisions to handle for many days."

By September 13 the Navy Board had finished its work in Hawaii and was on its way to San Francisco. Here, two days later, it met at the Federal Building for interrogation of Admiral "Terrible"

Turner. At first he stated he knew nothing about an execute of the "winds" message but later corrected himself. "Admiral Noyes called me up on the telephone. What day or time of day I don't recall. I think it was December 6. He said something like this: 'The Winds message came in,' or something of that sort." Was Stark told of the message? "Not from me. I believe Admiral Noyes informed him."

Did Turner consider that the message was of such high significance that action should be taken immediately to transmit that information to Kimmel?

"No, I assumed that he had it."

Then came a rather startling piece of information. Lavender asked if Turner knew that Kimmel was not receiving the decrypted, intercepted Japanese diplomatic messages. "I have never received such information." He had assumed that Kimmel was reading *all* the intercepts.

There was much more to come. Turner reiterated that he had thought a Japanese air attack on Hawaii was a possibility, wasn't "in the least" surprised when it came. "I knew our carriers were out, and with the warnings which had been given, I felt we would give them a pretty bad beating before they got home by our shore-based aircraft and by our carriers."

It was apparent that Turner had let his mouth run away with him. And those who knew him intimately wondered if he had been drinking again.

The judge advocate was puzzled by Turner's remarks since no warnings had been sent to Kimmel since November 27. "Well, if you felt this strongly, Admiral," he asked, "did you discuss this probability with the Chief of Naval Operations?"

Turner did not answer this direct question but rambled on, first admitting that the Navy Department knew Kimmel didn't have enough patrol planes, and then acknowledging that the Japanese attack on Pearl Harbor could not have been averted. "I think the destructive effect could have been considerably lessened, but I don't believe that the attack could have been stopped from coming in, except by luck."

The three admirals must have been stunned by such talk from the former head of Navy War Plans. Turner not only thought an air attack on Pearl Harbor was a lively possibility but recognized that Kimmel had neither sufficient planes for a proper search nor a strong enough force to avert an air attack when it came. Lavender and Hanify found it unnecessary to cross-examine Turner. His testimony couldn't have been better for their client.

The following morning Admiral Noyes was interviewed at the Federal Building. He confused matters by denying he had received any "winds" execute and had not even talked to anyone about it; and then by charging that Admiral Turner must have known Kimmel was not getting the intercepts. "It is my remembrance that Admiral Turner asked what was our set-up in regard to intercepted messages and it was fully explained to him." The session was adjourned at 12:30 P.M. and plans were made to leave for Washington.

5.

On September 19 Stimson was preparing his testimony before the Army Board, which would probably come the following Monday. "General Marshall came in in the last part of the morning and he with McCloy, who happened to be present, and I talked over the same matter, Marshall telling me what had developed in his two hearings before the Army Board and the Navy Board respectively, and I telling him what I had dug up in regard to my own testimony." In the afternoon he attended a meeting with American and British scientists. "The meeting lasted for three hours and was a pretty long strain. Part of the time we called in General Groves to give us information." The conversation with Groves, overseer of the Manhattan Project, obviously was about the atom bomb.

On Monday the twenty-fifth the Navy Inquiry was winding up its investigation where it had begun, on Constitution Avenue, but the Army Board was by no means finished. The following day Stimson was interrogated at the Pentagon. "I am somewhat in the position, roughly speaking, of a district attorney in his relations with the grand jury," he told them. "And, by becoming a witness, I have to 'watch my step' very carefully that I do not get into a position of advocacy or bias towards any person who may afterwards be proceeded against or concerned with the action which your report may recommend."

General Grunert said the Board thoroughly understood his position, adding, "And the Board is not a bit timid!"

General Russell demonstrated this by aggressive questions on the warning to Short, which Russell termed ambiguous. Then he asked if Stimson had envisaged an air attack from Japanese carriers at the time the warning message went out.

"Well, I envisaged it as one of the possibilities. . . ."

"Then you were not surprised at the air attack on the 7th of December?" prodded Russell.

"Well, I was not surprised, in one sense, in any attack that would be made; but I was watching with considerably more care, because I knew more about it, the attack that was framing up in the southwestern Pacific."

Stimson could not have been altogether happy with the treatment he got from the three generals, but he wrote Roosevelt, later that day, a reassuring letter. "I was sorry to learn . . . that you had been worried by rumors as to what the Army Pearl Harbor Board might find in its report." That morning he had spent two and a half hours before the Board "and I think satisfied them on the subject matter of some of these speculations. One can never tell but I felt at the end of the hearing that they were satisfied with my account of the sequence of the events. I had the advantage which, so far as I know, none of the other witnesses have had of having kept a daily account of my meetings and work during that critical period so that my testimony was all based upon records and thus lifted above the danger of faulty memory. For myself, I can hardly imagine a picture of more close cooperation and anxious desire to warn our outposts of impending attack than was shown by this documented record. According to my memory, you were yourself so painstakingly on the job throughout that period that I should be greatly distressed if you were victimized now by ignorant or malicious rumors."

The Board returned to the Munitions Building on Friday, September 29. At ten-thirty that morning Marshall returned to admit that he had not considered telephoning Short on December 7.

And if he *had*, he would certainly have called MacArthur first and then the Panama Canal. Besides, from his own experience it took too long to get a telephone call through. "You put the other thing through in a hurry." And, if Short, who was waiting outside to testify, had been present, he would have found it difficult not to interject that the "hurry" message had not arrived until hours after the attack.

In the afternoon Short appeared and it was obvious that he had taken Kimmel's warning to heart, for he was now looking upon Marshall not as a friend and protector but as an enemy. He brought up the final part of Admiral Kimmel's testimony before the Army Board. "He makes a statement that I would like to have read to the Board, and then I would like to comment on it."

Short's counsel read the Kimmel testimony revealing that there had been considerable information regarding the imminence of war that had not been transmitted to either Kimmel or Short.

"I feel that Admiral Kimmel would not have made that statement," Short said, "unless he had factual data to corroborate it. I haven't had access to that data, and, from reading Admiral Kimmel's testimony, it does not appear that the Board has been furnished with it." He had written a letter that day to the Secretary of War asking that a search be made of War Department files; and if not found there the Navy should be required to furnish it.

"General," said Frank, "are you putting the Board in the position of working for you?"

"I am putting the Board in the position, I hope, where I feel that they should want to consider everything, that this should not be a one-sided investigation; but that here is something that is tremendously important from my point of view."

Frank took offense. "Have you found anything in the proceedings of this Board that has indicated that this Board has not tried to conduct an impartial proceeding?"

"No, I have not; but I have found nothing in this Board's proceedings—now, they may have done it; the Board may have had access to everything that Admiral Kimmel has in mind, but I feel that he definitely would not have made that statement without he had data to support it." He was so upset, his tongue had got twisted. If the Board had such information and it was off the record, then he hoped the letter to Stimson would cause it to be made available to him. "I do not know what the Board has had, off the record. They may have had everything I am asking for." He turned indignantly to Frank. "I do not think your statement is a fair one that I am trying to have the Board work for me. I am really just hopeful that they will get everything before the Board that is necessary for a complete understanding of the case."

"That is just what we are endeavoring to do," said Frank.

The Board responded by sending Marshall a list of questions to be answered either in person or by a signed statement by the following Monday. Was there information in the War and Navy Departments on December 6, 1941, "that the order of attack was momentarily imminent"? Had the Chief of Staff known that between November 27 and December 7 the alert in effect in Hawaii for the Army forces provided security for sabotage only? Why wasn't the telephone used on December 7 to warn Short? What warnings were sent to Short from October 21, 1941, until November 27? There were many other questions but none directly asking that the Japanese intercepts be released and put on record by the Board.

6.

On Saturday, the last day of September, Colonel Rufus "Togo" Bratton was called before the Board. Serious, competent and meticulous—if not brilliant—the industrious Bratton was well qualified for his position in 1941 as chief of the Far Eastern Section of Army Intelligence. He was responsible for Japanese matters. His interest in all things Japanese had come from three long terms in Japan. Being a scholar as well as a soldier, he had delved into the history and customs of the Japanese and could write as well as speak the language. He and Colonel Otis Sadtler, a senior intelligence officer of S.I.S., had also been involved in a minor uprising as a result of the Bomb Plot message from Tokyo to the Japanese consul in the fall of 1941. Like their Navy colleagues involved in the mutiny on the Second Deck, they too felt this important message should be transmitted to the Pacific commanders. After the Navy failed to get permission to send off their warning, these two West Point colonels managed secretly to transmit theirs through a special channel to Spencer Akin, MacArthur's chief signal officer. This information alerted General Charles Willoughby, MacArthur's G-2, who later wrote, ". . . this was no longer a case of diplomatic curiosity; coordinate grid is the classical method for pinpoint target designation; our battleships had suddenly become 'targets.'" Spencer Akin was uneasy from the start. "We drew our own conclusions and the Filipino-American troops took up beach positions long before the Japanese landings." This was the information denied both Kimmel and Short.

The involvement of Sadtler and Bratton in this and succeeding incidents had made them outcasts. Bratton, a heavy-set bear of a man, had confided his concern to Colonel Ivan D. Yeaton in early 1942. Yeaton, a Far East expert, had just been assigned to the War Department General Staff. Bratton felt, Yeaton wrote in his unpublished memoirs, "that he had given both G-2 [General Miles] and the chief of staff sufficient warning that they should have been sleeping in their offices instead of comfortable at home. He was well aware that this testimony would be considered disloyal by Marshall and probably mean the end of all chance of promotion."

Later in 1943, Army Intelligence had been ordered by the White House to produce a study on Japanese preparations for war from 1935 to Pearl Harbor. Bratton wrote it. "The morning after it had been sent up to the chief of staff," recalled Yeaton, "I found Bratton at his desk with his head in his hand, looking down at the Far Eastern manuscript. Looking over his shoulder, I could see the margin notes and lined out words and phrases. 'Who dun it?' I asked. 'The Old Man himself,' he answered. Marshall had edited out all the parts most damaging to him, leaving the remainder too vague to be interpreted as cause for immediate concern over Japanese intentions. I urged Bratton for his own protection to have the entire volume photostated at once and to keep the evidence in a safe place." This he did.

Bratton, a sophisticate who talked like a college professor, had a ruddy complexion with a face that reminded one colleague of a "friendly bulldog." He had already been interrogated by Marshall's special investigator, Colonel Carter Clarke, and must have been apprehensive by the time he faced the Army Board that Sat-

urday. He told how he had received the translations of the two
Japanese intercepts between eight-thirty and nine on the morning
of December 7. These were immediately apparent as of such importance that he had telephoned Marshall's quarters only to be informed he was riding horseback. "I requested his orderly to go out
and find him at once and ask him to call me on the telephone as
soon as practicable, as I had an important message to deliver to
him." He finally got the call from Marshall sometime between ten
and eleven. "He said to report to him in his office, as he was on his
way there. I reported to him at his office at about 11:25, immediately upon his arrival."

Over the weekend there was discussion at the War Department
on how to handle General Short's request to release secret material
to the Board and his own counsel. If the request were denied for
reasons of national security, one staff officer warned Marshall,
"politicians may question our motives and thus embarrass the
President." This advice may have influenced Marshall to recommend that Stimson send Short a letter permitting his counsel to
examine the records "in the presence of a member of the Board."
Stimson did so on Monday, the day Marshall was to appear a third
time before the Board.

The witness preceding him was Captain Safford. He told how
Kimmel had managed to get permission to inspect files for some
sixty or so Japanese intercepts—he was referring to the forty-three
messages Lavender had discovered—and how these documents had
finally, after many efforts, been introduced as evidence in the Navy
Inquiry.

"Who has the official custody of these sixty messages at the moment?" asked Frank. The recorder of the Navy Court of Inquiry,
answered Safford. "If it was the desire of these Boards to get a
copy of those sixty messages, to whom should the request be
made?" The Secretary of the Navy. Safford was then asked if the
"winds" execute was among these messages. "That is still missing." He told how he had discovered its absence from the files. He
also told how Kramer had told him all about delivery of the Japanese fourteen-part message on December 6 and 7.

"When did he make these statements upon which you base your evidence now?" asked Russell.

"Kramer made his statements the 8th or 9th of December immediately after the event, when I discussed it fully with him. I called for statements. I talked to everybody concerned, to see if my people had been negligent in any way, that this thing had in any way been our fault. I made a very careful investigation." Russell credited Safford's testimony, as well as his claim that the "winds" execute had been purposely done away with. "It is my personal belief that it was destroyed for a reason," wrote Russell later. "Neither Marshall nor Stark wanted it to be made public. Marshall knew about it."

In the afternoon Marshall returned with answers to the questions submitted by the Board. He told of regulations regarding the extreme secrecy to be used regarding ultrasecret information. That was why they had to be so cautious in sending messages to Short and Kimmel in 1941.

Then General Frank asked why the thirteen-point message of December 6 had not been delivered to Marshall that night.

Russell was amused that today Marshall's attitude was different. "No longer was he the talkative salesman. Now he was the somewhat irritated executive, very brusque and direct in his answers, employing just as few words as possible. Apparently my criticism of General Marshall about his treatment of the Board had reached him."

Russell took over the interrogation. The Board had learned, he said, that there had been a G-2 investigation of Pearl Harbor shortly after the attack. It appeared that a lot of things discovered at that time were not transmitted to the Army Board and had just come to the Board's knowledge the past week. He was referring, of course, to the intercepts.

Marshall's close friend, Grunert, now joined in. The G-2 witnesses, he said, had all had the opportunity of giving this information to the Board but had not. "Now, evidently they either forgot or didn't recall, or else they didn't tell us this information which we have gotten of late."

Marshall hedged. "Well, I don't know." He hadn't seen or talked to General Miles, the G-2.

Grunert told how the Navy Board had managed to pry their information out of the Navy. "Of course, naturally, the Board thought that; well, if they held out from the Board information which is now coming up, what do we know but that something else is being held out?"

"And information that is rather vital, too," added Frank.

"Well, I don't know," said Marshall.

"I cannot imagine that it is intentional," said Grunert.

"The only thing that I can think of in connection with that," said Marshall, "is that everybody that is concerned with this top secret thing is very cagey about saying anything about it."

"That is what I attribute it to," said Grunert.

"And naturally he feels no freedom whatever to speak about it unless he is specifically authorized," said Marshall; and then ended the session with a curt "I have nothing else I can think of."

He was followed by Bratton, who was asked about a message sent out to Hawaii on December 5. He admitted he had seen it that very morning but was unable to get it.

"And it is over there in the files, but they won't let you have it?"

"Well, they wouldn't let me bring it over here, if that is what you mean, sir."

"Now, do you know who has issued the instructions that we are not to be given those messages, Colonel?"

"No, sir. I mean by that, I don't know the ultimate authority."

After sidestepping that question, Bratton admitted he had received the first thirteen parts of the long message on the night of December 6 and had delivered it to Marshall's office as well as to the watch officer in the State Department. He remembered when he turned it over at the State Department—about half past ten; but had no recollection of exactly when he placed the message on Marshall's desk.

Bratton was obviously under stress and, after further probing about delivery of the message, finally said, "I am trying to remember, sir, what I did with the copies that went to General Miles and General Marshall and General Gerow. I can't verify it or prove it, at this time, but my recollection is that those three officers got their copies the evening of the 6th."

"By 'the three officers,' you mean whom?"

"General Marshall, General Miles and General Gerow," he said fearfully, as if, one witness recalled, expecting to be struck by lightning. All at once he seemed to remember everything. "Now, it was my practise to deliver to them their copies before I went to the State Department." That would make it before 10:30 P.M.

Did he deliver a copy to Marshall personally that evening?

"No. I very seldom delivered it to him in person. I gave it to his secretary, in a locked bag."

"And what is the name of the secretary to the Chief of Staff?"

If Togo Bratton had been concerned for his future before, he must have blanched that day. "Colonel Smith, Bedell Smith, now Lieutenant General," he said. Yes, he was the one who got Marshall's copy on the night of December 6.

7.

The following day the three members of the Board increased pressure for release of the secret material. Russell could see only one reason for not doing so: "Marshall and his close associates on the General Staff did not want the Army Pearl Harbor Board to know that they were in possession of so much important information, none of which had been sent to Short on the Islands."

During the day Grunert did something definite about it. "May I call on War Department agencies to produce files and personnel having knowledge thereof, without in each case getting some higher-up's O.K.?" he asked Marshall's deputy. The answer was, "Yes," and Grunert promptly wrote back a top secret letter stating that the Board had verified that the Army had a file of these intercepts. "It is requested that the file referred to be made available for the Board's examination. . . ." If permission was denied, Grunert requested "that that decision be communicated to the Board in writing."

The next day Grunert's request was approved. At last the Army Board had Magic. It came in time to be recorded at the last interrogation of witnesses on October 6, which featured the testimony of Colonel O. K. Sadtler who, like Bratton, still held the same rank he had in 1941.[3]

Sadtler told the Army Board that he was telephoned by Admiral Noyes on the morning of December 5 and told, "Sadtler, the message is in!" It was a "winds" execute and Noyes wasn't sure which enemy was indicated. He thought it meant the Japanese were going to war with Great Britain. "I asked him for the Japanese word, and he didn't know it, but to please tell G-2."

Sadtler reported all this to General Miles "and then I went down to see General Gerow, who was head of the War Plans, told him to the effect of what Admiral Noyes had said, and didn't he think we should send a message to Hawaii. I don't mean Hawaii— to Panama, the Philippines, and Hawaii. He says, 'I think they have had plenty of notification,' and the matter dropped. I then went in to the Secretary of the General Staff and talked to Colonel [Bedell] Smith about the same thing, and he asked me what I had done, and I told him I had talked to G-2 and War Plans; and he didn't want to discuss it further."

Why, asked Russell, was Sadtler so concerned that he went the "second mile" to discuss the matter with both Gerow and Smith? "I was sure war was coming, and coming very quickly." The previous day, December 4, at a meeting of the Defense Communications Board he had been asked by the Assistant Secretary of the Treasury what he thought about the imminence of war "and I said that I thought they would have war within 48 hours. He turned to Captain Redman, who represented Admiral Noyes at the meeting, and asked him what he thought, and he said he agreed with Colonel Sadtler."

So ended the Army Pearl Harbor Board hearings. Now there was the task of writing a report. The Navy was well along with theirs and it was submitted to the Secretary of the Navy on October 19. It completely reversed the findings of the Roberts Commission. Kimmel had not received all available information from Washington and could not be blamed for something he could not

[3] "We knew nothing of the reasons for continuing them in their grades of colonel," commented Russell, "but we do recall that in one of our informal conversations, some officers said that the pattern was perfectly clear. If an officer wanted to be condemned forever it was only necessary for him to have guessed Pearl Harbor correctly."

expect. Admiral Stark, however, had "failed to display the sound judgment expected of him in that he did not transmit to Admiral Kimmel . . . important information which he had regarding the Japanese situation."

The following day came the Army report. To Russell's delight, his two colleagues had supported his own conclusions. He was gratified that they had not flinched from the truth even if it might "undermine such faith as the great masses of the people still had in the Army." Russell himself did not care what Marshall might think. "There was nothing that he could do to or for me which concerned me in the least."

Although the Army report stated that Short had made an "earnest and honest" effort to implement plans for defense, he was criticized for adopting only a sabotage alert. He was also charged with failing to reach an agreement with Kimmel to implement joint Army-Navy plans. But these were mild scoldings compared to the counts against Marshall:

1. Failure to keep Short fully informed as to the international situation and the probable outbreak of war.

2. Failure to note Short's message that he was only preparing for sabotage without taking any action.

3. Failure to alert Short on the evening of December 6 and the early morning of December 7 that an almost immediate break with Japan was coming.

4. Failure to investigate and determine the state of readiness of Short's command after the November 27 warning despite the impending threat of war.

But the most scorching criticism came in a supplemental top secret report. Marshall and the War Department were censured for sending Hawaii so little of the mass of information it had of impending war. "The messages actually sent to Hawaii by either the Army or Navy gave only a small fraction of this information. No direction was given the Hawaiian Department based on this information except the 'Do-Don't' message of November 27, 1941. It would have been possible to have sent safely information, ample for the purpose of orienting the commanders in Hawaii. . . ."

Much vital information, which had been distributed to the War, Navy and State Departments, "did not go out to the field, with the possible exception of the general statements in occasional messages which are shown in this Board's report. Only the higher-ups in Washington secured this information."

The report went on for several more pages about the "winds" execute and the poor handling of the fourteen-point message, ending with a devastating list of Marshall's delinquencies.

> There, therefore, can be no question that between the dates of December 4 and December 6, the imminence of war on the following Saturday and Sunday, December 6 and 7, was clearcut and definite.
>
> Up to the morning of December 7, 1941, everything that the Japanese were planning to do was known to the United States except the final message instructing the Japanese Embassy to present the 14th part together with the preceding 13 parts of the long message at one o'clock on December 7, or the very hour and minute when bombs were falling on Pearl Harbor.

At the Pentagon that October 20 there were anger, indignation and consternation. The repercussions were felt even more at the White House. With the Roberts report so dramatically turned about by both the Army and Navy inquiries, the new findings would have to be suppressed until they could be refuted. And in little more than two weeks the nation would go to the polls to elect a President.

That evening James Forrestal did publicly reveal that the Navy Court of Inquiry report had been presented to him. For the present, at least, he told the press, it would be kept confidential. He had asked Admiral King to ascertain how much of this material sufficiently affected present military operations as to merit a security classification.

Rugg sent Forrestal this telegram:

I REQUEST IMMEDIATE RELEASE OF FINDINGS OF NAVY COURT OF INQUIRY AS TO INNOCENCE OR GUILT OF ADMIRAL KIMMEL. FOR NEARLY THREE YEARS HE HAS BORNE PUBLIC BLAME FOR PEARL HARBOR DISASTER. HE HAS REQUESTED AND BEEN DENIED COURT MARTIAL. HIS TREATMENT HAS BEEN UN-AMERICAN. IN YOUR LETTER TO ADMIRAL MURFIN RELEASED TO PRESS ON OCTOBER 20 YOU INTIMATE THAT FACTS, NOW THREE YEARS OLD, FOUND BY NAVY COURT MAY BE

WITHHELD AS "SECRET" OR "TOP SECRET" ON GROUND DISCLOSURE WOULD INTERFERE WITH WAR EFFORT. CERTAINLY RELEASE OF FINDINGS OF COURT AS TO KIMMELS INNOCENCE OR GUILT CANNOT AFFECT WAR. PAST INJUSTICES CANNOT NOW BE REMEDIED. SIMPLE JUSTICE AND COMMON DECENCY REQUIRE IMMEDIATE PUBLIC ANNOUNCEMENT OF COURTS FINDINGS AS TO KIMMELS INNOCENCE OR GUILT.

But there was little doubt in knowledgeable Washington circles that the Navy would find it all top secret, and the Pearl Harbor cover-up would continue.

Chapter Eight

"YOU DO NOT HAVE TO CARRY THE TORCH FOR ADMIRAL KIMMEL" JUNE 1944–SEPTEMBER 1945

1.

A month before the Army and Navy inquiries opened, it appeared as though an event only distantly related to Pearl Harbor would endanger Roosevelt's attempt to win his fourth presidential election. It was a curious case in camera, unique in the American experience. A young U.S. code officer in the London Embassy had been seized on May 20, 1940, by British police; and, with the connivance of Ambassador Joseph Kennedy, arrested. The officer, Tyler Gatewood Kent, was then secretly tried in Old Bailey under the Official Secrets Act of 1911 for stealing official documents and sentenced to serve seven years in a British prison.

Kent was a clean-cut, good-looking young man from a well-known Virginia family. A descendant of Davy Crockett, he was born in Newchwang, Manchuria, where his father was the American consul. He had been educated at the Kent School, Princeton, the Sorbonne, the University of Madrid and George Washington University. Six years earlier he had entered the consular service. He was sent to Moscow as a code and cipher clerk and became alarmed by the dispatches of his ambassador, William C. Bullitt, as well as the cables sent on from Warsaw by Ambassador Anthony Drexel Biddle urging the Poles to resist Hitler. To Kent this was all evidence that American diplomats were "actively taking part in the formation of hostile coalitions in Europe . . . which they had no mandate to do."

Being an isolationist as well as an anti-Communist, he began to think of ways he could reveal such information to the U. S. Senate or the press. This resolve was strengthened, soon after being transferred to London in October 1939, upon reading the secret correspondence between Churchill and Roosevelt which, contrary to protocol, by-passed the British Foreign Office. These messages were far more alarming than anything he had yet seen. Here was the President of the United States and the First Lord of the Admiralty conniving to oust Chamberlain as Prime Minister so that they could put an end to the "Phony War" carried on by Chamberlain. They were both dedicated to a genuine all-out war against Nazism. The messages also indicated that Roosevelt was in touch with Eden, Duff Cooper and other members of the "War party" who were vigorously opposing Chamberlain's attempts to make a compromise peace with Hitler.

This secret correspondence continued even after Churchill became Prime Minister in the spring of 1940. Convinced that Roosevelt would draw America into the war unless he were exposed, Kent felt it was his duty to do so no matter the cost to himself. Recently he had met a Russian émigrée, Anna Wolkoff, whose father had been naval attaché in London at the time of the 1917 revolution. She shared Kent's detestation of Communism and introduced him to Captain A. H. M. Ramsey, a hero of the First World War and a Tory member of Parliament who was equally anti-Communist. He also was convinced that a vast Jewish conspiracy had taken over England from within.

Kent showed copies of some of the Roosevelt-Churchill correspondence to Ramsey, who thought they might be made the subject of a question in Parliament. This would not only expose Churchill's plot against Chamberlain but reveal to a peace-minded American public that their President was secretly working to that end. At this point Kent made the mistake of letting Anna Wolkoff borrow some of the messages. At his trial Kent testified that he thought she was going to take them to Ramsey.

Two days before Kent's arrest, a Scotland Yard officer informed Ambassador Kennedy that one of his code clerks "had become the object of attention by Scotland Yard through his association with a group of persons suspected of conducting pro-German activities." One was Anna Wolkoff, who was believed to be in communication with the Germans. This raised the question of whether Kent had been giving the Germans, through Wolkoff, secret cables involving the President. Since Kent was an American citizen, entitled to diplomatic immunity, and the documents were American property, the Scotland Yard man wondered what should be done.

Without consulting Washington, Kennedy waived Kent's immunity and then asked permission from Hull to do so. The approval came in a "very secret cable" two days later. In the meantime Kent, despite the serious charges against him, had been allowed to carry on his duties.

On the morning of May 20 he was arrested at his flat at 47 Gloucester Place. Two Scotland Yard detectives and an officer of British Military Intelligence searched the room and found some fifteen hundred copies of confidential documents in an unlocked cupboard and a brown leather bag. Kent was arrested and soon was facing Kennedy. How on earth, asked the ambassador, could Kent break trust with his country? Confident that he had only acted to prevent his country from being driven into a catastrophic war, Kent "never batted an eye." Then Kennedy asked why he had taken all this material. The reserved Kent said he did so because they were "important historical documents."

Now, by the choice of his own government, Kent was a British political prisoner with no American rights. It was not until two months later that he was finally formally charged in a closed session of Bow Street Police Court. "I don't think there was any intention originally of pressing any charges against me," Kent later said. "I believe it was done as a result of pressure from officials of the United States." This was likely since, three days after his arrest, the Home Office had issued a deportation order indicating the British were willing to expel him from the country.

Admiral J. O. Richardson (extreme right), commander of the U. S. Pacific Fleet. He is forcefully protesting to Secretary of the Navy Frank Knox on October 10, 1940, that continued basing of the fleet at Pearl Harbor is not a deterrent but an incitement to Japanese aggression in the Pacific. Roosevelt disagrees, and Richardson is replaced by Admiral Husband Kimmel. To Knox's right, Admirals Harry Yarnell (left) and Harold Stark. *(Naval History)*

The Atlantic Charter is signed, August 1941, aboard the British battleship *Prince of Wales*. Roosevelt and his advisers also agree to join Britain in preventing "further encroachment by Japan in the southwest Pacific" even though such measures "might lead to war." Left to right: General George Marshall, Army Chief of Staff; Franklin Roosevelt; Winston Churchill; Admiral Ernest King, commander of the Atlantic Fleet, and Admiral Stark, Chief of Naval Operations. *(National Archives)*

Henry L. Stimson, Secretary of War. *(Nation* *Archives)*

Harry L. Hopkins, the President's close friend a *adviser. (National Archives)*

Cordell Hull, Secretary of State. Hull, Stimson, Knox, Marshall and Stark constituted Roosevelt's War Cabinet. *(National Archives)*

Admiral Kimmel, commander of the Pacific Fleet in 1941, conferring with his chief of staff, Captain William Smith, right, and his operations officer, Captain W. S. DeLany. *(Naval History)*

By early December 1941 Kimmel has raised the Pacific Fleet to battle efficiency. *(Naval History)*

Lieutenant General Walter C. Short, commander of the U. S. Army ground and air forces in Hawaii. (*National Archives*)

Aerial view of Pearl Harbor from the north, showing the Pacific Fleet clustered near Ford Island. Battleship Row is on the east side of the island. Ensign Takeo Yoshikawa, the lone Japanese naval spy in Hawaii, posing as a consular employee, took similar pictures from a sightseeing plane. (*National Archives*)

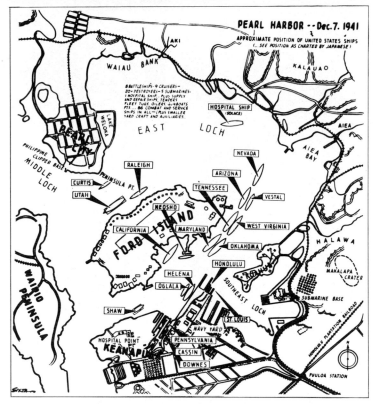

Chart of Pearl Harbor as it was on the morning of December 7, 1941. *(National Archives)*

Japanese planes begin taking off from six carriers at 6 A.M. *(National Archives)*

Great Raid On Hawaii

The Imperial Navy's air unit, mass-raided Pearl Harbor, Hawaii, the greatest and Pacific concentration center for the United States Navy. Its raid annihilated the American Pacific Fleet on December 8, and blew up Wheeler Field and Hickam Field, destroyed practically all the planes there.

The Imperial Navy's torpedo-planes and dive-bombers instantaneously sank five battleships, two cruisers, and a tanker. They also disabled or badly damaged four battleships and four light cruisers. The Navy air arm not only wiped out the American Pacific Fleet but also shot down or de-roped at least 464 enemy planes.

These photographs were taken by the Navy men participating in the repeated Battle at Hawaii, and are reproduced here through the courtesy of the Navy Office.

The black areas on the surface of the sea indicate petroleum flowing from badly hit enemy battleships. In addition, the tracks of torpedoes as well as bursts of shells where on land, are clearly shown.

Explanation Of Diagram I

Explanation Of Diagram II

Explanation Of Diagram III

Explanation Of Diagram IV

Through Japanese Eyes

(Pictures, sketches, diagrams and translated captions as published in Japan) *(National Archives, Suitland)*

Through Japanese Eyes

Boyer, radioman at the Wailupe naval radio on near Pearl Harbor. At 7:58 A.M., Hawaiian , he tapped out the signal heard around the world: RAID ON PEARL HARBOR. THIS IS NO DRILL. *(Karl r)*

Lieutenant Earl Gallaher, pilot of a scout bomber from the carrier *Enterprise*, approached Pearl Harbor during the attack. He reported that the Japanese were returning on a northwesterly course. But conflicting information sent the U.S. search to the south. At the Battle of Midway, Gallaher's bomb hit among the parked planes on the carrier *Kaga*. As he saw his bomb explode he thought, "*Arizona*, I remember you!" Later in the day he led the bombers that sank a second carrier, *Hiryu*. *(Rear Admiral Earl Gallaher)*

Admiral Kimmel watched the attack from the second floor of the submarine base. A spent Japanese bullet came through an open window and struck Kimmel in the chest. "I wish it had killed me," he said. *(Naval History)*

Through American Eyes. *(U. S. Navy)*

The *Arizona*, sunk and still burning, but with her flag flying. Nearly half of the 2,403 killed on December 7 were lost on this battleship. *(National Archives)*

"Yesterday," Roosevelt tells Congress, "December 7, 1941—a date which will live in infamy—the United States of America was suddenly and deliberately attacked. . . ." *(National Archives)*

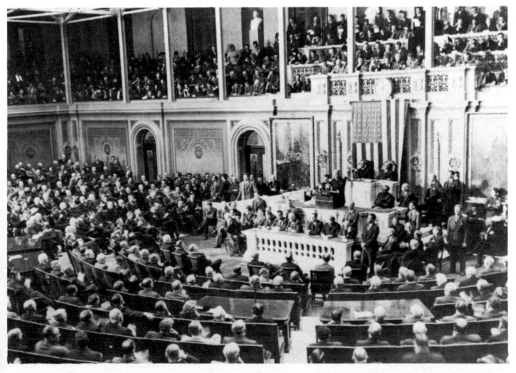

The Roosevelts' Christmas card to friends. *(Rear Admiral Lester Robert Schulz)*

Admiral Chester Nimitz relieves Kimmel as commander of the Pacific Fleet twenty-four days after the attack. *(Naval History)*

Knox visits the new commander at Pearl Ha: *(Naval History)*

The Navy Building on Constitution Avenue, Washington, D.C. Here, on the second floor, took place the "mutiny" of October 1941.

Rear Admiral Richmond Kelly Turner, brilliant Chief of War Plans, nicknamed "Terrible Turner," for his sulfuric temper. He refused the request of Captain Alan Kirk to send warning of possible attack on Pearl Harbor to Kimmel. Kirk was "detached" from his position as head of Navy Intelligence. *(National Archives)*

Rear Admiral Theodore "Ping" Wilkinson, Kirk's replacement, was also bullied by Turner. This picture was taken in Japanese waters on September 21, 1945. He met a tragic death soon after testifying at the congressional investigation of Pearl Harbor when his car plunged off a ferry. *(National Archives)*

Rear Admiral Leigh Noyes, Chief of Navy Communications, also feuded with Turner. *(National Archives)*

Commander Charles C. Hiles, one of Safford's close postwar friends and confidants. Their voluminous correspondence, available at the Archive of Contemporary History, University of Wyoming, is an invaluable source for researchers. *(Mrs. Charles C. Hiles)*

Commander (later Captain) Laurance Safford, one of the subordinates on the second deck who persisted in trying to send warnings of Pearl Harbor to Kimmel. A talented cryptoanalyst, he later risked his reputation and career to prove that Kimmel was innocent of responsibility for the Pearl Harbor debacle. *(Commander Charles C. Hiles)*

William Friedman, a close friend of Safford's and leader of the talented team of codebreakers that solved the Japanese Purple code. *(George C. Marshall Research Foundation)*

The machine constructed to break the Purple Code. *(National Archives)*

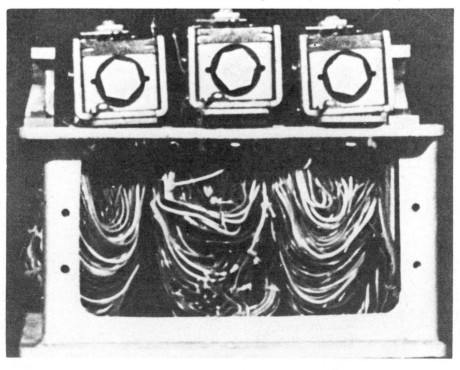

The Roberts Commission placed the burden of blame for Pearl Harbor on Kimmel and Short. Left to right: Major General Frank McCoy, Admiral William Standley, Associate Supreme Court Justice Owen J. Roberts, Rear Admiral Joseph Reeves and Brigadier General Joseph McNarney. Standley, the highest-ranking officer on the commission, later felt he had been grossly betrayed by Roberts and called his performance as head of the commission "as crooked as a snake." *(Wide World)*

Kimmel selected retired Navy Captain Robert Lavender as assistant defense counsel in his efforts to clear himself. Lavender, second from left, is shown as a member of the crew of one of three Navy planes involved in the historic transatlantic flight of 1919. *(Naval History)*

Charles Rugg of Boston, the chief defense counsel for Kimmel. *(Edward Hanify)*

In early 1944 Admiral Thomas Hart began a one-man investigation. His principal witness was Captain Safford, who revealed that early in December 1941 he had seen the intercept of the Japanese "East wind, rain" message which meant that Japan was about to wage war on America. *(David Richmond)*

Admiral William Halsey, one of the many high-ranking defenders of Kimmel. He wrote Kimmel, "As you know I have always thought and have not hesitated to say on any and all occasions, that I believe you and Short were the greatest military martyrs this country has ever produced, and that your treatment was outrageous." *(National Archives)*

That July the three members of the Navy Inquiry are sworn in. Left to right: Vice Admiral Adolphus Andrews, Admiral Orin Murfin and Admiral Edward Kalbfus. When they learned to their amazement and indignation that Kimmel had been deprived of vital information they reversed the Roberts findings and exonerated Kimmel. *(David Richmond)*

Members of the Navy Inquiry talk with Admiral Nimitz (back to camera) at Pearl Harbor. *(David Richmond)*

But this would have meant a trial in the United States at a time when Roosevelt was preparing his 1940 campaign for re-election. Since a secret trial in America at this time would have been impossible, the revelations in open court could have meant Roosevelt's defeat. But in England all trials under the Official Secrets Act were held in camera. That October Kent was taken to the Old Bailey. He told how disillusioned he had become with American foreign policy, and that Roosevelt had not been straight with the people. They "were not being adequately informed, they were . . . being told half-truths, instead of the strict truth." Alarmed by the cables he read, he had decided to reveal Roosevelt's chicanery to the U. S. Senate or the press; and had finally decided the only way he could do so was through Captain Ramsey.

Didn't he feel he owed allegiance to his employer, Ambassador Kennedy? Yes, he replied, but this was not his only duty. "To whom did you consider you had another duty?"

"Well, putting it in a dramatic way, to the American people."

"Which duty did you consider the higher of the two?"

"Naturally, the one to the people of America."

Despite Kent's admission that he had let both Ramsey and Wolkoff borrow some of the documents, it would be difficult to convict him under the Official Secrets Act unless it could be proven to the jury that Wolkoff was a foreign agent. The only evidence to show this was an intercepted letter addressed to "Lord Haw-Haw," who broadcast anti-British propaganda over the German radio; the letter contained advice to launch stronger attacks on the Jews. Even flimsier was evidence that Wolkoff had been friendly with a military attaché at the Italian Embassy in London *before* Italy declared war. The Solicitor General, the Earl Jowitt, later admitted "there was no evidence that she had passed any secret information to such attaché." Even so Wolkoff was named a "foreign agent" by the court under the special definition contained in the Official Secrets Act that such an agent was anyone reasonably suspected of having committed an act prejudicial to the safety or interests of the state. Jowitt admitted that "Anna Wolkoff was not employed by any foreign power, nor did she ever receive any payment from any foreign power."

Still, by definition, she was a foreign agent; and Kent, found guilty, was sentenced to seven years in prison. He was still convinced he was a loyal citizen of the United States. He admitted he had committed an offense "but the motive or purpose of an act that is committed is of prime importance." While the British claimed it was for a purpose prejudicial to the interest and safety of the state, Kent never believed it was at all prejudicial to the interest and safety of his own country. Quite the contrary. The majority of Americans wanted to stay out of war in Europe.

From the beginning Kent's mother, Mrs. Anne H. P. Kent, waged a battle to return her son to America where he could be tried under U.S. law but her letters to Roosevelt and the State Department brought no satisfaction. It was not until June of 1944 that the news of Kent's imprisonment was released by chance. It came after a member of Parliament asked a question about Captain Ramsey, who had been imprisoned the past four years without charge. It was then revealed that Kent had given him some of the secret Roosevelt-Churchill messages. An American reporter filed this story, which surprisingly passed the British censor. The result was a tempest in Washington on June 19. "I cannot understand how an American citizen could be tried in a British secret court," Burton Wheeler stated in the Senate. What would happen, "if we should arrest a member of the British Embassy here and endeavor to try him in an American secret court? Of course, the British Government would immediately protest, and we would not try him in a secret or a public court."

The chairman of the Senate Foreign Relations Committee, Democratic Senator Tom Connally of Texas, replied, "The State Department says that the British government before prosecuting submitted the documents to the United States Government, and before the prosecution was begun our Government examined the documents and concluded that Kent ought to be prosecuted and waived his diplomatic immunity." Connally said he had no pity for Kent. "It is all very well to beat your breasts and say, 'We will try Americans in American courts,' but here we find a man who is conspiring, and under the British law he is concluded to be guilty. I have no tears to shed for him." He also claimed the stories of the so-called Churchill-Roosevelt private correspondence were only gossip.

"This is not gossip," retorted a Republican senator. "I am amazed that the British censor should pass it, but since he has, I assume it has the imprimatur of the British Government. No one on the floor of Parliament denied the statements." Another Republican observed that the reported secret negotiations between Churchill and Roosevelt preceded the President's 1940 campaign pledge "again and again and again" that American boys would not be sent to fight foreign wars.

This stung. "Why can we not have unity until the war is over?" pleaded Connally. "Why cannot we stop this sniping and shooting behind the lines?"

The heated Senate debate was echoed in the House where a Republican declared that Roosevelt and Churchill, then First Lord of the Admiralty, "were carrying on a correspondence, the purport of which was to involve us in the present war." He also revealed that he had been informed of the case more than two years earlier by Kent's mother. "I was unable at the time to get accurate information as to the facts but, if the story is false, the facts should be spread upon the record. No harm could possibly be done to the military effort."

Concern among Democrats preparing for the presidential election in the fall was echoed across the Atlantic. In a memorandum to the Foreign Office, Viscount Halifax noted that the isolationists in Congress had generated a sizable issue out of the Tyler Kent case. "If any fact about the Kent-Ramsey case could be made public without prejudice to security it would do much to clear the air. Otherwise there is considerable danger that issue re: alleged collusion between President and Mr. Churchill behind backs of United States Congress and people to make American entrance into war inescapable will be injected into election issues to our detriment and continue to cloud pages of journalists and historians long after."

The State Department received so many letters inquiring whether Tyler Kent had been fairly treated that it was felt necessary to release a statement early in September, most of which was accurate, but it read more like a spy thriller than a sober State Department report with its injudicious mixture of suspicions and proven facts. For example, at one point it intimated that Kent was a spy by stating that the police had "established that some of the papers found had been transmitted to an agent of a foreign power."

Mrs. Kent protested to Secretary Hull. "Very few persons besides his mother are interested in Tyler Kent *per se*," she wrote, "but 130 odd million Americans are vitally concerned to learn whether or not it is true that in time of peace, one year before the Lend-Lease bill and other measures were put before the Senate, they had been planned 'between the American President and the British Navy head.'"

The incident was inflamed the next day by former Ambassador Kennedy, who had just visited Franklin D. Roosevelt, whom he had endorsed in a surprise, last-minute radio speech in 1940. In an exclusive interview with Scripps-Howard reporter Henry J. Taylor, Kennedy mentioned matters that were never touched upon in the Kent trial and made unfounded allegations that far exceeded those in the State Department statement.

When asked how and why Kent transmitted the secret information to Germany, Kennedy said, "Kent's reported friendliness with the Russian girl, Anna Wolkoff, had its place in his attitude but apparently she didn't have safe and regular channels into Germany. . . . But Kent used the Italian Embassy to reach Berlin. For the most part he passed our secrets out of England in the Italian diplomatic pouch. Italy, you recall, didn't enter the war until after Kent was arrested. If we had been at war I wouldn't have favored turning Kent over to Scotland Yard or have sanctioned his imprisonment in England. I would have recommended that he be brought back to the United States and been shot."

He gave a dramatic twist also to his version of the discovery in Kent's flat of "a locked box" containing fifteen hundred copies of cables in an unbreakable code.

> That night America's diplomatic blackout started all over the world. I telephoned the President in Washington saying our most secret code was no good any place, and I told Mr. Roosevelt that the Germans and Italians, and presumably the Japanese, had possessed the full picture of the problems and decisions and everything else sent in and out of the White

House and the State Department for the past eight months, as critical a period as any in the history of the war. . . .

The result was that for weeks, right at the time of the fall of France, the United States Government closed its confidential communicating system and was blacked out from private contact with American embassies and legations everywhere. At this critical time, with decisions of the highest importance needing to be made and communicated hourly, no messages could be sent or received by the President, Mr. Hull or anyone else. This lasted from two weeks to a month and a half—until a new unbreakable code could be devised in Washington and carried by special couriers throughout the world. . . .

Nobody "railroaded" Kent. The British sentence that put him on the Isle of Wight for seven years was mild beyond measure. The only thing that saved Kent's life was that he was an American citizen and we were not yet at war.

This concoction of fact and fiction, labeled by Taylor as "the most important spy case yet revealed in this war," successfully ended Republican efforts to make Kent an election issue. It also ended whatever public sympathy there had been for Kent. The man was an out-and-out spy who had betrayed his country, probably for the love of a glamorous Mata Hari. (She was, in truth, middle-aged and described by one observer as "the ugliest woman" he had ever seen.)

Kent managed to cable his mother that the Kennedy statement was a tissue of lies. It was. The story that Kent had smuggled American secrets in the Italian diplomatic pouch was sheer conjecture based on the fact that Wolkoff knew an Italian Embassy employee. In his trial Kent was not even accused of conspiring with her. In a letter, produced at Old Bailey, the Public Prosecutor declared that he had no intention of charging that Kent "participated in, or had any knowledge of, her attempt to communicate with Germany."

The diplomatic blackout caused by Kent was another fabrication. Kennedy himself, during the days following Kent's arrest, sent very confidential cables which would eventually be published by the State Department. Moreover, to describe the code used to transmit the Churchill-Roosevelt messages as "unbreakable" and

"our most secret code" was ludicrous. This was the notoriously un-
confidential Gray code which had been read with ease by the Germans and other foreign powers since 1918. It became so familiar
to American Foreign Service officers that in the late twenties a senior consul in Shanghai made his retirement speech in Gray.

2.

Although the Kent case had been successfully submerged, Pearl
Harbor remained the most volatile issue of the election. It came to
a climax in late August through a mistake in judgment by the
Democrats' candidate for Vice-President. In the August 26 issue of
Collier's, Senator Harry Truman called for a consolidation of the
Army and Navy, opening his argument with the statement that
the Pearl Harbor attack revealed "the danger that lies in a division
of responsibilities." He went on to imply that Short and Kimmel
were not on speaking terms prior to the attack, and stated that at
no time "did Admiral Kimmel ask or receive information as to the
manner in which the Army was discharging its highly important
duty." He also charged that Kimmel had never conducted any distant air reconnaissance except during drills and maneuvers. Nor
had General Short ever ascertained how the Navy was handling
this task.

Kimmel wrote Truman that his allegations were false since they
were based on the Roberts report, which did not contain the basic
truths of the Pearl Harbor catastrophe. "I suggest that until such
time as complete disclosure is made of the facts about Pearl Harbor, you refrain from repeating charges based on evidence that has
never met the test of public scrutiny. I ask for nothing more than
an end to untruths and half truths about this matter, until the
whole story is given to our people, who, I am convinced, will be
amazed by the truth."

Publication of Kimmel's letter, which was never answered, set
off a storm of controversy, with Republicans and anti-Administration forces rushing to his defense. The author, Rupert Hughes,
made a speech over radio calling the plight of Kimmel and Short
an American Dreyfus case. "Dreyfus was on Devil's Island for four
years. Kimmel and Short will have been in purgatory for three

years in December." The Administration was covering up the entire affair. "Of course, if Thomas E. Dewey is elected," he promised, "the fur will begin to fly. . . . It took a new President of France to get Dreyfus out of his cruel inferno."

Republicans in the House took the ball from there, one charging that Truman, the possible "assistant Commander in Chief," had himself reopened the question of Pearl Harbor responsibility and, moreover, "had prejudged it, in allocating the blame, before all the facts have been made known." Full disclosure of the controversial incidents surrounding the catastrophe was demanded.

A few days later another Republican charged that Short had only acted according to information transmitted from Washington. "There appears to be an abundance of evidence that 72 hours before the attack, the Australian Government advised the American Government in Washington that an aircraft carrier task force of the Japanese Navy had been sighted by Australian reconnaissance headed toward Pearl Harbor."

House Majority Leader McCormack responded. "A dangerous rumor of this kind cannot be treated lightly or brushed aside, as most political statements are, with a smile," he said, and produced an official denial that Washington had received the alleged Australian warning. "There would appear to be a bottomless cavern wherein cheap politics begets unforgivable war rumors."

To counter this accusation a Republican two days later read into the record a statement by Colonel Sidney Graves, son of the commanding general of American forces in Russia in 1918–20. He claimed he had heard Sir Owen Dixon, then Australian ambassador to the United States, discuss the warning at a Washington dinner on December 7, 1943. Dixon said, in substance, "About 72 hours before Pearl Harbor, I received a flash warning from my Naval Intelligence that a Japanese Task Force was at sea and Australia should prepare for an attack; 24 hours later this was further confirmed with a later opinion of Intelligence that the Task Force was apparently not aimed at Australian waters and perhaps was directed against some American possessions."

Dixon denied he had made any such remarks and in his press conference on September 22 Roosevelt made a joke of the matter. "There will be lots of things like that, flocks of them—morning, noon and night—until the seventh of November." Although his airy dismissal of the Dixon case was successful, Roosevelt remained concerned about other rumors or charges that might be revealed before Election Day. Stephen Early, the presidential press secretary, had already informed him that Charles Rugg was supplying information on Pearl Harbor to Senator Robert Taft and the Republican National Committee. The White House was also getting large numbers of letters urging the Administration to stop hiding the truth about Pearl Harbor and reveal Washington's part in the disaster. "The American People demand the TRUTH be told about Pearl Harbor before November 7, 1944," wrote one citizen. "Did Harry Hopkins transfer 250 Navy planes which were needed at Pearl Harbor before the attack?"

What worried Roosevelt most, according to Stimson, was "fear there would be an adverse report by the Army Pearl Harbor Board" just before the election. "The President rather characteristically isn't worried at all about the Navy Inquiry but is worried about the Army and was anxious to have the termination of the inquiry postponed until after Election." But the Army Board still had a few weeks to go and Stimson knew it would be impossible to stop proceedings. All he could do was hope that it would not include politically damaging information.

There were also rumors that Dewey had already gathered many facts about Pearl Harbor and would use them in his next major speech. The man who took action on this was not the President but George Marshall, who feared revelation of secret material might endanger the security of the Purple code. On September 25, the day Dewey was scheduled to speak in Oklahoma City, he drafted a letter of caution to Dewey and sent it to Admiral King with this note: "A recent speech in Congress had deadly implications and I now understand much more is to be said, possibly by Governor Dewey himself. This letter, of course, puts him on the spot, and I hate to do it but see no other way of avoiding what might well be a catastrophe to us." The whole thing, he added, was "loaded with dynamite but I very much feel that something has to be done or the fat will be in the fire to our great loss in the Pacific, and possibly also in Europe." The letter was approved by

King, and Marshall decided to have it hand-delivered by Colonel Carter Clarke, a trusted assistant of Marshall's.

That evening Dewey made a strong speech that put the Democrats on the defensive. He claimed that Roosevelt was accountable for "the shocking state of our defense programs" in the months preceding Pearl Harbor. America was grossly unprepared for war.

The following afternoon Carter Clarke, in civilian clothes, arrived in Tulsa where arrangements had been made to meet Dewey in a private room at the Tulsa Hotel. Clarke made sure they were alone before handing over the letter from Marshall. "Well, Top Secret," said Dewey. "That's really top, isn't it?" He began reading:

> I am writing you without the knowledge of any other person except Admiral King (who concurs) because we are approaching a grave dilemma in the political reactions of Congress regarding Pearl Harbor.
> What I have to tell you below is of such highly secret nature that I feel compelled to ask you either to accept it on the basis of your not communicating its contents to any other person and returning this letter or not reading any further and returning the letter to the bearer.

Dewey looked up from the letter and asked Clarke, "Are you a Regular Army officer?" He was. Would Clarke give his word that he had been sent by Marshall? Yes. At this point, so reported Clarke, the governor said he did not want his lips sealed on things he already knew about Pearl Harbor. "He then asked if I were authorized to say to him in the name of Gen. Marshall that if he read the letter through and then stated to me that he already had in his possession the identical information that was contained in the letter, that he would then be released from all obligations to keep silent."

After Clarke said he had no such authority, Dewey said, "I cannot conceive of General Marshall and Admiral King being the only ones who know about this letter." Nor could he conceive of Marshall approaching an "opposition candidate" and making such a proposition. "Marshall does not do things like that. I am confident that Franklin Roosevelt is behind this whole thing." The letter had been lying in his lap. He picked it up. "Let me read those first two paragraphs again." He started to read, laid down the letter. "I have not reread them because my eye caught the word cryptograph. Now if this letter merely tells me that we were reading certaiṇ Japanese codes before Pearl Harbor and that at least two of them are still in current use, there is no point in my reading the letter because I already know that." He paused. "That is the case and I know it, isn't it?"

"Governor," said Clarke, "I am merely a courier in this case."

"Well, I know it and Franklin Roosevelt knows all about it. He knew what was happening before Pearl Harbor and instead of being reelected he ought to be impeached." He handed back the letter. "I shall be in Albany on Thursday and I shall be glad to receive you or General Marshall or anyone General Marshall cares to send to discuss at length this cryptographic business or the whole Pearl Harbor mess."

Marshall responded by writing a second letter requesting Dewey only to agree not to disclose information of which he was not already aware. He was persisting in the matter, he wrote, only "because the military hazards are so serious that I feel some action is necessary to protect the interests of our armed forces."

This letter was delivered by Clarke on September 28 at the Executive Mansion in Albany. But Dewey refused to look at it unless his personal adviser could also read it. He then suggested Clarke phone Marshall. Clarke replied that he did not want to do so from the Executive Mansion but would go to a pay booth. "Oh, hell," said Dewey, "I'll phone Marshall. I've talked to him before and this will be all right." He conversed several minutes with Marshall before handing the phone to Clarke. Marshall authorized the colonel to give the letter to Dewey, to leave it with him and to discuss the case technically in the presence of his personal adviser. A moment later Dewey put the letter down. "Well, I'll be damned if I believe the Japs are still using those two codes."

Clarke assured him that they were and that one of them was America's lifeblood in intelligence. Dewey read how vital the Purple code was to the war effort, and a final appeal from Marshall to help keep it a secret. "You will understand from the foregoing the utterly tragic consequences if the present political debates regarding Pearl Harbor disclose to the enemy, German or Jap, any suspicion of the vital sources of information we possess." Further speeches such as the one recently delivered in Congress by Representative Forest Harness of Indiana would clearly reveal to the Japanese that we were reading their codes. "I am presenting this matter to you in the hope that you will see your way clear to avoid the tragic results with which we are now threatened in the present political campaign."

Dewey still believed Roosevelt's administration was responsible for Pearl Harbor but, despite urging from some Republicans to expose what he already knew about the codes, he promised to keep this issue out of the campaign—and did.

Another issue kept from the public was Roosevelt's failing health. A photo taken at the Democratic Convention had revealed a haggard President with mouth hanging listlessly open. *Time* and *Life* kept hinting about his fragile health since Henry Luce was now unabashedly supporting Dewey. Yet early that month he made a decision that might have won Roosevelt the presidency. *Life's* managing editor showed Luce some two hundred Roosevelt pictures for upcoming issues. "In about half of them he was a dead man," recalled Luce. "We decided to print the ones that were the least bad. And thereby—by trying to lean over backward being fair or something, or kind—we infringed our contract with readers to tell them the truth. Actually the truth *was* in the pictures." The big irresponsibility of the American press, confessed Luce, "came when we did not indicate, especially in *Life's* pictures, that Roosevelt was a dying man."

Lies about his health had been coming from the White House since early in the year. That March a checkup on Roosevelt at Bethesda Naval Hospital had confirmed indications of "hypertension, hypertensive heart disease, failure of the left ventricle of the heart, and fluid in both lungs. FDR had a persistent cough, a grayish pallor on his face, a noticeable agitation of the hands, a blue cast to lips and fingernails." And yet a month later Admiral Ross McIntire, his personal physician, assured a reporter from *Time* that Roosevelt was in good health. "Considering the difference in age, his recent physical examination is equally as good as the one made on him twelve years ago."

And so, on November 7, the American public went to the polls unaware that the Army Pearl Harbor Board and the Navy Inquiry had just placed the burden of blame for Pearl Harbor, not on Kimmel and Short, but on Washington. Nor did the voters know that one of the candidates was a dying man. As a result the President won thirty-six states with 432 electoral votes. Dewey took only twelve states with 99 electoral votes. The Democrats won seven more senatorial seats than their opponents, with two races still in doubt. In the House the score was 242 to 185 in favor of the Democrats. It must have particularly pleased Roosevelt that two of his favorite enemies, isolationists Hamilton Fish and Gerald Nye, were defeated. Upon his return to the capital from Hyde Park the President was greeted by a crowd of several hundred thousand despite a downpour. He was in a jovial mood, remarking that he hoped news writers "won't intimate in the papers that I expect to make Washington my permanent residence for the rest of my life."

3.

By Election Day MacArthur had landed a substantial force on Leyte with more than 100,000 tons of cargo. In the great naval battle that followed in Leyte Gulf, the Americans sank some 300,000 tons of combat shipping. It was the virtual end of the Imperial Navy.

In Europe the Allies, confident of imminent victory, were preparing to storm the Siegfried Line, unaware that Hitler was preparing a surprise counterattack in the Ardennes designed to reach Antwerp and destroy thirty U.S. and British divisions.

The morning before the election Forrestal and Stimson had conferred about Pearl Harbor for an hour and a half. "We each told the other the substance of the reports of our respective investigating boards," Stimson wrote in his diary. "I was relieved to find that the Navy were apparently not going to try to whitewash their people and Forrestal seems to look at the matter in a very cooperative spirit." By afternoon Stimson had "finally gathered myself together and decided practically what my decision will be in the

Pearl Harbor case." Having reached the decision, Stimson "took the bit in my mouth" and told the Judge Advocate General and the assistant recorder of the Pearl Harbor Board that he was going to reverse the Board's findings. "To my relief I found that they agreed with me and were very helpful in working out the general outlines of it. In fact I think we were all finally agreed on it by the time the long talk of the afternoon was over. It was a great relief to my mind to have gotten that far."

At Navy Headquarters, Admiral King was presented with a proposed endorsement to the Navy Inquiry report for his signature. In it Stark was criticized for not keeping Kimmel properly informed and the latter for not being sufficiently alive to the dangers of the situation. "Since trial by general court-martial is not warranted by the evidence adduced, appropriate administrative action would appear to be the relegation of both of these officers to positions in which lack of superior judgment may not result in future errors." Although he had not yet read the proceedings of the Navy Inquiry, and although he felt that Kimmel had been made a scapegoat, King signed the endorsement.

The Secretary of War, with the help of two assistants, worked diligently to finish his endorsement to the Army Board report and by the following Monday he could write that "by the grace of God by the end of the day we had done so practically." What concerned him most were the "pinpricks" in the Army Board's conclusions about Marshall. "That's what makes all the trouble." Although Marshall was held in the highest of esteem throughout the Army and the Administration, the charges against him would damage his position. They also would reflect on Stimson and Roosevelt. Marshall himself had only recently read the report and was despondent. On November 14 he told Stimson that the shocking conclusions of the Board had destroyed his usefulness in the Army. "I told him that was nonsense, to forget it."

Later in the day Stimson had lunch with Forrestal at the Navy Department. Afterward Stimson brought out the draft of his statement. Forrestal read it, then handed over the endorsement signed by King. The two Secretaries concluded they were "not very far apart and that there was to be no clash between the standards and views of the two Departments in regard to the situation."

On the twentieth Stimson sought advice from General Alexander Surles, who handled Army Public Relations. First Surles read Stimson's latest draft, then the Secretary read him the conclusions of the Army Board. Surles had not seen these before and was so staggered that "his first reaction was to try to keep back the findings. He was afraid that the Navy will somehow or other ride in behind our publicity and escape it themselves and leave us to bear the whole brunt of it." Although Surles approved of Stimson's statement he was not sure they could "afford to take the big publicity" that would surely result from the criticisms of Marshall. "This was natural and not unexpected but of course it was a heavy blow to me to have to carry the whole load alone myself. Surles has usually been such a support and his judgment has always been so good that this was another staggering swipe to me."

Throughout the night he was also troubled because he hadn't yet heard from the Navy. He had shown Forrestal his own report but still had no idea what his fellow Secretary was going to say. "So this morning I called him up and said that I wanted to have their report before I saw the President or at least to know what they were going to do." Stimson knew Forrestal had seen Roosevelt the previous week and he suspected the two had come together "more or less."

Forrestal revealed that he had not finished his report but would send it over before Stimson saw Roosevelt. When it arrived late that morning Stimson was appalled. "After all the preliminaries, the preambles, and recitals, it consisted of just one sentence in which he said that, owing to the situation and the circumstances which existed, it was not in the public interest or something like that to take any proceedings against any naval officers. Well, my group who at once got together again, as well as myself, decided that in the face of that, if the Navy put that out, why our report with our frankness and our frank criticism of our own people would get all the publicity and unfavorable publicity in the sense that the people would do all the speculating about the big names that have been mentioned."

By then it was time to go to the White House. Stimson had lunch with the President in his penthouse with Roosevelt's daughter, Anna Boettiger, present. "That of course cramped a little bit our style . . . so during the luncheon I sat quiet and listened to the chitchat that went on." Finally Roosevelt brought up the Pearl Harbor report. "I think," he remarked, "the less said the better."

Stimson guessed the President must have seen and approved Forrestal's draft. "I told him that I had been completely cut off from my proposal by that plan because we could not afford to go ahead and be frank when the Navy was not being frank." Stimson explained his own plan and argued that frankness was the best policy. Then he handed the President the conclusions of the Army Board.

Roosevelt read them very carefully. "Why, this is wicked!" he said. "This is wicked." He studied Stimson's report carefully and at length. Very good, he said, but still thought it would be safer to follow Forrestal's line.

After Stimson expressed fear that Congress would get at the papers and the facts, Roosevelt said they should take every step against that, and also must refuse to make the reports public. "He said that they should be sealed up and our opinions put in with them and then a notice made that they should only be opened on a Joint Resolution of both Houses of Congress approved by the President after the war, this resolution to say that it was in the public interest to do so."

Stimson left the White House disgruntled. His influence there was apparently waning. He knew that Harry Hopkins was conniving against him on the grounds that he was ill and too old. What stung most was that Forrestal's method had been chosen, not his. Stimson reluctantly complied with the President's order to prepare a shorter news release, but was stubborn enough to include that the Army Board had found that "certain officers in the field and in the War Department did not perform their duties with the necessary skill or exercise the judgment which was required. . . ." He also criticized Short by name.

In a covering letter to the President, he wrote, "The enclosed draft goes as far in condensation as I believe I can properly go. To say merely that I believe that the facts do not warrant the institution of any proceedings against any officer of the Army would, I believe, inevitably give the impression that I was trying entirely to absolve all Army officers from any criticism including General Short. . . . This is an impression I am unwilling to father."

The proposed news release and the letter were sent to Hyde Park by a courier who had been instructed by Stimson to wait for an answer. But the President said he couldn't reply that day and would like to compare it with the Navy proposition since he wanted both departments to coordinate. "His wish for coordination . . . is reasonable," Stimson wrote in his diary, "but I have gone a long long step towards giving up what I think is the wisest plan and I think it is time for the Navy to come and meet me. In any event I do not feel like yielding to him at all. In fact it is a matter of conscience—any yielding to the Navy form. I can't help feeling that if I did that I would lose the respect of the people whom I most value because they would say that I was doing a complete whitewash of the entire Army in a situation where such a position was untenable. That criticism will come to Forrestal if he doesn't change his form of statement."

Although the next day was Thanksgiving, Stimson went to his office as usual. He talked on the telephone to Forrestal, whom he found "not as stiff as the draft statement which he sent me the other day." The Navy Secretary was also in favor of admitting there was something wrong in the Navy but Stimson had his doubts and these were strengthened upon hearing rumors that the Navy was going to whitewash everyone including Kimmel. And so Stimson called back on the twenty-fourth. Forrestal assured him he was going to admit the guilt of some of his officers. But there was still nagging doubt in Stimson's mind. He would have "an uneasy feeling" till the thing was done.

On the way home he read the new critique of the Judge Advocate General on the Army Board's report. It was, thought Stimson, "really a humdinger," since he "handled the Pearl Harbor Board without gloves and had analyzed very carefully and yet fairly all their mistakes."

The Judge Advocate's memorandum largely reconfirmed the findings of the Roberts Commission. It also stoutly defended Marshall, stating baldly that none of the Board's criticisms of the Chief of Staff was "justified."

Forrestal was far more sensitive to the Army's problem than

Stimson realized. If the Navy criticized Stark that would reflect unfavorably on Marshall. Yet it would not be fair only to place blame on Kimmel. "The exercise of hindsight is probably the easiest intellectual function available to man," he wrote in his diary on the twenty-seventh but he was still forced to conclude that neither those officials in the Navy Department nor those in Hawaii had taken adequate precautions for the Japanese attack. At the same time he had to protect the reputation of the Navy.

His dilemma apparently weighed so heavily on him that when he talked on the phone to Stimson the latter got the impression that Forrestal was backsliding, for he bitterly noted in his diary that the Secretary of the Navy was "turning back to his old form of impossible statement or rather a statement the form of which is impossible for me. It was another body blow to me."

Still another came that day with the announcement that Hull was being replaced by a much younger man, Edward Stettinius. "The departure of Mr. Hull means a tremendous loss to me personally and officially. Hull, Knox and I have kept so close together all through these four years that it has saved many a bad slip, and now both Hull and Knox have gone. So tonight I felt pretty solemn and alone." It must have made him aware of his age—and of Harry Hopkins' continuing efforts to get rid of him.

His differences with Forrestal were solved in the next few days; Stimson found Forrestal's latest draft to be "a very good job." On the last day of November they met to make their two statements "as parallel as they could be under the circumstances." After final tinkering the two men called up the President at Warm Springs, Georgia, and read aloud their reports. Roosevelt approved and authorized release to the press. "Now I feel as if I had a burden off my back for the present," wrote Stimson, yet still felt it was a grave mistake not to have made a frank and full statement—"but it is as much as Forrestal and I could accomplish under the President's direction that we should not go too far."

This was one time Stimson's political instinct was superior to his chief's. The general editorial response to the two statements on December 1 was negative. Newspapers and magazines attacked the Administration for continuing to suppress the Pearl Harbor story. Great numbers of letters and telegrams flooded into the White

House. "What do you think Americans are?" a man from Edge-wood, Rhode Island, asked the President. "Just ignorant and dumb cattle? Freedom of Speech: Freedom of Press? . . . Can't tell us now about the responsibility for the Pearl Harbor catas-trophe because it will undermine the morale? The Government's cover-up of the responsibility for that catastrophe has done more to undermine morale than any other single event of the past three years. The thinkers of America, and there are millions of them, won't stand for such guff. I am but one of the millions of Ameri-cans today who are shocked, humiliated and indignant because of this announcement."

In his column in the New York *Daily News*, John O'Donnell wrote that a police court aroma hovered over the case. Partisan debate in Congress broke out anew. The Democrats defended the two press releases. What more should be disclosed during a war? The Republicans repeated their charge of suppression of vital in-formation. In any case, it was obvious that full revelation of facts and an open investigation of Pearl Harbor could not come about until the war was over.

Neither Rugg nor Kimmel had been surprised by the news releases since the latter had been kept informed of the rumors floating around the corridors of the Navy Building and the former had collated this information into an accurate prediction. The Roosevelt-Stimson-Forrestal tactic aroused the admiral's fighting spirit and he immediately demanded an audience with the chief of Naval Operations. It was fitting that the interview was granted on the third anniversary of the Japanese attack. Kimmel found the crusty King in a friendly and sympathetic mood, treating an ad-miral-in-disgrace as if he were still in the inner circle. With disarm-ing frankness Ki, as he was known to a few intimates, stated that it was he who had recommended to Forrestal that Betty Stark be relieved of his command and placed on the retired list. "He strongly implied, without definitely stating it as a fact," Kimmel wrote in his memorandum of the interview, "that the Court of In-quiry had completely cleared me of all blame in connection."

King's frankness even extended to revelation that the Army Board had vigorously censured Marshall "for his action or lack of action" in the days preceding the catastrophe, and that Stimson himself had "sweat blood" over his news release. "The publication of any part finding any fault of Marshall's was voted down," confessed King. The President, he said, had not only turned down King's proposal to relieve Stark on the ground that he was performing valuable services, but made it clear that Marshall was irreplaceable. "He would not consent to the publication of any remarks in the slightest degree derogatory to Mr. Marshall." Roosevelt, in fact, had been "fit to be tied" when he read the Army Board report.

After King asserted he had also recommended against publication of the Army and Navy findings, Kimmel bluntly asked what assurances King could give that the record and findings of the Navy Inquiry would not be tampered with or destroyed. The Navy commander in chief indignantly replied that he was amazed at such a question. Under no circumstances could the findings be tampered with! "You need not be amazed," retorted Kimmel, "as such things have happened and might happen again." He told how he had heard Stark commit perjury at the Navy Inquiry. "And after hearing that, I think anything might happen."

King showed such shock that Kimmel asked him point-blank, "Have you read the record of the Court of Inquiry? Stark's lies are spread there for anyone to read, and the fact that he was lying is unmistakable."

King admitted he had not read the testimony. Kimmel assured him that at least half a dozen other witnesses had heard Stark's testimony. "I am convinced that Stark lied before the court under oath," said Kimmel. "After listening to Stark I was ashamed of the Navy."

4.

The criticism that followed the news releases impelled Stimson to seek new information that would refute the Army Board charges. He turned over the job to Major Henry Christian Clausen, who had served as assistant recorder for the Board. An attorney before he entered the Army, he had served as assistant U.S. attorney for the Northern District of California and then become chief counsel for the chief engineer during the construction of the

Golden Gate Bridge. At the outbreak of war, Clausen, already in
the Army Reserve, volunteered his legal services. He had prosecuted a court-martial involving an air scandal in Ohio, bringing
about ultimate convictions. This, together with a letter of recom-
mendation to the War Department from Senator Truman, had
resulted in his assignment to the Army Pearl Harbor Board. Currently he was on the staff of the Judge Advocate General, a strong
dissident of the Army Board findings, who submitted to Clausen a
list of unexplored leads to be followed up. Among the most important witnesses to be "subjected to further questioning" were the
controversial Colonels Bratton and Sadtler.

To be selected by Stimson for the new mission was an honor.
The Secretary of War was the great man of the war to Clausen,
and he himself had not been in total agreement with the Army
Board report, finding the condemnation of Marshall too severe.
Clausen was, in short, a very appropriate choice from Stimson's
point of view for a difficult and sensitive task.

After preparing himself, he began interrogations in Washington
in February 1945, concentrating on the "winds" execute. Colonel
Moses Pettigrew, Bratton's assistant in the intelligence branch before Pearl Harbor, testified that someone he did not now recall
showed him "on or about 5 December 1941" the "winds" execute
"which indicated that Japanese-U.S. relations were in danger." He
had taken this message "to mean that anything could happen"
and, consequently, at the request of someone he did not recall, he
had prepared a message to Hawaii.

Colonel Carlisle Dusenbury then signed an affidavit that he was
the one who had instructed Pettigrew to draw up the message,
which read: "Contact Commander Rochefort immediately
through Commandant Fourteenth Naval District regarding broadcasts from Tokyo reference weather."

"The reason which I recollect for sending the secret cable,"
testified Dusenbury, "was that the trend of translated intercepts
which had been received by G-2, especially the 'Winds Code,' indicated danger to the United States."

Clausen was keeping Stimson periodically informed of his progress. In early March he reported that he was uncovering important
evidence that Short had more information about imminent war

with Japan than he had admitted. He knew about the "winds" code and had advance notice that the Japanese were going to destroy their secret codes and papers at embassies just before the attack.

Convinced that Clausen, now a lieutenant colonel, was on the trail of discrediting the Army Board findings, his superiors sent him on to Pearl Harbor for more proof.

At Yalta the Big Three had agreed on the perimeters of the postwar world. Victory was in sight. The Russians had crossed the Oder River and the Americans, after recovering from a setback in the Battle of the Bulge, crossed the Rhine. In Berlin Hitler was living like a mole in his bunker, nurturing an impossible dream— that the British and Americans would come to their senses at the last moment and join his crusade against Godless Red Russia.

The efforts to bury the facts about Pearl Harbor were being turned over to loyal Democrats in the Senate. Both Stimson and Forrestal sent identical bills to the chairmen of the Senate and House Armed Services Committees prohibiting disclosure of any coded matter. On March 30 Senator Elbert Thomas introduced his bill in the Senate.

The next day Kimmel happened to read an obscure item in the New York *Herald Tribune* about the bill. He immediately telephoned Rugg in Boston and then hurriedly packed and left his apartment in Bronxville for Washington. While he was attempting to find out what was going on, he received a call from Rugg. The bill, he said, had been passed in the Senate while Senator Ferguson was in the Caribbean; it had been sent to the House.

In desperation Kimmel began telephoning congressmen and senators only to learn that if the House followed the Senate's example that was the end to all disclosures about Pearl Harbor. As a last resort he telephoned the publisher of the Washington *Post*, Eugene Meyer, to whom he had been introduced by Admiral Harris in New York. By the time he reached Meyer's office the publisher had two of his top writers on hand. The four discussed the matter and the next morning headlines in the *Post* attacked the Thomas bill. A stinging indictment of the Democratic attempt to hide the facts of Pearl Harbor followed in the April 12 issue. "It is regrettable to note that we can no longer depend upon the Senate to protect the Nation against executive deprivation of our liberties." Only one hearing had been held prior to the bill's passage and that in camera. "Either from inertia or somnolence, either from lack of interest or just plain complacence, the Senators approved the say-so of Chairman Thomas of the Military Affairs Committee. Yet this bill would gag anybody who would publish any information which originally took the form of a coded message. The effect would be to put the history of this storied period under wraps, for all of that history could be traced back to a coded message. And you may be sure, if this bill is enacted, almost everything that it sought to keep from the prying eyes of the public will first be put in code."

Later in the day came news that Franklin Delano Roosevelt was dead in Georgia. It was shocking to all, friends and foes, for it was the end of an era.[1]

Rugg came down from Boston and, with the help of Hanify and Lavender, wrote speeches for their friends in Congress. These were so effective that the Senate approved Ferguson's move to reconsider the Thomas bill; and by the time the bill to gag the facts was brought to the floor of the House, the matter had been aired so thoroughly that it was defeated by that body. "I have wondered always," Kimmel later wrote, "if we would have been successful if Franklin Roosevelt had not died on April 12, 1945."

On the eighteenth of April Forrestal met with the new President. He informed Truman that Admiral H. Kent Hewitt had been selected to pursue the Pearl Harbor investigation. "I told him that I felt I had an obligation to Congress to continue the investigation because I was not completely satisfied with the report my own Court had made. . . ."

The Hewitt Inquiry began amidst national rejoicing over the unconditional surrender of Germany six days earlier. Although Admiral Hewitt was the nominal head of the inquiry and would do

[1] That day MacArthur talked to his military secretary, Brigadier General Bonner Fellers, as they drove to their quarters. "Well, the old man has gone," said MacArthur, "a man who never told the truth if a lie would suffice."

much of the interrogation, the real work was carried on by John F. Sonnett, a special assistant to Forrestal, and his own assistant, Lieutenant John Ford Baecher.

His most important witness was Captain Safford, who was first informally quizzed in Room 1083A of the Navy Building. Sonnett, a New York lawyer of some distinction, asked many questions pertaining to Safford's testimony before previous investigations and they discussed the discrepancies between his testimony and that of other witnesses.

"It was apparent to me on my very first meeting with Lieutenant Commander Sonnett," Safford wrote in a Confidential Memorandum for the record, "that he was acting as a 'counsel for the defense' for the late Secretary Knox and Admiral Stark rather than as a legal assistant to the investigating officer. His purpose seemed to be to refute testimony (before earlier investigations) that was unfavorable to anyone in Washington, to beguile 'hostile' witnesses into changing their stories, and to introduce an element of doubt where he could not effect a reversal of testimony. Above all, he attempted to make me reverse my testimony regarding the 'Winds Execute' message and to make me believe I was suffering from hallucinations."

Safford again talked informally to Sonnett on May 18 and a day or so later. "On these latter occasions, like the first, Sonnett tried to persuade me that there had been no 'Winds Execute' message, that my memory had been playing me tricks, that I had confused the 'False Winds message' with what I had been expecting, and that I ought to change my testimony to permit reconciling all previous discrepancies and thereby wind up the affair. In some cases the idea was stated outright, in some cases it was implied, and in other cases it was unexpressed but obviously the end in view."

During the course of the three conferences Safford distinctly recalled Sonnett using these statements:

> "You are the only one who seems to have ever seen the Winds Execute message."
> "How could the Winds Execute be heard on the East Coast of the U.S. and not at any of the places nearer Japan?"
> "It is very doubtful that there ever was a Winds Execute."

"It is no reflection on your veracity to change your testimony."

"It is no reflection on your mentality to have your memory play you tricks—after such a long period."

"Numerous witnesses that you have named have denied all knowledge of a Winds Execute message."

"You do not have to carry the torch for Admiral Kimmel."

But the clever barrage of assorted suggestions, insinuations, veiled threats and wheedlings had no effect on Safford when he appeared officially before Admiral Hewitt on May 21. He repeated the testimony he had previously given with only a few minor changes.

As he was leaving the room Safford asked Hewitt if there were still any doubts in the admiral's mind that there had been a "winds" execute. Hewitt, according to Safford's memorandum, looked startled but before he could reply Sonnett said, "Of course, I am not conducting the case and I do not know what Admiral Hewitt has decided, but to me it is very doubtful that the so-called Winds Execute message was ever sent."

Hewitt thought a moment or so before replying to Safford: "You are not entitled to my opinion, but I will answer your question. There is no evidence of a Winds Execute Message beyond your unsupported testimony. I do not doubt your sincerity, but I believe you have confused one of the other messages containing the name of a wind with the message you were expecting to receive."

For his part, Safford did not doubt Admiral Hewitt's integrity, "but I do believe that Sonnett has succeeded in pulling the wool over his eyes."

Safford was also convinced that Sonnett used similar tactics on Alwin Kramer, now a captain. That same afternoon he summoned Kramer to a private conference and showed him a number of intercepts. But what had failed with Safford succeeded with Kramer, who was recovering from illness and mental fatigue. The following day he drastically altered the positive testimony he had given before the Navy Court that he had seen the "winds" execute in early December and it read, "East wind, rain."

Although he admitted he had seen the "winds" message, he now could not recall the wording. "It may have been, '*Higashi no kaze ame,*' specifically referring to the United States, as I have previously testified at Pearl Harbor, but I am less positive of that now than I believe I was at that time." He explained that he had revised his original statement after thinking it over.

"For that reason, I am at least under the impression that the message referred to England and possibly the Dutch rather than the United States, although it may have referred to the United States, too."

A little later he admitted that his memory had been refreshed the previous afternoon by Sonnett, who had shown him a number of messages. If Kimmel and his counsel had been allowed to be present their cross-examination could have brought out full details of the informal meeting with Sonnett, and whether pressure had been applied on Kramer to change his testimony.

Rugg would also have vigorously protested Hewitt's announcement at the next session that, in view of the testimony of Kramer, it was decided not to call Admiral Noyes as a witness; the admiral's previous evidence was good enough. Moreover, it appeared from Safford's own testimony that he only "*thought* that a 'Winds' message relating to the United States was received about 4 December 1941, and was shown to him by Captain Kramer and a watch officer and then delivered to Admiral Noyes. . . . There is yet no other evidence to the effect that a 'Winds' code message relating to the United States was received."

In late June Safford was recalled by Hewitt but was asked no questions about the "winds" execute. That, apparently, was a dead issue in the eyes of Hewitt and his assistants. Safford left Washington for a vacation in Marblehead and on July 3 called on Charles Rugg. He told about his ordeal with Sonnett and his belief that the same measures were being used on other witnesses favorable to Kimmel, particularly Rochefort and Kramer.

Rugg asked what would be the probable results of the investigation. Safford thought Hewitt would file a report absolving Washington of all responsibility and divide the blame between Short and "an act of God." He had no opinion as to whether they would try to pin any errors of judgment on Kimmel.

As he was leaving Safford asked if Rugg would act as his counsel if he got into any trouble in connection with anything that he might have done. "One of the reasons why he suggested this," noted Rugg·in a memorandum, "was that that relationship with me would make it possible and legal for him to talk freely to me about matters of interest."

In his official report Hewitt concluded that "no message was intercepted prior to the attack which used the code words relating to the United States [East wind, rain]." Stark was criticized for not warning Kimmel of other intercepted Japanese messages, particularly during the week prior to the attack, but Hewitt still found that Kimmel had "sufficient information in his possession" to indicate that the outbreak of war was imminent.

Even before he learned of the conclusions Kimmel was bitter. He had specifically asked Hewitt if he could appear but had been refused. "I studied carefully every word of testimony in each of the earlier investigations, including, of course, all the statements of Admiral Kimmel himself," Hewitt later wrote to Kimmel's biographer, Donald Brownlow. "As to his appearance before me, I would have been glad to hear him, although, frankly, I did not see how anything of import could be added to what had already been said. However, Secretary Forrestal himself disapproved of the Admiral's further appearance. It was an unfortunate decision, for the result was misunderstanding and bitterness and the loss of some old friendships." By laying the blame on Forrestal, Hewitt had raised a point that was never resolved. Although the Secretary of the Navy had refused to allow Kimmel to cross-examine witnesses and have counsel, he had authorized the admiral's appearance before Hewitt as a witness "whether it be at his request or on your own initiative." Had Forrestal privately instructed Hewitt to ignore this written permission or had the admiral acted on his own initiative?

Hewitt had never felt that Kimmel was in any way guilty of dereliction of duty and in his conclusions praised him as "energetic, indefatigable, resourceful and positive in his efforts to prepare the Fleet for war." He had neither intended to whitewash the Navy Department nor make Kimmel a scapegoat. But as Forrestal read the Hewitt report he took it as corroboration of his own misgivings about the conclusions of the Navy Inquiry.

5.

By this time another one-man investigation was under way at the instigation of Marshall. During his interrogation by Hewitt, Safford had mentioned a third-hand story that the "winds" execute message had been destroyed by a Colonel Bissell "on the direct orders of General Marshall." This account had come, he reluctantly revealed, from William Friedman, the man credited with the solution of the Purple code. Hewitt subsequently interviewed Friedman, who testified that he had heard this story from Colonel Sadtler.

Colonel Carter Clarke, who had brought Marshall's letters to Dewey, was again utilized by the Chief of Staff, this time to find evidence refuting this and other charges. On July 14 Sadtler confirmed that he had been told about the destruction of messages. "Some time during 1943 General Isaac Spalding at Ft. Bragg, North Carolina, told me something to the effect that J. T. B. Bissell had told him that everything pertaining to Pearl Harbor was being destroyed or had been destroyed."

Three days later, on July 17, General Spalding admitted to Clarke that he had discussed the matter with Sadtler but first wanted it to appear on record that it was his "full belief that the Secretary of War, Mr. Stimson, and the Chief of Staff, General Marshall, are not involved in any way whatsoever with the testimony which I am about to give, and it is my belief that neither one knew anything of it."

After this cautious disclaimer, which anyone who has served in the armed forces would understand, Spalding related that in 1943 he had talked to Colonel John T. B. Bissell at Fort Bragg about the Pearl Harbor incident. Spalding had expressed amazement that General Miles and the Navy had not been able to track the Japanese task force. "I was astounded at their ignorance or inability to detect that! I remember shooting off my mouth about Sherman Miles for whom I didn't have a very high regard professionally, and I think I remember telling him . . . that I thought Sherman Miles was a 'stuffed shirt.' . . ." Spalding also revealed that Bissell had told him "certain messages had been received and were in the files of G-2 and he deemed it most necessary to destroy them. I got the impression that these messages were derogatory to the War Department and that he [Bissell] on his own responsibility destroyed them. I had the impression that they were secret information which it was most desireable that the President, Congress, the public, Mr. Stimson and Gen. Marshall not know about. I had the feeling that Bissell destroyed them without even Gen. Raymond Lee, the G-2 at that time, knowing they were in existence."

Next it was the turn of Bissell, now a brigadier general, to testify. He admitted discussing Pearl Harbor with Spalding and confirmed he had heard Miles called a stuffed shirt. But he denied saying that any messages had been destroyed. Nor had he ever heard of any messages being destroyed except in 1940 when the World War I files were cleared out.

"Did you tell Gen. Spalding at any time, in substance, that you had destroyed what you would call vital records, records which if known to exist would be very unpleasant to the War Department?"

"I did not."

As far as the War Department was concerned this categorical denial closed the incident. But it seems reasonable to assume that, if Bissell had done anything improper or illegal, he would have denied the allegation under any circumstances. It is just as likely to believe that he was probably telling the truth to Spalding, an old friend, never dreaming that the story would be investigated officially.

6.

Colonel Clausen had been traveling to the Pacific and Europe. In Frankfurt am Main he had interviewed Bedell Smith, now a lieutenant general and Eisenhower's chief of staff, early in June.[2]

[2] Earlier that year Lieutenant Richmond, Stark's counsel, chanced to ride in the same car with Smith and General Marshall in Malta. "I don't know if you remember me, General," Richmond said, "but I had a little set-to with you down in Washington." Marshall thought he had seen Richmond someplace before. "I was Admiral Stark's counsel at the Court of Inquiry, and I assisted Admiral Hart and asked you some questions."

"Oh yes," said Marshall. "By the way, they got me all tangled up in that thing." He couldn't remember anything about the weekend of December 6 and 7.

At first Smith objected to being interrogated. He "pulled rank" on Clausen, a mere lieutenant colonel, insisting the matter go up to Ike. But Clausen was not one to be intimidated, having a directive from someone of higher rank, Stimson. During the interview Smith flatly denied Colonel Sadtler's claim that he had asked Smith and Gerow on December 5 to authorize him to send Hawaii a warning, and both had refused. He also denied Colonel Bratton's claim that he had delivered the thirteen-part message to him on the eve of Pearl Harbor. He had left his office, he said, about 7 P.M. on December 6 and therefore could not have been in his office when Bratton delivered it.

Several weeks later Clausen saw Gerow in Cannes. He too denied the Sadtler testimony. Moreover, he had never seen any "winds" execute. "If I had received such a message or notice thereof, I believe I would now recall the fact, in view of its importance." He also denied that Bratton had ever delivered to him the thirteen-part message on the night of December 6.

Bratton was now chief of Intelligence of the staff of Berlin District. The chief of staff of Berlin District, Brigadier General Paul Ransom, regarded him as "an exceptionally good officer and especially well qualified in the field of intelligence. He did excellent work in Berlin under circumstances made difficult by Russian intransigeance."

That July Bratton was on the Autobahn encircling Berlin, on his way to the British Sector headquarters, when a British car overtook and flagged him down. Colonel Clausen stepped out, told what his mission was and that he had authority to interrogate Bratton. Once they had settled in Bratton's billet, Clausen discovered he had left papers necessary for the interrogation in Paris. He radioed Army Intelligence requesting the papers be flown to Berlin by courier but was informed this material was top secret and the interrogation would have to take place in Paris.

In a state of trepidation, Bratton went to a friend, Lieutenant

---

Smith interrupted. "General, there's a book that has all that in it. You had everybody write a memorandum the day after Pearl Harbor about everything they could remember about that pre-Pearl Harbor period and the day itself, and it was all put away in a single volume. I did it."

Marshall wanted to know what in the devil happened to the book and Smith said it was still in the safe at the Chief of Staff's office.

Colonel William F. Heimlich, head of Combat Intelligence, Fifteenth Army. Bratton related how he had to go to Paris with a Colonel Clausen and he feared he might not return. He then described in detail the events preceding the Japanese attack as he saw them unravel at the Munitions Building; and of his problems with Marshall later. Removing a carefully wrapped brown envelope from his office safe, he explained that the contents were copies of intelligence summaries submitted to Marshall in the months preceding Pearl Harbor. They had been prepared for the President, and Bratton called Heimlich's attention to numerous paragraphs which had been crossed out and initialed on the side "G.C.M."

"In the event he did not return," recalled Heimlich, "I was to hand-deliver them to his family. He did not give a reason why he might not return and I assumed he might continue on directly to Washington from Paris."

The interrogation took place at the Hotel Prince of Wales on July 27. Clausen showed Bratton a number of affidavits he had collected in his travels. After seeing those of Generals Bedell Smith and Gerow, Bratton promptly changed his previous testimony that he had delivered the thirteen-part message on Pearl Harbor to one of these two officers. In the affidavit refuting himself, he said, "Any prior statements or testimony of mine which may be contrary to my statements here . . . should be modified and considered changed in accordance with my statement herein. This affidavit now represents my best recollection of the matters and events set forth, and a better recollection than when I previously testified before the Army Pearl Harbor Board, and is made after having my memory refreshed in several ways and respects."

Chastened, Bratton returned to Berlin where he reclaimed his photostats from Heimlich without comment.

Clausen's next witness was Sadtler. On August 13 they met in Washington and he, like Bratton, repudiated his previous testimony. No, he had never conferred with Generals Gerow and Smith on December 5 concerning a warning to Hawaii. Nor had he ever seen any "winds" execute message.

Three days later the indefatigable Clausen, who had already

journeyed some fifty thousand miles in his quest for information, went to Boston to see Miles. The general denied that he had ever met with Colonels Sadtler and Bratton on December 5 concerning information supposedly received by Sadtler from Admiral Noyes of a possible "winds" execute.

Clausen's findings pleased Stimson. Although the peripatetic colonel had uncovered some evidence which raised serious doubts as to the extent of information Washington had sent Short, the War Secretary's mind was eased by the refutation of Bratton's and Sadtler's damaging testimony concerning Marshall's assistants. And no new information had come up that would further implicate the Chief of Staff himself. Indeed, the net result of both the Clausen and Clarke reports was to acquit the War Department of the charges made by the Army Pearl Harbor Board.

7.

In another part of the Pentagon, Forrestal was similarly relieved by the conclusions of Hewitt. In his endorsement to the admiral's report, Forrestal found no negligence on the part of Washington officials with respect to withholding from Kimmel vital information clearly indicating an attack on Hawaii. And he particularly denied the existence of any intercepted "winds" execute. But he did censure Kimmel and Stark for failing to demonstrate "the superior judgment necessary for exercising command commensurate with their rank and their assigned duties."[3]

Forrestal was so satisfied with the Hewitt report that he felt there was no reason to withhold any longer from the public the report of the Navy Inquiry. He discussed this three days after V-J Day, August 17, with President Truman, who had gotten himself mixed up in the Pearl Harbor controversy with his attack on Kimmel and Short in the *Collier's* article. He regretted that act and was now determined to detach himself and his Administration

[3] In a taped interview in the Oral History Collection, Columbia University, Hewitt later stated, "Secretary Forrestal had some very set ideas about the thing. And he wanted me to find certain things which I couldn't find and didn't find. I think he was disappointed that I didn't make a report in accordance with some of his ideas." It is unfortunate Hewitt didn't say what Forrestal's "ideas" were.

from the issue. After all, he had not been involved in prewar policy and wouldn't have to defend his own action. The problem, as a loyal party man, was to protect the Democratic Administration from new attacks without causing further acrimony. He agreed with Forrestal that the best solution was to terminate the entire issue as soon as possible: and the first step should be disclosure of the Army and Navy reports. No longer could the excuse be made that Pearl Harbor secret data must be concealed for the sake of national security now that the war was over. The denial of such material, said the astute Truman, "only added to and accentuated the atmosphere of mystery surrounding such an event of broad national interest as Pearl Harbor."

Stimson may not have liked the idea but he made no protest, and on the morning of August 29 Truman, his advisers, and officials from the War and Navy Departments began working out the final details of releasing the two reports. But Forrestal, apprehensive that Truman was being "stampeded" into action, had second thoughts. The two endorsements of the Navy Court's report by himself and King were so critical of Kimmel that Forrestal feared their release might prevent the Hawaiian commander from receiving the unbiased court-martial promised by Knox in 1942. At the same time the Secretary of the Navy realized that withholding release of the Navy Court findings could result in charges of a cover-up.

The solution of this dilemma, Forrestal told Truman, would be either courts-martial for Kimmel and Short or formation of another commission to study the case. While announcing a new trial for the commanders, he suggested, why didn't the Army publish its report and the Navy publish nothing?

Stimson's two representatives at the meeting both objected strenuously. Why should they accept a proposal that placed the burden of culpability on the Army? At this point the President ended the controversy. Kimmel, he promised, would receive a fair trial despite all the publicity.

At his press conference that morning Truman announced that the two reports would be released with the endorsements. He noted that there were criticisms of General Marshall in the Army Board report to which Stimson, in his statement, took sharp issue and characterized as entirely unjustified, and that the Chief of Staff had "acted throughout with his usual 'great skill, energy and efficiency.' I associate myself wholeheartedly with this expression by the Secretary of War." Then he added, "Indeed, I have the fullest confidence in the skill, energy and efficiency of all of our war leaders, both Army and Navy."

The release to the public of the Army and Navy reports was done in such a manner that they were overshadowed by the endorsements from Stimson and Forrestal condemning them. In fact, some readers got the impression that the Army and Navy had confirmed the guilt of Kimmel and Short.[4] The majority of newsmen and radio commentators found fault with the disclosures. The Navy Department's own Office of Public Information found unfavorable reaction from 64 per cent of the editorials, 54 per cent of the columnists, and 68 per cent of the radio commentators. The *Kiplinger Washington Letter* called it a cover-up. "These high-ups are now sitting in judgment on their own acts. They are ducking all blame, and applying the whitewash to each other, and tell partial truths. This may be natural but it is not honest. . . ."

Political commentator Gabriel Heatter's instant reaction over the Mutual Broadcasting System was typical of those defending both the Roosevelt and Truman administrations. "If anybody were to ask tonight who stands with complete confidence behind General George C. Marshall, I would reply: Put me down . . . with tens of millions of other Americans."

Truman did nothing to stem the tide of dissatisfaction at his press conference the next day. From the opening he was bombarded with pointed questions: Why had the reports been put out on the day American troops entered Japan? Were they a whitewash as some charged? Was he ordering courts-martial for Kim-

[4] When one of the members of the Army Board, General Russell, read the first dispatches from Washington he was disgusted. "As the stories were 'rigged' in Washington little was said in the press about the Board's findings. The criticisms of those findings were featured. In a small way the President and the Secretary of War defended Mr. Hull, who was criticised very mildly in our report, but Marshall was the one to whose rescue they went in a big way. Poor old Stark, whose derelictions were almost identical with Marshall's, was completely forgotten. In fact, the findings of the Navy Board, which resulted in driving him from all responsible official duties, were actually approved. How strange it is that conduct which virtually eliminated Stark from the Navy—was described by the President and Secretary of War as the exemplification of great skill, energy, and efficiency on the part of Marshall."

mel or Short? Why had communications broken down between Washington and Hawaii? To this last question he gave an answer that would only generate more suspicion. "I came to the conclusion that the whole thing is the result of the policy which the country itself pursued. The country was not ready for preparedness. . . . I think the country is as much to blame as any individual in this final situation that developed in Pearl Harbor."

This statement was received with widespread indignation, typified by that expressed by the Nashville *Banner*: "The attempt to place the blame on the American people is a national insult." But what promised to be the most devastating result of the reports was the demeaning of George Marshall. "There is no getting away from the fact that the public reputation of General Marshall has been smirched," reported an Office of War Information press summary; ". . . his name has been bracketed with Kimmel and Short, the two men whom [sic] the American public has long been led to believe were primarily responsible for the Pearl Harbor tragedy." There were rumors throughout Washington that Marshall planned to retire and demand a court-martial to clear his name. This story was branded as "poppycock" by officials but the Washington rumor mill took this as only confirmation.

In any case the demand was growing from many sources for a final and thorough investigation of Pearl Harbor. By the beginning of September it seemed likely that Congress would approve a full and impartial inquiry. On the fifth two investigation bills were introduced in the House and one in the Senate was expected the next day from Senator Ferguson. Speaker Sam Rayburn made a feeble effort to halt any congressional investigation. "I wish Congress could forget about it," he remarked wistfully, then added, with a sigh, "But I guess it can't."

It couldn't. And Majority Leader Barkley asserted that the President not only approved a full investigation but urged it. At his press conference Truman confirmed this. His only purpose, he said, was to get the truth, the whole truth and nothing but the truth.

"While the name of the late President Roosevelt was not mentioned in the debate," declared the Chicago *Tribune*, "the remarks of Barkley, Ferguson and several other senators indicated clearly an awareness that only a Congressional inquiry could be expected to fix responsibility upon Mr. Roosevelt, if the evidence brings it out."

The Senate measure was sent to the House where prompt consideration was promised by Rayburn. Overwhelming passage was assured and the public was at last to be admitted to an open hearing of a controversy that had threatened the unity of the United States since December 7, 1941.

Part 3

CONGRESS DANCES

Chapter Nine

"IF I HAD KNOWN WHAT WAS TO HAPPEN . . . I WOULD NEVER HAVE ALLOWED MYSELF TO BE 'TAGGED'"

William D. Mitchell

NOVEMBER–DECEMBER 1945

1.

By the beginning of September a Joint Congressional Committee to investigate Pearl Harbor had been appointed, composed of five senators and five representatives, three of each being Democrats and two Republicans, thus giving the Administration about to be investigated a majority of six to four.

It also gave the majority members the choice to pick the committee counsel. They chose a nominal Democrat, William D. Mitchell, who had also served with Stimson in the Hoover Cabinet and shared many of his beliefs. A lawyer from New York, he was seventy-one and held the conviction that Army and Navy officers did not lie. He was serving without fee, as was his chief assistant, a young retired New Dealer, Gerhard A. Gesell, at that time a $35,000-a-year partner in the law firm of the Under Secretary of State, Dean Acheson.

John Sonnett, who had so effectively assisted Admiral Hewitt's investigation, no longer headed the influential Navy Pearl Harbor Liaison Group. He had been promoted to Assistant Attorney General of the United States and replaced by his able assistant. The Army Liaison Group included several bright young lawyers with New Deal leanings.

Such a line-up would give the Democrats a decided edge in the hearings and among some Republicans there was fear that Mitchell, a man with a prestigious record, would lean decidedly toward the majority views. From the first preliminary meeting of the committee there were sharp arguments, particularly over the release of classified material to individual members. The argument was carried to the Senate on the second of November with the senior minority member, Senator Owen Brewster of Maine, complaining that under a ruling of the majority of the committee that morning no member was to be permitted to look at records.

Brewster, an aggressive anti-New Dealer, whose voice could be heard in the farthest seat, angrily charged during the heated two-hour debate that the Democrats were blocking the probe of Pearl Harbor by this measure. "I simply ask the right to go to the chairman of the committee, tell him there are certain records and files which I should like to examine, ask him to designate a member of the counsel's staff to accompany me—I would not desire to go there alone, and be allowed to examine the records and see whether any rumors or reports I had received were correct."

The second Republican senator, Homer Ferguson, was equally irate. "It is absolutely impossible for the committee to function properly to cross-examine witnesses, if we don't have the records. The fact that files are missing and that records are missing is material to this investigation." The composition of the committee, charged Ferguson, was unfair. Every controversial issue at executive session that morning had been decided by a strict vote along party lines and therefore favored the Democrats. In addition, he said, Chief Counsel Mitchell had "taken it upon himself to say what is competent and what is not competent."

The Republican imputations continued a few days later with Brewster's revelation that he had been advised by Mitchell that files of four government monitoring stations covering the critical period before Pearl Harbor were missing, and the records of one had been destroyed for lack of storage space. The following day, November 6, the two Republican representatives on the committee brought other charges to the floor of the House. Representative Bertrand Gearhart of California, an anti-New Dealer and isolationist whose chief claim to fame was advocacy of Iceland as the forty-ninth state, charged that a key message, known as the "winds" execute, was also missing; and Frank Keefe of Wisconsin declared that he was not allowed to see an important witness, a Captain Kramer, who was in the psychopathic ward at Bethesda Naval Hospital and that "whole legions of stories have arisen about the manner in which he was broken down in mind and in health." Another Republican congressman, not on the committee, added dark hints. "I'm surprised they've only locked him up. I'm surprised he hasn't been liquidated."

In the Senate the Republicans were also demanding freedom to examine the personal files of Roosevelt. This brought fire from Scott Lucas, one of the Democratic senators on the committee. A reliable New Dealer; except for one lapse in 1937 when he denounced Roosevelt's court-packing scheme, he had since consistently supported the Administration's internationalist foreign policy. "I shall never grant permission to any single member to examine these files. I cannot understand why any member of the Senate would wish to go down and look over by himself, the personal files of a former President of the United States. I simply cannot understand it—any more than I would want to look at the personal files of the Senator from Michigan."

In an effort to placate the Republicans, President Truman signed a directive on November 9 authorizing disclosure of additional information to individual members of the committee. Sam Rosenman and the Attorney General protested that this went too far, but the Republicans were not at all satisfied. Brewster said that Truman's modification "seemed to have been designed by the President's advisors with devilish ingenuity to leave the heads of executive departments in doubt as to what they are to do."

Brewster's protest was joined by one from Senator Burton Wheeler, a long-time foe of Roosevelt's interventionist policies. The gag being imposed on the Pearl Harbor investigation, he said, was unprecedented in his twenty-two years' experience in the Senate. "The Teapot Dome investigation in which I played a part, would have been a complete failure if such tactics had been permitted."

Senate Majority Leader Alben Barkley retorted next day, "Neither I as chairman nor the committee as a whole will countenance any effort to keep from the public any fact material to the inquiry. Our task, as I see it, is to lay all the facts before the public, no matter whom they hurt in high or low places, and we propose to conduct the inquiry accordingly."

William Mitchell was so upset by the rancor aroused that he wrote a close Republican friend, "It is very distressing to me to have these charges and countercharges publicly made. When I took this job I told the Committee that I wanted it understood there was to be no hush-hush stuff, and there was to be no restraint on me in getting the truth out, and they were unanimous in saying they would back me in that to the limit. I have seen no trace among the Democrats of the slightest inclination to suppress anything or to place any restraints on me. . . . It is a tough situation, and if I had known what was to happen, and that political feelings and charges of suppression were to be bandied about, before anyone had a look at what my staff can produce, I would never have allowed myself to be 'tagged.'"

A shadow of doubt was cast on the hearings and the Republican minority still had hopes that the whole truth might be extracted if they were aggressive enough. At least they would finally have the chance of cross-examining Stimson, Hull, Forrestal and other Administration leaders. The proceedings began on November 15 in a Hollywood atmosphere at the Senate Office Building's stately, bechandeliered caucus room where national scandals like Teapot Dome had seen light of day, and where the classic picture of a midget on J. P. Morgan's lap was taken. Large maps and charts hung about for the benefit of the members, their counsel and the witnesses who sat at long tables placed in T formation. In front of each man was a microphone. A hundred reporters sat at tables paralleling each side of the T. Behind crowded some four hundred onlookers, straining to see the principals, while five newsreel cameras, aided by glaring klieg lights, filmed the scene.

The proceedings began on an inauspicious note. Just as Chairman Barkley rapped for order the room went black. A fuse had blown. After a considerable wait the lights came on and Chief Counsel Mitchell began his opening remarks. Few could hear what he said since the poor loudspeaker system could not compete with the grinding of cameras and bursting of flash bulbs.

The first session featured a narrative by an admiral and a colonel of the conditions that prevailed at Pearl Harbor on December 7 and the events of that momentous day. Perhaps the most intent listeners were Admiral Kimmel and General Short, both wearing civilian clothes. They sat at a small table with their lawyers.

It was not until the second day that the spectators were treated to the first lively exchanges. To questions as to whether Washington ordered Kimmel, Short and MacArthur in the fall of 1941 "not to fire unless the Japs fired first," the Navy narrator could only reply that he did not know. Gearhart was so exasperated, he shouted, "Is the reason that they have you people up here to read hearsay testimony so you can always reply you were only sent up to say that is 'not in my province to answer'?"

Barkley, ordinarily affable, became so annoyed at Gearhart's effort to get the Navy narrator to admit there was "something strangely significant" in some orders from Washington in November 1941 that he couldn't help blurting out that Gearhart was using the hearing for a political sounding board. This remark was not recorded.

There were half a dozen other flurries and by the end of the day the Republicans were in a rebellious mood. Ferguson had requested that the committee be furnished copies of all exhibits at least ten days earlier. Yet more than a thousand pages without any index had been dumped on them on the first day. Was this deluging tactic part of a plot to prevent intelligent questioning by the minority?

At a press conference that day the Republicans charged that the investigation of the Democrats' plan was merely an attempt to whitewash the Roosevelt Administration. The Democrats retorted this was just "a sneak attack upon the grave of Franklin D. Roosevelt." Robert Hannegan, the Democratic National Committee chairman, called it a "tactic of desperation by a party without a program."

To newsmen it was apparent that the hearings were going to degenerate into a battle royal between the two parties. From their conduct thus far, wrote W. H. Lawrence in the New York *Times*, "it seems almost certain that they will remain split into Democratic and Republican blocs throughout the investigation and the result will be a majority report by the six Democrats and a minority report from the four Republicans."

The early days had proved a disappointment to the press, for it seemed as if the inquiry were degenerating into inconsequential bickering. But this changed on the nineteenth with the appearance of the first genuine witness, Admiral Richardson, Kimmel's predecessor, who had previously denounced Pearl Harbor as a "damned mousetrap" and expressed his conviction that President Roosevelt, not Kimmel and Short, was responsible for the debacle. He created a stir when he told the committee of a luncheon with Roosevelt on October 8, 1940—less than a month before the presidential election—during which the admiral had urged that the Pacific Fleet should be returned to California. The President, he said, insisted that it be retained in Hawaii "to exercise a restraining influence on the actions of Japan." Richardson argued that Japan had a military government which knew that the American fleet was undermanned and unprepared for war. So how could it exercise any restraint?

"Despite what you believe," Roosevelt had replied, "I know that the presence of the fleet in the Hawaiian area has had, and is now having a restraining influence on the actions of Japan."

"Mr. President, I still do not believe it, and I know that our fleet is disadvantageously disposed for preparing for or initiating war operations." Richardson then asked the President if they were going to war. He had replied that if the Japanese attacked Thailand, or the Kra Peninsula, or the Dutch East Indies America would not get into the war, but sooner or later the Japanese would make a mistake as the area of operations expanded "and we would enter the war."

The next morning readers of the Washington *Post* were greeted with this headline:

. . . ROOSEVELT PREDICTED JAP WAR, KEPT FLEET AROUND HAWAII AS "RESTRAINT," RICHARDSON SAYS. . . .

"I have been greatly disturbed and still am about the Pearl Harbor investigation," Eleanor Roosevelt wrote Harry Hopkins that day, "because I have a feeling that none of those people are looking after the President's interests." She was referring to her husband, not Truman. "I am sure, in the long run, it will all come out all right but you have got to remember that all of the witnesses are going to look after themselves."

2.

By this time the Republicans had gathered themselves for the attack. Although Brewster was a shrewder interrogator, Ferguson had taken over the leadership because of a keener interest in the case. He had put aside his personal and social obligations and all but the most important of his other congressional duties. His chief assistant was Percy L. Greaves, Jr. (pronounced Graves). A graduate of Syracuse in 1929 *magna cum laude,* he had been head of public relations research for the Metropolitan Life Insurance Company before becoming associate research director of the Republican National Committee in 1943. Greaves and six helpers had been retained to assist all the minority members in their efforts to ferret out the essential facts which had been withheld. The money for the operation had been raised by John T. Flynn, author and columnist. A staunch foe of Roosevelt, he had devoted his energies to the fight to keep America out of the war. Now he was equally dedicated to proving that Roosevelt and his advisers had deliberately plunged the country into war by the back door, Japan.

"Since Senator Ferguson devoted more time and effort to this investigation than any other minority member," Greaves recalled, "my work simmered down to working constantly with him while reporting to Senator Brewster and maintaining liaison with Republican Representatives Keefe and Gearhart."

Most of the members of the committee had been inundated with so much material that they relied on the testimony and what little they could read in spare moments between other congressional duties. But Ferguson had instructed his staff and secretary not to interrupt him except in cases of supreme emergency. He settled down to a routine, devoting most of his waking hours to Pearl Harbor.

He and Greaves would work together about an hour before each day's hearing opened. For every witness it was necessary to know the phases with which he was familiar, what he had previously testified and what others had testified about him or the facts with which he was familiar. The previous night Greaves would have gone over his voluminous files for such information and made special note of any conflicting testimony. Just before ten every weekday morning they walked down the corridor to the caucus room with several assistants helping Greaves lug the many documents needed for the session. Once they arrived at the committee table they were usually greeted with a new stack of documents. While Ferguson was doing the questioning, Greaves sat at his side to supply the needed documents and make suggestions, should the answers take an unexpected turn.

After morning recess they would return to Ferguson's private office where a secretary would bring them soup, sandwiches and ice cream. And as they ate they would discuss procedure for the afternoon session. Often Ferguson would telephone his wife, who was ill, and she would give the senator encouragement. Following the afternoon session the two men would return to Ferguson's office, discuss the events of the day and plan the next day's program. Greaves would then hand the senator a pile of material to be read that night and they would leave at six or seven.

On November 22 the aged and ailing Cordell Hull appeared as a witness. He brought with him a 22,000-word statement to be offered in evidence to support his contention that he had striven ceaselessly to avoid war with Japan. He did not read it since the committee had been advised by Hull's physicians that it would constitute an undue strain.

Senator Walter George of Georgia, like the other two Democratic senators on the committee, had been a reluctant convert to Roosevelt's interventionist policy but once war broke out he supported the President loyally; and it was unlikely that he would now join in the Republican criticism of a foreign policy he had grown to accept. There was no reason to read the statement, said

George, since all the members had been given copies. All the Democrats concurred but Brewster said Hull's remarks were so important they should be read aloud. He also suggested that Hull return at 2 P.M. for questioning. Predictably the other Republicans voted with Brewster. At that point came the first break in party uniformity. Chairman Barkley voted with the minority.

Hull, pale and shaking from long illness, was back at 2 P.M., topcoat draped over his shoulders, and underwent forty-five minutes of considerate questioning from Gesell, Mitchell's chief assistant. In a tired voice the former Secretary revealed that he had failed to foresee any attack on Pearl Harbor and denied he had known of any U.S. pledge to defend British possessions in the Pacific until early November 1941.

The Republicans had to content themselves with having a joint memorandum from Marshall and Stark read into the record. Dated November 27, 1941, it stated that, should current negotiations with Japan end unsuccessfully, "Japan may attack the Burma Rd., Thailand, Malaya, the Philippines, the Russian maritime provinces." They saw blows at five possible spots—but not at Hawaii.

The following Monday Hull appeared for another questioning by Gesell and friendly Democrats. His answers were those of an exhausted old man until someone read an excerpt from the Army Board report describing his November 26 reply to the Japanese as an ultimatum, and concluding, "It was the document that touched the button that started the war as Ambassador [Joseph] Grew so aptly expressed it." These words infuriated Hull and he erupted. Although his voice scarcely rose, the words crackled. "If I could express myself as I would like I would want all of you religious minded people to retire!" Restraining himself from using the sulphuric language at his command, he continued, his voice tired but ominous, "I stood under that infamous charge for months, when every reasonable minded person knew that the Japs were on the same march of invasion in the Pacific area to get supreme control over it in every way so that we could not even land a boatload of goods on the other side of the Pacific except under extortionate terms—" He paused for breath, almost overcome with angry indignation. Everyone, he went on, knew the

Japs were on the move of conquest. ". . . and yet, somebody who knows little and cares less, now says, 'Why didn't the United States make concessions and save us from the war,' when any person knows, and if you look back on the situation as it existed during those last 10, 12, 14 days, any rational person knows just what the Japs were doing. They were off on this final attack and no one was going to stop them unless we yielded and laid down like cowards, and we would have been cowards to have lain down." His hour was up and he walked out of the room to the accompaniment of resounding applause.

It was an exit worthy of a Barrymore and effectively prevented the frustrated minority from cross-examining a witness they still felt was officially responsible for the disastrous negotiations that led to Pearl Harbor.

Despite the absence of new revelations or dramatics, interest in the investigation remained high. A hundred reporters from newspapers throughout the country, jammed shoulder to shoulder, poured out reams of copy over the four crowded wires in the Senate Office Building. "The quality of this extravagant coverage," reported *Time*, "was something else. The painful Pearl Harbor story was confused at best. It was complicated by contradiction, by varying recollections and by bitter bouts of political swordplay." The testimony was tailored to fit old prejudices. FDR PEARL HARBOR SMEAR PLOT BLOWN SKY HIGH BY EVIDENCE was the headline in New York's *P.M.* But the Washington *Times-Herald* and many other papers regarded the first week as a war-criminal trial with Roosevelt convicted daily. "One becomes appalled and frightened at the one-man, all-out ignorance and mental arrogance of the late Franklin D. Roosevelt," wrote John O'Donnell in the New York *Daily News*. "The evidence builds up to the simple brutal fact that F.D.R., the Big Brain, through blind stupidity . . . was directly and personally responsible for the blood and disaster."

SAY HULL EDICT DECIDED JAPS TO OPEN WAR, proclaimed the New York *Journal-American*. Yet the same afternoon the New York *Post* saw it differently: JAP WAR PLANS SET BEFORE TALKS. And so it was throughout the nation.

Little of importance was disclosed in the next few days and Representative Gearhart charged that the Democrats on the committee were "deliberately" unfolding testimony in driblets to "hamstring a real investigation." They had already accomplished their purpose, he told reporters on December 1. "They have turned this into a judicial body without any investigative duty."

A modicum of interest was added to the proceedings three days later with the arrival in Hoboken of Tyler Kent. He had come by the British freighter *Silver Oak* after serving more than five years in prison. He brought with him a copy of his secret trial which he had placed in his suitcase. The suitcase had been carried out of the prison by an unwitting Scotland Yard agent who neglected to search its contents.

As soon as Kent left ship, he was escorted by two policemen to his mother, waiting at Pier 3. They kissed and she said, "It is so nice to see you." Then he was taken to a room crowded with more than forty reporters who began firing questions at him. Why had he taken the Roosevelt-Churchill documents? "I considered that these documents contained information which the Senate and the people of the United States should know about." Someone else asked if he were going to testify at the Pearl Harbor investigation. He said he would be willing but hadn't been asked. "Not as to the Pearl Harbor phase but as regards America's entry into the war."

He admitted he should not have taken the documents to his London flat. "But under the special circumstances I considered I had a moral right." Finally he broke free from the reporters and went off, guarded by two private detectives hired by his mother. "Where are you going?" was the last question flung at him. "We're just disappearing," said Kent.[1]

3.

There was renewed interest in the proceedings once it was announced that Marshall, recently retired as Chief of Staff, would appear before the committee in early December. On November 28 Truman bestowed on him the Oak Leaf Cluster to the Distinguished Service Medal as the man who exercised "greater influence

[1] Years later this author asked Kent if he would do it all over again. Yes, he said, but this time he wouldn't be caught. "If I had more experience I wouldn't have gotten into that situation. I would be more circumspect and careful." But he would still do it because Roosevelt had to be prevented from getting America into the wrong war.

than any other man on the strategy of victory." The following day, after Patrick J. Hurley resigned as ambassador to China, the President selected Marshall as his special envoy to China with ambassadorial rank.

The Marshalls were at their home in Leesburg, Virginia. At about 2 P.M. as Mrs. Marshall was starting up the stairs for a rest the telephone rang. Marshall answered it. When she came down at three the radio was broadcasting the news that her husband would leave immediately for China. She stood rooted to the floor.

Marshall got up from a chaise longue. "That phone call as we came in was from the President," he said. "I could not bear to tell you until you had had your rest."

Marshall left immediately for Washington and summoned Captain Robert Diggs, a lawyer in private life, who had been assigned the responsibility of preparing the general for his testimony before the Joint Congressional Committee. For the past two months Diggs, a graduate of Hamilton and the Yale Law School, had been preparing a summary of all the evidence from previous investigations which related to matters that would have been within Marshall's knowledge. Diggs was under no time pressure, since the general was scheduled to be the last witness, and was plodding through the tedious task of documenting the summaries with copies of all the relevant orders, memoranda and correspondence.

Diggs had not heard the news about China and was astounded to learn that Marshall would have to testify in a week. This meant Diggs would not only have to rush through his preparations for Marshall but also hurriedly prepare Mitchell and Gesell, who would question the general.

Marshall told Diggs that his testimony before the committee was his "number one priority until it was completed and that I was to feel free to barge into his office anytime I wished to consult with him even though someone else might be there." They immediately began a series of sessions of several hours a day. "I would sit across his desk from him and he would read through the material I had prepared. He seldom made any comments or asked any questions, and so I had very little idea of how much he was absorbing or to what extent he agreed or disagreed with the statements

in the material. I was heartened by occasional remarks that he
thought I didn't have the entire story or didn't have it in proper
perspective and he would give suggestions of further avenues of
research."

Theirs was an unusual relationship. Diggs was treated not as a
lowly captain but as the former Chief of Staff's lawyer, his equal.
One day they were interrupted by a group planning the trip to
China. "Instead of asking me to step out he simply joined the
group at a table at the far side of his office and then rejoined me at
his desk as soon as he was able to oust them."

Another morning Diggs arrived at the Pentagon a few minutes
early to be told by the general's secretary that he was with the Chinese ambassador. Diggs waited in the anteroom until the ambassador left. Marshall was annoyed. "Diggs," he said tartly, "at the
very beginning I told you that you were to walk in at any time, no
matter who was here." It was the first time Marshall had been critical or cross with the young lawyer. "I've been trying to get rid of
that boring ambassador for ten minutes or more but knew you
were to come at eight-thirty and give me an excuse to get rid of
him. But instead of coming in you sit across the hall waiting for
him to leave."

On the day before Marshall was scheduled to appear, Gerow,
now promoted to lieutenant general, was brought in to testify out
of order, and he caused a mild sensation by taking all the blame
for the confusing war warning sent to Short on November 27.

Was he sure, asked Mitchell, that it wasn't the responsibility of
Marshall and Stimson? "It wasn't their function to follow up
things like that?"

"No, sir," said the bemedaled Gerow, a hero in the Normandy
landing. "I was a staff adviser to the Chief of Staff, and I had a
group of 48 officers to assist me. It was my responsibility to see
that these messages were checked, and if an inquiry was necessary,
the War Plans Division should have drafted such an inquiry and
presented it to the Chief of Staff for approval. As I said, I was
chief of that division, and it was my responsibility." It was
refreshing to hear someone at last taking responsibility but Gerow
was, in fact, only responsible for War Plans, not for sending off
confusing messages to Hawaii. And the minority only saw Gerow's

admittance of malfeasance as a ploy to relieve Marshall from any part of the blame and prepare the way for the former Chief of Staff's own testimony.

Just before Marshall was scheduled to start his testimony on Tuesday morning, December 6, he asked Diggs about the format of the proceedings and what was expected of him. Diggs said that the top people of the Navy had sat at a table with two or three assistants at their sides whom they would consult, sometimes at considerable length, before answering questions. "I said that I felt this created an unfavorable impression and that I thought he should sit there alone and give his own answers to the questions, pointing out that he could always say that he didn't recall as to any particular question but would be glad to furnish later on whatever additional information was requested. He agreed emphatically."

As Chairman Barkley called the committee to order, Marshall was sitting alone, in the brilliance of klieg lights, an impressive and reassuring figure. Diggs was a mere spectator in the back of the room. "Naturally I had a great deal of trepidation concerning his performance, having very little idea as to how he might fare." Marshall began his testimony, unperturbed and at ease. He answered all of Chief Counsel Mitchell's questions briskly and with authority.

"It was thrilling to me," recalled Diggs, "to hear his complete command of every question put to him—reflecting not only total absorption of all the materials prepared for him but also his own perspective and grasp of the bigger underlying factors. I felt that his performance was masterful and my reaction was being proud of him not of myself."

Although Marshall had confided to Diggs that he felt Short and Kimmel "had let Washington down terribly," he was careful not to criticize either of them openly. When Mitchell asked a question about which he was uncertain he would reply, as he had before the Army Board, "I do not recall." Did he know that a week prior to Pearl Harbor the Navy had lost complete track of the Japanese carriers? "I have a faint recollection that I did not know all the time where all the Japanese ships were. I do not recall being aware of the fact that it was the carrier divisions that were the missing ones. It may be I knew it, but I do not recall." Nor could he recall at Friday's session where he was on the night of December 6. "The only definite thing I have is that I had no dinner engagement." His wife's engagement book showed there was nothing for that night. "Also they checked on the post movie. It was about our only recourse for relaxation, and I had never seen the picture. So I was not there. We were not calling. We were leading a rather monastic life."

"You are sure you were not at the White House that evening?" asked Mitchell.

"No, sir; not at all," he said, which could mean he might have been or he might not have been.

After Mitchell finished, the Democrats took over with friendly, respectful questioning. In midafternoon Barkley wondered if they could conclude the testimony the next day. What were the general's plans to leave for China? "All I can do, sir, is have a plane in readiness as soon as you release me."

"So your plans are to go forward at once as soon as we are completed?" said Barkley.

"Yes, sir."

The minority members were unhappy with what appeared to be an attempt to rush Marshall through the committee before they had time to interrogate him fully but they did get their chance the next morning. Their first interrogator, Senator Brewster, had been called out of town because of the sudden death of his father and Ferguson took over. Fortunately he had devised, with the help of Greaves, what he called a "blue plan" for questioning the general. He had it typed into a loose-leaf binder with a full set of questions on each phase of Marshall's involvement in the case. He did not mean to let him go until every single question was answered.

By the end of what must have been a most trying time for Marshall, Ferguson had succeeded in getting him to admit these damaging facts:

1. That Gerow was in charge of war plans and had no authority over Short; and therefore could not take the blame for the confusing messages to Hawaii. Moreover, Gerow had no responsibility for sending or not sending a proper alert to Short.

2. That Marshall, as Chief of Staff, was the only Army officer

with authority over Short; and was therefore the only one responsible for not properly alerting Short.

3. That there was no responsible Army officer on duty on the night of December 6, or Sunday morning, who could take action before Marshall's arrival after his long horseback ride. Therefore the Army was not on full alert even though it was known the situation was critical.

4. That Marshall had appointed General Miles as head of Army Intelligence, although aware he did not have proper qualifications.

5. That Marshall knew the British were privy to the Purple code before Pearl Harbor, and that "we have been trying to keep that quiet as much as we could."

6. That Marshall did not know why Kimmel had not been getting the information from the Purple and other codes.

7. That before the Roberts report "was made public there were certain things withdrawn and the complete Roberts Report went to the President before portions were withdrawn."

8. That the United States initiated the Anglo-Dutch-American agreements which called for unified action against the Japanese; that Marshall, Stimson and Knox had approved them; and that the agreements had gone into effect before the attack.

9. That officers of the United States, the Flying Tigers, were furnished to China for combat duty against Japan before Pearl Harbor.

At last Ferguson's relentless grilling, which visibly annoyed the Democrats, was ended for the day. The Vice Chairman, Representative Jere Cooper, a strong party man used as a Democratic trouble-shooter in the House, had said so little thus far that he was nicknamed "The Sphinx" by reporters. Now he asked if he could inquire something of General Marshall. "I understand he stated yesterday his plane was waiting to take him to his duties in China."

"It will have to continue to wait," said Marshall equably. "I am to be at your disposal until you have finished."

"Under these circumstances," said Barkley, "the committee will recess until ten o'clock Monday morning."

Ferguson resumed his bulldog tactics on the tenth, unperturbed by majority attempts to deride and discredit his interrogation. He was also back on Tuesday, "blue plan" in hand. Finally, late in the day, Marshall was excused to see the President but not before Ferguson gave warning that the Republicans were by no means through with him. In the remaining time, General Miles was recalled. Described in *Time* as "balding, bumbling," he admitted he had read the thirteen points on the night of December 6 and later said he did not believe "it was necessary to arouse the Chief of Staff at that time of night for that message."

Ferguson ordinarily was at the extreme right end of the long table, but in Brewster's absence he moved one chair to the left. Greaves, who hitherto had sat at the head of the table, had moved over into Ferguson's original seat. During the Miles interrogation, Greaves smiled at something Senator Lucas said.

Lucas, aware that Greaves had been prompting the Republican senators, flared up, protesting that the gentleman sitting to the right of Ferguson was ridiculing him. "I would like to know who the gentleman is and what right he has to sit alongside of the committee table and chuckle at a member of the United States Senate. . . . I do not propose to sit around this table and permit some individual that I do not know anything about, who is constantly in this case and constantly reminding Senators of the type and kind of questions they should ask, to give a hearty chuckle to something I might suggest in connection with this hearing. I think it is about time that the committee find out just who he is and what his business is."

Ferguson said Greaves was in charge of Senator Brewster's Pearl Harbor files. Lucas wanted to know where Greaves had worked before that. "Was he the Republican National Committee research man in the campaign of 1944? Let him answer that."

Greaves replied that he was; and Barkley wondered who was compensating him for the services being rendered to Brewster and Ferguson.

"He is not rendering any services to me," said Ferguson.

"Not much!" said Lucas sarcastically.

Ferguson insisted he could not say who was paying Greaves but Senator Brewster surely could as soon as he returned from his father's funeral.

But Lucas had the last word: "Mr. Chairman, I do not appreciate the gratuitous insults that have been made a couple of times by this gentleman, and I do not propose to take it much longer."

After adjournment Greaves was surrounded by reporters and photographers. He said that anyone who wanted to know the whys and wherefores of his salary would have to ask Brewster, who would not be back until Friday. Lucas also had the last word with the press. "It seems strange to me that a man so recently and so closely identified with the Republican National Committee should be sitting here, doing all the research work for two Republican Senators—especially when they so loudly claim that they want politics kept out of it." He promised the reporters that he was going to find out "who's paying for Mr. Greaves, how much, and who's responsible for moving a prominent Republican into a non-partisan hearing."

The next morning Greaves was back at the caucus room, this time sitting in his usual place at the head of but not behind the committee table. It was Keefe's turn to question Marshall. The Wisconsin representative was a big, imposing man. At the University of Michigan he had been president of the Glee Club and his clear, baritone voice dominated the room. Famed as a trial lawyer, it was said he could hypnotize juries with his logic and eloquence.

At first he was smiling and affable but soon he assumed the role of district attorney, which he had once been. Somewhat flustered, Marshall excused his lapses of memory. Things were being brought up "that have been, to a large extent, rubbed out by 4 years of global war. I have not investigated these things to refresh my memory until the past few days. . . ."

At the afternoon session Keefe, with punctilious courtesy, quizzed Marshall on the ambiguous warning to Short on November 27. Should not he, as Chief of Staff, have investigated further and given further orders to General Short once it appeared that he was only alerted against sabotage?

"As I stated earlier, that was my opportunity to intervene and I did not do it."

"Well, now, you say that was your *opportunity*," said Keefe pointedly. "That was your *responsibility*, was it not?"

"You can put it that way, sir."

"Well, I don't want to put it that way. I am asking *you*. You used the words, 'that was your opportunity.'"

Hiding any resentment he might have felt, Marshall again made an excuse. "Mr. Keefe," he said, "I had an immense number of papers going over my desk every day informing me what was happening anywhere in the world. . . . I noted them and initialed them; those that I thought the Secretary of War ought specifically to see I put them out for him to see, to be sure that he would see it in case he by any chance did not see the same message." He quickly added, "I was not passing the responsibility on to the Secretary of War. I merely wanted him to know. Now the same thing related to these orders of the War Department. I was responsible." He repeated that he had full responsibility in the matter, but General Gerow had "a *direct* responsibility."

"Well, now, then," said Keefe, "the fact remains that on this most important matter . . . when you and everybody else in the exercise of ordinary care must have known that war with Japan was imminent and that they might strike any time or any place, as you have said, and yet this important message comes back from Short and through some misadventure or dereliction some place no further message went to General Short or no further investigation was made." Short, sitting only a few feet away, must have been as impressed by Keefe's line of questioning as were Kimmel's attorneys, Rugg, Lavender and Hanify.

Keefe was not finished and minutes later abruptly asked Marshall if it was fair to conclude from his testimony that he fixed the responsibility for the Pearl Harbor tragedy on General Short so far as the Army was concerned.

"I have never made that statement, sir. I feel that General Short was given a command instruction to put his command on the alert against a possible attack by the Japanese. The command was not so alerted."

"Well, I will ask the same question, from a full and complete knowledge of the situation and the responsibility involved, do you assume any responsibility for this disaster at Pearl Harbor?"

He would only assume responsibility in not detecting that Short's reply "did not indicate a full alert."

Marshall's ordeal ended the next day but not before Gearhart, taking over from Keefe, asked why Japanese intercepts, particularly those between Honolulu and Tokyo, had not been sent to Short and Kimmel. "Don't you think the specific inquiry from Tokyo in reference to ship movements in Honolulu and Pearl Harbor was sufficiently important to convey to the commanders in Hawaii?"

He replied that "a great many messages about a great many places" were coming in and that if he had the final responsibility of reading all of the Magic messages, "I would have ceased to be Chief of Staff in practically every other respect, so that that was an absolutely impractical proposition."

By 12:45 P.M. the Republicans had finished with Marshall and he was free to leave for China. Chairman Barkley thanked him for his patient cooperation and wished him, on behalf of the committee, as high a degree of success in his new mission as he had had in other fields. An adept master of ceremonies, Barkley ended with a joke. "The Chair would like to say personally that if after you get to China, you discover that you cannot successfully cultivate your Leesburg farm from Chungking and need a good farmhand, the Chairman of the committee feels that by spring he will be available." For once the caucus room was united—everyone laughed.

The majority and the legal staff all felt that Marshall's testimony had been convincing. "Totally honest," was Gesell's conclusion. "I felt that his performance was masterful," recalled Diggs, "and my reaction was being proud of him not myself." But many Republicans, and practically all isolationists, were convinced he had lied.[2] "The General left a sorry impression on those who heard him," reported John T. Flynn in the New York *Journal-American*. "One left on me was that he revealed a surprising readiness to blame his subordinates."

Marshall himself must have been greatly relieved to leave the caucus room where, he later complained to a friend, he had to "sit and take it."

By the end of the afternoon session Chief Counsel Mitchell was in a glum mood. He called Barkley into his office to announce that he and his staff were resigning. They had been promised that the proceedings would be over in a month yet the end was far

[2] According to Percy Greaves, Ferguson told Greaves and Brewster before one of the sessions that the previous night he had overheard Marshall remarking to Barkley in the men's room at a social affair that he could not say where he was on the night of December 6 because it might get "the Chief" in trouble. Ferguson took "the Chief" to mean Roosevelt.

from in sight. Barkley urged Mitchell to reconsider, to at least sleep on the matter.

The next morning, December 14, Mitchell announced to the committee his decision to quit. Only eight witnesses had been examined after a month of sittings and there remained at least sixty more. Therefore he and his staff would have to be replaced since they had taken on the assignment with the understanding that the final report of the committee would be made not later than January 3, 1946. He complained that "extensive examination by some members of the committee" had gone "far beyond" what he had anticipated. And so he and his staff felt they could not see the job through to the end. "This outcome is a source of deep concern and regret to me and to the other members of my staff. I did not want the place as counsel, but under the circumstances I felt I could not refuse it." He and his staff had worked days, nights and Sundays for two and a half months, and had produced much pertinent information never before introduced by other inquiries. "We are all depressed that because of the course of the proceedings we have not been able to present it." He didn't say so but it was his quarrels with the Republicans which had forced his decision. He regarded them as obstructionists who were only playing politics, while they felt Mitchell was openly partisan to the Democrats on all important issues.

Barkley praised Mitchell and his staff and deeply regretted their decision. He himself was thinking of quitting. "I must, in my own mind, decide whether I have any further duty in regard to this investigation, and whether, if I have any duty, it outweighs my duty on the floor of the Senate in the capacity in which I have been chosen by that body, and in which I have served for more than 8 years."

Senator George added his criticism of the extended examinations by the Republicans. "Of course, I recognize the right of all members of the committee to cross-examine witnesses at any length, but I have wondered whether or not we were confusing the issue rather than arriving at any answer in which the public could have any confidence."

Mitchell did agree to stay on until early January, and business resumed with more testimony of General Gerow. Despite the tension of the morning, by afternoon both Mitchell and Barkley were in a joking mood. In discussing how safe a fortress was from attack, Mitchell noted that Fort Ticonderoga was one of the strongest British fortresses in the Revolution. "The Commander, as I remember it, was caught in bed. . . . I think he even had his trousers in his hand."

"Was he about to put them on, or take them off?" asked Barkley to the delight of the spectators.

Reaction to Mitchell's resignation depended on which newspaper was read. Pro-Administration journals denounced the minority members of the committee for unnecessarily delaying the proceedings for political gain. But opposition papers like the Cedar Rapids *Gazette* took another view. "Who in the world ever made a deal with Mitchell and his staff that the hearings wouldn't last beyond January 3? What kind of investigation did whoever made that agreement think this was going to be anyhow? An investigation of this kind is vital to America and it should be given all the time necessary to do the job right if it takes five years."

William S. White, in the New York *Times*, revealed that Mitchell's decision was not wholly unexpected by those associated with him.

> What was indicated in his statement was much more evident in his manner for at least two weeks.
>
> This was his growing impatience with committee examinations which left counsel with little more to do than to obtain data and hand up exhibits, and his hardly repressed anger at many pointed questions from the Republican side suggested that he had perhaps not brought out all that was material on this or that point.
>
> His exchanges, especially with Senator Ferguson, Republican of Michigan, were edged since the first week of the hearing.

4.

The following Monday Brewster explained to the committee that Greaves worked for him and had had no connection with the Republican National Committee for many months. Then he read a letter from Greaves stating that "there never was any intention on my part to insult or reflect on any members of the United States Senate by thought, word or action. . . . I am sure that the Senator from Illinois misconstrued an unconscious and which I thought was a silent smile that went unnoticed by anyone else."

Not at all appeased, Lucas said he was going to find out more about Greaves in executive session. "I think this committee is entitled to know who every individual is, what his background is, what his motives and purposes are, how much he is being paid, and by whom."[3]

Brewster retorted with a threat that if there was going to be an investigation of Greaves there could also be one "of the associations and connections of those more actively identified with the committee, but I am sure we will be embarking on something that will carry us a rather long way."

"Yes," said Lucas. The two were like fighting cocks.

"There are a good many things that have occurred which have not impressed the minority. They are matters of record. If we are going to start on that we will make a complete job of it."

What threatened to be a storm only turned into a tempest in a teapot. It was agreed that Greaves could stay but never again sit behind the committee table. Barkley left the caucus room shortly after the noon recess. He had a fever, he said, and his doctor had ordered him to bed. He called off the executive session that was to have been held later that afternoon. He hoped to be back next day. But instead of going home Barkley went to the White House. After a conference with Truman he told reporters he had not yet made up his mind whether he'd resign as chairman.

The following morning, the eighteenth, Admiral Wilkinson caused consternation among the majority by revealing that there had been an intercepted German message informing the Japanese that the Americans could have broken some of their codes. "Several messages that were sent from Japan indicated that they wished their agents to be particularly careful in their reports to protect the code." Greaves watched to see how Mitchell would react. A month earlier Ferguson had asked the chief counsel for

---

[3] Later Democratic Representative Clark, who had been relatively quiet during the sessions, put an arm around Greaves's shoulder. "If you ever need a counsel," he said affably, "let me know."

any information indicating that the Japanese knew the United States had broken their code. Mitchell had replied a day later in the negative.

Brewster now asked whether counsel had located these messages. Gesell, answering for Mitchell, said they had not. Whereupon Brewster turned on Mitchell like a district attorney. "Well, I have a letter from Mr. Mitchell saying there was no evidence that the Japanese had any knowledge that we were breaking their codes or suspected it, and that the evidence was all to the contrary. Do you recall that letter, Mr. Mitchell?"

"Yes," said Mitchell. "That is based on a report from the department of whom we made inquiry." He had forwarded the negative report to the minority.

Brewster held up a paper. It was an intercepted message from Tokyo to Mexico. He read it: ". . . American surveillance will unquestionably be vigilant. There are also some suspicions that they read some of our codes."

Mitchell paled and Greaves thought he was going to faint.

"Now that," continued Brewster, "of course, is squarely in conflict with the report which apparently the Navy Department gave you, is it not, indicating that at least the Japanese suspected that we were breaking their code?"

Mitchell was flustered. "I assume the Navy kept right on cracking them, so we can assume the Japs did not know that. I suppose that is why they made that statement. Obviously that one message contains a suspicion that we might be."

Brewster's voice was sharp. "Now the intercepts run from July 1 to December 7 and I asked some time ago for the earlier intercepts, after I was refused permission to examine the files, as I was reliably informed that there were five cablegrams which made very specific reference to this matter of which the admiral now speaks, that the Germans had apparently discovered something of this kind. . . . I say I am at least surprised that the Navy would give you the information that there was nothing to indicate this, if there are four or five messages of this character in their files." After Mitchell asked exactly what information Brewster was really looking for, the Republican said that was obvious: he wanted all messages indicating the Japs suspected their codes were broken. Why, he repeated, had Mitchell given him a negative report to his request for information?

The harried chief counsel replied that he had merely transmitted the report the Navy had given him. "I never asked them what their evidence was, but I assumed it was a fact because we kept on breaking the code, indicating that the Japs were not aware of it."

Brewster repeated what Admiral Wilkinson had just testified about the warning tip from Berlin to Tokyo. "I think it is unfortunate that the Navy should have given you a report of this character, if what Admiral Wilkinson says now is correct."

At last a majority member came to Mitchell's aid. "This is two or three times that the statement is in the record," protested Representative John W. Murphy of Pennsylvania. The eleventh of twelve children, he was an aggressive Irishman who relished combat.

Brewster raised his voice. "I can quite understand the concern of the gentlemen over anything which seems in any way to be in conflict here, but I think it is a rather important point, on which great emphasis has been laid, and I would like to know whether or not these messages exist. . . . I have been trying for more than a month to get them. I spoke to counsel about this in executive session ten days ago, and now I am advised that they would like to know just what it is I am after."

"You are using that microphone rather loudly," chided Murphy. "This is three times that that statement is in the record now."

Vice Chairman Cooper, taking over for the ailing Barkley, tried to bring order. "I think counsel understands, Senator. I am sure they will continue to cooperate in every way possible."

Brewster was ready to resume the questioning of Wilkinson but Ferguson entered the fray. He produced the memorandum that Mitchell had written to him stating that there was "no information or indication" that Japan ever knew their code had been broken.

Mitchell looked his age but now he was angry. He could not see the significance of the matter. Why were they making such a fuss? "I am probably dumb about it, but I do not grasp it. . . ."

"I should be very happy to give you what is in my apparent simple mentality," boomed the senator from Maine. First, if Admiral

Wilkinson was correct, the Navy had not been giving the chief counsel complete or accurate information. Secondly, when Marshall was examined regarding the Dewey matter, great importance was attached to' the fact that Magic was a great state secret and the Japanese had no suspicion their codes were being broken. "I cannot understand why the Navy will tell you there was nothing to indicate it. If it is not of any importance, why do not they simply give us the facts and the messages, and if it is of importance, and there is any suggestion of concealment, that is something we must take into account." A third point Brewster could have added, but left unspoken, was the lively suspicion that the Navy had held back or destroyed other messages on even more important issues.

Murphy cut in to say that yesterday twenty minutes were spent "on tirades" concerning Percy Greaves, "and now we have spent 20 minutes in trying counsel, talking about the Dewey episode. I suggest we talk about Pearl Harbor. . . ."

But Keefe had complaints of his own about the delivery of requested material. He himself had made at least twenty-five requests and only two or three had been complied with. And now a month had passed on the information Ferguson asked about code breaking. "We cannot help but wonder as to what is the cause of this great delay. This has caused me great exasperation and I can only say we have been receiving spoon-fed evidence."

By the end of the day Mitchell was in such a pitiable state that his wife approached Mrs. Brewster to ask if the minority senators might be a little easier on him because of his health.

In the morning the chief counsel opened the session with an embarrassing apology. "Now, yesterday I made the mistake, without checking up on the fact, of saying or thinking that I had submitted that request to the Navy or the Army, and they had reported and it was on the basis of their report that I made that statement, and as a result of that there were some imputations made on the good faith of the Army and Navy in not producing what we asked for." His voice was weak in his humiliation. "I want to say that imputation is not justified because I now find I never did ask for that material. . . . I am quite willing to be open to criticism for not following it up, although at that time we were pretty busy getting started, and possibly I might be forgiven for that."

"I am sure we all recognize that," said Vice Chairman Cooper sympathetically. Nor were there any sharp remarks from the minority, thanks either to the good offices of Mrs. Brewster or sheer pity. Mitchell then read in the record eleven messages Admiral Wilkinson had unearthed from the files proving beyond any doubt that the Japanese indeed feared America had broken their codes.

After Wilkinson was dismissed, Admiral Turner was called, and it was remarkable that he walked into the room without a tremor. He had been a house guest of his former aide, Captain William Mott, who had been desperately trying to sober up Turner for the hearings. After the Battle of Savo Island his drinking problem had degenerated into alcoholism. During the Battle of Okinawa he was drinking straight alcohol mixed with grape juice. He would send out for quantities to sick bay "for my foot," and would become so drunk that Mott often could not wake him during a kamakaze raid. To Mott, Turner was the brightest and most forceful admiral in the Navy and he had protected him for months. But the matter became so serious he finally reported it to the fleet surgeon. Turner was relieved. On the trip back to Guam, he drank nothing but orange juice. Arriving sober, he managed to convince Nimitz there was nothing wrong with him and that he should be task force commander for the invasion of Japan.

He exhibited the same recuperative powers at the hearings. Although some of his testimony was mixed up, no one realized what his condition had been the day before. On Thursday, December 20, he repudiated the testimony he had given before the Navy Inquiry: that Admiral Noyes had reported to him a "winds" execute had been received; and that this meant a break in relations or more probably war between Japan and the United States. Now he testified that Noyes telephoned him on December 5 to say that the first weather message had come in and it read "North wind, clear."

Turner said he had been a little confused in his testimony before the Navy. But now he was clear. Under cross-examination by Brewster the next day, the twenty-first, he explained his changed testimony. Recently he'd been straightened out by several officers who had studied the matter. Listeners wondered which testimony should be accepted: Turner's own remembrance of the "winds" incident or the repetitions of conversations he had heard in San Francisco?

Turner also claimed that Noyes had assured him on three occasions prior to Pearl Harbor that Kimmel and Short were receiving the same decrypted information that Washington had. Since Noyes had denied this at the Navy Inquiry, Turner said, "The only conclusion that I can arrive at is that I did not make my question to Admiral Noyes clear and that he misunderstood what I was trying to do." It was peculiar that two high-ranking Navy officers couldn't make each other understood on three separate occasions. "However, as a result of those three conversations at three widely separated times during 1941 I believed and so informed Admiral Stark that those officers were receiving the same information on all decrypted messages, at least concerning the Pacific, that we had here in Washington." By now, of course, he knew that there was no Purple machine in Hawaii.

Even so Turner harshly criticized Kimmel. If he had carried out the November 27 war warning he could have defeated the Japanese or greatly reduced the effects of their attack. Asked if Kimmel had sufficient equipment and material to have accomplished that result, Turner said, in conflict to considerable testimony to the contrary, "Yes, sir, to have inflicted very serious damage on the Japanese Fleet."

The session went on until 5:40 P.M., at which time Vice Chairman Cooper thanked the witness, excused him and said, "The Committee wishes the press and all others who have worked with us a Merry Christmas and a Happy New Year, and the Committee now stands adjourned until December 31, at 10 A.M."

Chapter Ten

THEIR DAY IN COURT
DECEMBER 31, 1945–
JANUARY 31, 1946

1.

When the committee next met on the last day of the year, a new chief counsel had finally been selected to replace Mitchell as of January 15, 1946. The unanimous choice was Seth Richardson, a staunch Republican from North Dakota, who had served the present Administration as chairman of the Subversive Activities Control Board. Long associated with the two isolationist senators from his state, Gerald P. Nye and William Langer, he himself had been a critic of Roosevelt but the majority had approved his selection to give the hearings that air of impartiality they had so far lacked. Lucas, his frequent golf partner, felt that he would not be harmful to the majority cause.

His selection created a minor mystery in Washington circles. Had it been a coincidence that his law office did business with the government and that he and Mitchell were old friends? Richardson had been selected by Herbert Hoover as Assistant Attorney General under Mitchell; and the retiring chief counsel had prepared for his successor a "Revised Order of Proof and List of Witnesses, and Explanatory Memoranda." It revealed Mitchell's own judgment of witnesses not yet interrogated and evidence not yet completed. In one section it was critical of Kimmel and in another it expressed near certainty that the "winds" execute message had never been received. Still another dealt with the White House papers of Roosevelt which the minority had been so anxious to get. Mitchell had requested that Grace Tully, the late President's secretary, extract from the files for the year 1941 all papers relating to Japan, the imminence of war in the Pacific, or general Far Eastern developments. "Counsel has not yet had nor requested physical access to the files," wrote Mitchell, "but has relied upon Miss Tully's extraction of documents coming under the broad headings noted above." Not all of the Roosevelt files had been checked, "but, of course, those considered likely to contain material relevant to the inquiry have been read." Reliance upon a President's loyal secretary to extract documents that could be embarrassing was naïve at best.

To ease himself into the task, Richardson, a bulky six-footer, was on hand to watch Mitchell and his staff interrogate Stark on December 31. Stark, relieved of duty by King at Forrestal's order, was again counseled by Lieutenant Richmond. He had urged the admiral to "go after" Marshall in his opening statement. Richmond was angry because the former Chief of Staff was "coming through this looking like a hero, and he didn't deserve it, and I wanted to take a good, sound whack at him." But Stark refused. "I know you and George are good friends," said Richmond, "but we're trying to do something here that's of tremendous historical significance."

"Well, Dave," said Stark, "let's tell the facts about me, and if somebody wants to point the finger at someone else, let them do it, not me." And so he refused to make adverse comments about Marshall, Roosevelt, Hull, Kimmel or others. He would leave evaluations to the committee. In his statement, Stark did introduce into the record a number of letters he himself wrote in 1941. Many were personal, and some so much so that he had suggested the recipients burn them. In one he wrote that he had told Roosevelt after Hitler invaded Russia, "I considered every day of delay in our getting into the war as dangerous, and that much more delay might be fatal to Britain's survival."

During the afternoon session Seth Richardson, who would soon replace Chief Counsel Mitchell, sat between Ferguson and Greaves, to get an idea of what was going on at the committee table. Later Greaves wrote a friend that Keefe was very enthusiastic about the new chief counsel but that Gearhart was much opposed "and feels that if he did anything against the Administration, he would be cutting off his chief source of income as a Washington attorney. Ferguson feels that they can't do anything about it, so they might as well make the best of it." Richardson, noted Greaves, had conversed in a very friendly manner with Ferguson, who had neglected to introduce him. "As yet Richardson has not decided on any assistants and I do not know that any serious effort was made to get minority help, as Lucas is branding Richardson as a Republican."

For three more days Stark was forced to submit to harsh questioning. Unlike Marshall, he was treated by the Democrats as a defendant who was as guilty as Kimmel and Short. Then a Republican, Gearhart, queried him about his loss of memory on the night of December 6. "In view of the fact that the Chief of Staff cannot remember where he was on that night is it possible that you and he could have been in each other's company that night?"

"I think we had no such conspiracy at that time, sir," replied Stark, causing some stir by the use of the word "conspiracy."

"Well, do you shut it out as being an utter impossibility that you and he could have been in each other's company that night?"

It was not an utter impossibility, admitted Stark, "but I think we were not." The "think" was provocative to some observers. On January 5, Ferguson questioned him on the controversial staff conversation with the British and Canadians early in 1941 which had led to a Joint Basic War Plan directed against the Japanese. In Stark's original statement it was noted that this plan was approved by the Secretaries of War and Navy, and by the President. Stark had put a line through "and by the President."

"I want to know," said Ferguson, "when you put that in there, whether you were of the opinion personally that that had been approved by the President?"

"Yes," replied Stark. "He approved my sending it out, although he had not officially approved it."

This not only ended Stark's interrogation but was also the last appearance for Chief Counsel Mitchell at the hearings. In ten days the investigation would lie in the hands of Richardson, who was well meaning if ill prepared.

2.

The hearings were recessed to give Richardson a chance to study the case. His first witness on January 15 was Kimmel. Now at last the admiral would have his day in court. What had concerned the attorneys for both Kimmel and Stark was the bad feeling between the two admirals. Stark had already written Kimmel to offer anything in his files. He had also invited Kimmel to his home for lunch, but both offers had been declined. Even so, Stark told David Richmond that he was to consider himself Kimmel's lawyer just as much as his own. "I want the truth to come out. Don't spare me in any way."

At his first meeting with Kimmel's attorneys Richmond had remarked that it was an awful shame that their two principals were at such odds. "It wouldn't take much for Stark to be a good friend of Kimmel. He's not mad at him." The reply was that their fellow was pretty mad at Stark. Richmond proposed they do something and their efforts had some effect. Kimmel and Stark did shake hands and on that morning managed to greet each other publicly.

Dressed in a dark suit with a bright blue tie, the sixty-three-year-old Kimmel began to read a 25,000-word statement asserting that Washington had denied him information that might have made Pearl Harbor an ambush for the Japanese. His voice was strong and he punctuated points with aggressive finger-pointing. He had come not with bowed head but full of fight. He was angry that the committee had already released to the press his and Short's testimony given at previous investigations. "This was unquestionably done with the object of lessening the impact of my statement when it was read."

The next day Kimmel told of the abuse and threats to his life that followed the Roberts report. Asked by Richardson if there had been a close personal relationship with Stark before Pearl Harbor, Kimmel said he'd had the highest regard for him. "I trusted him, and I felt he was one of my best friends. I had that feeling, but I cannot forget the fact"—he paused as if restraining himself—"well, events that have occurred since then."

During four and a half hours of questioning by Richardson and Vice Chairman Cooper the admiral flung back quick, authoritative answers. "I could have saved the fleet if given facts," he said. "Had they given me those dispatches, dispatches that were my primary concern—the people in Washington had other things to do—I can say without reservation they would have changed my ideas considerably. My staff still feels the same way. We were there—on the ground."

Friday, January 18, was a harrowing day for Kimmel, who had trouble hearing some of the sharp questions by Lucas. Several times he protested that he was deaf. This disability was compounded by the district-attorney manner of the senator. To wind up his interrogation Lucas asked, as if it were an accusation, "From November 24 until the hour of attack did you exercise that superior judgment necessary for one of your rank and position when you knew the war was practically imminent?"

"I did."

"In other words, Admiral, you are now telling the committee under solemn oath that you did not commit any mistakes or commit any errors of judgment from November 24 to December 7?"

"I would say that is a reasonable conclusion, and it is a conclusion that the Naval Court of Inquiry, composed of three Admirals, selected by the Secretary of the Navy came to when they submitted their report to the Secretary of the Navy."

On Saturday Representative Murphy of Pennsylvania continued the aggressive Democratic interrogation of Kimmel. But pressure on the admiral was relieved by an argument between Murphy and Keefe. Since the beginning of the hearings the two Irishmen had crossed swords good-naturedly but lately bitterness had crept into their colloquies.

"Now, Mr. Chairman," said Murphy, "the gentleman on the left has made a statement before I started a question and he was going to try to cut me off." Though he was a head shorter than Keefe, he was sharp of tongue and as feisty as Jimmy Cagney. He had tried forty-five murder cases as Assistant District Attorney without losing one. "We are all men. Now let us not have this needling going on. I want to conduct a fair examination and I do not propose to be cut off."

Murphy continued his acute and contentious interrogation of Kimmel for another hour before Brewster finally took over for the Republicans. At last Kimmel had an ally. "I appreciate as you do that perhaps necessarily over the past few days, this entire week now, there has been much that is repetitious in the very extended examination. I do not want to single out any of my colleagues by undue mention, but I do want to say Mr. Cooper, who is perhaps of the most belligerent variety, has questioned you in his customary style." He smiled. "When I went before him as a witness one time in the House he offered to throw me out of the room." There was laughter.

"I can appreciate the belligerency," said Kimmel. "I may have indulged in that sometimes myself. I do not object to it." What he objected to privately was the deletion of some of his own remarks from the record.

Brewster continued with questions that Kimmel was pleased to answer. Until then the committee had only been told of the defensive duties of Kimmel's Pacific Fleet. Now he was asked to enumerate the fleet's considerable offensive responsibilities. These included support of Allies in the Far East by diverting enemy strength away from the Malay Barrier; protection of sea communications of the Allies within the Pacific area; support of British naval forces in the area south of the equator; and protection of Allied territory within the Pacific area "by destroying hostile expeditions and by supporting land and air forces in denying the enemy the use of land positions in the Hemisphere."

"Now those are rather large orders, are they not?" said Brewster.

"Yes, sir," said Kimmel, and charged that Rugg had twice pointed out to Mitchell and Gesell that the true picture of Kimmel's offensive responsibilities had not been presented to the committee.

Brewster asked what reply Gesell had made to Rugg regarding that request.

"I do not know as he made any reply, but he did not do anything about it."

A volume containing the war plans of the Pacific *had* been delivered to the committee, but only one copy made available. It was so bulky that no one had time to read it and Mitchell had kept it out of the record. Now, thanks to Brewster, Seth Richardson finally let it be entered. "It contained the first inkling of what Admiral Kimmel had been ordered to do in the so-called 'war-warning' message, first mentioned in the Roberts Report," recalled Greaves. "Unfortunately, no copies were given or shown to the press until the entire proceedings were printed many months later."[1]

"Murphy took up most of today but got nowhere in particular," Greaves reported to columnist John T. Flynn, who was spending much of his working day on Pearl Harbor. Greaves told of Brewster's success in bringing out Kimmel's offensive responsibilities. "Both Mitchell and Gesell tried to keep it out, but it is now in evidence. . . . Brewster brought out that no one would be able to judge whether Kimmel carried out his assignment without knowing what it was and there had been attempts to suppress what his full duties were. Rugg seemed very enthusiastic about the results so far."

On the following Monday Kimmel's testimony ended, this session highlighted by Gearhart's lengthy criticism of the war warning message on November 27. How could Kimmel be condemned for being caught by surprise, said Gearhart, "when everybody above him, the Commander in Chief of the armed forces of the United States, the Chief of Naval Operations, the Chief of Staff of the Army, all insisted that they were surprised."

To Kimmel it was a satisfactory ending. He wrote his brother, Colonel Manning Kimmel, that although only a very small part of the evidence had so far been presented, he had finally had the chance to tell completely his story about Pearl Harbor; and had it not been for this investigation he was "confident that the Navy Department would never have permitted me to disclose this story. They would have kept it under wraps on the plea that any disclosure would jeopardize our code breaking activities and that would have left me hanging in the night. So I suppose I should be

[1] This important document was buried among exhibits on pages 2882–883 of Vol. 18, Joint Committee Hearings. See Notes.

thankful for small favors and certainly telling my story in public has relieved my mind and reduced my blood pressure considerably."

3.

The next day it was Short's turn. He was now represented by a young Army captain; his former counsel, General Green—whom both Kimmel and Rugg had suspected of connivance with Marshall—was now the Army Judge Advocate General. Short declared that he had been treated unjustly by the War Department. "I was singled out as an example, as the scapegoat for the disaster. I am sure that an honest confession by the War Department General Staff of their failure to anticipate the surprise raid would have been understood by the public, in the long run, and even at the time. Instead, they 'passed the buck' to me, and I have kept my silence until the opportunity of this public forum was presented to me."

The burden of examination was handed over to Samuel Kaufman, the associate general counsel. It was obvious to Greaves that Kaufman was already convinced of Short's guilt and was doing his best to shift the blame for the wrong alert from Marshall to Short by skipping over that part of the war warning message that placed full responsibility on the Chief of Staff. "He even tried to ignore Washington's instructions to look out for sabotage. He omitted entirely the shabby way the General's retirement had been handled. From his questioning you would have thought the Hawaiian commander was a dunce while those in Washington were wise men."

Short's fourth day on the stand was the most dramatic and moving. In the presence of his son, Major Walter Dean Short, he described the Roberts Commission hearings as "star chamber" proceedings at which he had no opportunity to hear the testimony of other witnesses or cross-examine them in his own defense. In a voice still weakened by recent illness, he said, "When I read the findings of the Roberts Commission in the newspapers on the morning of January 25, 1942, I was completely dumfounded." It was beyond his comprehension to be accused of dereliction of duty after almost forty years of loyal and competent service. "I immediately called General Marshall on the telephone."

Tears came to Short's eyes as he told how his old and trusted friend of thirty-nine years' standing said he had not seen the Roberts report until that minute. "I asked him what I should do, having the country and the war in mind, should I retire? He replied, 'Stand pat but if it becomes necessary I will use this conversation as authority.' I told him I would place myself entirely in his hands, having faith in his judgment and loyalty." But the next day Marshall had sent a memorandum to Stimson stating, "I am now of the opinion that we should accept General Short's application for retirement today. . . ." Short dabbed quickly at his eyes with his handkerchief; sitting behind him, his son did likewise. ". . . and to do this quietly," continued Short, "without any publicity at the moment."

Brewster asked if the Marshall memorandum to Stimson indicated a radically different position than the Chief of Staff had taken the day before. "Yes, sir," said Short. He seemed more hurt than angry. "And the day before he had told me to stand pat."

Later he did show anger and indignation when asked to comment on a list of possible charges to be brought against him in a memorandum compiled by the Adjutant General's office in 1942. To every charge, Short answered with spirit, "Not guilty!" and then gave his reasons. He concluded by stating that he had "never at any time tried to pass the buck to a single subordinate." He may have been tempted to add "like the War Department," but didn't.

It was fitting that the next witness be Justice Roberts. He had come reluctantly and became testy under badgering by the minority, apparently resenting the fact that a justice of the Supreme Court should be forced to endure such indignity. To Brewster's question whether there had been any mention in the commission's hearings of the "winds" message, Roberts replied curtly, "I have no recollection of any such thing. And I think you will search the testimony in vain for any reference to it."

Ferguson picked up a transcript of the testimony before the Roberts Commission. "You were the chairman, and this is your language," said the senator, and began quoting: " 'It has been reported to me that about ten days before the attack a code was intercepted which could not be broken, but it was forwarded to Washington to the War Department to be broken, and the War Department found out it could be broken and did break it, and found it contained three important signal words which would direct the attack on Pearl Harbor, and that the War Department subsequently intercepted over the radio those three signal words and forwarded them to the military authorities here as an indication that the code had been followed and that the attack was planned.'" Ferguson extended the document to Roberts. "I wish you would look at that."

"You don't need to show it to me," the justice replied testily. Ferguson asked what he was talking about in that quote. "I was talking about some information that had been given me somewhere around Pearl Harbor. People were coming to me all the time telling me there was such and such a rumor. You see I say 'It has been reported to me.'"

"Wouldn't this describe the 'winds' code message?"

"Very likely it would," admitted the justice. "Very likely so."

Did Roberts follow up on the matter? asked Ferguson.

"Yes, sir. We asked for all the messages there were about any broken codes and we were told we had all they had except this Magic thing."

"Do I understand that you did not get the Magic?"

"No, we were never shown one of the Magic messages," said Roberts, then admitted he knew the Army or Navy had been cracking a super code of the Japanese. "They did not show us the messages, any of them, and I didn't ask them to."

"That being true," said Ferguson, "how was this finding possible . . ."

Roberts angrily interrupted. "Now, Senator, is this an investigation of the Roberts Commission or an investigation of what happened at Pearl Harbor?"

Ferguson was somewhat intimidated. "I am trying to get the facts."

"When you ask 'How is this finding possible?' I don't find you criticizing me a bit," retorted Roberts sarcastically.

"I am not criticizing," said Ferguson. "I want to know on the facts you had before you . . ."

"How we could make a certain finding," interrupted Roberts.

"Yes."

"I think that is criticism."

Though cowed, Ferguson returned to the attack. He read from another document that the Secretary of State had fulfilled his obligations by keeping the War and Navy Departments in close touch with the international situation and fully advising them respecting the course and probable termination of negotiations with Japan. He turned to Roberts and asked how the commission could make a finding if it didn't have the facts.

Roberts replied that he had spent an entire day in Hull's office. ". . . Secretary Hull showed me his personal memorandum where he had noted that on a certain day he had told the Secretary of War and the Secretary of the Navy this, that and the other thing, and where he got that information. I didn't ask him, but I was perfectly convinced, and our commission was convinced from my report to them of the testimony he brought to me, that Secretary Hull had been warning the War and Navy Departments day by day and day by day that something might happen this day or that day, that the situation was degenerating, and so on."

"All right," said Ferguson. "Now, Justice, that part of the testimony is not in the testimony furnished to us, is it?"

"Certainly not. They had a stack of memoranda of the State Department that high, or Hull's personal memoranda and in order to recap it I asked him to write the letter which is in our record." He explained that his commission had not gone into any question of Hull's or the President's policy and was limited solely to the Army and Navy.

"All right," said Ferguson. "Then we come to the next finding in your conclusions." He read:

" 'The Secretary of War and the Secretary of the Navy fulfilled their obligations by conferring frequently with the Secretary of State and with each other and by keeping the Chief of Staff and the Chief of Naval Operations informed of the course of negotiations with Japan and the significant implications thereof.'

"Now," continued Ferguson, "without having the intercepted Magic messages, did you make this finding? I will put it that way."

"Why, certainly. The Chief of Staff and Admiral Stark told us and the Secretary of War and the Secretary of the Navy told us that every time Hull gave them a warning they would go and repeat it to the Chief of Staff and to the Admiral. I did not need to look at any messages to find out whether Marshall and Stark had been sufficiently warned. That is all I was interested in."

But, asked Ferguson, did he not know that Knox, Stimson, Hull, Stark and Marshall were all being furnished the Magic?

"I did not know it and I would not have been interested in it," said Roberts.

Ferguson was taken aback, as were some of the spectators.

Roberts reverted again to sarcasm. "Let's investigate the Roberts Commission. I would not have been interested in it, Senator. I wanted to know whether the military men were put on full warning and put on their toes by the men who had the information. I got a unanimous statement that they were."

"Well, then, Justice, if your commission was not furnished all the data that we had here in Washington, how could you make a finding on whether or not they were on their toes out in Hawaii and knew all the facts?"

The justice was becoming openly belligerent. He repeated he had not seen the Magic. "I would not have bothered to read it if it had been shown to us. All I wanted to know was whether the commanders [Kimmel and Short] had been advised of the criticalness of the situation." He had found from the messages sent them that they had ample warning and that they had orders from headquarters. "Now, they could have been sent more, of course," he said, adding derisively, "They could have been sent a message every two hours."

Ferguson took him literally. "Well, now, wait. If there was a message coming in every two hours and that information would have given them more warning wouldn't there then have been neglect on those here who did not send it?"

"Now, do you want me to make your report?" Roberts was losing his temper.

"No."

"Well, I have made my conclusions. My commissioners joined me in making the conclusions. If you reach a different conclusion, certainly that is your privilege but don't ask me to check your conclusions."

He may have been intimidated, but the senator pointed out that the oral evidence of the commission amounted to 1,887 typewritten pages while the photostatic copy only had 1,862. There were twenty-five less. He asked the justice to look at the page with this information.

"I do not need to, sir."

"Can you answer it if you do not need to look at it?"

"Yes; I can answer it. I do not know why the discrepancy."

Obviously ill at ease, Ferguson pressed on. "On the day you spent some two hours with the President, the day you made your report, did you have a discussion of the facts?"

No, said Roberts.

"Well, will you try and give us what took place there and that will answer the question."

"Well, I think it a highly improper thing but if you ask it I suppose I am bound to answer it." Reluctantly Roberts told of the conversation, which revealed nothing startling.

"Well, now, Justice, what was wrong with the question I asked you, to tell me what the President had said?"

"Well, now, Senator," mimicked Roberts, "I am not going to indicate whether Senator Ferguson is wrong. We have been inquiring about how wrong Roberts is. Don't let us get clear off that line."

"I was wondering why we shouldn't have the facts as a committee."

"Well, I'm not going to argue it with you, Senator. I said I was going to try to answer your questions."

Ferguson appeared disheartened to Greaves. "My personal reaction," recalled the latter, "was that the Senator was deeply shocked by such conduct. The Senator's own judicial background had led him to revere all Supreme Court Justices." Ferguson laid down Greaves's question list and left the battleground to Brewster. Definitely not one to be intimidated, he approached the task with relish. "I would like to take up one further matter, Justice, and I think you will understand that it is very rare for us to have an opportunity to examine a former Justice of the Supreme Court."

"Well, I hope they are having as much fun as I am."

"It is rarely we can suggest that a witness may be unduly sensitive, although without positive—"

"Oh, no," interrupted Roberts, "I am just plain Mr. John Citizen now; you know that. I haven't the high exalted position that you hold now."

Brewster hoped the justice would appreciate the difficulty of the commission's situation; and then asked why General Marshall had testified that portions of the Roberts report had been suppressed for reasons of military security.

Roberts' momentary show of good nature dissolved. He snapped, "Well, I have testified to the facts. Now if you want me to say, which I think is a very improper thing, that General Marshall was wrong, I will say General Marshall was teetotally wrong. I have given you facts. The facts are all typed, they are not my word against General Marshall's word."

Brewster would not submit to Roberts' testiness. Raising his voice, he sharply counterattacked. "I do not think it is questioning the integrity of General Marshall or criticizing you when your attention is called to the testimony of General Marshall before this committee, and it was called to your attention for any comment you desired to make, and I do feel very confident, in examining your distinguished record both as investigator and justice of the highest court in this country for many years, that you have found that this [situation] could be duplicated many times."

Bowing sardonically, Roberts retorted, "Thank you for those kind words." A few minutes later Barkley attempted to make a joke out of an embarrassing afternoon. "Mr. Justice, the committee thanks you for your cooperation. It regrets the necessity of bringing you from what Horace in his 'Odes' said is a Sabine farm."

Roberts smiled. "I cannot get back in time to milk, Mr. Chairman."

"I would like to have a photograph of you in that operation," said Barkley.

"I think that is the most irrelevant of anything that the commit-

tee has asked me for." There was a burst of laughter and Justice
Roberts was excused.

Monday the twenty-eighth of January had provided an entertaining if sorry spectacle to the reporters and spectators in the
crowded, smoke-filled room. To some it was an outrage that a justice of the Supreme Court should be treated so roughly. To others
Roberts' behavior was a blow at the vaunted objectivity of that
court. But an even higher drama seemed in sight with the announced appearance in a few days of Captain Laurance Safford. It
was expected that he and Kramer would consume more than a
week of high-tension testimony which would settle the crucial
issue of the "winds" execute one way or the other.

Chapter Eleven

SAFFORD AT BAY
FEBRUARY 1–11, 1946

1.

The public interest in Safford, Kramer and the "winds" execute
had been whetted since the previous November when Representative Keefe had charged he had proof that a Navy intelligence
officer was being "badgered" to change his testimony about the
"winds" message. The officer was Captain Kramer and he was
being held in the neuropsychiatric ward of the Bethesda Naval
Hospital. "He entered the Naval Hospital under orders," Keefe
told the Associated Press. "They took away his uniform and gave
him pajamas, bathrobe and slippers." He was convinced that
Kramer, with whom he had had three conversations, was chafing
under this restraint.

But Kramer had denied that he was being held incommunicado.
"I have been a patient at the hospital for some weeks and as for
being beset and beleaguered as the newspapers said, I'm feeling
very well. My treatment by the Navy has been as fair and considerate as it could possibly be." He said he could leave the hospital
at his discretion and was ready to testify at the congressional hearings whenever he was called.

Richardson had been well briefed by his predecessor on the "winds" execute. In a memorandum Mitchell had stated that, although previous testimony and available information left the issue in doubt, he felt it was an unimportant issue. "Our whole reaction to the whole 'winds' code episode was, and still is, that it is all much ado about nothing, because even if such a signal was sent out in a broadcast by the Japs and [had] been received by the War and Navy Departments, it would have added nothing to what our people already knew." While hoping the whole matter would be dropped, Mitchell wrote that he was aware that the sensational publicity already surrounding the issue made it necessary to continue the search for evidence.

This remained the attitude of the Democrats, who not only ridiculed the significance of the "winds" execute but were convinced it had never existed. The Republicans, as well as some neutral observers, contended that Safford's evidence could not be treated so cavalierly and that the existence of the message proved that Washington had sufficient warning of the Pearl Harbor attack to have repulsed it.

Perhaps the person most interested in the matter, except for Safford himself, was Chief Warrant Officer Ralph T. Briggs, for he clearly recalled receiving the "winds" execute in early December 1941. At that time he was one of the qualified operators assigned to monitor all Japanese intercepts at the Navy's East Coast intercept installation, Station M. A *katakana* (the Roman style of the Japanese alphabet) instructor, he was the only one on duty at Station M that night who understood the significance of *"Higashi no kaze ame,"* which meant "East wind, rain."

Briggs had come to Washington just as the congressional hearings were about to begin. He was assigned to Safford's former command, the Security Intelligence Section of Naval Communications, presently located at the ex-girls' school out on Nebraska Avenue. Concerned as he was by the innuendoes in the press that Safford was lying or confused about the "winds" execute, Briggs felt there was nothing he could do. Like others in intelligence, he was extremely security minded, having signed an oath never to reveal what he knew without official approval and release. He had no idea Safford was in a little office only a few minutes away until early in December 1945 when he got a telephone call from the captain, who asked if he'd be kind enough to come to his office in Building 18. "I want to go over some things with you that you may be able to confirm, and help me out in reference to some intercepted messages, some Orange [Japanese] traffic I'm looking for."

It was only a short walk to the south side of the grounds. Briggs found a mild-mannered, soft-spoken man who showed him some notes, then abruptly asked, "Was your sign RT?"

"Yes, sir," admitted Briggs. "I was RT." Receivers had to put their sign on every incoming message.

"I've pinned that down from the record," said Safford. "I believe you were the one who copied this particular message, this 'winds' execute message."

Briggs was edgy. "Well, it could be." He had no idea how much had already been revealed in previous investigations and was under the impression that everything was still classified Secret or higher.

"Well, do you recall getting that message?"

"I guess I did."

Safford said he didn't have the execute. Somehow it had become lost but he recalled seeing it for the last time when he had assembled it with a batch of related material for submission to the Roberts Commission hearings. "That is why I wanted to confirm this with you."

For many months Safford had searched in vain for the "winds" execute message. And at last he was sure he'd found the operator who had received it.

But the issue had already raised a storm of controversy. Could he now convince Briggs to reveal his involvement?

To his great relief Briggs admitted his role as one of the Orange intercept operators who had been alerted by Safford's own office to the three possible "winds" execute messages. He noted that the captain had a list of the names and signs of the other operators involved. Safford also brought out testimony taken at previous hearings. "It's in here," he said. "Some of it but not all of it."

It was obvious to Briggs that the captain knew what he was talking about; he had everything right. Then Safford identified Briggs

as the one who had received the "winds" execute. "Of course,"
recalled Briggs, "I admitted I did." Late on a night in early December 1941, he had found himself copying down *Higashi no
kaze ame.*" He quickly checked his watch supervisor's classified instructions and felt sure this was one of the three anticipated exe-
cutes. In addition to the original message, he made two carbon
copies. He entered the message in the log and then telephoned his
superior, Chief Radioman DW,[1] who had quarters at the station.
DW said, "Get it on the circuit right away to downtown Washington's 20G terminal." This was Safford's office, Op-20-G.

After explaining his dilemma, Safford asked if Briggs would be
willing to testify as a witness at the present hearings. Briggs
reasoned that Safford must have some authority to see him as well
as to ask for his testimony. Therefore he agreed to appear.

A day or so after their meeting, Briggs was ordered to report
to Captain John S. Harper, commanding officer of the Naval
Security station. He was austere and dignified, the epitome of military bearing and firmness. A stickler for discipline and the chain of
command, he felt that only one man on that post was entitled to
the title of captain—himself. "Briggs," he said, "I understand you
have been holding meetings with Captain Safford in reference to
the hearings." Why hadn't he, the commanding officer, been informed? "Who authorized you to do this?"

"Well, no one, sir—other than Captain Safford."

Harper's stern expression indicated this was no excuse. Didn't
Briggs know that *he* was the commanding officer of the station,
not Safford?

"Yes, indeed, sir, but Captain Safford didn't allude to the fact
that you weren't aware of my meeting with him."

Harper didn't pursue the point but remarked that too much had
already been revealed at the hearings. "I'm not at liberty to disclose the reasons for what I am about to tell you," he said. "You
are not to confer with Safford any further on this subject. You are
specially prohibited from meeting with him in his office, and if
there are any further inquiries or requests with reference to this

[1] Certain names and restricted material have been deleted by the U. S. Navy from
an official taped interview of Briggs on January 13, 1977. These deletions only
concern security and in no way affect Briggs's narrative.

matter, you are to report to me at once!" Then he added, "You are not to be called as a witness at any hearings. Is that clear, Briggs?"

Briggs was taken aback. Harper himself was uneasy. "Well, Briggs," he said, softening his tone, "perhaps someday you'll understand the reason for this." He paused as though wanting to say something further in clarification but then straightened up, ramrod erect. "You understand what I've told you? That is all!"

Briggs mulled over the situation. Had Harper called in Safford and discussed this with him? There were a number of questions to be answered but Briggs realized further contact with Safford would damage his career. He had no choice but to obey Captain Harper's order. And he had an added responsibility. Recently his wife had lost her sight and required the use of a guide dog. What if something happened to him? Even so he felt he had to talk to Safford once more. He telephoned the captain and told him what had happened. There was a long, strange silence on the other end of the line.

Safford seemed stunned, at a loss for words. He finally expressed regret that the efforts to assist him had resulted in Briggs's being called on the carpet by Harper. He promised to look into the matter and get back to Briggs later. After a few days Safford did so. This time he was in complete control of himself. The decision to reject Briggs's testimony, he explained, had possibly originated from someone on the staff of the Joint Congressional Committee. Safford concluded that "higher authority" had probably been responsible for canceling any further rebuttal witnesses. He once more thanked Briggs for his information and support. Since the captain had not identified by name who he thought the "higher authority" might be or what channel had been used to pass the order down to Harper, Briggs guessed that Safford had been intentionally bypassed. The only logical explanation was that a definite effort had been made to cover up the truth. But why? And what had happened to the missing messages?

It was about this time that Lieutenant Hanify was called from the caucus room to answer a telephone call from Safford. Would Hanify please come out to his house? There was such urgency in the captain's voice that Hanify immediately took a cab to 2821 Dumbarton Avenue. No sooner had he rung the front doorbell than he was met by both Saffords in lounging robes. They hastily pulled him inside, explaining that Drew Pearson, the columnist, lived in the neighborhood. If he saw a visitor in naval uniform he might draw conclusions.

Mrs. Safford, a distinguished and imposing woman, was in great distress and it appeared to Hanify that her husband was distraught because of her.[2] They both looked as if they had spent an anxious,

[2] By now the seemingly endless Pearl Harbor controversy had frayed her nerves. During a recent party one of Safford's colleagues, Prescott Currier, started to talk to him. Mrs. Safford put both hands on Currier's chest and pushed him back so forcefully that he almost fell backward. "Leave him alone," she said. "You can't monopolize him."

Mrs. Safford suffered even more than her husband during his tribulations at the hearings. Although he never held it against Kramer and other associates who repudiated him, Ruth Safford was bitter. Once she told the wife of one of Safford's colleagues over the telephone, "Your husband is a Judas Iscariot!"

After the congressional hearings she would not permit any talk of Pearl Harbor, and several times physically ejected colleagues and reporters who called at the Safford home. One such was Helen Worden Erskine, a contributing editor of Collier's. In 1954 she arrived unannounced at the Saffords' to gather material for an article in the Boston Traveler.

She was met at the door by a man with a kindly face and gentle voice. "I am Captain Safford. What can I do for you?"

"I understand you're the real hero of Pearl Harbor."

There came a scream from the upper floor: "Not Pearl Harbor, not Pearl Harbor!" Mrs. Safford rushed down the stairs shouting, "Get out! Get out!"

"Ruth, be quiet," said Safford, and turned to the reporter. "I've said all there was to say at the Pearl Harbor inquiry."

"Stop talking!" exclaimed his wife.

Safford continued politely. "I have my own opinions, but I'm not in a position to comment any more."

Abruptly Mrs. Safford grabbed Erskine by the shoulders and pushed her toward the door. "Get out!"

Safford was extremely upset by the story that appeared in the Traveler, particularly since both he and his wife were Bostonians. He protested in a letter to Erskine that he was not, as described, "a lonely and tragic figure" who had sacrificed his career for the truth. This, he objected, tended "to make me appear forlorn and pathetic—which I am certainly not. . . . If I had it all to do over again, I would not change a jot of it; even to the decision to give up all hopes of being an admiral. . . . It is a matter of deepest personal regret to me that you wrote so unkindly of Mrs. Safford."

Safford continued an obsessive interest in Pearl Harbor until his death, and wrote voluminous letters for years to a group engaged in publishing a revelatory history of Pearl Harbor. Their replies to Safford had to be sent to a series of mail drops, the last the National Space Agency library, where the wife of an old friend, Major General William O. Reeder, worked.

For this project, which was headed by revisionist historian Dr. Harry Elmer Barnes, Safford wrote articles and lengthy memoranda. These had to be composed outside the home, for if his wife found any such papers she would burn them. She would check letters addressed to him at their home, and those to which she objected "went down my wife's private memory hole."

"Like all women Mrs. Safford is curious and suspicious," he warned Commander

sleepless night. Safford explained that they were concerned over possible repercussions or reprisals if he testified as planned.

Hanify reassured them. All Safford had to do was tell the truth and stick to the evidence. The information about the Japanese intercepts was now in the record and he could speak openly on the subject. "I had a very good idea that Laurance Safford was not going to be the most popular character in the American Navy for a long time," recalled Hanify. "There was no doubt about that in my mind. On the other hand, I did not expect that anyone would dare bring proceedings against him, because the case was already beginning to get into the public domain."

Safford said nothing about the order preventing Briggs from appearing as a witness, in fact, never mentioned his name. And Hanify drove back to the Senate Building somewhat perplexed.

2.

There was an atmosphere of expectancy in the caucus room at 2 P.M. on the first of February even before Seth Richardson began interrogating Safford. After his briefing by Mitchell the new chief counsel was convinced he was about to deal with a brilliant but confused witness who stood alone in the belief that a "winds" execute had been received. The professorial-looking Safford was visibly nervous as he began to read a 28-page statement of his involvement with the "winds" code. He told his story in halting bursts and was so obviously upset that once Richardson thoughtfully asked if he were "scared." Safford said the frequent flashes of photographers bothered him. The picture taking was halted. But as he continued his nervousness remained and he would occasionally pause to bite his lips and sip from a glass of water.

His story, heightened by his own excitement, caused a sensation.

Charles Hiles in 1962. "Unlike other women she goes into hysterics at the mention of Pearl Harbor or the idea of another book about it. Fortunately I got the mail which included your letter so no harm has been done."

By 1967 Mrs. Safford had become so disturbed that the captain warned those working on the new book that "it would take very little to send her to the snake-pit." More secure measures, such as the use of code names, were taken to keep the correspondence secret. This continued until Safford's death in 1973. Mrs. Safford died seven years later.

"Capt. L. F. Safford, a timid, graying code expert," reported the Washington *Times-Herald*, "tossed a bombshell into the Congressional Pearl Harbor inquiry yesterday, when he declared positively that a Tokyo 'Winds Execute' message (meaning war between Japan and the U.S.) was received in Washington on December 4, 1941." Without mentioning Briggs, Safford had stated categorically that the message came in Morse code and was intercepted by a Navy listening post on the East Coast, Station M. "Safford's dramatic revelations were contrary to everything which the Congressional Inquiry has been told about the Winds messages by the Army-Navy high command—Gen. Marshall, Adm. Stark, Vice Admiral Wilkinson, then director of Naval Intelligence, and Major Gen. Miles, former War Department G-2." Equally sensational was Safford's claim that, less than a week after Pearl Harbor, the Navy Department ordered all personal memoranda concerning the disaster destroyed.

The next day, Saturday, brought new sensations. Safford accused John Sonnett, legal assistant to Admiral Hewitt, of having attempted to get him to reverse testimony before the Navy and Army boards that a "winds" execute had been intercepted. "It was apparent to me on my first meeting with Lieutenant Commander Sonnett that he was acting as a 'counsel for the defense' for the late Secretary Knox and Admiral Stark, rather than as the legal assistant to the investigating officer. His purpose seemed to be to refute testimony [before earlier investigations] that was unfavorable to anyone in Washington, to beguile 'hostile' witnesses into changing their stories and to introduce an element of doubt where he could not effect a reversal of testimony. Above all, he attempted to make me reverse my testimony regarding the 'Winds Execute' message and to make me believe I was suffering from hallucinations."

A little later he told Richardson that all copies of the "winds" execute were missing; and the one in Kramer's safe must have been stolen.

"Well," said Richardson in a tone that made it obvious he did not believe Safford, "do you think that there was a general conspiracy running from the White House through the War Department and Navy Department and through Kramer's section to destroy these copies?"

"I have never indicated the White House at any time in my testimony."

"Well, do you think there was a conspiracy between the Navy Department and War Department to destroy these copies?"

"There is an appearance of it," said Safford nervously.

"And whom do you suspect as individuals who took part in that conspiracy?"

"I have no first-hand knowledge."

"All you have is a suspicion?"

Safford said he had more than that and told in detail of his search for a copy of the controversial message. The men in charge of the files of his section did not know it was missing; "they had no record of it being missing, they had no authority for destruction and no record of destruction." Repeated searches were made but no copies ever showed up. "They had simply evaporated from the face of the earth. They were gone, and no records of them. It was an unwritten law in that section that we retain the original intercept forever, because we could never tell when it would be useful or how many years we might want to go back to verify something." Then he tried to find the original teletype at both Station M and the Bainbridge Island station near Seattle but there was no trace. Letters in connection with the search had also disappeared without a trace. "It was not only the Winds message itself; it was everything connected with the Winds message which had disappeared."

Richardson did not take any stock in these accusations. "Now, it is a fact, isn't it, Captain, that every single witness who has testified on the Winds code, on the subject of having received or seen a Winds Execute message, testifies that they never saw one; isn't that a fact? Every single one of them."

That was not true, retorted Safford. The assistant chief of Naval Operations before Pearl Harbor, Admiral Ingersoll, for one, testified he had seen it and that it meant war with the United States. The admiral wasn't sure whether he saw it before or after Pearl Harbor, but he definitely saw it and it was in writing.

Richardson brushed aside the Ingersoll testimony. "Why," he

asked, "would anyone want to press the veil of secrecy, destruction, on this Winds Execute message that you say came on the 4th of December, why would they?"

"It is human to try to cover up mistakes."

"Well, what was the mistake that was made with reference to that message?"

"The fact that no war warning was sent," said Safford. "The fact that an attempted war warning in the Navy Department was suppressed by higher authority and that the War Department didn't even attempt to get a war warning out."

"Then it is your idea that, with a message in the hands of the officers of the Navy, the officers of the Army, and the President of the United States, that everybody forgot that they were interested in the war and forgot to make use of this message?"

"I do not know why the warning did not go out."

"I suggest, Captain, that the reason the warning didn't go out was because there never was a Winds Execute message on the 4th of December. You disagree with that?"

"I disagree with that," said the harried Safford.

Richardson kept asking repetitious questions until Safford could restrain himself no longer and exclaimed that the chief counsel was trying to get him to change his testimony and wasn't the first one who had tried to do so.[3]

By the time Safford left the caucus room that afternoon, he was exhausted. Now at least he would have a day of rest before returning on Monday to what was likely to be even more severe interrogation by the majority.

In a statement to the press Sonnett denied the charge that he had attempted to get Safford to change his testimony. Now promoted to Assistant Attorney General of the United States, he said, "I was instructed by the Secretary of the Navy to secure all of the facts concerning the 'Winds messages' in order to clear up the

[3] This part of the interrogation cannot be found in the published record. "I was sitting right behind Safford and heard every word of what was said and it was so unusual that I remember the whole thing distinctly," Lavender wrote Kimmel. This came as no surprise to the admiral. Many of his own remarks had been deleted and misquoted in the record. Greaves also recalled that key material had been deleted from the record.

apparent mystery as to that message about which there has been so much rumor. I discovered that Captain Safford was the source of the erroneous rumors concerning the existence of such a message. . . . It should be borne in mind that, of the many people named by Captain Safford in previous testimony as having knowledge of the 'Winds message,' not a single one recalled the existence of such a message. It is impossible to believe that all those witnesses could be wrong." It was also hard to believe that Sonnett didn't know that not only Ingersoll but two others, Colonels Moses Pettigrew and Carlisle Dusenbury, had testified that they saw it. So had Kramer until his memory was altered at the Hewitt Inquiry.

3.

On Monday morning, February 4, the Democrats converged on Safford. Lucas began by asking if he had communicated with Kramer about the "winds" message. Safford admitted he had written his friend a letter about the end of 1943 but did not have a copy. "Your memory would be better then than it is now, would it not?" asked Lucas.

"As far as that aspect was concerned."

"And if in that letter you said this whole thing was somewhat vague and uncertain—I don't know whether it did or not, I haven't seen the letter but maybe we can get it—that would be true, would it not?"

"I believe I did not go into details at all. . . . And I did not suggest anything to Kramer. I was trying to ask a question."

"I see," said Lucas, and then dramatically called out, "Is Captain Kramer in the room?"

"Yes," said a voice that Safford recognized as Kramer's.

"Do you have a copy of that letter, Captain?"

"Yes, sir, I do. I made it available to counsel, Senator." Kramer put his hands in front of his face as a photographer took his picture.

It was a moment for theater with Safford and Kramer facing each other. One can only imagine what conflicting emotions Safford endured. He had fallen into Lucas' trap—because of a trusted friend. Agitated, he admitted he had destroyed his copy of the letter and then had to listen to Lucas reading out that he was preparing a secret paper and was getting details from available records. "'My memory is bad as to details . . . ,'" quoted Lucas and stopped. Was that true of the "winds" execute? he asked.

"That is true on the details," admitted Safford. "You will see I had not been able to establish the date at that time, the exact day. I knew it within two or three days."

Lucas read on: "'My memory is bad as to details, which is the reason for preparing this memorandum, and I have forgotten or am very vague as to certain things which I clearly recalled a year ago.'"

All of the Safford-Kramer correspondence was read aloud, including the code to be used giving numbers to persons, messages and places. With obvious relish Murphy, the feisty Irishman from Pennsylvania, took over the questioning. His aggressive tactics had already brought him press commendation as the ablest majority member who "has shown himself fast and shifty on his feet." Safford had previously testified that he had left his office about four-thirty on the afternoon of December 6, had gone out with friends that night and was having late breakfast on the seventh. "You were still in your pajamas the next afternoon at 2:20 having breakfast, on December 7, is that right?"

"That is right."

"At 2:20 you were still in your pajamas having breakfast?"

"That is right."

Murphy began savaging him. "And you are home at a time when you think war is coming, because you have told this committee that war was coming on Saturday or Sunday, you knew that there is going to be a time fixed which will fix the deadline and you leave on Saturday afternoon at 4:30, and you do not inquire as to anyone under you until after the war has started; that is right?"

Safford explained that one of his subordinates had sent the thirteen parts of the Japanese message to the Army for translation. That was the day the Army was supposed to do translations of Magic. Also another of his officers had called Kramer to tell him what was in the message.

"We are talking about you, in charge of 200 men!" exclaimed Murphy. "You, the one who has been accusing everybody else!

We are now talking about you." The fact was, he said, that
Safford had no translator on hand on December 7—"on the day
you expected the war to start, did you?"

Safford admitted he had no translator in the office at that time
but was not given a chance to explain that he had a watch officer
on duty at all times to decrypt promptly whatever came in. And it
was Kramer's responsibility to provide translation.

"And you are still in your pajamas having breakfast at 2
o'clock?" accused Murphy.

"Yes, sir."

"Do you have any sense of responsibility for the failure of this 1
o'clock message to get to the proper people in time? Do you feel
responsible?"[4]

"Not in the least. . . . Three official naval investigations have
listened to all the facts and none of them found me responsible."

"Not one of them have gone into this, have they? Whoever
asked you about your responsibility and failure to be there on Sunday; whoever asked you that question before?"

"That question was not specifically asked."

"You believe that the best defense is an attack, don't you?"

Safford could have replied that this was exactly what Murphy
was doing. "It is the oldest trick in the book," he later wrote, "—to
try to put the chief witness for the prosecution on the defensive or
to try to make the victim responsible for his own murder." The
reason the warning to Short and Kimmel arrived too late was by
no means Safford's or Kramer's fault but that of Stark and
Marshall. The one o'clock message had been translated and in the
hands of Stark a little after 10 A.M., three hours before the first
bombs fell on Pearl Harbor.

But all the flustered Safford could think to say was, "I believe
the best defense is telling the truth."

---

[4] Murphy's accusations were grossly unfair. It was Safford who, before December
1941, had set up a twenty-four-hour watch to decrypt Magic traffic. He told an assistant that if the Japanese started anything it would be over a weekend. And if
things broke Op-20-G would be held responsible for unprocessed traffic even if it was
the Army's date of responsibility. He thereupon instructed his people to decrypt
Army date traffic after all Navy date had been run.
    Safford's vigilance and foresight paid off on December 6. The Army decrypters
closed at noon but Op-20-G stayed on duty and began decryption of the message
from Tokyo. Otherwise the first thirteen parts would have remained undecrypted
until Sunday.

Murphy then turned to another of the letters Safford had written Kramer. He read:

"'. . . What a break for you, as well as to the cause, to be ordered to Halsey's staff. I can see the hand of Providence in it.'

"What was the *cause?*" asked Murphy. The cause of Admiral Kimmel, explained Safford. Murphy then called attention to another paragraph.

"'. . . Be prudent and be patient. I am just beginning to get things lined up at this end. No one in ✕15 [the code for Office of Naval Operations] can be trusted.'

"Will you give us who you felt was not trusted in the Navy of the United States during the course of the war on January 22, 1944?"

"That is a rash statement," admitted Safford. "I will not expand on it."

Murphy pressed him to name names. Safford refused. "You will not?" exploded Murphy. "You refuse? I ask you to tell us. You are now under oath. Please tell us, sir, who you say there cannot be trusted, because, sir, that is an important accusation. It is an accusation against one of the important departments of the United States Navy during the war. You are making assertions. This is going into the papers of the country as well as are your other statements. You say 'they cannot be trusted.' Who were you saying could not be trusted? Names, please. Who could not be trusted?"

"He says all of them," said Lucas, joining in the attack.

"I would like to have names," said Murphy. "Here is a man making an accusation in writing." He made it sound as if Safford had made a public statement, not a comment in a private letter. "This is going to the papers. You, sir, a captain in the United States Navy, say: 'No one in ✕15 (Opnav) can be trusted.' Who did you mean? I don't want any sweeping statement. We are going to get down to details. Who could not be trusted?"

The harried Safford had no counsel to advise him. Rugg had to be careful not to talk or write to him before he testified, and would not even exchange glances with him during his testimony. Behind his horn-rimmed glasses, Safford's brown eyes darted warily with what seemed to Hanify "a combined comprehension and apprehension born of secrets known and secrets not to be told." It was an alert guardedness, a mannerism that probably came from his years as a cryptologist. It was obvious to Hanify that this unassuming man had a strong will. He appeared diffident and retiring but was as malleable as steel. Under his inquisitor's relentless quest for names, Safford kept silent.

Murphy kept at it like a terrier. "Names, please. I am still waiting. Waiting. Will you please give us the names as to who could not be trusted in Opnav? Please, sir. What did you mean by saying no one in ✳15, Opnav, can be trusted?"

"Do you wish to answer?" asked Barkley.

"I would prefer not to answer," said Safford. Rugg, Hanify and Lavender must all have heaved a sigh of relief.

"The Chair thinks you should answer if you can answer," said Barkley. Safford had no right to conceal anything that was pertinent.

"That was a private letter to Commander Kramer," said Safford stubbornly.

Murphy tried another angle. He read the next sentence.

"'. . . Premature action would only tip off the people who framed ✳31 (Admiral Kimmel) and ✳32 (General Short) and will also get ✳8 (Safford) and ✳10 (Kramer) into very serious trouble.'

"What did you mean by that?" asked Murphy. "How would it get Safford into trouble if he was doing the right thing? Will you answer that, sir? Still waiting."

"Go ahead," said Barkley. "Answer if you can. You must have some sort of answer to that."

"What I meant was that nothing should be done in the way of making any statement or anything of that sort until the expected court-martial or the expected investigation at that time which had been directed by Congress had taken place, so I could come on the witness stand, or Kramer could come on the witness stand and present the facts."

"And spring a surprise," said Murphy. "Is that right?"

"Not necessarily. . . ."

"How would you get into trouble, what trouble could you get into for telling the truth, if you were telling the truth: Who would make trouble for you?"

"I was standing almost alone at that time."

"Who would make trouble for you, sir?"

The answer obviously was: the higher-ups. Safford had no one to advise him. Today he was really alone. "Anyone who doubted the accuracy of my statements," he finally said.

Who did the framing of Kimmel and Short? pressed Murphy relentlessly. "Name names, please. That also is a serious accusation. Names. Do you know that to frame anyone is one of the meanest and lowest crimes?"

Safford had no trouble in answering this. "Yes, sir."

"Now, then, you say some people did frame these two people, Admiral Kimmel and General Short. Who framed them?"

"I do not know."

"Whom do you refer to and whom are you cautioning Kramer against? Whom were you referring to?"

"I was referring to the War and Navy Departments in general, but not to any specific individual that I can identify."

"Captain, you wouldn't accuse the whole War and Navy Departments with the stigma of the vile crime of framing anybody? Can you narrow it down?"

"Well, I will narrow it down to the people concerned, the General Staff and officers."

Murphy was triumphant. "In other words, you felt that the General Staff of the United States Army under General Marshall, and the General Staff of the Navy under Admiral Stark had framed Kimmel and Short. Is that right?"

Safford licked his lips and wiped his forehead with his handkerchief. "I felt that way."

Murphy was set for the kill. "And my question is now: Can you give to the committee the name of any single witness . . . to furnish absolute proof or overwhelming proof of the guilt of Opnav and the General Staff of the United States Army?"

Safford said he could name four people who, he believed, "will give me some support if not complete support," and listed Kramer and three colonels, Sadtler, Bratton and Pettigrew.

"Did Sadtler ever say anything to you that he felt General Marshall had violated the criminal laws of the United States?"

"Not directly."

"What did he say that would make you think that he believed General Marshall, General Gerow, and the other generals would commit crime by ordering the destruction of—withdraw that. What did he say that would lead you to believe that those men were guilty of what you were referring to in this letter to Kramer? I am speaking of Sadtler."

Harried as he was, Safford had never raised his voice or displayed temper. "I cannot estimate anything that Colonel Sadtler will say specifically," he said courteously.

"Well, what do you have to offer to the committee by way of generalization as to what he might say that will prove the guilt of the General Staff of the Army? Have you any lead? Have you any suggestion? Have you any idea, that led you to believe that they will testify and support you and corroborate you in these charges? Upon what do you base your statement here today that these men will corroborate you? This is going into the papers, the statement that you made that four men will corroborate you in these charges."

"Colonel Sadtler knew of the Winds Execute," he said.

"What else?" pressed Murphy. "What will he say about the guilt of General Marshall or anybody on the staff, if you know?"

"I believe that Colonel Sadtler knows about the destruction of documents in the War Department." He had been told this by William Friedman, the code expert.

"What evidence can he give as to the guilt of the General Staff of the Army?" hammered Murphy. "You see, there is quite a difference between the alleged or actual existence of a Winds Execute and the violation of the criminal laws of the country in destruction or pilferage, stealing from the files. What evidence can he give on that subject? You say he is a reliable witness as to the guilt of the General Staff of the Army."

At last Safford got help. Keefe motioned to Cooper, who had replaced Barkley in the chair. "Mr. Chairman, I don't want to object, but aren't Colonel Sadtler and Colonel Pettigrew and these other people going to be witnesses, and won't their testimony be the best this committee can get as to what they are going to testify, instead of speculating as to what this witness may think they will say?"

A little later the committee recessed for the day and Safford, still shell-shocked, gathered his papers. Kimmel's three lawyers did not acknowledge him but their feelings were with him. Lavender thought the afternoon's grilling was cruel and gruesome. Hanify had suffered through Safford's inept testimony about his whereabouts on December 6 and 7. Why had he mentioned he was in pajamas? The majority had had a field day with that slip. They had made him look like a fool. "That's where he betrayed the inexperience of a person who has been in a quasi-academic atmosphere all his life, and not in a competitive atmosphere," recalled Hanify. "He was not a forensic type. He was not a debater. He was not argumentative." He was helpless without counsel in the hands of a Murphy or Lucas. But there had been something noble, thought Hanify, in the way Safford had stood up alone against all the forces arrayed against him and refused to back down. He was a modern Don Quixote.

The reporters crowded around Murphy, who was triumphant and exultant. "We haven't touched the real meat of this," he told them. "There's real, genuine tenderloin in it." And tomorrow he would go after it.[5]

When Briggs read the stories of Murphy's "hard-hitting, hammering cross-examination" of Safford and how he and the other Democrats were making a mockery of his testimony about the "winds" execute, "it became increasingly evident to me that the poor man was really being taken for a ride and not given an opportunity to prove his points." If it had been within Briggs's power to help Safford find one of the copies of the missing message, he would have done so. But he didn't know where they were or who had them.

The next morning, February 5, Murphy resumed the attack on Safford's inaction on December 7—the day he slept late and was in his pajamas even after bombs were dropping on Pearl Harbor. Safford tried to explain why he was not responsible for the delay in sending the warning message to Kimmel and Short on December

[5] Two months later, President Truman would nominate Murphy to be U.S. district judge for the Middle District of Pennsylvania. Murphy had been Truman's floor manager in the 1944 convention that nominated him for Vice-President.

7. It was true he slept late that morning but he was not responsible for the translation of the fourteenth part and the 1 P.M. message.

"There was not one translator in the Navy that day, was there, outside of Kramer?" said Murphy.

"I cannot answer for the translators," said Safford.

"In other words, you weren't so concerned about getting the message translated?"

"It was not my responsibility," said Safford patiently, "and I had no responsibility to issue any orders about translators."

"Weren't you interested in protecting the American Navy? You said war was going to start that day. Do I understand you to say you were not responsible for anything at all that might help with winning the war?"

Keefe objected. "Mr. Chairman, I don't think that the answer bears any such interpretation. I think it is an unfair question." There was rustling among the spectators, mostly women, who were beginning to have sympathy for Safford. "The witness is entitled to some degree of fairness and fair play."

"I expected Mr. Keefe to be concerned, and I expect he will have more trouble all day. What is the objection?"

Keefe's voice boomed out. "I object because the witness has testified that under the set-up he had no responsibility for translators. You are trying to make it appear that he did have and had no interest in protecting the welfare of the nation." The onlookers could no longer control their emotions. A wave of spontaneous handclapping swept around the big room. Vice Chairman Cooper rapped a large ashtray on the table. "The committee will be in order," he called out. "That applies to the guests."

"Mr. Chairman," said Keefe, "I have sat here all during this hearing without hardly opening my mouth. I think it is unfair on the part of the Congressman to say he expected to be interrupted by me all the time. But there is a limit to fairness even with this witness." There was another burst of vigorous applause.

Murphy was angry at the sudden turn. "I think I understand what is happening, and I am not going to be taken off the track by either certain people in the audience, or by the objection. I will proceed. I will get the facts regardless of any hindrances, sir." He

turned to Safford. "The fact is, sir, that you were head of communications, and you felt war was going to start on Sunday." And
it was also a fact that the translators were Kramer's responsibility,
not his.

Some steam seemed to have been taken out of the Irishman
from Pennsylvania and he dropped that unproductive line of inquiry. He asked if Safford ever had any trouble with Admiral
Stark.

"No, never."

"Well, when was it you first turned against him? You have
turned against him, haven't you? You feel he is guilty of a crime,
don't you? You said he could not be trusted, didn't you? You said
he was guilty of a frame-up . . ."

"I said that in a private letter . . ."

"Well, sir, you always speak the truth privately or publicly,
don't you?"

"You try to," said Safford almost to himself.

"Yes. Well, now, was it or was it not your feeling when you said
that you felt that Admiral Stark was guilty of a frame-up?" Safford
didn't understand the question and asked for it to be reread. "Will
you answer the question, sir?"

"Yes."

"Your answer is 'Yes,' Captain?" asked Cooper.

"No. I said I would answer the question." He begged Cooper's
pardon.

"Take your time," said Murphy, who might have been
impressed by Safford's unfailing courtesy under stress. "I will
wait."

"I want a chance to get that straight."

"I don't want to ask you these questions but my job here is to
get the facts." Murphy's adversary tone was dropped. "I don't want
to embarrass you at all. I would rather not be here, but being here
I am obliged to get the facts."

"It was not my feeling at the time," said Safford, "and if I
wronged Admiral Stark I regret it. . . ."

"At any rate, you did state as an officer of the United States
Navy that the leading officers, the commanding officers of the
Navy were guilty of a frame-up and that, in your judgment, a

frame-up is about as vile and low a thing as can be done to a human being, isn't it, or by a human being?"

"It is."

"And do you feel now, sir, today, that Admiral Stark and the members of his staff did bring about a frame-up of Admiral Kimmel?" Safford did not answer. "I won't press you upon that point."

"All right," said Safford. "Thank you."

"You have answered a good many others," said Murphy. He continued the questioning but his hammering ceased and so had hope of the tenderloin envisaged yesterday. Then the minority took over and both Ferguson and Keefe began bringing out points that supported Safford.

Keefe said one thing puzzled him: "Captain Safford, I am unable to understand any possible interest, personal interest, that you might have in this controversy, and if you have any such personal interest, I would like to have you state it."

"I have no personal interest, except I started it and I have got to see it through."

This brought a third spirited round of applause.

"The guests of the committee will be in order," warned Cooper.

"You realize, of course," went on Keefe, "that in view of the implications that have been stated in the cross-examination of you, especially by the gentleman from Pennsylvania, that you have made some rather strong charges?"

"Yes, sir."

"That may well mitigate against your career as a naval officer. Did you realize that when you came here as a witness?"

"I realized that every time I testified."

"And despite the fact that you have nothing to gain, and everything to lose, you have persisted in this story every time you have testified."

"I have."

Yesterday had been a day of trauma for Safford, today one of satisfaction. But upon his return on December 6, the Democrats made another attempt to break him. This attack was launched by Lucas and it was in the form of a threat. Didn't Safford realize that when he sent the private code to Kramer giving numbers for the President and other notables he was doing something wrong and was violating naval regulations?

This time Safford answered promptly. "Yes, sir."

"That is what I cannot understand, Captain Safford, how a man who is as intelligent as you are, and who is such a brilliant officer as you have appeared before this committee, would take a chance on the violation of naval regulations in order to help a man that you never saw or knew intimately, in order to help Admiral Kimmel, an individual whom you never served under, that you slightly knew, but you did all of this taking a chance of ruining your own career to help a man that you hardly knew. Can you explain that to me?"

Safford said that he had first been very bitter against Kimmel, assuming he was guilty for Pearl Harbor. Then he learned that Kimmel had not been sent the "winds" execute and other vital information.

As a result of this change, Lucas asked Safford, "you then felt it your duty to go all out and do everything you could for him?"

"I did."

"And in so doing you realized that Captain Kramer was probably the most valuable man you could get on your team in the defense of Kimmel?"

"Yes. That is, if Kramer was so disposed."

And if Kramer had answered Safford's second letter, using the personal code against Navy regulations, the two of them might have been court-martialed for it?

"Yes, sir," said Safford. "Kramer used better judgment on that occasion than I did."

If Kramer *had* answered the second letter, said Lucas, then he would have been in the same boat as Safford was now in. "Isn't that right?" Safford insisted Kramer was always a free agent. "I do not want to infer," went on Lucas, "that you haven't given us your best understanding of this whole transaction, but there is a lot of testimony here against you on this Winds message and if Captain Kramer had been with you on this completely from beginning to end—which he would have had to have done, if he had answered the second letter—this committee would have had a pretty difficult time making any determination upon that question."

Brewster protested.

"I will withdraw it, if the Senator objects to it. Please don't take it, you men, for the newspapers. I will withdraw the whole thing. I do not want to get into any arguments with the Senator from Maine."

"I quite appreciate your request to the newspapers," said Brewster, "but I am afraid it will be difficult for them to completely disregard it." Lucas had implied that Safford was involved in a plot. By using pejorative words, Lucas had accused Safford of "laying a *net* for Captain Kramer and also the fact that if Kramer had responded to his letter, then Captain Safford would have had him at his *mercy*, certainly those things imply that Captain Safford was plotting in this situation, and I understand you do not mean any such insinuation. If Kramer had innocently and not evilly answered Captain Safford, that would not imply anything at all, that Captain Safford would have blackmailed Captain Kramer, or that Captain Kramer would have yielded to Captain Safford. I think all of these implications are unwarranted and unfair."

The audience applauded briskly.

"The Chair desires to say to the guests that this is not a political convention," said Barkley, who had returned to duty, "and any further outbursts in the midst of this testimony will be dealt with accordingly, no matter in whose behalf they are or in response to whose questions." He added that the Chair had made no objection to demonstrations on the part of the audience when a witness had concluded his testimony. "This was true in regard to Secretary Hull, General Marshall, and the others, but the audience has repeatedly broken into the testimony of the present witness to make demonstrations. If they want to applaud when he finishes, that is their business."

By early afternoon the committee was through with Safford and this time the sustained applause brought no objection from Barkley. As the captain, exhausted and nervous, was getting to his feet, Richardson said, "Mr. Chairman, I would like to present Captain Kramer."

"Captain Kramer," said Barkley, "come around, please."

Kramer and Safford passed each other. The latter, stunned a few days earlier to learn that his friend had turned over all their private letters without informing him, did not feel that he had been betrayed. He figured that the pressure of the past year had cracked Kramer and he was a sick man. Safford felt no resentment, only sorrow that his friend had been forced to undergo such harassment. They exchanged friendly words and had their picture taken together.

As Kramer prepared to testify, his wife, standing in the rear of the room, watched nervously. The minority members and Greaves were equally tense. Kramer had previously testified both ways. Which way would he go today? He began by admitting he had seen a "winds" execute. But it was on the fifth of December, not the fourth.

"Now it is testified here," said Richardson, "that you came into Captain Safford's office with the watch officer and that you said, 'Here it is,' and handed to Captain Safford a message on yellow teletype paper in Japanese, about 200 words, 'War with United States.'"

"If I had written anything on that piece of teletype paper I would most positively have not used the word 'war,'" he said, flatly denying not only Safford's recent testimony but his own at the Navy Inquiry. The original "winds" message setting up the code, he explained, did not specify "war," merely "strained relations" with America, England or Russia.

"What country do you recall, if you do recall, was involved, in the one you recall?"

"To the best of my belief it was England." He was quite sure it was "West wind, clear" and not "East wind, rain."

It was apparent when Kramer returned to the stand the next day that he had once more had his memory refreshed—perhaps by counsel, Richardson and Kaufman, or the Democrats. This time he retreated even further from Safford. "In the last few weeks, I have had occasion to see some interrogations conducted by General MacArthur's headquarters in Japan of high Japanese officials who were concerned with these broadcasts. In view of their statements that no such weather signal [a "winds" execute] was made, it is my present belief, in the light of my recollections on this matter, as well, that what I saw Friday morning in December before Pearl

Harbor was also a false alarm on this Winds system." This statement, reversing his avowal the day before that the message *was* a
genuine "winds" execute, caused a stir. Some were wondering why,
if he had known about MacArthur's interrogations of the Japanese
for several weeks, he hadn't mentioned them the day before. Others,
who knew about the interrogations, wondered why he did not add
that these same Japanese officials also denied even setting up a
"winds" code. Kramer's next words added to the mystery. "It was,
nevertheless, definitely my conception at the time that it was an
authentic broadcast of that nature. I am still of that opinion, that
it used that precise wording, keeping in mind, as I indicated this
morning, that my recollections on that are that only one country
was involved." What did he mean? First he said that he presently
believed the message was a false alarm, and now he implied it was
not.

"What country was that?" asked Cooper.

"To the best of my recollection, it was England."

He became irascible under cross-examination and turned openly
irate when asked if anyone had tried to get him to change the testimony he had given at the Navy Inquiry. "There never was any
such person," Kramer exclaimed, denying the charges that Sonnett
had put pressure on him.

"Have you ever been 'beset and beleaguered'?" asked Murphy,
referring to Keefe's charge after an earlier visit to Kramer at
Bethesda Hospital.

"At no time," said Kramer sharply, "have I been beset and
beleaguered."

"Did anyone 'badger' you?"

"That statement, sir, is false," he said.

He was equally upset when Cooper asked if he felt the General
Staffs of the Army and Navy were crooks or would "frame" Kimmel or anyone else. "Such phenomena are inconceivable to my
mind."

That evening Kramer listened to radio commentator Fulton
Lewis, Jr.'s broadcast in which he referred to Kramer's testimony
as "very irate," "antagonistic" and "reluctant." The following
morning he was chastened, prefacing his testimony with an apology. "It may well be that he [Lewis] is accurate in this regard,

inasmuch as I left this witness chair at 5 P.M. yesterday afternoon, after testifying for approximately six hours, with a slight headache, undoubtedly due to the fact that I am somewhat out of condition physically. Mr. Chairman, my effort has been to be as objective and cooperative with this committee as I possibly could. In pursuance of this policy I have been as truthful as I could. . . . If I have created any impression of irrationalism, antagonism or reluctance, I feel I am under obligation to apologize to this committee and assure the members that my only intention in tone of voice or manner was emphasis on points I was making. I will endeavor to amend my tone and manner during further inquiry."

He proceeded to apologize to Keefe for a gruff remark during the discussion on his stay at Bethesda Hospital. Keefe good-naturedly said no apology was called for.

During the afternoon session Kramer produced what the Washington *Times-Herald* described as "new fireworks" by producing from a little black satchel a hitherto secret letter which Kimmel had written to Halsey four months before the opening of the Navy Inquiry. In this letter Kimmel asked his fellow admiral to have Kramer answer a list of enclosed questions about the "winds" execute and other matters, and sign an affidavit. "I will assure him that I will make no use of the affidavit without his permission so long as he is alive."

Kramer testified that after Halsey showed him the letter he did promise to write the affidavit, then changed his mind and, instead, wrote a memorandum for Admiral Halsey setting down what he recollected and asking for Halsey's advice. Keefe strode over to the witness chair to look at the memorandum to the accompaniment of photographers' flash bulbs. It was mighty funny, he said, that Kramer had been allowed to disclose "at the tail end of this examination, what appears to be a very important and vital instrument which has been in the possession of the Navy and no one knew anything about it. Now how are we ever going to be sure unless these things are going to be turned over to our counsel in advance, what facts there are? I haven't read it, I don't know what is in it, but it seems to me, if we are to believe what Captain Kramer says, that it represents his idea as to what the facts were when he wrote this in the spring of 1944."

Kramer then revealed that he had had no intention of introducing the Safford letters or that day's material into the hearing until they were specifically requested. Ferguson was angry. "Now, is there any doubt, from now on, Captain, that you are going to give the truth, the whole truth, and nothing but?"

Kramer related that he had taken the memorandum to Halsey, who read it and handed it back. "I thought about it in fact all through the summer of 1944, and it was only after my testimony before Admiral Murfin's court of inquiry that I felt no further necessity of even thinking about that. I simply kept those papers with me."

"And up to the time you testified before Admiral Murfin's court of inquiry you had been giving a lot of thought to this question?" asked Keefe.

Only to what disposition he could make of the papers. "Not to the subject matter of that piece of paper."

"You were satisfied that the statements which you made in this memorandum prepared out there in the South Pacific were the truth?"

"Yes, sir, as of that time." He had not read the memorandum since he prepared it for Halsey.

"You mean you have had it in your possession all this time, and you haven't read it until now?" Keefe was incredulous.

"I have not read it to this moment, sir."

The committee adjourned to the Judiciary Committee room for an executive session. They decided not to put the memorandum in the record because of security; and later declined to reveal their decision to the press. They did announce that they might hold night sessions, in view of the surprising developments, with the aim still to wind up the inquiry by February 15.

The following morning, Saturday the ninth, Keefe read Kramer's testimony at the Navy Inquiry. When questioned which Japanese words were used in the message Kramer had replied: "*Higashi no kaze ame*, I am quite certain. The literal meaning of *Higashi no kaze ame* is East wind, rain. That is plain Japanese language. The sense of that, however, meant strained relations or a break in relations, possibly even implying war with a nation to the eastward, the United States."

And now, asked Keefe, the captain was testifying that the Japanese words in the message were not *Higashi no kaze ame?*

"No words referring to the United States."

"Well," asked Keefe, "were there any words at all in it that you remember?"

"Yes, sir," he said, but when asked if he remembered what the words were said, "I do not, sir."

Keefe was skeptical. "Now, you, as the man in charge of translations of these messages, with the knowledge that the whole government was set up to pick up this very vital and important message, who handled that message, who saw it, who read it, who checked the interpretation of the watch officer on that message, sit here before us today, and say you can't tell us what that message said, you have no recollection of what it said at all; is that correct?"

"That is correct, sir. However, I would like to point out to you, Mr. Keefe, that I think that an entirely unwarranted emphasis and importance is being attributed to that message, not only in this hearing but in past hearings, and in the press." This had been the thesis of Mitchell, who successfully passed it on to Richardson. And now Kramer had accepted it as his own.

Later that afternoon the decision to withhold the memorandum Kramer had written to Halsey was reversed. With the exception of one question, it was introduced into the record. Its importance lay in the fact that it represented Kramer's best memory of the "winds" execute in 1944 after much thought. Kramer now testified that he later showed the memorandum to Admiral Wilkinson, Captain Rochefort and a Marine colonel in charge of the Far Eastern Section of Naval Intelligence. The three occasions had occurred from December 6, 1945, to January 9, 1946. Yet Kramer insisted he himself had never reread it.

Brewster, who had been conducting this inquiry, was equally skeptical. "Do you expect that it can be credited that during this month that elapsed from December 6 to January 9, during this period when you were showing these papers to three different men because of your very great concern, apparently, over your name being used in connection with this, asking your friend the captain about it, and asking for an interview with the colonel, that during all that period you never once examined, yourself, this memorandum which you present here now?"

"I did not, Senator."

"You realize how difficult it is for anyone to credit a statement of that sort, Captain, when you were really disturbed, that you never examined this paper which you present?"

"By 'examine,' if you mean to infer that I read this paper, I did not." He repeated, "I did not." Credulity was further stretched when the distraught Kramer said, "I have, without question, looked at certain points that I may have pointed out or that they may have pointed out. I do not believe that that occurred, though, sir, I think in each case, Senator, there was practically no conversation throughout this paper."

"You were taking this to them without a statement of the background, and your recollection and your action?" asked Brewster with utter disbelief. "We are going to recess over the weekend. I wish you would ponder that question, from the standpoint of the difficulties which we face. I can see no reason why you should not have examined it. I do not think you would be subject to any criticism if you had examined it. I have been amazed from the beginning that you insisted that you did not see it, that you base your entire present recollection on the refreshment you received with officers who examined that document; that under those circumstances it must have seemed proper for you to refresh your recollection from something you wrote more than a year and a half ago in Noumea. I think it would make it far easier for us to credit your story if we could believe you examined that paper at some time in the last month."

On Monday morning Brewster was unable to attend and the questioning was taken over by Ferguson. He said he would give Kramer the opportunity to explain what had been left up in the air over the weekend. Kramer said he had pondered Brewster's request and would like to read a statement. It went on so long and was so diffuse that Richardson was visibly impatient. And when Kramer began reading from his own diary, the chief counsel interrupted. "Is there any need of carrying this on?" The only question that had been asked by Senator Brewster "was the question of keeping this memorandum in your possession without reading it." Kramer tried to explain why he had been so long-winded. "Go ahead," said Richardson. "Get through with it."

Now Murphy protested. "Mr. Chairman, in fairness to the witness, the senator from Maine did ask him to ponder."

The vice chairman was also impatient. "Go ahead, Captain," he said.

"In November last year my wife came to Washington from Miami and remained with me until our departure on November 14 for Miami. On my return alone to Washington in early December to await the pleasure of this committee I determined to keep notes in some detail of my activities, people I met, old acquaintances seen again, and so forth, so that on my expected return to Miami for the Christmas holidays she could read them over and I would thus be able to acquaint her of the above in detail without depending on memory alone." He went on and on and finally answered Brewster's question in a long, tangled sentence swearing that he had definitely *not* read the memorandum. More than half an hour had been taken up to arrive at an explanation which by no means satisfied the minority. Even some neutral observers were finding their credulity taxed. The question to most observers now was who was more likely to be telling the truth about the "winds" execute—Kramer or the quixotic Laurance Safford? Late that afternoon it was announced that the latter, in ceremonies at the Navy Department, had been awarded the Legion of Merit for "exceptionally meritorious conduct" in cryptographic research from March 1942 to September 1945. "A dynamic leader combining strong purpose and creative imagination with a profound knowledge of mechanical and electrical science and their cryptographic applications, Captain Safford was the driving force behind the development of the perfected machines which today give the United States Navy the finest system of encipherment in the world." He had, read the citation, "contributed essentially to the successful prosecution of the war." It was a shocking rebuff to those attempting to discredit and demean Safford, and indicated there were men in high naval posts who not only regarded him highly but openly supported him.

In his broadcast that night Fulton Lewis, Jr., said, "The net significance of the whole thing is a practical demonstration that the Navy has nothing against Captain Safford for what he has said before the Pearl Harbor Committee. . . . A gorgeous gesture, on very high ground, indeed, and it calls for a bow of respect to the Navy officials who were broad-minded enough to do it."

The Democratic members of the committee were indignant at the award and suggested that Kramer be granted "some medal of higher dignity than that which was given to Captain Safford."

Chapter Twelve

"TO THROW AS SOFT A
LIGHT AS POSSIBLE ON
THE WASHINGTON SCENE"

1.

On Lincoln's birthday a far different breed of witness appeared. Lieutenant Colonel Henry C. Clausen was not at all daunted by the committee and its battery of counsel. A lawyer himself, he faced cross-examination with refreshing cockiness. When it was suggested that Stimson and the War Department had meant him to "slant" his one-man investigation, he bridled. "No, sir. I would not have conducted it if they had." Were there instructions that he should in any way attempt to have a witness change his evidence? "No, sir," briskly.

A query from Ferguson on the pre-war American agreement with the British, Chinese and Dutch was revelatory. Clausen said that an investigation of this nature "would lead to the White House and I was told that it was beyond the scope of my functions to investigate there."

The next day Clausen talked frankly about his relationship with Stimson, whom he admired greatly. "When you made your investigation," asked Ferguson, "did you ever look into his diary?"

"No, sir."

"Why not?"

"Well, you mean I should investigate the investigator? That would be like the grand jury investigating the grand jury. You told him to do the job. If you wanted somebody else to investigate Stimson you should have said so in the law."

On February 14 Clausen assured Gearhart that he had been "as free as the wind as to what I could do so far as uncovering evidence was concerned. I mean by that, Mr. Gearhart, and I want you to believe this, there was no compulsion, no restraint, nothing put upon me except that in which I agreed."

During the day Senator Lucas read Keefe's statement in the House the previous November that Clausen "at the instigation of the War Department and Secretary of War" had apparently "browbeat" Colonel Bratton into signing an affidavit changing his previous testimony.

Then Lucas turned to Clausen, a man of average size. "What I want to specifically know is whether or not you browbeat this 225-pound Colonel here into giving evidence that was other than what he considered at that time the truth."

It was a comical concept from a physical aspect.

"No, sir."

The next witness was the burly Bratton, who had first made a statement to the Army Board that he had delivered the thirteen-part message to Bedell Smith and General Gerow. Now, under the grilling of the associate general counsel, Samuel Kaufman, Bratton was trying to explain why he had changed his testimony to Clausen. "This is the point at which my memory begins to go bad on me. I cannot state positively whether there was any delivery made that night or not at this time. . . . At the time when I made the statement to the Grunert Board I had not remembered, or I did not remember, that Colonel Dusenbury was working with me in the office that night." Since making the statement to the Army Board Clausen had shown him affidavits from Bedell Smith and Gerow denying that they had received the thirteen-part message that Saturday night. "Now, I know all these men. I do not doubt the honesty and integrity of any one of them, and if they say that I did not deliver these pouches to them that night, then my memory must have been at fault."

It was odd that after such abasement he was preparing to challenge Marshall himself. Just before leaving Berlin to testify at the hearings, he had vowed to his friend, Colonel Heimlich, that he was going "to blow the roof off that inquiry!"

He began by testifying that it was Marshall who, sometime in August 1941, had ordered him not to send Magic to the overseas theaters. But Bratton became so convinced by subsequent Magic messages that war was coming that he decided to take a chance and send a warning to Hawaii.

Then he produced the carefully wrapped package of photostats he had brought from Berlin; it was the long memorandum requested by Roosevelt on Japanese and German preparations for war from 1937 to Pearl Harbor. This was the report Bratton had discussed in 1943 with Colonel Yeaton, who had advised him to have the entire volume photostated at once and kept in a safe place.

Now at last he had nerved himself to reveal that Marshall personally had deleted vital portions of the memorandum. One stricken part dated 1937 was read aloud by Ferguson:

" 'There is a possibility, fantastic as it may seem, that Japan contemplates military action against Great Britain in the Orient at a time when she is involved in Europe, with the idea of seizing Hong Kong and Singapore, and ultimately acquiring the Dutch oil fields and control of trade routes to the Orient . . . it is not improbable that this country will be compelled to apply the Neutrality Act and ultimately become involved.'

"Now who struck that out of the report?" asked Ferguson.

"To the best of my knowledge and belief it was stricken out by General Marshall in person."

"Well, now, will you tell us whether or not that was a false report that you had inserted in there or was it true?"

"The report was true to the best of our knowledge and belief and was based on intelligence that we had secured from various sources. . . . All of the items that were stricken out of this book, to the best of our knowledge and belief, were supported by documents now on file in G-2. . . . I may say this is a document that has been referred to a number of times by my chief, General Miles. He attempted to get this committee to take cognizance of this document on a number of occasions while he was testifying but nobody seemed to take an interest." He explained that the Far Eastern volume was supported by more than ten volumes of photostats of original documents on file in G-2.

Richardson ridiculed the entire matter. "Here is a review made by a person two years after Pearl Harbor. It is of no more importance than a review made by the Washington *Post* or the Chicago *Tribune.*" His equation of an official War Department report based on voluminous secret material with a newspaper review was ludicrous. Equally so was his misunderstanding of the seriousness of deleting material for the eyes of the President foreseeing war with Japan over a period of years from 1937, an action interpreted by Bratton to Yeaton as a cover-up by the Chief of Staff of the Army.

Not a single thing in the volume was fact, charged the chief counsel with some heat. "Everything is conclusion of this witness, historically, as to what happened. I don't care how many times it has been referred to here, but I am wondering as counsel how far the committee is going to go into the hindsight of some historian as to what the situation was at Pearl Harbor when we have all this trouble here trying to get foresight."

Murphy and Ferguson, usually antagonists, joined in pressing the issue. The former moved that Bratton be allowed to read a letter explaining the import of what had been stricken out of the volume. The colonel read a memorandum, dated August 26, 1943, for General George Strong, the Army Intelligence Chief.

> The attached tab does not comply with the directive in that it contains much material other than the MA reports. The Chief of Staff desires it to be revised to contain only MA reports.
>   By direction of the Chief of Staff
>   (signed)   W. T. Sexton
>   Colonel, General Staff
>   Secretary, General Staff

"Do I understand everything was stricken out except MA's?" asked Ferguson. "What is an MA? That is a military attaché?"

"Yes, sir," said Bratton. "The book was all torn to pieces by the Chief of Staff and everything deleted therefrom except the raw MA and MO reports, MO meaning military observer."

Asked for an example, Bratton read parts of a confidential lecture delivered to the faculty and students of the Army War College which gave the opinion of the Far Eastern Section as to the approaching war. He then gave other examples showing partial as well as total deletions in what he claimed was Marshall's own handwriting. "There are numerous comments on the margin, all through the book which I believe, and General Strong also believed, to have been made by General Marshall in person." Strong, he said, had told him this upon the return of the volume from the Chief of Staff in 1943.

There were no more questions from the committee. It was already after 10 P.M. The matter was dropped; and Bratton disappeared into obscurity.[1]

2.

Colonel Sadtler was the next witness. As bitter and disillusioned as Bratton, he also was determined to at last fight back. To the committee's surprise he reverted to the first testimony he had given the Army Board. Yes, he *had* told Gerow about the "winds" execute on December 5 and it undoubtedly meant a Japanese break with Britain and America. Then he *did* see Bedell Smith. "I said, 'The Winds message is in,' as I recall the wording."

"So you told him the Winds message was in," said Ferguson. "And did you ask him to get it to General Marshall, that word that it was in?"

"As I remember it, he asked me what I had done and I told him I had talked to General Miles and General Gerow. . . . He said he didn't care to discuss it further."

"What did that really mean, that he didn't want to discuss it further?"

[1] He retired in 1952, still a colonel, and moved to Hawaii. Six years later, an embittered man, he died at Tripler Army Hospital.

"That I was through. . . . Had done as much as I could possibly do."

". . . Did he say as to whether or not he would convey this to General Marshall?"

"No, sir."

"Then, I assume, you thought your mission had been performed, when you told them that the Winds message was in?"

"I think I had gone a little too far in talking to either General Gerow or Colonel Bedell Smith."

Had Sadtler considered it was a genuine message? Yes. "So far as you were concerned, the Winds message was in and it meant war."

"Yes, sir." He also verified that, before the rebuff from both Gerow and Smith, he had prepared a warning message to Hawaii, Panama and the Philippines that read:

> Reliable information indicates war with Japan in the very near future Stop Take every precaution to prevent a repetition of Port Arthur Stop Notify the Navy. Marshall.

"And you did it because of the mounting tension and flow of information which you had together with the Winds Execute at that time?" asked Ferguson.

Yes, but the message was never sent. "I did not show it to anyone. I do not know where the message is now, and I made no copy at the time."

This was the testimony that Sadtler had given to the Army Board and then, after being confronted by written denials from Gerow and Smith, had reversed to Clausen. Keefe asked for a clarification of the confusing double reverse. Did Sadtler now mean to tell the committee "positively and without question" that he was challenging the denials of Gerow and Smith?

"Absolutely," said Sadtler. "I talked to both of them." This unequivocal statement was not only an attack on the credibility of Gerow and Smith but a covert admission that Sadtler had reversed himself to Clausen out of fear of opposing the Army hierarchy.

He also declared that the "winds" intercept "was the most important message that I think I ever handled in my life." Murphy challenged its importance. After the messages that preceded it, what exactly did the "winds" message do? "It capped the climax," said Sadtler.

"In what way?"

"That everything is here. Now we have the whole thing. . . . Now, there was nothing but the Winds message, which was a message that we had been straining every nerve to get; we had everybody listening for that message."

The dramatics provided by Bratton and Sadtler were surpassed by revelations from the surprise naval witness who followed. He was Commander Lester Robert Schulz, who had taken a message to Roosevelt on the night of December 6, 1941.

In late November 1945, after a request by Ferguson to locate witnesses who had been at the White House, the Navy Pearl Harbor Liaison group, headed by Commander John Ford Baecher, had requested that Schulz, chief engineer of the U.S.S. *Indiana* docked at Puget Sound Navy Yard, Bremerton, Washington, be ordered for temporary duty in connection with the congressional investigation. Since Schulz was needed at Bremerton, it was decided to retain him on the West Coast until the committee was ready for him to testify. A week later Commander Baecher telephoned Schulz and learned that he had been on watch at the White House on Pearl Harbor eve; and that he had received the thirteen-part message delivered by Kramer at about 9:30 P.M. Schulz revealed that he had personally carried the message to the President and stood by while he read it.

Having spent the night of February 14 on board a Navy transport plane from San Francisco, Schulz had slept very little. He arrived in the capital about 9 A.M. to be met by a Navy officer who took him to the Navy Department where he talked briefly with Commander Baecher. Schulz had been reading about the hearings and disagreed completely with any innuendoes that the President could have known in advance of the Japanese attack. Not yet being aware of the significance of the Magic messages, he didn't feel that he had much to offer as a witness.

As Schulz entered the caucus room, Keefe was winding up his interrogation of Sadtler. Informed that Schulz had arrived, Ferguson hurriedly escorted him to the reception room of the Judi-

ciary Committee for a short talk. When Ferguson returned to his
seat he leaned over and whispered to Greaves, "This is it!"

After Schulz met Richardson, whom he did not then know, he
was brought into the caucus room. The appearance of the mystery
witness kindled interest and the explosion of flash bulbs surprised
the young commander.

Richardson asked if Schulz recalled Captain Kramer coming to
the White House on the evening of December 6 to deliver some
papers.

"He handed them to me," said Schulz. "They were in a locked
pouch. . . . I took it from the mail room, which is in the office
building, over to the White House proper and obtained permission to go up on the second floor and took it to the President's
study." An usher announced him and left. "The President was
there seated at his desk and Mr. Hopkins was there. . . . I informed the President that I had the material which Captain
Kramer had brought and I took it out of the pouch." As Schulz
recalled, Mr. Roosevelt was expecting the material. There was a
hush of expectation in the room. Schulz's open, bright face
radiated credibility. The committee members listened in rapt silence. "The President read the papers, which took perhaps ten
minutes." Then he handed them to Hopkins, who had been slowly
pacing back and forth. "Mr. Hopkins then read the papers and
handed them back to the President. The President then turned toward Mr. Hopkins and said in substance—I am not sure of the
exact words, but in substance—'This means war.' "

There was an excited murmur, a stirring of chairs. Several photographers moved within a few feet of Schulz and began taking
pictures. Startled by the flash bulbs, Schulz wondered what the excitement was about. The photographers, under orders to take no
pictures once testimony began, were reprimanded and Murphy
told Schulz to relax.

"Mr. Hopkins agreed," he continued, "and they discussed then,
for perhaps five minutes, the situation of the Japanese forces, that
is, their deployment and—"

"Can you recall what either of them said?" asked Richardson.

"In substance I can. There are only a few words that I can
definitely say I am sure of, but the substance of it was that—I be-

lieve Mr. Hopkins mentioned it first—that since war was imminent, that the Japanese intended to strike when they were ready, at a moment when all was most opportune for them—"

In the excitement, Barkley could not hear. "When all was what?"

"When all was most opportune for them. That is, when their forces were most properly deployed for their advantage. Indochina in particular was mentioned, because the Japanese forces had already landed there and there were implications of where they should move next. The President mentioned a message that he had sent to the Japanese Emperor concerning the presence of Japanese troops in Indochina, in effect requesting their withdrawal. Mr. Hopkins then expressed a view that since war was undoubtedly going to come at the convenience of the Japanese, it was too bad that we could not strike the first blow and prevent any sort of surprise. The President nodded and then said, in effect, 'No, we can't do that. We are a democracy and a peaceful people.' Then he raised his voice, and this much I remember definitely. He said, 'But we have a good record.' The impression that I got was that we would have to stand on that record, we could not make the first overt move. We would have to wait until it came."

Schulz heard no mention of Pearl Harbor. "The time at which war might begin was not discussed, but from the manner of the discussion there was no indication that tomorrow was necessarily the day. I carried that impression away because it contributed to my personal surprise when the news did come."

Neither Roosevelt nor Hopkins mentioned sending any further warning or alert to overseas posts. "However, having concluded this discussion about the war going to begin at the Japanese convenience, then the President said that he believed he would talk to Admiral Stark. He started to get Admiral Stark on the telephone." The President, so recalled the commander, was told by the telephone operator that Stark could be reached at the National Theater "and the President went on to state, in substance, that he would reach the admiral later, that he did not want to cause public alarm by having the admiral paged or otherwise when in the theater, where I believe, the fact that he had a box reserved was mentioned and that if he had left suddenly he would surely have been seen because of the position which he held and undue alarm might be caused, and the President did not wish that to happen because he could get him within perhaps another half an hour in any case."

"Was there anything said about telephoning anybody else except Stark?"

"No, sir, there was not."

"How did he refer to Admiral Stark?"

"When he first mentioned calling him, he referred to him as 'Betty.'"

Schulz had made an excellent impression on all the members of the committee as well as the observers. No one doubted that he was telling the truth. As he left the room no reporters or photographers followed. They were busy with the next witness. He left alone but was soon invited by Admiral Noyes to ride with him back to the main Navy Building. Schulz was glad the ordeal was over and still couldn't understand why there had been so much excitement. It was an uneasy ride. He was somewhat in awe of the admiral and did not feel comfortable conversing with him. Schulz was also somewhat concerned about his recent testimony. Had the committee really understood Roosevelt? After all, there was a big difference between feeling war was imminent and expecting it to begin with an attack on Pearl Harbor. So much could be inferred from the tone of voice. The President, for instance, had said, "This means war," calmly without emotion. Could he possibly have unwittingly harmed the President, whom he admired and held in high esteem?

3.

Five days later, after uneventful interrogations of eleven more witnesses, the hearings were suspended. "The committee had some differences with respect to procedure," commented peacemaker Barkley in closing, "but these differences were no doubt inherent in the situation; but they have not been too serious. . . . I might say that the committee and counsel have a vast amount of work yet to do before we get our report ready for the Congress, and I am sure we will pursue that phase of this task with the same diligence and I hope the great thoroughness with which we have concluded the hearing." Whereupon, at 5:15 P.M., February 20, the committee adjourned, subject to call of the Chair. The committee now had until June 1 to assess the evidence it had received and prepare their report.

Over a period of three months and five days there had been sixty-seven days and three nights of public hearings. The testimony of thirty-nine witnesses comprised almost 14,000 pages. Even so, many witnesses deemed important by the minority were not called. These included Bedell Smith, Forrestal, the judge advocates of the Army and Navy who had instigated the Clausen and Hewitt investigations, Marshall's orderlies and two top State Department Far East advisers, Maxwell Hamilton and Stanley Hornbeck. The latter, sent off recently to Holland as ambassador, had more to say about the Pacific Fleet than the Navy itself, according to Admiral Richardson's testimony. Hull was not recalled for Republican cross-examination on medical grounds, and Secretary of War Stimson had a heart attack the day it was announced he was to be summoned.

"The Congressional Pearl Harbor investigation, one of the longest and most extraordinary in the history of any country," commented William S. White in the New York *Times*, "closed this week, but the fog of doubt and accusation that has hung so long about that disaster has been dispelled only in part."

The day was marked by a tragedy involving an important witness. That morning Vice Admiral Theodore Wilkinson, former head of Navy Intelligence, drove a borrowed Cadillac sedan off the ferry *West Point* at Norfolk. As the car rolled down the port side at about twenty miles an hour, a deckhand, Luke Piland, shouted, "Stop that car, man, you're driving too fast!" Piland threw a block beneath a wheel of the car but the Cadillac went over this obstruction, crashed through the forward chain and gate to plunge into the Elizabeth River. Piland saw the admiral bent over the wheel. ("I thought he would open the door and make a leap out," he later testified. "He never did straighten up any more.")

As the car hit the water, Wilkinson shouted to his wife to open her window. She did and was halfway through when the car sank. She surfaced and was rescued, but a diver found the admiral's body stuck behind the wheel. Wilkinson was still clutching the steering post. His window was wide open. "He died at the peak of his career," said Secretary of the Navy Forrestal. "There goes with him on his last journey the heartfelt 'well done' of all hands."

The freak accident sparked rumors that Wilkinson had committed suicide because he had defied the military hierarchy during his earlier testimony to the committee. He, it will be recalled, had insisted there had been messages indicating the Japanese feared the Purple code had been compromised—and then produced eleven intercepts which Marshall and others had testified did not exist.

Some supporters of Safford reasoned that, being a man of honor, Wilkinson had not been able to live with the fact that he had not come forward with the truth about the "winds" execute. Safford himself believed this. Referring to the October 1941 Mutiny on the Second Deck, he wrote, "Wilkinson was the only decent one in the lot, the only one to show any remorse." The Wilkinsons had been close friends of the Saffords and, after the tragic incident at Norfolk, the admiral's widow had come to Mrs. Safford to accuse her husband of "causing Ping's death" by his dogged persistency in the Pearl Harbor controversy.

A Naval Board of Investigation, after a thorough inquiry, concluded that his drowning was accidental "and was not the result of his own misconduct, and that his death was not caused in any manner by the intent, fault, negligence or inefficiency of any person in the naval service."

By late March Baecher reported to Forrestal that Seth Richardson had submitted a draft of a proposed report concluding that "Washington must bear a large share of the burden for what occurred on 7 December 1941." However, his assistant, Sam Kaufman,[2] would submit a draft "more in keeping with the views of the Democrats. It places the primary responsibility for the Pearl Harbor disaster on the command in Hawaii, chiefly because of failure to take reconnaissance and other action after receipt of the war warning message."

[2] Kaufman further demonstrated his pro-Administration sympathies during the first trial of Alger Hiss.

A few days later there was a surprise move. George Marshall, recently returned from China, was summoned to another session at the caucus room. He and Stark arrived on the morning of April 11. The admiral still could not remember where he was on the night of December 6 despite testimony that he had been at the National Theater attending a performance of *The Student Prince*. "It does not ring any bell with me that I was there that night, but I can assume, in view of the testimony of Commander Schulz and of others who tried to contact me, and my remembrance of having seen the revival, that I probably was there." Nor did he recall getting any telephone message later that night from the President.

On May 23 written answers to questions by the minority to Hull and Stimson were entered in the record. The latter responded only to those questions he felt worth answering. At twelve-fifteen the work was finished and Barkley announced that the record of the investigation was now officially closed. The inquiry, editorialized the New York *Times*, "has ended as it began on a note of Republican suspicion," and it seemed inevitable that a "majority report and a minority report—along strictly party lines—will be written."

But there was the one final dramatic surprise in this inquiry of surprises. On May 25 Captain Harold Krick and his wife had dinner with their old friends, the Starks. Krick had been the admiral's flag lieutenant and the Starks had treated the Krick children as if they were grandchildren. As the admiral was carving he casually mentioned how happy he was that the hearings were over at last. But one thing bothered him. He hadn't been able to tell the committee where he was on the night of December 6.

"Well, we know," said Krick. "We were with you at dinner; and then we went to the National Theater." The Kricks both reminded Stark that after the show the President had called. They would never forget it.

Stark did recall the dinner party and the show but, although he racked his mind far into the night, the Roosevelt telephone call remained a blank. The more he thought about his previous testimony the more convinced he became "that the committee should have this, the record should have it straight, and I got up around two or three in the morning, thinking this thing over. . . ." He wrote a letter to Barkley in longhand stating that he wanted this new evidence placed before the committee.

Five of the members of the committee were out of town but, since Stark was scheduled to leave for London on May 31 to receive a decoration, Barkley called an emergency meeting for 10 A.M. of that day in Room 312 of the Senate Office Building. Only Barkley, George and Lucas were present. Keefe promised to come later but the others were unavailable.

"Admiral," said Richardson, "if the President had told you in his talk with you that night, assuming that you talked to him, and had told you that it was his opinion that this thirteen-part message meant war, thereby impressed you with his serious estimate of it, what would have been, in accordance with your custom, the action for you to have then taken, with that information?"

"I don't know, sir, that I would have, that we would have sent anything more. I think that I should have gotten in touch with Ingersoll and with Turner. . . . We thought, and the President knew every move we had made, that we had sent everything possible, on that premise, that war was in the immediate offing. I don't know that I would have done anything. I couldn't say."

At last Keefe arrived. He was disturbed and unhappy at the last-minute notice. Barkley explained that the admiral was leaving for London that night and it wasn't right merely to file his letter with the committee. "I raised the question," said Keefe, "because I had understood that the hearings had, by action of the committee, been closed, and that the testimony had been closed, and I want to keep the record clear, in the absence of my colleagues, none of whom are present here this morning."

After Krick was duly sworn by the chairman, he told about the dinner, the theater and the return to the Stark home.

"What occurred when you went into his house?" asked Richardson.

"One of the admiral's servants advised the admiral that—"

"What did he say?"

"That there had been a White House call during the evening, sir. . . . The admiral excused himself and retired to his study on the second floor and returned."

"How long was he there?"

"I would say approximately between five and ten minutes."
Then he came downstairs.

"Did he say anything to you?"

"Only to the extent that the conditions in the Pacific were serious; that was the substance of it, that conditions with Japan were in a critical state, something of that sort, sir."

"Did he say anything to you, as near as you can recall, that he had had a telephone message, on the second floor?"

"That is my inference. There is absolutely no doubt in my mind about it, sir. But I do not recall the exact statement. I do not recall that he stated, 'I have talked with the President of the United States.' But I heard, of course, the statement of the servant that there had been a White House call, and the admiral retired immediately, and he may have stated that he was going to call the White House; but I have the distinct impression that the conversation was with the White House." Did he have any impression that upon his return from upstairs Admiral Stark made any statement that his talk had been with the White House? "My impression very definitely was that; yes, sir."[3]

The interrogation was accelerated with only Lucas asking a few questions, and at 11:15 A.M. the committee adjourned, this time for good. What would have been a sensational revelation several months earlier was interred by exasperation and a desire by all parties to make an end to the matter. And so the hearings ended not with a bang but a whimper.

4.

Besides the two memoranda submitted by Richardson and Kaufman there were two others designed to assist the committee in making its report. One, by assistant counsel John Masten, concentrated on the diplomatic phase and echoed the opinions of the Democrats; the second, by another assistant counsel, Edward P. Morgan,[4] also represented the Administration's viewpoint.

These last two memoranda displeased the four Republicans. And when Barkley told reporters, after a lengthy closed session on

[3] In an interview with the author his wife confirmed the impression.
[4] Morgan later wrote the Tydings Committee report, described by Republicans as a whitewash of the State Department.

July 6, ". . . my hope is that we can make a unanimous report," Keefe announced that he was positive there would be more than one report.

Within a week a majority report based on the Morgan memorandum was concluded. But there were important modifications. Morgan had stated, "Indeed, had the keen awareness of Japanese deceit and beastiality voiced by the Secretary of State characterized thinking elsewhere, the disaster of Pearl Harbor as we know it might never have occurred." This was changed to "The President, the Secretary of State, and high Government officials made every possible effort, without sacrificing our national honor and endangering our security to avert war with Japan."

Morgan's flat statement that the disaster was the failure of "the Army and Navy in Hawaii" was modified by the removal of the words "in Hawaii." Again where Morgan charged that Kimmel and Short "were fully conscious of the danger from air attack," the final report read, "Officers, both in Washington and Hawaii, were fully conscious of the danger from air attack."

On July 16 the violently anti-Administration columnist, John T. Flynn, received a startling telephone call from a Washington correspondent: Congressman Gearhart was about to join the majority in its report.

Flynn immediately wrote Gearhart that he was profoundly shocked.

> I earnestly hope there is no truth in the somewhat round-about rumor that came to me, but it was enough to surprise and grieve me. Recalling so many of the things that you said during the hearings, I simply could not credit it. . . . I would be horrified beyond expression if I could be made to believe that you had changed your mind after so much that you said appears in the record itself, to take part with these fellows in the job they were appointed to perform and which apparently they are now about to complete.
>
> If I could believe this rumor that has come to me to be true, it would help to explain so much that has happened to this country and the Republican Party in the last dozen years. I begin to tremble for the fate of this country.

Flynn wrote Keefe about the rumor. "It confirmed what you told me yourself and I was so greatly disturbed that I wrote

The Army Pearl Harbor Board was simultaneously convening. The members were equally appalled by similar evidence. Moreover, two of General Marshall's closest subordinates, Colonel (later General) Bedell Smith (left) and Brigadier General Leonard Gerow (right) were involved in controversial testimony. Consequently the Army Board also reversed the Roberts findings, placing much more blame on Marshall than on Short. *(National Archives)*

James Forrestal, successor to Knox as Secretary of the Navy, put an endorsement on the Navy Inquiry report repudiating its findings. Secretary of War Stimson did the same to the Army's report. *(National Archives)*

Tyler Kent, right, in Russia prior to transfer to London as a code officer in the American Embassy. He was imprisoned by the British in 1940 for possession of secret Roosevelt-Churchill messages. *(Tyler Kent)*

Mrs. Anne Kent worked tirelessly to free her son. The revelation that he was still in a British prison caused a stir during Roosevelt's campaign for the presidency in 1944. *(Tyler Kent)*

Vice-President Harry S. Truman also inserted himself into the campaign controversy by implying in *Collier's* that Short and Kimmel were not on speaking terms prior to the Pearl Harbor attack; and he made the false statement that at no time did "Admiral Kimmel ask or receive information as to the manner in which the Army was discharging its highly important duty." Kimmel wrote Truman for a correction of the mis-statements but never received a reply. *(National Archives)*

THE INVESTIGATIONS, 1945–46

In a special investigation conducted by Vice Admiral Henry Hewitt, Captain Safford charged that he was pressed to repudiate his previous testimony about the "East wind, rain" message. Captain Alwin Kramer, who had supported Safford in the Navy Inquiry, did reverse his testimony. *(Naval History)*

Marshall testifying on December 6, 1945. The table for the congressional committee is perpendicular to Marshall. Percy Greaves (extreme left), chief researcher for the Republicans, leans over to confer with Senator Homer Ferguson. Next to Ferguson, almost obscured, is the other Republican senator on the committee, Owen Brewster. *(Wide World)*

Rear view. Behind Marshall are General Short's counsel (hand to face), the general, and Counselor Rugg. Extreme right center, Admiral Kimmel leans back. Both Short and Kimmel show their disbelief of Marshall's testimony. *(Wide World)*

Republican Congressman Frank Keefe chats amiably with Marshall, but moments later his aggressive cross-examination puts the general on the defensive. *(National Archives)*

Marshall insists he cannot remember where he was on the night before Pearl Harbor. Investigators failed to check the December 7, 1941, issue of the Washington *Times Herald.*

Percy Greaves with Senator Ferguson (left) and Senator Brewster (right). Greaves causes a tempest in a teapot on December 10 by smiling at something Democratic Senator Scott Lucas says. "I would like to know who the gentleman is," storms Lucas, "and what right he has to sit alongside of the committee table and chuckle at a member of the United States Senate." *(Wide World)*

At last, in early January 1946, General Short, weakened by illness, has his day in court. As he tells how his old friend of thirty-nine years, George Marshall, advised him "to stand pat," tears come to Short's eyes. "I told him I would place myself entirely in his hands, having faith in his judgment." Until mid-1944 Short had regarded Marshall as his friend. Then Kimmel told him about the intercepted messages. "Short, Marshall is your enemy. Haven't you found that out yet? He is doing everything he can to double-cross you and has been right from the very beginning." *(National Archives)*

Chief Warrant Officer Ralph T. Briggs with his wife and her Seeing Eye dog. He told Captain Safford he had received the controversial "East wind, rain" message a few days before the attack. Briggs offered to testify at the hearings but was forbidden to do so by his commanding officer, who told him, "Maybe someday you'll understand the reason for this."

```
                                        M  2  DEC  41
                                        OPR-RS

FROM   REMARKS _ _ _ _ _ _ _ _ _ _ _ _ _ _   TIME_ _ _
                                        Ø4Ø2
                                        1243ØE

    RS  OFF  TO (RT.)
      COPY  PRESS  SKDS  HR  ON(SEE        Ø5ØØ
                        OTHER  LOGS)        12275
    RT  OFF  TO  SE                         13ØØ
```

Below Comments added on 12/5/60

> I, RALPH T. BRIGGS, NOW ON DUTY
> AT A NAVSEC GAUDET AS OINC, duly
> NOTE that all transmissions intercepted
> by me between 0500 thru 1300 on
> the above date are missing from these files &
> that these intercepts contained the
> "Winds message WARNING Code. My Operation
> SIGN WAS RT"
>
> RT

In 1960 Briggs, then officer in charge of all U. S. Navy World War II communications intelligence and cryptic archives, found what he believed to be his log sheet of the "East wind, rain" message. He felt he had no right to make a copy, but did write his comments on the bottom. At the request of the author, the classified Briggs material was released by the U. S. Navy.

Safford swears that his superiors ordered him to destroy all the notes he had made of the circumstances concerning the "East wind, rain" message (left). Other sensational revelations by Safford bring forth a savage, relentless cross-examination by Democratic Congressman John W. Murphy (right). "We haven't touched the real meat of this," the triumphant Murphy tells reporters after the session. "There's real, genuine tenderloin in it." The next day he continues his attack until Republican Keefe protests so eloquently that the onlookers spontaneously applaud. They do so twice more until rebuked by the chairman. *(Wide World)*

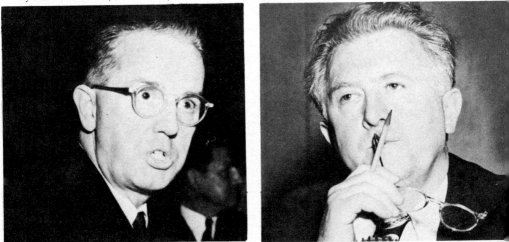

Safford chats with his friend Captain Kramer just before the latter testifies that there was no "East wind, rain" message. *(Wide World)*

mer Lieutenant Colonel Henry C. Clausen tes-
s that he had been "as free as the wind" in his
-man investigation for Stimson. He also denies
rges that he had browbeaten witnesses, including
onel Rufus Bratton, into changing their testi-
1y. *(Wide World)*

Colonel "Togo" Bratton admits he was not browbeaten by Clausen—and then reveals new testimony
damaging to his former chief, General Marshall.
(Wide World)

Commander Lester Robert Schulz—pictured ab
with his wife and child when he was communicati
assistant to Roosevelt's naval aide in 1941—caus
sensation on February 15 by revealing that on P
Harbor eve he had delivered an intercepted Japan
message to Roosevelt that caused him to say, "T
means war." *(Rear Admiral Schulz)*

Republican Congressman Bertrand Gearhart ca
consternation among the Republicans when he s
the Democratic findings. He did so, accordin;
Washington gossip, to save his seat in Congress
November. *(Wide World)*

Admiral Stark on a boat ride with the Krick family in
1939. On the last day of the hearings, Captain Harold
Krick testifies that he recalls Stark's telephoning the
President late evening of December 6, 1941. *(Harold
Krick, Jr.)*

On December 2 Lieutenant Ellsworth A. Hosner and his assistant, of 12th Naval District Intelligence, get cross bearings on mysterious signals in the Pacific. Figuring these might be from the missing Japanese carrier task force, they alert their chief, Captain Richard T. McCollough, a personal friend of the President. By December 6 the unidentified task force is tracked to a position approximately 400 miles north-northwest of Oahu. *(Seaman First Class Z)*

. A. Berndtson, Commodore of the Matson Fleet d captain of the luxury liner *Lurline*. His first assist nt radio operator, Leslie Grogan, picked up suspici s Japanese signals as the ship headed toward Hon ulu. *(Matson Navigation Co.)*

On December 3, 1941, the *Lurline* docks near the Aloha tower. Grogan and the chief operator walk the few blocks up Bishop Street to the downtown Intelligence office of the 14th Naval District and turn over their data to a naval officer. *(Matson Navigation Co.)*

Hosner's assistant, Seaman First Class Z, an electronics expert at twenty, had already designed a device being used on all U. S. Navy landing craft. *(Seaman First Class Z)*

Hosner's office on the seventh floor of 717 Market Street, San Francisco. *(Seaman First Class Z)*

On December 2, 1941, Captain Johan Ranneft, the Dutch naval attaché in Washington, is informed by U. S. Naval Intelligence that two Japanese carriers are proceeding east and are now about halfway between Japan and Hawaii. On December 6 Ranneft again visited the Office of Naval Intelligence and asked where the two Japanese carriers were. An officer put a finger on the wall chart some 300–400 miles northwest of Honolulu. Ranneft reported all this to his ambassador and to his superiors in London. (*Rear Admiral Johan Ranneft*)

Excerpt from Captain Ranneft's official diary, supplied to the author by the Historical Department of the Netherlands Ministry of Defense. After the U.S. officer pointed out the position of the carriers just northwest of Honolulu, Ranneft reports: "I ask what is the meaning of these carriers at this location: whereupon I receive the answer that it is probably in connection with Japanese reports of eventual American action. No one among us mentions the possibility of an attack on Honolulu. I myself do not think about it because I believe that everyone in Honolulu is 100 percent on the alert, just like everyone here at O.N.I."

2-12-41. Bespreking op Navy Dept, men wijst mij op de kaart de plaats van 2 Japanse carriers uit Japan vertrokken met Oostelijke koers.

3-12-41. Am. vloot te Balik Papan. Duitsland begint te verliezen. 's Avonds dinner Gezant bij in Honor of Secr. of the Navy Knox, aanwezig o.m. Senator Pepper, Walter Lippmann (journalist).

5-12-41. Bespreking op State Dept. van Kurusu en Nomura. Er is een gerucht, dat Am. zal aanvallen in beide gevallen:
1. Japan valt Thai aan.
2. Japan "beschermt" Thoi.

Zaterdag 6-12-41.
Te 0200 's morgens bespreking op Br.Ambassade met Admiral Danquest. Hij is juist terug van conferentie op Navy Dept. Men gelooft niet aan directe aanval van Japan nu, uitgezonderd Admiral Turner U.S.N., die een plotselinge Japanse aanval vreest op Manila.
Te 1400 naar Navy Dept., het departement is gesloten behalve de afdeling O.N.I., waar ook nachtwacht zal worden gedaan. Allen aanwezig op O.N.I. spreek Director Adm. Wilkinson, Capt. Mac Collum, LtCdr. Kramer. Krijg nadere gegevens omtrent Japanse eskaderbewegingen in Zuid Chinese Zee, Golf v. Siam. Men wijst mij - op mijn verzoek - de plaats aan van de 2 carriers (zie 2-12-41) beW. Honolulu. Ik vraag, wat het idee is van deze carriers op die plaats waarop geantwoord: vermoedelijk i.v.m. Japanse rapportage bij eventuele Amerikaanse actie Er is niemand van ons, die spreekt over een mogelijke vliegaanval op Honolulu. Ikzelf denk er niet eens over, omdat ik geloof, dat iedereen te Honolulu 100% on the alert is, zoals iedereen hier op O.N.I. Er heerst op O.N.I. een zeer gespannen stemming.
Te 1600 naar legatie.
's Avonds te 2100 conferentie bij Gezant - aan huis - met Mil Att. Weyerman. Verneem van Gezant, dat President rechtstreeks aan Mikado s zeinde teneinde conflict te voorkomen. Indien Maandag geen antwoord zou zijn gekomen, wordt toestand hoogst ernstig.
Te 2300 terug naar huis.

Soon after the war, Ranneft, now a rear admiral, is presented the Legion of Merit for outstanding service to the United States by Admiral Nimitz. *(Rear Admiral Johan Ranneft)*

NAVY DEPARTMENT

IMMEDIATE RELEASE
PRESS AND RADIO   AUGUST 21, 1946

REAR ADMIRAL JOHAN E.M. RANNEFT, ROYAL NETHERLANDS NAVY,
RECEIVES LEGION OF MERIT, DEGREE OF COMMANDER

Rear Admiral Johan Everhard Meijer Ranneft, Royal Netherlands Navy, today was presented the Legion of Merit, Degree of Commander, for outstanding service to the Government of the United States while on duty as Naval Attache at the Netherlands Embassy from December, 1941, to September, 1945. Fleet Admiral Chester W. Nimitz, U.S.N., Chief of Naval Operations, made the presentation at a ceremony in the Navy Department.

The text of the citation reads:

"For exceptionally meritorious conduct in the performance of outstanding services to the Government of the United States as Naval Attache of the Netherlands in Washington, D.C., from December 1941, to September 1945. Discharging his responsibilities with great skill and initiative, Rear Admiral Ranneft rendered invaluable assistance in prosecuting the war against our common enemy and in strengthening the holds of friendship and understanding between the Netherlands and the United States. His brilliant handling of many problems in connection with shipping control and the arming of merchant vessels was an important factor in the success of Allied operations in the Atlantic area, and his contributions to the development of Naval ordnance were of inestimable aid to ships of Allied Navies carrying out defensive and offensive measures against the enemy."

Rear Admiral Ranneft, who is continuing on duty as Naval Attache at the Netherlands Embassy, resides at 7114 Alaska Avenue, Northwest, Washington D.C.

(Photographs available, Pictorial Section, Office of Public Information).

In early December 1941 General Hein Ter Poorten, Commander of the Netherlands East Indies Army, informs Brigadier General Elliott Thorpe, the American Military Observer in Java, that a Japanese message in the consular code has just been intercepted informing their ambassador in Bangkok that attacks would soon be launched on Hawaii, the Philippines, Malaya and Thailand. The signal for war against the United States would be "East wind, rain." *(Netherlands Department of Defense)*

1943 General Albert C. Wedemeyer was told by ce Admiral Conrad E. L. Helfrich that the Dutch ew the Japanese were going to attack Pearl Harbor l that his government had warned the United tes. *(General A. C. Wedemeyer)*

Some of the Javanese students who helped Dutch Colonel J. A. Verkuhl and his wife solve the Japanese consular code. *(Karel Rink)*

General Thorpe (pictured here with MacArthur [center] in 1945) transmitted the full information from Ter Poorten to Washington. There is no record that this, or a second message, was ever received. No one ever admitted seeing them. A few days later Thorpe sent a third message through the American consul, but the latter omitted mentioning the location of the attacks and added that he "attached little or no importance" to the intercept. Thorpe sent out a fourth message a few days before the attack, which was acknowledged by Washington. He was ordered to send no more dispatches on the subject. The fourth message was found in War Department files, but the paragraph warning of the Hawaii attack was, curiously, deleted in transmission. *(General Elliott Thorpe)*

Early in December 1941 FBI agent Robert L. Shivers (seen here with Colonel Kendall Fielder, General Short's Intelligence officer) warned Lieutenant John A. Burns of the Honolulu police that Pearl Harbor was going to be attacked in a few days. *(Brigadier General Kendall Fielder)*

...ns, head of the Honolulu Espionage Bureau, later ...me three-time Governor of Hawaii. *(Mrs. John ...urns)*

In Cairo on December 6, 1941, Colonel Bonner F
lers (foreground), later MacArthur's Military Sec
tary, was told by the British Air Marshal in charge
the Middle East: "We have a secret signal Japan w
strike the United States in twenty-four hours." *(C*
lection of Mrs. Bonner Fellers)

At the emergency Cabinet meeting on the evening of
December 7, 1941, Secretary of Labor Frances Perkins
was extremely perturbed by the President's strange
uneasiness. "I had a deep emotional feeling that something was wrong, that this situation was not all it
appeared to be. . . . His surprise was not as great as the
surprise of the rest of us." *(National Archives)*

Gearhart. I did not, of course, mention that you had talked to me."

The news about Gearhart was true. Much more astounding was Keefe's signature on the majority report. He had signed after promises to alter other Morgan conclusions. Whereas Morgan had found that Hawaii had been "adequately and properly alerted on the basis of the November 27 warnings," the majority agreed to conclude that "The Intelligence and War Plans Divisions of the War and Navy Departments failed" in this respect. The majority also consented to state as their final conclusion: "Under all of the evidence the War and Navy Departments were not sufficiently alerted on December 6 and 7, 1941, in view of the imminence of war."

The Washington gossip was that Gearhart had been intimidated. In 1934 he had won both the Democratic and Republican nominations and held them both until losing the Democratic primary that June. This had come about after the Administration, knowing he represented a strong anti-Japanese California district, launched an attack charging Gearhart was pro-Jap and even wore a kimono. Now to save his seat in November he had gone along with the Democrats.

The case of Frank Keefe was far different. He tried to explain to Flynn in a letter why he had signed the majority report.

> I did succeed in getting many ideas incorporated through changes of language and interpretations and in the addition of conclusions. . . . However, because the whole report is slanted in the wrong direction, in my opinion, I have filed my own views in a separate report. My signature to the committee report is with reservations. Gearhart has unfortunately signed the report without any reservations, and although he thoroughly agrees with the views which I have expressed in a separate report, he could not sign the same for reasons that are best known to himself. (The fact that he may have an election coming up may have something to do with his decision.)

Keefe's 24-page "Additional Views" statement condemned not only Marshall and the Administration but also the bias of the majority report. "The committee report, I feel, does not with exactitude apply the same yardstick in measuring responsibilities at Washington as had been applied to the Hawaiian commanders. I cannot suppress the feeling that the committee report endeavors to throw as soft a light as possible on the Washington scene." Rugg and Hanify helped Keefe draft his "Additional Views," and according to the anti-Administration historian, Charles A. Beard, they "constitute an arraignment of the Roosevelt Administration's management of affairs during the months before December 7, 1941, which is, in many ways, sharper in tone than the 'propositions' filed by the two Republican Senators, Mr. Ferguson and Mr. Brewster. Indeed, in phrasing, Mr. Keefe's statement is even more like an indictment than the essentially historical Conclusions advanced by the minority. . . ."

Unfortunately for Keefe, the press sensationalized his signing of the majority report but almost completely ignored his "Additional Views," which were not released until the following day.

Unlike Beard, Flynn could find no excuse for Keefe, and wrote a blistering reply.

> Why did you have to sign a report which contained so much which according to your letter you did not agree to? Why could you not have done what any reasonable man would do —refuse to sign the report and file your own, which by the way, is what you said you would do?
>
> I know, of course, that you were angered at Senator Ferguson[5] for what you believed was the manner in which he conducted his part of the investigation and that you were annoyed at Senator Brewster for not being around. But what possible excuse could this be for you to put your signature to a document containing this complete exoneration of the President and Hull and the verdict that they "did all in their power to avert war with Japan," when you know that they did not and when you repeatedly said not only to me but to many others that they did not. You will see .what a mess you have made of the Republican share in the investigation when you

[5] Keefe was handicapped throughout the hearings, wrote Percy Greaves, "by committee rules which permitted every other member prior opportunity to question each witness. Many of the questions he had worked up were exhausted by Senator Ferguson before Keefe's turn. Time after time, Keefe saw the Senator getting credit for uncovering many important points he, himself, had been prepared to reveal. Piqued by this fact, he was determined not to sign a report sponsored by the Senator."

see the newspapers of the country and the use they will make of your incredible folly.

Flynn's prediction was accurate. *P.M.* wrote, "When two Republicans joined with six Democrats in signing a majority report which absolved the late President of blame in the disaster, any claims the partisans could make that the Congressional investigation under Democratic leadership was a 'whitewash' were knocked out."

The less partisan New York *Herald Tribune* agreed. The majority report dissipated all the wildest rumors and suspicions "and even the minority report by Senators Ferguson and Brewster offers no clear or convincing criticism of the basic course of the Administration policy. We are left with the intricate story of what happened upon which all are now substantially agreed, and that story in turn leaves us about where we began four and a half years ago." Now the public had the facts on record but there was no valid guide to the future conduct of both war and diplomacy. "The committee failed to produce that searching critique and synthesis for which some hoped. Perhaps it was a hope too high to place on any politically-appointed investigation, unavoidably involved in partisan ends."

Despite differences expressed by the two reports, it was now obvious that the wartime debate on Pearl Harbor was over. The avid critics of Roosevelt still remained vocal but, as a partisan political question and a public issue, Pearl Harbor was dead.

The principals in the affair were still left in limbo; Short, for one, felt he had been partially vindicated. Kimmel refused to comment to reporters but privately both he and Rugg felt that they had accomplished their purpose. They had placed the bulk of the material concerning the attack on record so that some historian in future years could study it with objectivity and reach conclusions. Preservation of the material to them both meant success.

Even so, many colleagues of Kimmel's remained indignant. "The most disgraceful feature of the whole affair," said Admiral Harry Yarnell, former commandant, Pearl Harbor Naval Base, "was the evident determination on the part of Washington to fasten the blame on the Hawaiian commanders. The incomplete and one-sided Roberts report, the circumstances of the retirements of

Kimmel and Short, the attempts of the War and Navy Departments to deny access to the intercepted messages by the Naval Court of Inquiry and the Army Board of Investigation, the appointment of secret one-man boards to continue investigations, and finally, the inability of the Joint Congressional Committee to secure access to pertinent files, constitute a blot on our national history."

The fate of Captain Laurance Safford was perhaps the hardest to bear. In spite of the considerable evidence to the contrary, it was believed that he was mistaken about the "winds" execute. Even friends and colleagues were convinced there had been no such message. To them it was a tragedy that a man who had done practically everything right in the years before Pearl Harbor, and had built an organization which produced a wealth of solid intelligence which later helped win the Battle of Midway, could have risked his career by the fanatic pursuit of the "winds" execute. Now his achievements were all but forgotten and he was generally regarded as a brilliant eccentric whose obsession with cryptology had affected his judgment, and who had, indeed, suffered from hallucinations. The testimony of those others who had seen the "winds" execute was so buried in the complexity and verbiage of the inquiry that the general impression was that Safford and only Safford had ever seen the message.

Less than a month after the appearance of the Joint Congressional reports, Safford visited his old friend, William Friedman, the code expert, to view a ciphering machine. After the demonstration, Friedman asked him to autograph a copy of the statement on the "winds" execute Safford had prepared for the committee. Friedman asked how Safford *now* felt about the "winds" execute.

The captain looked at him rather intently, then said, "I feel I didn't *prove* it existed." He himself had prepared a war warning to send in case higher authorities did not do so.

"But," said Friedman, "it *might* have been based on an erroneous or false 'winds' execute."

"When you're going to by-pass higher authority," retorted Safford, "be damned sure your facts are right." Not only had he prepared the warning message but he had it encoded. And the man who encoded it remembered the message.

Was this introduced into evidence at the hearings? asked Friedman. No, said Safford, the encoder had been out of the country and unavailable until the hearings were over. Safford had not wanted to bring up the matter at the time since he could produce no corroborating witness. "In case the subject is reopened," said Safford, "I know I can get him to tell his story."

Friedman later wrote on the back of the statement autographed by Safford: "It is clear that S is of firm conviction there was an authentic 'Winds Execute', that it was intercepted, decoded, passed around—and has disappeared."

And so the majority of Americans, by midsummer 1946, were convinced that the "winds" execute was either a fabrication or a delusion, that Kimmel and Short should carry the burden of blame for Pearl Harbor, that George Marshall had been maligned cruelly, and that Hull, Stimson and Roosevelt had done their best to prevent war with a nation run by bandits.

Although all these conclusions had been disproved in the course of nine investigations, the truth had become so distorted by reversion of testimony, cover-up and outright lies that the only chance for it to emerge could come if all the secret records of Pearl Harbor were declassified; and those with special knowledge, like Ralph Briggs, had immunity to talk openly. Only then could a tenth investigation, carried out in full freedom, be made.

Part 4

THE TENTH
INVESTIGATION

"The truth must be repeated again and again because error is constantly being preached around us," Goethe told a friend in 1828. "And not only by isolated individuals, but by the majority! In the newspapers and encyclopedias, in the schools and universities, everywhere error is dominant, securely and comfortably ensconced in public opinion which is on its side."

Chapter Thirteen

OPERATION Z
1932–NOVEMBER 27, 1941

1.

An American hunchback, who became a Chinese general and helped organize the revolution that crushed the Manchu dynasty, published an imaginative history in 1909 exposing Japanese plans to conquer the United States. Homer Lea's *The Valor of Ignorance* inspired a demand among certain American military and naval circles for a preventive war against Japan. Lea foresaw that the Japanese would not only make easy conquest of the Philippines but seize Hawaii and Alaska, thus gaining control of the North Pacific. This extraordinary book accomplished something not intended by the author. It inspired those Japanese who felt that Asia was being held in bondage by the West to rise against their oppressors. The Japanese publisher of the book, which bore the title *The War Between Japan and America,* managed to sell 40,000 copies. No wonder, considering its advertising appeal: "More interesting than a novel, more mysterious than philosophy, this is excellent reading material for Oriental men with red blood in their veins." It became required reading for Army and Navy officers.

In 1918 Lenin predicted that Japan and America, though presently allies, were fated to be bitter enemies. "The economic development of these countries over the course of several decades has stored up a great mass of inflammable material which renders inevitable a desperate conflict between these two powers for mastery of the Pacific Ocean and its shores."

Seven years later a novel came out in England; *The Great Pacific War* provided further inspiration to the Japanese and was studied at their Naval War College. Hector C. Bywater, naval correspondent for the London *Daily Telegraph*, described a Japanese surprise attack on the U. S. Fleet in Pearl Harbor, with simultaneous assaults on Guam and the Philippines, and with landings on Luzon at Lingayen Gulf and Lamon Bay. Isoroku Yamamoto ,was serving as naval attaché in Washington in 1925 when the novel was reviewed on the first page of the *New York Times Book Review* under the headline, IF WAR COMES IN THE PACIFIC. Undoubtedly Yamamoto, an obsessive student of naval affairs, had the book called to his attention.

American naval experts took such a surprise attack even more seriously following the Grand Joint Army and Navy Exercise held in Hawaiian waters in February 1932. Involving the major portion of the Battle Force, United States Fleet, the exercise was designed "to train the two Services in the joint operation involved in the defense of such an area. More specifically it is to determine the effectiveness of an air, surface and land attack against Hawaii and the adequacy of the air, surface, sub-surface and land defenses of Hawaii to repel such an attack."

The commander of the attack force, Admiral H. E. Yarnell, revolutionized naval strategy by leaving battleships and cruisers behind while he raced from California with two carriers, *Saratoga* and *Lexington*, and an escort of destroyers. By tradition the commander of a fleet would have his headquarters on a battleship but Yarnell, an air-minded officer, was on *Saratoga*.

The defenders were expecting the traditional naval attack but Yarnell launched 152 planes half an hour before dawn, in the dark, forty miles northeast of Kahuku Point. It was Sunday the seventh of February. Although expecting some sort of air attack, the defenders were caught by surprise when planes, hidden by rain clouds over the Koolau Range, suddenly swooped down on the

Army airfields and the area near Pearl Harbor as dawn was breaking. Yarnell had gained complete air supremacy, for most of the
defender's planes were on the ground in dispersed and cam-
ouflaged positions.

It should have been a cautionary lesson but the Chief Umpire
concluded: "It is doubtful if air attacks can be launched against
Oahu in the face of strong defensive aviation without subjecting
carriers to the danger of material damage and consequent great
losses to the attacking air force."

The Japanese took a different view and by 1936 their Navy War
College produced *Study of Strategy and Tactics in Operations
Against the United States,* which stated: "In case the enemy's
main fleet is berthed at Pearl Harbor, the idea should be to open
hostilities by surprise attacks from the air."

The following April another U.S. exercise was held. One hundred and eleven warships and 400 planes left San Pedro Naval
Base to "attack" Hawaii by surprise. Again planes bombed Oahu's
airfields into submission, enabling troops to land the next day
without opposition. The attackers lost only one ship, a battleship.

Still, so little had been done to defend against a surprise attack
on Pearl Harbor that H. H. (Hap) Arnold, an Army Air Corps
general, sounded a public warning in 1939 after a visit to Hawaii.

> On our return to Washington [he wrote] I was quoted by the
> newspaper commentators as having said I would have liked
> nothing better than to have a chance to take a crack at Pearl
> Harbor from the air with all those ships lying at anchor.
> Whether I really said it or not, the target presented was an
> airman's dream—a concentration difficult to find. But worse,
> it seemed to me—though about this I could say nothing
> publicly—was the lack of unity of command in Hawaii. Here
> the dismal idea of "responsibility of the Army and Navy being
> divided at the shoreline" was as sadly evident as I had ever
> seen it. Actually, nobody was in over-all command, and thus
> there was no over-all defense.

Early in 1941 Admiral Richardson, about to be relieved of his
command of the Pacific Fleet because of opposition to Roosevelt's
insistence that the fleet remain stationed at Pearl Harbor, complained to Stark of the inadequacy of defense against air attack.

He also complained that there did not appear to be "any practicable way of placing torpedo baffles or nets within the harbor to protect the ships moored therein against torpedo plane attack without greatly limiting the activities within the harbor, particularly the movements of large ships and the landing and take-off of patrol squadrons."

This alarmed Stark, who wrote the Secretary of the Navy on January 24: "If war eventuates with Japan, it is believed easily possible that hostilities would be initiated by a surprise attack upon the Fleet or the Naval Base at Pearl Harbor." He listed the dangers envisaged in their order of importance. First came "air bombing attack" and second "air torpedo attack."

Knox replied that he completely concurred as to the importance of defending against a surprise attack on Pearl Harbor. The Army, he said, was best equipped to give full protection to the fleet; he was, therefore, passing on the information to General Short, "directing him to cooperate with the local naval authorities" in making proper defensive measures effective. From then on it became Short's turn to beg in vain for adequate material and manpower.

Despite the pleas of younger air-minded officers, the basic strategical plans of Japan's leading admirals in the thirties had been to let her enemy, America, sortie from Pearl Harbor to make the initial attack: by the time the forces met in Japanese waters, the Americans would be so weakened by harassing submarine attacks that they could be defeated in one great surface battle somewhere west of Iwo Jima and Saipan.

But once Yamamoto assumed command of the fleet he and the younger officers, influenced by the writings of Homer Lea and Bywater, began to think offensively. After observing successful fleet maneuvers in 1940, Yamamoto told his chief of staff as they paced the deck of the flagship *Nagato*, "I think an attack on Hawaii may be possible now that our air training has turned out so successfully." With one sudden blow they could cripple the American fleet at Pearl Harbor, and before it could be rebuilt Japan would have seized Southeast Asia with all its resources.

This concept of achieving decisive victory by a single surprise blow lay deep in the Japanese character. Their favorite literary form was the *haiku*, a poem in seventeen syllables expressing with discipline the sudden illumination sought in the Japanese form of Buddhism. Similarly, the outcome in *judo*, *sumo* and *kendo*, after long preliminaries, is settled by a single stroke. In 1904, Yamamoto's hero, Admiral Togo, had, without declaration of war, assaulted the Russian Second Pacific Squadron at Port Arthur with torpedo boats while its commander was at a party.

Preliminary discussions at naval headquarters of a surprise raid on Pearl Harbor were probably overheard. On January 27, 1941, Dr. Ricardo Rivera Schreiber, the Peruvian envoy in Tokyo, chanced to meet Max Bishop, third secretary of the American Embassy, in the lobby of a bank. Bishop was changing his money in preparation for returning to Washington. Schreiber whispered that he had just learned from his intelligence sources that the Japanese had a war plan involving a surprise attack on Pearl Harbor.

Upon return to the embassy, Bishop drafted a telegram warning the State Department of the attack, then presented it to Ambassador Grew, who was most impressed. After making a few minor changes, he ordered Bishop to have the message encoded at once and dispatched to Washington. Grew remarked that he doubted the warning would get "a hot reception" but he regarded it as serious. Later that day he wrote in his diary, "There is a lot of talk around town to the effect that the Japanese, in case of a break with the United States, are planning to go all out in a surprise mass attack on Pearl Harbor. I rather guess that the boys in Hawaii are not precisely asleep."

As Grew feared, the warning was not taken seriously in Washington. One of Stark's subordinates passed on the message to Kimmel but added, "The Division of Naval Intelligence places no credence in these rumors. Furthermore, based on known data regarding the present disposition and employment of Japanese naval and army forces, no move against Pearl Harbor appears imminent or planned for in the foreseeable future."

That same day Yamamoto wrote an official letter to the chief of staff of the Eleventh Air Fleet, outlining his surprise attack plan and requesting a secret study of its feasibility. The problem was turned over to Commander Minoru Genda, one of the Navy's most promising officers. He had already won fame for his brilliant innovations in mass long-range fighter operations. He reported ten days later that an attack on Pearl Harbor would be difficult to mount and risky, but contained "a reasonable chance of success."

Only a gambler would accept the challenge and Yamamoto was certainly that. Gambling, he told a staff officer, was half calculation, half luck. As for the Pearl Harbor attack, he said, the odds were too good not to take. "If we fail," he said fatalistically, "we had better give up the war." Whereupon he outlined his plan to Captain Kanji Ogawa of Naval Intelligence with a request that he collect as much data as possible about Hawaii. Ogawa already had a few spies in the islands—a timid German named Otto Kuhn who needed money, a Buddhist priest and two Nisei. But they were only supplying unimportant bits of information. Ogawa decided to send in a Naval Intelligence expert who had already been prepared for such a mission, Ensign Takeo Yoshikawa. He was to pose as a consular official. On March 20 Yoshikawa arrived in Honolulu.

By April the Pearl Harbor plan had a new name—Operation Z, in honor of the famed Z signal given in 1905 by Admiral Togo at Tsushima when he annihilated the Russian fleet: ON THIS ONE BATTLE RESTS THE FATE OF OUR NATION. LET EVERY MAN DO HIS UTMOST. Now it was time to turn the operation over to those who would have to put it into effect—the First Air Fleet.

Early that May Roosevelt asked Marshall to prepare an assessment of the defense of Hawaii against a Japanese attack. The latter wrote:

> The defense of Oahu, due to its fortification, its garrison, and its physical characteristics, is believed to be the strongest fortress in the world.
> *Air Defense.* With adequate air defense, enemy carriers, naval escorts, and transports will begin to come under air attack at a distance of approximately 750 miles. This attack will increase in intensity until when within 200 miles of the objective, the enemy forces will be subject to attack by all types of bombardment closely supported by our most modern pursuit.

Hawaiian Air Defense. Including the movement of aviation now in progress Hawaii will be defended by 35 of our most modern flying fortresses, 35 medium range bombers, 13 light bombers, 150 pursuit of which 105 are of our most modern type. In addition Hawaii is capable of reinforcement by heavy bombers from the mainland by air. With this force available a major attack against Oahu is considered impracticable.

At the bottom of the report Marshall had handwritten in reference to the 35 flying fortresses: "Due to make a mass flight to Hawaii May 20. A number of this type of planes could be dispatched immediately if the situation grew critical."

This reassuring report was never passed on to Kimmel who, later that month, complained to Stark that he found himself "in a very difficult position . . . as a rule, not informed of policy, or changes of policy . . . and . . . as a result . . . unable to evaluate the possible effect upon his own situation." He was not even sure what force would be available to him.

Although Roosevelt was reassured by the report, he still resisted the pleas of Stimson and others to put pressure on Japan with more economic sanctions. "There will never be so good a time to stop the shipment of oil to Japan as we now have," argued Secretary of the Interior Harold Ickes, on June 23. The public, he said, would applaud the move. When Roosevelt refused to act, Ickes offered his resignation. The President argued that Japan was experiencing an internal struggle to decide whether to invade Siberia, attack Southeast Asia or make peace with America. "No one knows what the decision will be but, as you know, it is terribly important for the control of the Atlantic for us to help to keep peace in the Pacific. I simply have not got enough Navy to go round—and every little episode in the Pacific means fewer ships in the Atlantic."

Stimson was also urging the President to immediate action, this on the other side of the world where Hitler had just invaded the Soviet Union. "For the past thirty hours I have done little but reflect upon the German-Russian war and its effect upon our immediate policy," Stimson wrote Roosevelt. The Nazis, he argued, would be "thoroughly occupied in beating Russia for a minimum of one month and a possible maximum of three months." He strongly recommended that "this precious and unforeseen period of respite should be used to push with vigor our movements in the Atlantic theater of operations." On July 3 the Secretary went further, this time urging Roosevelt immediately to ask Congress for a declaration of war. But once more the President resisted any overt move.

His refusal to act in the West may have left him more vulnerable to the arguments to act in the East. The Japanese made up his mind on July 23 by forcing the Vichy government to agree to the peaceful entry of Japanese troops into French-occupied Indochina.

Stanley Hornbeck, who presided over the making of Far Eastern policy at the Department of State, regarded the Japanese as a "predatory" power run by arrogant militarists. He assured the Secretary of State that the Japanese were bluffing and so Hull, in turn, added his voice to the Stimson-Ickes demand for economic force. On the night of July 26 the President ordered all Japanese assets in America frozen, thus cutting off the main supply of oil to Japan.[1]

As a result Naval Chief of Staff Nagano, a cautious and sensible man, was caught up in the near hysteria which seized the Supreme Command.[2] He warned the Emperor that Japan's oil stock would only last for two years, and once war came, eighteen months; then concluded, "Under such circumstances, we had better take the initiative. We will win." The Emperor asked if they would win a

[1] Admiral Turner, then Navy Chief of War Plans, testified that the freezing order came out of a clear sky. "I had expressed the opinion previously, and I again express it, that that would very definitely bring on war with Japan. There was no possibility of composing matters after that unless Japan made a complete backdown, which it was very apparent she was not going to do."

The Economist of London later commented: "When President Roosevelt told the Americans in the 1940 election that 'I shall say it again and again and again: your boys are not going to be sent into any foreign wars' he had already committed the United States to a huge program of military aid to Britain, and had drawn up the Rainbow contingency plans for a simultaneous war with Germany and Japan, and was soon to slap on Japan the embargoes which some people still believe pushed the Japanese into their attack on Pearl Harbor."

[2] On February 13, 1915, a group of Japanese army and navy officers lunched with their American counterparts at the residence of the superintendent of the U. S. Naval Academy. The signature in the guest book of Commander Osami Nagano appears just above that of Captain Douglas MacArthur. One wonders if they ever went beyond "pass the salt" to discuss the situation in the Pacific.

great naval victory like the Battle of Tsushima. "I am sorry, but that will not be possible."

"Then," said the Emperor, "the war will be a desperate one."

In Washington Secretary of War Stimson was delighted. At last the Stimson Doctrine was in full effect. Japan would finally have to pay for her crimes of aggression.

The passage of five weeks without any compromising words from America increased the desperation of Japan's military leaders. "With each day we will get weaker and weaker, until finally we won't be able to stand on our feet," warned Admiral Nagano. "Although I feel sure that we have a chance to win a war right now, I'm afraid this chance will vanish with the passage of time." An initial surprise victory was essential. He was referring to Operation Z but kept this to himself. The fewer in on the secret the safer. "Thus our only recourse is to forge ahead."

The Chief of Staff of the Army agreed. "We must try to achieve our diplomatic objectives by October 10. If this fails we must dash forward." And so it was decided at an imperial conference to put a five-week deadline on diplomacy and then wage war. But the Emperor did what no other ruler of Japan had ever done. A few days after the deadline, even though there was no progress in the negotiations with America, he rescinded the decision of the imperial conference. The new Prime Minister, General Hideki Tojo, was ordered to "go back to blank paper," that is, start with a clean slate and continue sincere negotiations with America for peace. Even so the preparations for the attack on Pearl Harbor continued on schedule—just in case diplomacy proved impossible.

2.

Further warnings of a possible attack on Hawaii had already reached Washington. In June an interesting report arrived at O.N.I. from the American commercial attaché in Mexico City:

Related with my recent report on activities at Honolulu Pearl Harbor Hawaii Naval Base and the use of the word Molokai I

have run across the following vital information bearing on
that subject and related features.

Enclosed were two rough pencil drawings of a new type of small
submarine with a maximum radius of action of four hundred miles,
and fitted with remote-control electromagnetically activated diving valves and air valves. A dozen of these small submarines would
be hidden under water off the island of Molokai. And when war
came "the plan is to at once use this small fleet of submarines for
lightning attacks on the U. S. Navy fleet anchored in Pearl Harbor."

The American naval attaché had forwarded this report to Washington with the observation that it possibly contained "an element
of truth, in spite of its apparently fantastic nature, and in spite of
this officer's reluctance to report what may prove to be totally unfounded rumors."

A much more important report came to Washington from a
British double agent, code-named "Tricycle." He was a Yugoslav,
Dusko Popov, who had first been recruited by German intelligence. Being a patriot, he offered his services to the British. His
job was to feed the Germans controlled information.

That summer he was ordered by the Nazis to set up an espionage ring in the United States. He left England two days after the
invasion of Russia, stopping off at Lisbon to get orders. He was
asked to study a questionnaire.[3] The second heading startled him.
It was *Hawaii.* He was to locate ammunition dumps and airfields
on the island of Oahu and learn complete details of Pearl Harbor,
including pier installations, number of anchorages and depth of
water. Recently Popov had learned of Japanese interest in the British attack at Taranto which had put half the Italian fleet out of action in a single day by aerial torpedo attacks. Obviously Pearl Harbor was to be the Japanese target of a surprise attack.

Popov was ordered by the Germans to proceed to Hawaii as
soon as he had set up the spy network in America. "There was
some urgency about it," recalled Popov. "The action wasn't for tomorrow but it was for soon." He communicated the news of the
impending attack to the Lisbon office of British intelligence.
"They got on to London and I was instructed to carry my informa-

3 For complete questionnaire see Notes.

tion personally to the United States, since I was leaving in a few days. Apparently, they thought it preferable that I be the bearer of the tidings, since the Americans might want to question me at length to extract the last bit of juice."

On August 10 Tricycle left for New York on a Pan American Clipper carrying with him a brief case filled with the questionnaire, microdots and other material. Once aboard the plane he turned over the brief case to a British intelligence officer who promised to pass on copies to the F.B.I.

The morning after arrival in New York, Popov was escorted to the Manhattan office of the F.B.I. where, to his surprise, he was received coolly. The regional chief said he had received the material from the British and would forward it to Washington. "I refrained from asking why it hadn't gone yet. If the Americans were to counter a Japanese attack, every twenty-four hours would count."

When Popov asked if the F.B.I. wanted more details on the Pearl Harbor attack, he was told, "Well, it all looks too precise, too complete, to be believed. The questionnaire plus the other information you brought spell out in detail exactly where, when, how, and by whom we are to be attacked. If anything, it sounds like a trap."

The two main sources of his information, explained Popov, were very reliable. The first would surely warn him if the plan was a trap. The second, Baron Gronau, was an expert on Japan. "If his information is exact, there's no reason to doubt his conclusions. You can expect an attack on Pearl Harbor before the end of this year unless the negotiations with the Japanese produce a definite result." The questionnaire itself was the best source. "If that is a trap, then it means my whole mission to the United States is window dressing. And that is just not possible. The rest of my mission is too important to the Germans. They wouldn't sacrifice it and me with it. Sooner or later you'd learn you'd been had and I would be blown."

The questionnaire and corroborating material were examined by J. Edgar Hoover but he had already heard stories of Tricycle's extravagant life style. Even his code name was an affront. "It arose from his sexual athleticism," Hoover wrote. "He had a liking for bedding two girls at one time." Popov was just a Balkan playboy to Hoover, who also had no liking for double agents.

Consequently the director did not take the Pearl Harbor plan seriously[4] and refused to allow Popov to leave for Hawaii as ordered by his German masters. The Yugoslav's insistence on petitioning Hoover in person resulted in a disaster. "I'm running the cleanest police organization in the world," stormed Hoover. "You come here from nowhere and within six weeks install yourself in a Park Avenue penthouse, chase film stars, break a serious law, and try to corrupt my officers." He pounded the desk. "I'm telling you right now I won't stand for it."

Popov sought help from William Stephenson, Churchill's secret envoy in the United States, code-named "Intrepid," but he too failed to persuade Washington to take Popov's warning seriously, as did Sir John Masterman, head of the Double-Cross System whereby German agents captured in Britain were induced to become double agents and serve the Allies. The questions concerning Pearl Harbor in Tricycle's questionnaire, wrote Masterman, were specialized and detailed. "It is therefore surely a fair deduction that the questionnaire indicated very clearly that in the event of the United States being at war, Pearl Harbour would be the first point to be attacked, and that plans for this attack had reached an advanced state by August 1941."

Early that fall another direct warning of an attack on Pearl Harbor came to Washington. Kilsoo Haan, an agent for the Sino-Korean People's League, came to the CBS office of Eric Sevareid to announce excitedly that the Japanese were going to attack Pearl Harbor before Christmas. Friends in the Korean underground in Japan and Hawaii reported they had positive proof. "One piece of evidence in the jigsaw," recalled Sevareid, "—a Korean working in the Japanese consulate in Honolulu had seen full blueprints of our above-water and underwater naval installations—spread out on the consul's desk."

Haan told Sevareid of his frustration in trying to see the higher

---

[4] There are no available records in the F.B.I. concerning Popov's questionnaire. Hoover's second in command, Edward Tamm, never heard of it but if Hoover had received such information, he told the author, he would certainly have passed it on to Roosevelt.

officials at the State Department but he "always ended up seeing very minor officials who took a very minor view of his warnings."

Late in October Kilsoo Haan did manage to convince Senator Guy Gillette of Iowa that he had just discovered the Japanese were definitely planning an invasion for December or January. It called for not only an attack on Pearl Harbor but simultaneous assaults on the Philippines, Midway, Guam and Wake. Gillette alerted the State Department as well as Army and Navy Intelligence.

Information to the War Department also came from Major Warren J. Clear, sent in the spring of 1941 to the Far East by Army Intelligence, that the Japanese were planning to launch attacks against a chain of islands including Guam and Hawaii. He vehemently urged the garrisoning of the whole chain of islands from Oahu to Guam.[5]

3.

On the eighth of October Admiral Stark recommended to Hull that they should enter the war against Germany as soon as possible even if it meant a conflict with Japan. Eight days later, after a

[5] No record can be found of Major Clear's warnings of a Pearl Harbor attack. However, there is on file a lengthy memorandum dated November 2, 1941, which he sent to the Assistant Chief of Staff, G-2. In it he reports to the War Department on his meetings in Singapore with Air Chief Marshal Sir Robert Brooke-Popham and the G.H.Q. Military Liaison Office. This document indicates the importance of Clear's secret intelligence mission to the Far East and its high-level status. He was later promoted and awarded the Legion of Merit, the Distinguished Service Cross, the Purple Heart and the Order of the British Empire.

In 1967 Clear revealed in two letters that he was writing a book. ". . . you can be assured that my evidence re the P.H. tragedy and the related tragedies on all the islands . . . will show that Washington D.C. had solid evidence, prior to P.H. that Japan would take *the whole chain of islands*, including attacks on Guam and Hawaii. In view of this information at hand in Washington, but *not* relayed to Hawaii and Guam, it can be established that no culpability can be rightfully placed on Admiral Kimmel or Gen. Short." Clear's book, *Pearl Harbor—the Price of Perfidy*, was never published.

In 1968 Clear also stated that he had heard from several high-ranking generals that he was in line to be head of Army Intelligence. "I am referring to the matter of my promotion because it shows that the FDR cabal were blocking it all the way thru. It is not a matter of sour grapes with me. But the non-promotion shows the animus, the *fear*, that attached to anyone who might disclose facts." Like Ralph Briggs, Clear was ordered not to appear before the Pearl Harbor investigative committee.

He suffered a stroke and spent the last ten years of his life in a convalescent home. He died in 1980. His conservator, George Farrier, searched in vain at the author's request for a copy of his unpublished book.

meeting with Roosevelt, Stimson wrote in his diary, "We face the delicate question of the diplomatic fencing to be done so as to be sure that Japan is put into the wrong and makes the first bad move —overt move." The next day Admiral Claude Bloch, commander of the Fourteenth Naval District, Hawaii, wrote Stark that the deficiencies in the defense organization of Pearl Harbor described in a letter sent almost nine months earlier still existed. Bloch urged that, in view of the tense situation, small fast craft equipped with listening devices and depth bombs as well as at least one squadron of patrol planes be rushed to Hawaii. The request was strongly endorsed by Kimmel and Short but a reply would not be received for five weeks—and this would inform Bloch that no additional ships or planes could be assigned to Hawaii at the present.

In Tokyo Prime Minister Tojo was doing his utmost to carry out the Emperor's instructions to "go back to blank paper," even after Admiral Nagano observed somberly at the October 23 liaison conference, "We were supposed to have reached a decision in October and yet here we are." The Navy was consuming four hundred tons of oil per hour. "The situation is urgent. We must have a decision at once, one way or the other." Army Chief of Staff Sugiyama agreed. "We can't waste four or five days in study. We must rush forward!"

Tojo replied that the government preferred to review the matter carefully and responsibly. At a conference nine days later it was General Tojo who supported those seeking peace, and the militarists were forced to allow Foreign Minister Togo to negotiate until midnight, November 30.

Now the problem was to agree on what sort of final proposal should be sent to America. Togo said he had drawn up two. Proposal A was a somewhat watered-down version of their previous offers. In it the Army agreed to withdraw all troops from China, including those left as defense against Communism, by 1966. Proposal B was to be used as a last resort in case Hull turned down the first. It was designed to allay Hull's suspicions about the drive into Indochina and assure him that Japan was abandoning any idea of a military conquest of Southeast Asia. In Proposal B Japan also promised to make no more aggressive moves south; and, once peace was restored in China or a general peace was established in the Pacific, Japan·would immediately move all troops in southern Indochina to the north of that country. In return, America was to sell Japan one million tons of gasoline.

Sugiyama violently opposed Proposal B. For hours he and his colleagues refused to accede to any suggestion of withdrawal from Indochina, while insisting that Hull be asked to unfreeze Japanese assets. This was a ridiculous proposition and Foreign Minister Togo knew he could not possibly negotiate on such terms. In desperation he shouted, "We can't carry on diplomacy—but we still shouldn't start a war!"

Then proceed with Proposal A! demanded the Army and Navy.

But Togo refused to back down and Tojo reminded everyone that the Emperor had called for "blank paper" and they should bow to his wishes. Finally Sugiyama reluctantly acquiesced, but only if Proposal A should fail.

Next morning Togo called on Tojo and asked if the Prime Minister would persuade "those concerned to make further concessions" if Hull reacted favorably to either "A" or "B." Tojo did not disappoint him. He offered to make further compromises if the Americans also came part way.

Now it was Foreign Minister Togo's well-nigh hopeless task to engineer peace before the deadline. The only chance for success in Washington, he decided, was to send assistance to Ambassador Nomura, who had already made several diplomatic blunders. He chose Saburo Kurusu, an able diplomat, whose wife was an American, born of British parents on Washington Square, New York City. He set off for America on the night of November 4.

Before he arrived Togo cabled Nomura Proposals A and B along with secret instructions. It was in the Purple code and a translation was soon on its way to Hull. The opening sentence of the instructions gave the impression that the Japanese had given up on the negotiations.

WELL, RELATIONS BETWEEN JAPAN AND THE UNITED STATES HAVE REACHED THE EDGE, AND OUR PEOPLE ARE LOSING CONFIDENCE IN THE POSSIBILITY OF EVER ADJUSTING THEM.

Such pessimism was not in the original, for Togo had written:

STRENUOUS EFFORTS ARE BEING MADE DAY AND NIGHT TO ADJUST
JAPANESE-AMERICAN RELATIONS, WHICH ARE ON THE VERGE OF
RUPTURE. .

The translation of the second paragraph was even more mis-
leading:[6]

CONDITIONS BOTH WITHIN AND WITHOUT OUR EMPIRE ARE SO TENSE
THAT NO LONGER IS PROCRASTINATION POSSIBLE, YET IN OUR SINCER-
ITY TO MAINTAIN PACIFIC RELATIONSHIPS BETWEEN THE EMPIRE OF
JAPAN AND THE UNITED STATES OF AMERICA, WE HAVE DECIDED AS A
RESULT OF THESE DELIBERATIONS, TO GAMBLE ONCE MORE ON THE
CONTINUANCE OF THE PARLEYS, BUT THIS IS OUR LAST EFFORT.' . . .

The original was responsible in tone:

THE SITUATION BOTH WITHIN AND OUTSIDE THE COUNTRY IS
EXTREMELY PRESSING AND WE CANNOT AFFORD ANY PROCRASTINA-
TION. OUT OF THE SINCERE INTENTION TO MAINTAIN PEACEFUL
RELATIONS WITH THE UNITED STATES, THE IMPERIAL GOVERNMENT
CONTINUES THE NEGOTIATIONS AFTER THOROUGH DELIBERATIONS.
THE PRESENT NEGOTIATIONS ARE OUR FINAL EFFORT. . . .

The translation then stated that, unless these proposals succeeded, relations between the two nations would be ruptured.

. . . IN FACT, WE GAMBLED THE FATE OF OUR LAND ON THE THROW
OF THIS DIE.

Togo's actual words were:

. . . AND THE SECURITY OF THE EMPIRE DEPENDS ON IT.

Where Hull read—

. . . THIS TIME WE ARE SHOWING THE LIMIT OF OUR FRIENDSHIP:
THIS TIME WE ARE MAKING OUR LAST POSSIBLE BARGAIN, AND I HOPE
THAT WE CAN THUS SETTLE ALL OUR TROUBLES WITH THE UNITED
STATES PEACEABLY

—Togo had written:

. . . NOW THAT WE MAKE THE UTMOST CONCESSION IN THE SPIRIT
OF COMPLETE FRIENDLINESS FOR THE SAKE OF PEACEFUL SOLUTION,
WE HOPE EARNESTLY THAT THE UNITED STATES WILL, ON ENTERING

[6] Many Japanese are convinced that this and other diplomatic messages were
purposely mistranslated. No evidence could be found of this. It is far more likely
that the inaccuracies came from ignorance of the stylized Japanese used by diplomats.

THE FINAL STAGE OF THE NEGOTIATIONS, RECONSIDER THE MATTER
AND APPROACH THIS CRISIS IN A PROPER SPIRIT WITH A VIEW TO PRE-
SERVING JAPANESE-AMERICAN RELATIONS.

An even more inaccurate translation of Togo's specific instructions regarding Proposal A gave Hull the false impression that the
Japanese were deceitful and devious. It had misled Hull into believing that the Japanese were trying to avoid committing themselves to a formal agreement on any of the proposed points.

When Nomura brought Proposal A to Hull's apartment on the
evening of November 7 the Secretary of State glanced through it
hurriedly; he already knew all about it—or thought he did—and
was convinced it contained no real concessions. His attitude was so
obvious that Nomura asked for an appointment with the President.

Unlike Hull, Roosevelt was willing to negotiate. He had just received a joint appeal from his two military chiefs, Marshall and
Stark, urging him to do nothing to force a crisis. They pointed out
that the defeat of Germany was the major strategic objective. "If
Japan be defeated and Germany remains undefeated, decision will
still not be reached," they said and warned the President that war
with Japan could cripple the fight against "the most dangerous
enemy," Germany. They wanted no ultimatum to Japan for three
or four months, until the Philippines and Singapore were
strengthened.

Unlike Hull, Roosevelt was a practitioner of *Realpolitik* and he
responded to B with a *modus vivendi*, a temporary arrangement
pending a final settlement. He wrote it in pencil and sent it off to
Hull:

6 months

1. U.S. to resume economic relations—some oil and rice—
   more later.
2. Japan to send no more troops to Indochina or Manchurian
   border or any place South—(Dutch, Brit. or Siam).
3. Japan to agree not to invoke tripartite pact even if U.S.
   gets into European war.
4. U.S. to introduce Japs to Chinese to talk things over but
   U.S. to take no part in the conversations.

Later on Pacific agreements.

This *modus vivendi* brought about the first relaxation of American rigidity, the first real hope for a peaceful settlement. Hull dutifully, if without enthusiasm, began putting it into diplomatic form. Despite personal reservations about the newly arrived special envoy Kurusu (he didn't like Kurusu's looks and "I felt from the start that he was deceitful . . .") and suspicions of his superiors back in Tokyo, Hull was still willing to negotiate.

His suspicions were "confirmed" on November 22 by an intercept from Tokyo to Nomura extending the deadline of negotiations to November 30 (November 29 Washington time).

. . . THIS TIME WE MEAN IT, THAT THE DEADLINE ABSOLUTELY CANNOT BE CHANGED. AFTER THAT THINGS ARE AUTOMATICALLY GOING TO HAPPEN.

Even so, Hull felt it was his duty to advance his version of the President's *modus vivendi*. Upon meeting with Stimson and Knox for their usual Tuesday morning get-together on November 25, Hull explained that he was thinking of countering the Japanese demand with a proposal for a truce of three months. Stimson had opposed Roosevelt's original idea for six months but did not oppose Hull's new draft. "It adequately safeguarded all our interests, I thought as we read it, but I don't think there is a chance of the Japanese accepting it, because it was so drastic." Hull's terms were for the Japanese to evacuate their recent conquests, cease new aggressions, and in return America was to supply them with oil but only for civilian use.

The three men walked over to the White House for a noon meeting of the Cabinet. At one point Roosevelt remarked that they were likely to be attacked, perhaps as soon as Monday, December 1. The Japanese were notorious for striking without warning. "The question was," Stimson wrote in his diary, "how we should maneuver them into the position of firing the first shot without allowing too much danger to ourselves. It was a difficult proposition."

The previous day Hull had invited representatives of England, China, Australia and Holland to his office where he passed around copies of his own draft of the Roosevelt plan. The Dutch minister, Dr. Alexander Loudon, forthrightly declared that his country would support the *modus vivendi* but the other three had to wait for instructions. On the twenty-fifth the Chinese ambassador handed Hull a note from his Foreign Minister stating that Chiang Kai-shek felt that America was "inclined to appease Japan at the expense of China." Later in the day a cable for Roosevelt arrived from Churchill. He was disquieted about Chiang Kai-shek.

. . . IS HE NOT HAVING A VERY THIN DIET? OUR ANXIETY IS ABOUT CHINA. IF THEY COLLAPSE, OUR JOINT DANGERS WOULD ENORMOUSLY INCREASE.

These two reactions, coupled with Hull's own doubts and exhaustion after months of negotiating, caused him to scrap Roosevelt's *modus vivendi* that afternoon. Instead he contemplated offering the Japanese "a suggested program of collaboration along peaceful and mutually beneficial, progressive lines." His assistants began putting this new proposal into draft form.[7]

Stimson had returned to his office to find G-2 reports that the expected Japanese invasion expedition to southeast Asia was at last under way. Some thirty to fifty ships had been sighted south of Formosa. Stimson's adrenaline flowed. He prepared a paper on this invasion for Roosevelt. The time had come at last to act, for America to act.

The next morning, November 26, Hull was telephoning Stimson that he had "about made up his mind not to give . . . the proposition [the *modus vivendi*] . . . to the Japanese but to kick the whole thing over—to tell them that he has no other proposition at all."

Stimson promptly called Roosevelt to find out if the paper he had sent the night before about the new Japanese expedition force into Indochina had been received. Roosevelt reacted so violently that Stimson wrote in his diary: "He fairly blew up—jumped up in the air, so to speak, and said he hadn't seen it and that changed the whole situation because it was an evidence of bad faith on the part of the Japanese that while they were negotiating for an entire truce—and entire withdrawal (from China)—they should be sending that expedition down there to Indochina."

[7] At Sugamo Prison, after the war, Tojo told one of his most trusted advisers, General Kenryo Sato, that if he had received the original Roosevelt *modus vivendi*, the course of history would probably have been changed. "I didn't tell you at the time, but I had already prepared a proposal with new compromises in it. I wanted somehow to carry out the Emperor's wishes and avoid war." Then Tojo heaved a big sigh. "If we had only received that *modus vivendi!*"

Before long Hull arrived at the White House to recommend
that in view of the opposition of Chiang Kai-shek they drop the
President's *modus vivendi* and offer the Japanese a brand-new
"comprehensive basic proposal for a general peaceful settlement."
Roosevelt was still so indignant and angry at news of the Japanese
attack force that he approved. That afternoon Nomura and
Kurusu were summoned to the State Department. Hull presented
them two documents "with the forlorn hope that even at this ultimate moment a little common sense might filter into the military
minds of Tokyo."

The two Japanese expectantly read the first paper, an Oral Statement setting forth that the United States "most earnestly" desired
to work for peace in the Pacific but believed Proposal B "would
not be likely to contribute to the ultimate objectives of ensuring
peace under law, order and justice in the Pacific area. . . ." Instead Hull offered a new solution embodied in the second paper,
marked "Strictly confidential, Tentative and Without Commitment." Kurusu read its ten conditions with dismay. It insisted that
Japan "withdraw all military, naval, air and police forces from
China and Indochina"; support no other government or regime in
China except Chiang Kai-shek's; and in effect abrogate the Tripartite Pact among Japan, Germany and Italy.

It was even harsher than an American proposal submitted in
June, and Hull had drawn it up without consulting Marshall and
Stark, who happened to be in the act of drafting another mem-
orandum to Roosevelt begging for more time to reinforce the
Philippines.

Nomura was too stunned to talk. Kurusu foresaw that this
American reply to Proposal B would be regarded as an insult in
Tokyo. He didn't see how his government, he said, could possibly
agree to the immediate and unconditional withdrawal of all troops
from China and Indochina. Couldn't they informally discuss the
proposal before sending it to Tokyo?

"It's as far as we can go," said the tight-lipped Hull. Public feeling was running so high that he "might almost be lynched" if he
let oil go freely into Japan.

Dejected, Kurusu said that Hull's note just about meant the
end, and asked if the Americans were not interested in a *modus*

vivendi. This phrase had become an unpleasant one to Hull. We explored that, he said curtly.

Was it because the other powers wouldn't agree? Kurusu asked.

It was uncomfortably close to the truth. "I did my best in the way of exploration," said Hull.[8]

That same day Dr. Henry Field, an anthropologist, now serving as one of the President's bright, trusted young men, was summoned to Grace Tully's office. She acted strangely gruff and was very much to the point, in contrast to her normal friendly and relaxed manner. She told Field that the President was ordering him to produce, in the shortest time possible, the full names and addresses of each American-born and foreign-born Japanese listed by locality within each state. Field was completely bewildered and didn't know how to begin. She explained it was to be done by using the 1930 and 1940 censuses. Field was directed to go to the office of his friend, Under Secretary of Commerce Wayne Taylor.

"You will be the fourth person called after you arrive so as not to arouse any suspicion of a high priority interview." Field was to explain the situation to Taylor, who was, in turn, to notify J. C. Capt, Director of the Census, Suitland, Maryland, to expect Field shortly. "Call me if you need further help or authorization but try to avoid this. Final tabulations and addresses are of the utmost urgency. Use your own judgment to achieve results causing the least possible chance of a breach in security." Every hour counted so a twenty-four-hour program should begin immediately. "Arrange for delivery of the documents to yourself; then bring them, addressed to me, to the guard at the main gate on Pennsylvania Avenue. He will give you a receipt for each numbered envelope. Good luck! This is a major assignment!"

Field proceeded immediately to Taylor's office. No one seemed to take any notice of him as he awaited his turn. Taylor responded to his instructions graciously and enthusiastically. "I will call Mr. Capt at once to let him know you are coming. Break this request to him gently for the Census Bureau, to my knowledge, has never received a high priority order before."

---

[8] Three American admirals, Ingersoll, Noyes and Schuirmann, later testified that they had not expected the Japanese to accept the Hull terms.

Half an hour later Field was talking to Capt, a kindly, academic type who listened attentively to his instructions. "He gasped," recalled Field, "and said that that would take months especially for California. I told him it was a No. 1 priority of the Government and he had to do it as quickly as possible. If necessary, I said, he should shut down all other work of the Bureau to compile this information. He looked surprised and said he never had an order like that and he would go to work on it at once. He pressed all the knobs on a bank of switches to call his department heads in for a conference."

When Field returned after a call to Taylor there were twenty people with Mr. Capt. "There was a hush as I entered and every eye was on me." Capt's eyes were shining. "He told them that some of them could go home with full pay and that the others were to remain on a 24-hour basis to work only on this special project." The project had begun less than ninety minutes after Grace Tully had given the assignment. Field telephoned her that all was proceeding well but he needed security from the Marine Corps. Soon each entrance of the Census Building was guarded by an armed Marine. In the meantime a bank of IBM sorting machines was set up to extract the Orientals for each state from 110,000,000 cards; then they were to be resorted for the Japanese.

The Pearl Harbor Carrier Striking Force, *Kido Butai,* was now assembled some thousand miles north of Tokyo at an island in the Kuriles, Etorofu, which possessed a large deep bay, rough in summer but strangely calm in winter. It was an ideal clandestine rallying point. One of the six carriers, *Kaga,* had just arrived from the Inland Sea where it had been loaded with modified torpedoes with wooden fins from aerial stabilizers. Only with these fins could the torpedoes run shallow enough for the Pearl Harbor waters, which U. S. Navy experts still regarded as immune from aerial torpedo attack.

Late the previous afternoon more than five hundred flying officers from all of the carriers had jammed into the aviation-crew quarters of *Akagi* (*Red Castle*), a carrier converted from a battle cruiser which now displaced more than 30,000 tons. Admiral Nagumo outlined the attack. It was the first time most of the men had heard the words "Pearl Harbor." As the admiral spoke, excitement mounted and when he ended with a "Good fight and good luck!" there was a deafening cheer.

That night there was a giant *sake* party aboard *Akagi* but not attended by Nagumo. A compulsive worrier, he got out of bed long after midnight to arouse the commander, who had gone to Honolulu three weeks earlier to observe and take pictures of the Pearl Harbor entrance and the adjoining Hickam Field. He had also brought back answers to ninety-seven questions from the lone Japanese Navy spy, Yoshikawa.

Nagumo had to be reassured that Kimmel's fleet had not transferred from Pearl Harbor. "Is there any possibility the Pacific Fleet might assemble in Lahaina?"

"None."

The next morning—the twenty-sixth in Washington—dawned bright and clear with unusually high barometric pressure for this time of year. The seas had calmed. It seemed a good omen—until one of the giant screws of *Akagi* caught in wire just as the fleet was weighing anchor, and a sailor fell into the icy waters. Thirty minutes later *Kido Butai* finally got under way except for the man overboard, who could not be found. As the armada filed past Etorofu, the heavy cruisers and battleships test-fired their guns by throwing live rounds into a hillside of the island. The sound of the guns and the splashes of snow bursting on the hill like gigantic white flowers stirred the men.

At the State Department in Washington, Hull's uncompromising answer to the Japanese was being typed out for Nomura and Kurusu.

Chapter Fourteen

THE TRACKING OF *KIDO BUTAI*
NOVEMBER 26–DECEMBER 6

1.

By the time Colonel Rufus "Togo" Bratton had arrived at his office in the Munitions Building on the morning of November 26, he was convinced that war would soon break out. For the past six months he had plotted what looked surely like a Japanese deployment for war. From the intercepted Japanese messages both in the Purple and consular codes, he was almost dead sure that the Japanese would attack the following Sunday, November 30.

The next morning, Thanksgiving, Bratton's conviction that there would be war on Sunday was strengthened. Among the intercepts on his desk he had found a message from Nomura to Tokyo bemoaning Hull's curt reply: "Our failure and humiliation is now complete." Even more indicative were intercepts from the military and naval attachés advising their chiefs in Tokyo that the negotiations had collapsed and war with America apparently could no longer be delayed.

Since Marshall was vacationing in Florida with his wife, Bratton rushed these messages to Stimson along with a G-2 report evaluating a possibility that the Japanese "might be proceeding to the Philippines or to Burma to cut off the Burma Road, or to the

Dutch East Indies," or to "Thailand from which they could be in a position to attack Singapore at the proper moment."

Stimson telephoned Hull to learn what the diplomatic situation was. "I handed the note to the Japs," said Hull almost casually. "I have washed my hands of it and it is now in the hands of you and Knox—the Army and the Navy."

Stimson's call had interrupted Hull's conference with his three top advisers on the Far East, Hornbeck, Maxwell Hamilton and Joseph Ballantine. The first, as usual, was urging use of arms against Japan. Hull pointed out that Marshall wanted a delay of at least three weeks and Stark wanted three months. The Navy asked for six months last February, riposted Hornbeck, and the Secretary, through his negotiations, had got them that delay. Now they wanted three more. What the President should do, said Hornbeck, is "to stop asking the Navy, and tell it."

He assured Hull that yesterday's note would call the bluff of the Japanese. They weren't going to fight. He put his conviction on paper in a memorandum.

> Were it a matter of placing bets the undersigned would give
> odds of 5 to 1 that the United States and Japan will not be at
> "war" on or before December 15 (the date by which Gen-
> eral Gerow has affirmed that we would be "in the clear" so
> far as consummation of certain disposals of our forces is con-
> cerned); would wager 3 to 1 that the United States and
> Japan will not be at "war" on or before the 15th January (i.e.,
> seven weeks from now); would wager even money that the
> United States and Japan will not be at "war" on or before
> March 1. . . . Stated briefly, the undersigned does not be-
> lieve that this country is now on the verge of "war" in the
> Pacific.[1]

Even before Hornbeck began writing his memorandum, Stimson had made up his mind that Bratton could be right about war by Sunday. They must prepare for conflict. With Marshall out of town, Stimson himself would have to act. He asked Roosevelt for

[1] In Hornbeck's draft autobiography, he attempted to explain his faulty prediction: ". . . I made the mistake of yielding to an emotional urge and committing myself on record in terms of wishful thinking and gratuitous predicting." In mid-November 1941 he had rebuked a young colleague for prophesying that Japan would go to war in desperation: "Name me one country in history which ever went to war in desper-ation!"

authorization to send war warnings to the commanding generals of the danger zones: the Panama Canal, Hawaii and particularly MacArthur in the Philippines.

Roosevelt must have felt somewhat like a pawn in the hands of his belligerent Cabinet. He had planned to send a reasonable reply to the Japanese yet allowed his *modus vivendi* to be drastically altered by Hull. Hull, in turn, had been influenced by Hornbeck to think the Japanese were negotiating deviously; and, almost out of pique, had discarded his own *modus vivendi* to send a reply to Japan that would not be acceptable.

Ever since Stimson had accepted the post of Secretary of War, Roosevelt had been pushed further and further toward war with both Germany and Japan. Feeling he had little choice, the President ordered Stimson to send out "the final alert." Now the Secretary of War had what he wanted. No longer a mere civilian head of the War Department, he was Commander in Chief Roosevelt's deputy. Before long Knox and Stark were in his office along with Gerow. The last two begged for more time but Stimson cut them off. "I'd also be glad to have time but I don't want it at the cost of humiliation of the United States or of backing down on any of our principles which would show weakness on our part."

Gerow presented a draft of a warning to commanders in the Pacific he had already prepared. In his own hand Stimson added "but hostile action possible at any moment" to a sentence reading "Japanese future action unpredictable." He approved the rest of the message and at 11:08 A.M. the warning went out over the absent Marshall's name. Stark's warning to Kimmel was not dispatched until late in the day.

At Pearl Harbor Kimmel was conferring with his War Plans officer. "McMorris," he asked, "what is your idea of chances of a surprise raid on Oahu?"

"I should say none, Admiral."

The first news of Hull's note did not reach Tokyo until late morning. The message was sent at once to the palace, where a liaison conference was in session. Arriving just as the meeting adjourned for lunch, Tojo read it aloud. There was dumfounded silence until someone said, "This is an ultimatum!" Even Foreign

Minister Togo, who had held forth slight hope of success, never expected this. Overpowered by despair, he said something in such a stutter that no one could understand him; the Hull note "stuck in his craw." What particularly infuriated every man in the room was the categorical demand to quit *all* of China. Manchuria had been won at the cost of considerable sweat and blood. Its loss would mean economic disaster. What nation with any honor would submit?

Hull's proposal was the result of indignation and impatience, but this offending passage had been tragically misunderstood. To Hull, the word "China" did not include Manchuria and he had no intention of demanding that the Japanese surrender that territory. The American note should have been clear on this point. The exception of Manchuria would not have made the Hull note acceptable as it stood, but it might have enabled Foreign Minister Togo to persuade the militarists that negotiations should be continued; it could very well have forced a postponement of the November 30 deadline.[2]

And so two great nations sharing a fear of a Communist-dominated Asia were set on a collision course. Who was to blame? Japan was almost solely responsible for bringing herself to the road of war through the seizure of Manchuria, the invasion of China, the atrocities committed against the Chinese, and the drive to the south. But the United States did not fully understand that this course of aggression had been the inevitable result of the West's attempts to eliminate Japan as an economic rival after World War I, the Great Depression, her population explosion, and the necessity to find new resources and markets to continue as a first-rate power. How could the United States, rich in resources and land, free from fear of attack, understand the position of a tiny, crowded

---

[2] The author asked a number of Tojo's close associates what might have happened *if* Hull had clarified that point. General Kenryo Sato, learning the truth for the first time, slapped his forehead and said, "If we had only known!" Excitedly he added, "If you had said you recognized Manchuria, we'd have accepted!" General Teiichi Suzuki (director of the Cabinet Planning Board), Naoki Hoshino (Tojo's secretary-general), and Finance Minister Okinori Kaya would not go that far. Kaya, a leading politician in the postwar period, said, "If the note had excluded Manchuria, the decision to wage war or not would have been re-discussed at great length. There'd have been heated arguments at liaison conferences over whether we should withdraw at once from North China in spite of the threat of Communism." At least, said Suzuki, "Pearl Harbor would have been prevented. There might have been a change of government."

island empire with almost no natural resources, which was constantly in danger of assault from a ruthless neighbor, the Soviet Union? America herself had, moreover, contributed to the atmosphere of hate and distrust by excluding the Japanese from immigration and, in effect, flaunting a racial and color prejudice that justifiably infuriated the proud Nipponese.

There were no heroes or villains on either side. Roosevelt, for all his shortcomings, was a man of broad vision and humanity; the Emperor was a man of honor and peace. Both were limited—one by the bulky machinery of a great democracy and the other by training, custom and the restrictions of his rule. Tojo and Togo were not villains nor were Stimson and Hull. The villain was the times. Japan and America would never have come to the brink of war except for the social and economic eruption of Europe after the Great War and the rise of two great revolutionary ideologies— Communism and Fascism.

A war that need not have been fought seemed certain to begin.

In Tucson, William R. Mathews, the editor of the *Arizona Daily Star*, a close friend of General Pershing, was writing an editorial forecasting a surprise attack on the Philippines—and Pearl Harbor.

2.

The next day, Friday the twenty-eighth, Colonel Bratton brought Stimson information about Japanese movements in Southeast Asia amounting "to such a formidable statement of dangerous possibilities" that the Secretary decided to take it to the President before he got up. It was after nine o'clock but Roosevelt, suffering from a sinus infection, was resting in bed. After reading Bratton's reports, he said there were three alternatives: "first, to do nothing; second, to make something in the nature of an ultimatum again, stating a point beyond which we would fight; third, to fight at once."

The last two were the only ones, said Stimson. Roosevelt agreed. "Of the other two, my choice is the latter one," said Stimson, and waited in vain for the President to second the motion. But Roosevelt, apparently, was still leary of taking the final step to war.

At a noon meeting of the War Cabinet, consisting of Stimson, Knox, Hull, Stark and Marshall, the President read aloud the most alarming passages of Bratton's report envisaging an imminent Japanese attack on the Philippines, or Thailand, or Singapore, or the Dutch Netherlands. Roosevelt then said there was one more possibility, an attack on the Kra Isthmus, which would effectually block the Burma Road at its beginning.

In the discussion that followed, Stimson took the offensive. Strike at the Japanese force as it went by—*without warning!* The others preferred warning the Japanese that if their expedition "reached a certain place, or a certain line, or a certain point, we should have to fight."

The President approved of this and suggested sending a personal message to the Emperor asking him to help stop the senseless drift to war. Stimson thought little of this idea. One does not warn an Emperor, he said. It would be far better to send a message to Congress reporting the danger. Then, if he wanted, Roosevelt could dispatch a secret message to the Emperor.

Roosevelt didn't feel like arguing. He agreed. He was impatient to leave Washington and take his sinus problem to Warm Springs, Georgia. He said he wanted to have a belated Thanksgiving with the children there. Stimson disapproved—this was no time to leave the capital—but he said nothing, nor did anyone else. And so the President abruptly took himself out of the crisis.

No one in Washington had warned Short that he should be on the alert for more than sabotage from local Nisei. In fact, on that November 28, General Arnold wired the commander of the Hawaiian Air Force to initiate measures immediately "to provide the following: protection of your personnel against subversive propaganda, protection of all activities against espionage, and protection against sabotage of your equipment, property and establishment. . . . Avoiding unnecessary alarm and publicity protective measures should be confined to those essential to security."

Short took this message as confirmation that he was on the right alert. Army planes were bunched together for better protection from saboteurs.

On the last day of November Tokyo ordered their ambassador, General Hiroshi Oshima, in Berlin to inform Hitler immediately that the English and Americans were planning to move military forces into East Asia and this must be countered:

. . . SAY VERY SECRETLY TO THEM THAT THERE IS EXTREME DANGER THAT WAR MAY SUDDENLY BREAK OUT BETWEEN THE ANGLO-SAXON NATIONS AND JAPAN THROUGH SOME CLASH OF ARMS AND ADD THAT THE TIME OF THE BREAKING OUT MAY COME QUICKER THAN ANYONE DREAMS.

This Purple message was intercepted and promptly translated in Washington but neither Kimmel nor Short was informed.

At the War Department Hornbeck brought Stimson a draft for the President's proposed message to the Emperor. "I read it over," recalled Stimson, "and it was a comprehensive but very long and meticulous statement of the history of the United States relations with the Far East into which had been blended the suggestions that Knox and I had made. The whole paper was thirteen or four-teen pages long and had no punch for the requirements for which we had suggested it at the conference on Friday. Poor Hornbeck looked practically worn out. He had been working very hard and was evidently very nervous and tired. He said Hull was also very much worn."

In the evening Knox visited Stimson and they made their own draft for the finale of whatever message would be sent to the Emperor. "This was in the shape of a virtual ultimatum to Japan that we cannot permit her to take any further steps of aggression against any of the countries in the southwestern Pacific including China."

In Japan, where it was noon of December 1, the deadline had come twelve hours earlier. *Kido Butai* was well on its way to Hawaii and now, except for a last-minute diplomatic miracle, there seemed no chance that it would be called back.

The Matson liner *Lurline* was heading for the same destination but from the opposite direction. Ordinarily the ship would be crowded with tourists but on this trip there were far more defense workers aboard than passengers. She looked more like a transport than a luxury liner to Leslie E. Grogan, first assistant radio operator, who described himself as "a 260 pound blimp." The forty-seven-year-old Grogan, one of the most experienced radio operators of the Matson Line, picked up a faint signal which he could not identify. It came from northwest by west, a peculiar area for traffic at this time of year. What would anyone be doing in such northerly, rough waters? Suspicious, he strained to follow the signals. They increased, grew louder, and he could make out the call letters JCS, Yokohama. It was in some Japanese code. He stayed on after his watch ended at midnight helping Chief Operator Rudy Asplund log the signals. Grogan wrote down in his journal:

> The Japs are blasting away on the lower Marine Radio frequency—it is all in the Japanese code, and continues for several hours. Some of the signals were loud, and others weak, but in most every case, the repeat-back was acknowledged verbatum [sic]. It appears to me that the Jap is not using any deception of "Signal Detection" and boldly blasts away, using the Call letters JCS and JOS, and other Japanese based stations that have their transmitting keys all tied-in together, and controlled from a common source, presumably Tokio. . . .
>
> So much of the signals reaching us on the SS *Lurline* were good enough to get good R.D.F. [Radio Direction Finding Bearings]. We noted that signals were being repeated back, possibly for copying by crafts with small antennas. The main body of signals came from a Northwest by West area, which from our second night from Los Angeles bound for Honolulu —would be North and West of Honolulu.
>
> Having crossed the Pacific for 30 years, never heard JCS Yokohama Japan before at 9 P.M. our time on the lower Marine Frequency, and then rebroadcast simultaneously on the lower Marine frequency from some point in the Pacific.
>
> If anyone should ask me, I would say it's the Jap's Mobilization Battle Order. Rudy Asplund kept Captain Berndtson [the ship's master] informed and presume the Bridge Officers must have thought us "Nuts" with so much D.F. Tracking down of signals.
>
> It is now 3 AM and am trying to cool off after that hectic session earlier.
>
> Have jotted down all the particulars as they present them-

selves, and it is my desire to make a record of this because [I] sense things! Might prove worthy, who knows? GM 3.30 AM Dec. 1, 1941.

The next night, Monday, the Japanese signals were once more intercepted.

Again Rudy and I pick up without any trouble all the Japanese coded Wireless signals like last night—it goes on for two hours like before, and we are now making a concise record to turn in to the Naval Intelligence when we arrive in Honolulu, Wednesday December 3rd, 1941.

On Tuesday night the signals became even stronger as *Kido Butai* drew closer to its target.

We continue to pick up the bold Japanese General Order signals—it can't be anything else. We get good Radio Direction Finder bearings, mostly coming from a Northwesterly direction from our position. The Jap floating units continue their bold repetition of wireless signals, presumably for the smaller crafts in their vanguard of ships, etc. The Japanese shore stations JCS and JOS are keyed by remote tie-in, coming from Tokyo I presume, and if we had a recording device, it would only prove what we ourselves jot down, and we can't help but know that so much of it is a repeat back, letter for letter, because we have copied the original signals coming from Japanese land based stations, etc.

The Japs are so bold in using these low Marine frequencies too, but with all the tension we've seen up to now, it's safe to say something is going to happen, and mighty soon, but how soon? All this display means something—time will tell, and tonights Radio Detection signals have come from a NW by W from Honolulu, and from the signals, the Japs must be bunched up, biding time.

3.

The signals picked up by *Lurline* were only the shape of things to come. There was also excitement on the seventh floor of 717 Market Street in San Francisco, the main office of the Twelfth Naval District Intelligence. Lieutenant Ellsworth A. Hosner, a communications expert in civilian life, had recently been ordered to relocate the missing Japanese carrier force. For the past few days he had been feeding information to his assistant, Seaman First Class Z, a brilliant young man who had left college to volunteer in Navy Intelligence.[3] Z, an electronics expert at twenty, had already designed a device which was being used on all Navy landing craft. Z's task was to collate reports from commercial ships in the Pacific as well as the four wire services: Press Wireless, Globe Wireless, RCA, and Mackay. That morning they had received a report from one of the wire services wondering what was going on west of Hawaii. They were receiving queer signals that didn't make sense at such frequency. Hosner telephoned the other services and shipping companies. Were they getting any strange signals? Several confirmed they had.

Using a large chart, Z managed to get cross bearings on the mysterious signals. He told Hosner it could possibly be the missing carrier force. The lieutenant alerted the Chief of Intelligence, Captain Richard T. McCollough. Hosner felt assured that not only O.N.I. but the President would be promptly informed. It was common knowledge in the office that McCollough was Roosevelt's personal friend and had access to him through Harry Hopkins' telephone at the White House.

Across the Pacific in Bandoeng, Java, the Dutch Army intercepted a Japanese message from Tokyo to their ambassador in Bangkok. It was in the consular code, which had been broken by a Dutch colonel, J. A. Verkuhl, with the help of his wife and a group of students. The message told of attacks to be launched on Hawaii, the Philippines, Malaya and Thailand. The signal to begin all operations simultaneously would come from Tokyo in the form of a weather broadcast over Radio Tokyo. It was the "winds" code setup.

General Hein Ter Poorten, the commander of the Netherlands East Indies Army, hand-carried the long message to the next building where the American military observer, Brigadier General Elliott Thorpe, a close friend, had an office. Ter Poorten asked Thorpe's secretary to leave and, after locking the door, said, "I

[3] Seaman First Class Z, an officer after Pearl Harbor, is presently internationally renowned in his field for his accomplishments. His tapes have been monitored by Carolyn Blakemore and Ken McCormick of Doubleday & Co., and will eventually be open to researchers.

have something here I believe of great importance to your government."

Thorpe read the intercept. "Sir, this is so important that with
your permission I will go at once to Batavia and inform our senior
State Department representative of this and then send it directly
to Washington tonight."

By the time Thorpe arrived in Batavia the American Consulate
had closed, so he proceeded to the Hotel des Indes where Dr.
Walter Foote, the consul general and the senior naval attaché,
Commander Paul Sidney Slawson, lived. The former, nicknamed
"Uncle Billy," ridiculed the matter and advised Thorpe to forget
it. But Slawson was impressed. Since Thorpe's code book was in
Bandoeng, Slawson offered to send the message in naval code to
Washington. By the time it was encoded it was past midnight and
the main post office, which handled overseas communications, was
closed. The two pounded on the back door of the post office until
a member of the night staff appeared. Thorpe explained the urgency and asked that it be sent by cable; the Japs were probably
tapping the wireless. Since the message was in naval code it had to
go to the War Department through the Navy Communications
center. After its receipt was acknowledged Thorpe assumed that
both the Army and Navy had read the message and its warning of
an attack on Hawaii.[4]

On that eventful second of December Captain Johan E. M.
Ranneft, since 1938 the naval attaché of the Netherlands in
Washington, paid a visit to the Office of Naval Intelligence where
he queried Admiral Wilkinson and other intelligence officers
about the deteriorating situation in the Pacific. As usual they were
most frank with Ranneft since he had done the U. S. Navy a great
service. (After witnessing a demonstration of the 40-mm. Bofors
gun on a Dutch ship in the Caribbean, Captain W. P. H. Blandy,
chief of Ordnance, found it so far superior to all other anti-aircraft
guns that he was determined to get it for the U. S. Navy. But
there were complications. The weapon had been developed jointly
by the Netherlands Navy and two private companies, Hazemeyer-

---

[4] There is no record of this message ever having been received. No one has admitted seeing it; no copy has been found in any file.

Signaal and the Swedish firm of Bofors. Blandy realized how difficult it would be to get Swedish approval so he asked his friend Captain Ranneft for the blueprints. Without consulting his superiors in exile in London, Ranneft procured a set of blueprints from Batavia and turned them over to Blandy. Hours later a perturbed Swedish naval attaché protested this violation of patent rights. Ranneft assured him that the decision had been made by the Dutch government in London and any complaints should be lodged there.[5] A gun was made from the blueprints by a Baltimore firm, tested at Aberdeen Proving Grounds and would soon be installed on American warships.)

Ranneft was startled when one of the Americans pointed to a map on the wall and said, "This is the Japanese Task Force proceeding east." The position was halfway between Japan and Hawaii. Ranneft said nothing, only wondered how the Americans had managed to track the missing carriers. He cabled Dutch naval headquarters in London and also reported the information in person to Minister Alexander Loudon. Then he wrote in his official diary, "Conference at Navy Department, O.N.I. They show me on the map the position of two Japanese carriers. They left Japan on easterly course."

At Pearl Harbor Kimmel was asking his intelligence officer the whereabouts of the missing carriers. Lieutenant Commander Layton reported that there were a few carriers in Japanese home waters but the major force was still missing.

"What!" exclaimed Kimmel. "You don't know where Carrier Division 1 and Carrier Division 2 are?"

"No, sir, I do not. I think they are in home waters, but I don't know where they are. The rest of these units, I feel pretty confident of their location."

Then Kimmel looked at Layton as he occasionally did—with a somewhat stern countenance and yet partially with a twinkle in his eyes—and said, "Do you mean to say that they could be rounding Diamond Head and you wouldn't know it?"

[5] After the war, former Secretary of Defense Dekkers told Ranneft that it was lucky he had not asked London for the blueprints. "We should have been obliged to answer 'no.'" The U. S. Government eventually paid large sums to both Bofors and Hazemeyer-Signaal.

"I hope they would be sighted before now."

The information given to Captain Ranneft by O.N.I. was never sent to Kimmel. That day the admiral wrote Stark that the Pacific Fleet was so deficient in auxiliaries that it could not even start any attack west from Pearl Harbor before February of 1942.

4.

Stimson was worried on that Tuesday, the second. The President had returned from Warm Springs but as yet had sent no message to the Emperor or the Congress. Harry Hopkins reassured the Secretary that Roosevelt was not weakening. Stimson convinced himself this was true from F.D.R.'s attitude at the afternoon Cabinet meeting. "The President went step by step over the situation," he wrote in his diary, "and I think has made up his mind to go ahead." He was confident Roosevelt would now not only warn the Emperor but alert the American people through a strong message to Congress. The way was at last clear. Roosevelt's words would maneuver the Japanese into firing the first shot once they crossed that certain line in Southeast Asia. In a few days the line would be crossed and the British and Dutch would have to fight. And so, at last, would America.

Yet Roosevelt showed apprehension when he was interrupted during a later meeting with Donald Nelson, head of the Supply Priorities and Allocation Board, to be told that Kurusu and Nomura were outside with Hull. "How does it look?" asked Nelson.

The President shook his head gravely. "Don, I wouldn't be a bit surprised if we were at war with Japan by Thursday."

On the third of December he seemed almost cocky. He told Secretary of the Treasury Morgenthau that he had Kurusu and Nomura "running around like a lot of wet hens" after he asked them why they were sending so many military forces into Indochina. "I think the Japanese are doing everything they can to stall until they are ready."

The Census Bureau finally had the name and address of every Japanese in the United States, a total of 126,947: the California material alone consisted of some fifty single-spaced pages. Dr. Field telephoned the commandant of the Marine Corps that the job was finally completed and thanked him for his generous assistance. After congratulating Mr. Capt and his staff, Field then drove to the White House where he turned over the last envelope containing the California material to Grace Tully.[6] Copies were distributed to the F.B.I. and the governors and military commanders in each state.

That day Washington forwarded Kimmel two dispatches advising him of Japanese instructions to embassies and consulates to burn their code books. Nothing was sent about the approaching Japanese carriers.

At 9:00 A.M. the S.S. *Lurline* docked at its usual pier near Honolulu's famous Aloha Tower. Grogan and Asplund hurried the few blocks up Bishop Street to the downtown intelligence office of the Fourteenth Naval District in the Hotel Alexander Young Building. After introducing themselves to Lieutenant Commander George Warren Pease, they turned over their data. "He was a good listener," recalled Grogan, "and showed little outward reflection as to what we felt was a mighty serious situation, but nevertheless, Rudy and I felt relieved in our avowed duty to pass the vital information on to the Navy for whatever value they could derive from it." Pease promised to pass on the warning but there is no record that he forwarded the information either to the Fourteenth Naval District intelligence officer, Captain Irving Mayfield, or to Washington.[7]

Within sight of the docked *Lurline*, Police Lieutenant John A. Burns, head of the Honolulu Espionage Bureau, was entering the Dillingham Building. He proceeded up to the second floor to the

[6] Dr. Field, who became one of the world's leading anthropologists, recently revealed that years later he requested specific information on the project. "Dr. Conrad Taueber, director of the Bureau of the Census at the time, replied that no record of this assignment could be found! Apparently, our security measures were entirely successful." In 1980, the Freedom of Information Act notwithstanding, the associate director for administration, Bureau of the Census, wrote the author: "Apparently there is some misunderstanding regarding the assistance which the Bureau actually made. Our records indicate that no request for services was made to the Census Bureau prior to the attack on Pearl Harbor by President Roosevelt or any other administrative official." A request to Miss Tully for an interview on the subject was refused. "I'm sorry to tell you that I have nothing worthwhile to contribute to your project."
[7] Pease was killed in an air crash in 1945.

office of Robert L. Shivers, the F.B.I. agent in charge. "Close the doors," said Shivers. He was a small man who prided himself on being "a deadpan F.B.I. agent," but today he was patently agitated. "I'm not telling my men but I'm telling you this." There were tears in his eyes. "We're going to be attacked before the week is out." Pearl Harbor was going to be hit. The stunned Burns asked what he could do and was told to start contacting people in town to see if anyone had any foreknowledge of the Pearl Harbor attack. No one had.[8]

In San Francisco at the Twelfth Naval District Intelligence Office, Lieutenant Hosner and Seaman First Class Z had tracked the Japanese carrier force to a position northwest of Hawaii. Were they bound for the Aleutians or Hawaii? The information was passed on to Captain McCollough who, they assumed, informed Washington through intelligence channels as well as the President through Harry Hopkins.

Late that night Barnet Nover, associate editor of the Washington *Post*, was wakened by a telephone call from a British official who begged him to come at once to his room. Once Nover arrived the official, in great agitation, explained that a Dutch officer had told him two Japanese carriers had been discovered north of the Marshalls and were bound either for the Dutch Indies or Pearl Harbor.[9] The Briton confessed he could not sleep since he was certain the carriers' destination was Pearl Harbor.

Just after midnight, in the early hours of December 4,[10] Ralph Briggs was on duty at Station M, the Navy's East Coast intercept installation. Earlier Commander Laurance Safford had driven out to Station M to inspect the new land-line telegraph for direction-finder control. He knew that the Orange intercept team had been

8 Burns was later three-time governor of Hawaii. Taped interviews of the John A. Burns Oral History Project were conducted in 1975 by Stuart Gerry Brown, Daniel Boylan and Paul Hooper of the University of Hawaii Department of American Studies. Burns was cross-examined by all three on this issue. Professor Hooper told this author he was convinced Burns was telling the truth; he knew he was dying.

9 A full and more accurate account of this episode will appear in the forthcoming biography of Nover by his widow. Captain Ranneft asserts he was not the Dutch official mentioned above. It may have been Colonel F. G. L. Weijerman, the military attaché, now deceased.

10 Safford believed it was December 4 but Briggs today thinks it may have been earlier. See Notes.

alerted to watch out for any "winds" execute and was making a personal check of the watch assigned to that duty. He was assured that the Tokyo news and weather broadcasts were being monitored by qualified *katakana* operators.

Briggs had not met Safford on an earlier inspection but was well qualified to pick up any "winds" message. He could read Japanese and his superior, Chief Radioman DW, had instructed him to look out only for three terms: *Higashi no kaze ame, Kitano kaze kumori* or *Nishi no kaze hare.* DW privately explained to Briggs the significance of each term and that it probably would be the third, "West wind, clear," a diplomatic break with Great Britain.

Before dawn Briggs picked up on schedule the routine Japanese Navy weather broadcast from Tokyo and he began copying down in Japanese telegraphic code: *Higashi no kaze ame:* "East wind, rain." Momentarily he didn't realize its significance since he had been expecting "West wind, clear."

He quickly checked his watch supervisor's classified instructions. There was no doubt this was one of the war warning destruct messages to ministries and consulates. And it meant war with America.

He rushed to the next room and got the message on the TWX circuit to Safford's office. Then he telephoned his supervisor, who lived on the post. "DW," he exclaimed, "I think I got what we've been looking for!"

"Good. I'll be right up." Briggs was to get it on the TWX circuit downtown right away.

Briggs said he had already done that. He hung up and made an entry on his log sheet of the lead line of the message. He also included the warning characters, the date, time and frequency.

5.

During the fateful third of December an Army air corps captain had secretly brought to isolationist Senator Burton Wheeler a document as thick as a novel, wrapped in brown paper and labeled "Victory Program." The young captain, according to Wheeler's account, said he thought Congress had "a right to know what's really going on in the executive branch when it concerns human lives." As Wheeler scanned the top secret papers, his blood pressure rose. "I felt strongly that this was something the people as well as a senator should know about."

It looked to Wheeler like a blueprint for total war in Europe and Asia, contemplating total U.S. armed forces of 10,045,658 men. In righteous indignation he turned over the papers for publication to a Washington correspondent for the Chicago *Tribune*.[11]

The next morning, the fourth, it was 7:30 A.M. by the time that Major Albert C. Wedemeyer reached his office in the Munitions Building. He sensed an atmosphere of excitement. Officers were milling around amidst a buzz of conversation which ended abruptly as his secretary handed him a copy of the Washington *Times-Herald*. In consternation he read the banner headlines:

F.D.R.'S WAR PLANS

And in somewhat smaller type below:

GOAL IS 10 MILLION ARMED MEN:
HALF TO FIGHT IN AEF
Proposed Land Drive by July 1, 1943, to Smash Nazis

Wedemeyer hastily scanned the report. It was an exact reproduction of the Victory Program on which he had been working day and night the past few months. "I could not have been more astounded if a bomb had been dropped on Washington. . . . Here was irrefutable evidence that America was preparing to enter the war, and soon. President Roosevelt's promises to keep us out of war were interpreted as campaign oratory." Wedemeyer was the General Staff officer responsible for the preparation as well as the secrecy of the Victory Program, revelation of which might inevitably precipitate American participation in the war.

Privately he believed America should not intervene in the affairs of foreign countries unless national interest was in jeopardy.

11 According to the biographer of William Stephenson, the man called "Intrepid," the British had "planted" these documents with the help of a sympathetic American captain. "The primary aim of this deception was to use isolationist channels as a means of revealing to Hitler a 'secret plan' calculated to provoke him into a declaration of war. Even if the Japanese attacked British and American bases without warning, the British feared that the United States would not declare war on Germany."

And the United States, as professional military men generally agreed, was not in imminent danger. Despite his convictions, Wedemeyer had devoted all his energies to the planning of a war for which he felt the United States was unprepared. The first to be suspected of leaking the information, he was thoroughly investigated by the F.B.I., which found him completely innocent.

Official Washington was in panic on that fourth of December. By the time Stimson returned from a three-hour session with his dentist in New York, he found his assistants depressed. "Nothing more unpatriotic or damaging to our plans for defense could very well be conceived of and for the first time in my observation of him McCloy was sunk. But the picture of this occurrence during my own day of absence rather tickled my funnybones and I cheered them up. The thing to do is to meet the matter head on and use this occurrence if possible to shake our American people out of their infernal apathy and ignorance of what this war means."

He telephoned the President. "I gave him my views on the situation and was glad to find that he agreed that we should meet the crisis head on." Stimson was relieved to find Roosevelt "full of fight" and no longer vacillating. "So the evening's discussion ended with a note of fight and optimism."

William R. Mathews, who had recently predicted an attack on Pearl Harbor in his newspaper, was interviewing Knox. Mathews asked if the Navy was ready for a surprise attack. "Hell, yes," was the answer, "but they don't dare to make a surprise attack. They know they could commit suicide."

During the day Kilsoo Haan telephoned Maxwell Hamilton of the State Department that he had been warned by the Korean underground that the Japanese would attack Pearl Harbor the coming weekend. He was concerned enough to send Hamilton this long report:

> Pursuant to our telephone conversations regarding our agents' apprehensions that Japan may suddenly move against Hawaii "this coming weekend," may I call your attention to the following relevant and pertinent information.
>
> *One:* The publication of U. S. Army Air Corps maneuvers throughout the Hawaiian Islands by the Japanese daily *Nippu*

Jiji, Nov. 22, 1941. This timetable of air maneuvers is from November through Dec. 31, 1941, "every day except Sundays and holidays."

Two: The Italian magazine "Oggi" of Oct. 24, 1941, published an article in Rome forecasting war between Japan and America. The article forecast war between Japan and America by air and naval attack of the Hawaiian Islands and eventually attacking Alaska, California and the Panama Canal.

Haan also called attention to a Japanese book, *The Three Power Alliance and the U.S.-Japan War*, by Kinoaki Matsuo, published in October 1940. In a chapter entitled "The Japanese Surprise Attack Fleet," Matsuo had written that there was no doubt that in the event of war with the United States Japan would grasp the best opportunity to strike the enemy in advance.

> It is our considered observation and sincere belief, December is the month of the Japanese attack, and the SURPRISE FLEET is aimed at Hawaii, perhaps the first Sunday of December. . . .
>
> No matter how you feel toward our work, will you please convey our apprehension and this information to the President and to the military and naval commanders in Hawaii.

In Java General Thorpe had already sent a second message to Washington warning of the attack on Hawaii and the Philippines. But he was so disquieted, he decided, on the fourth of December, to send still another, this through Consul General Foote. But Uncle Billy deleted the entire first long paragraph mentioning the location of the attacks, and only set up the "winds" code. At the end Foote added: "Thorpe and Slawson cabled the above to the War Department. I attach little or no importance to it and view it with suspicion. Such have been common since 1936."

General Ter Poorten guessed that Foote would water down the warning and sent all the details to Colonel F. G. L. Weijerman, the Dutch military attaché in Washington, with instructions to pass the information on to the highest U.S. military sources.

Thorpe sent a fourth message a little later, one directly to the Army G-2, General Miles. This message was acknowledged by Washington; Thorpe was ordered to send no more dispatches on the subject.[12] "This might have been because the War Department felt my dispatches might reach the wrong hands or for some other reason they considered adequate."

Another drama was taking place to the north, in Manila. At Asiatic Fleet Headquarters, Lieutenant Kemp Tolley was instructed to set out on a mysterious mission ordered personally by the President. He was to arm a windjammer, the *Lanikai*, a two-masted interisland schooner, with a cannon, a machine gun and provisions for a two-week cruise—and be ready to sail in twenty-four hours. Tolley was aware that his was but one of three small ships on a joint mission, and that he was to relieve the *Isabel*, commanded by Lieutenant John Walker Payne, Jr., which was already on her way to the Indochina coast. Three days earlier Admiral Hart had received this extraordinary order:

PRESIDENT DIRECTS THAT THE FOLLOWING BE DONE AS SOON AS POSSIBLE AND WITHIN TWO DAYS IF POSSIBLE AFTER RECEIPT THIS DISPATCH X CHARTER THREE SMALL VESSELS TO FORM A QUOTE DEFENSIVE INFORMATION PATROL UNQUOTE X MINIMUM REQUIREMENTS TO ESTABLISH IDENTITY AS UNITED STATES MEN-OF-WAR ARE COMMAND BY A NAVAL OFFICER AND TO MOUNT A SMALL GUN AND ONE MACHINE GUN WOULD SUFFICE X FILIPINO CREWS MAY BE EMPLOYED WITH MINIMUM NUMBER NAVAL RATINGS TO ACCOMPLISH PURPOSE WHICH IS TO OBSERVE AND REPORT BY RADIO JAPANESE MOVEMENTS IN WEST CHINA SEA AND GULF OF SIAM. . . .

Hart had read this with consternation. "As a war measure the project was very ill-advised," he later told the Director of Naval History. "Pickets in such locations could not be useful because the Japanese were bound to have them marked down . . . which would mean no chance to let them see anything of value."

He had instructed Payne to observe the utmost secrecy. The two of them alone were to know the actual mission until the *Isabel* was at sea, and then only his executive officer, Lieutenant j.g. Marion Buaas, was to be informed of their true purpose. Their

[12] Of the four messages Thorpe sent, only two were found in War Department files: the censored one signed by Foote; and his own final message, which arrived without the paragraph warning of the Pearl Harbor attack. Somehow in transmission this vital information was deleted.

cover orders were to search for a downed Catalina. On the morning of December 5 the *Isabel* sighted a Japanese Navy plane which continued to reappear throughout the day as the ship, originally a private yacht, kept heading east. From the air the deck chairs gave the *Isabel* the appearance of a large yacht but it was obviously a warship because of four 3-inch guns mounted fore and aft as well as four Lewis machine guns on top of the pilot house.

At 7 P.M. Payne sighted the Indochina coast twenty-two miles distant. Ten minutes later he was ordered to return to Manila immediately. During the return voyage a message was received that Pearl Harbor had been attacked.[13]

In Washington it was early morning of December 5. Half of the front page of the Washington *Times-Herald* was occupied with the War Plan scandal:

WAR PLAN EXPOSÉ ROCKS CAPITAL, PERILS ARMY APPROPRIATION BILL: LONDON HAILS PROSPECT OF A.E.F.

The three subheadlines read:

> Congress in Uproar; Tinkham Declares Republic Betrayed
> British Press Headlines Sensational Disclosure
> Administration Fears Nation's Wrath Over Secret Project

Stimson called the President; he now disagreed with Roosevelt's idea of making no comment to the newspapers regarding the matter. "Go ahead," said Roosevelt. "Tell them." At his own press conference at 10:30 A.M. he said he had nothing to say but that the Secretary of War probably did. And when Stimson got to his own press room an hour later he found it jammed as never before. He

---

[13] After the war Tolley, whose ship was about to set sail when bombs fell on Oahu, was convinced the mission was only a trick to incite war with Japan. Lieutenant (later Captain) Buaas shared the belief that his ship was bait for the Japanese. "The true nature of our mission was to endeavor to locate Japanese ships and as such it was expected that our reporting would result in an incident in which the ship would probably be sunk." Although Admiral Hart had the opportunity to tell the truth about the three small ships at the congressional hearings he did not do so. Later he admitted to Tolley that the *Lanikai* had been sent out as bait. "And I could prove it. But I won't. And don't *you* try either."

Hanson Baldwin, the noted military analyst, also believed the three vessels had been intended as "tethered goats" to lure the Japanese. "In short, Roosevelt undoubtedly believed, like millions of Americans, that the United States' vital interests required the nation's entry into war, and in order to convince a large and reluctant portion of public opinion, he wanted the Japanese to strike first."

was very brief. First he asked two questions: "What would you think of an American General Staff which in the present condition of the world did not investigate and study every conceivable type of emergency which may confront this country and every possible method of meeting that emergency? What do you think of the patriotism of a man or a newspaper which would take those confidential studies and make them public to the enemies of this country?" Then he explained that the revelations were only unfinished studies. "They have never constituted an authorized program of the government."

During the day Roosevelt wrote Wendell Willkie, whom he had defeated at the polls the previous year, approving Willkie's proposed trip to Australia. "It would, of course, be of real value to cement our relations with New Zealand and Australia and would be useful not only now but in the future. There is always the Japanese matter to consider. The situation is definitely serious and there might be an armed clash at any moment if the Japanese continue their forward progress against the Philippines, Dutch Indies or Malaya or Burma. Perhaps the next four or five days will decide the matter."[14]

At the Cabinet meeting Roosevelt read Stimson's statement to the press. The latter was amused to find his fellow members extremely warlike. "They thought I was almost defensive in my statement. Harold Ickes grunted that it was entirely too defensive. Even Henry Wallace said that while he liked the main statement, he thought he didn't like the questions."

In his diary the Secretary of War did not mention the much more important discussion at the meeting concerning the approaching conflict. A rare detailed account of this was revealed by Secretary of Labor Frances Perkins in an oral history interview at Columbia University in 1955. She recalled that Hull was very sober and so lugubrious that the gloom fairly stood out all over him. He was disgusted with Kurusu and Nomura. "They don't mean business, Mr. President. I'm sure they don't mean to do anything. With every hour that passes, I become more convinced that they are not playing in the open, that what they say is equivocal

---

[14] The letter was not mailed until after the attack on Pearl Harbor. The President then wrote a postscript in longhand: "This was dictated Friday morning—long before this vile attack started."

and has two meanings to it. . . . They are the worst people I
ever saw." He continued in the strongest and most blasphemous
language Mrs. Perkins had ever heard him use.

As they started discussing how the Japanese would go about attacking the British, Knox suddenly interrupted. "Well, you know,
Mr. President, we know where the Japanese Fleet is?"

"Yes, I know," said Roosevelt and then looked around. "I think
we ought to tell everybody how ticklish the situation is. We have
information, as Knox just mentioned . . . Well, you tell them
what it is, Frank."

"Well," began Knox in his sputtering, excitable way, "we have
very secret information that mustn't go outside this room that the
Japanese Fleet is out at sea." He was extremely high strung.

Roosevelt, looking very serious and severe, kept nodding his
head in affirmation. He was scowling in a puzzled manner and as
Knox said, "Our information is . . ." cut him off and said, "We
haven't got anything like perfect information as to their apparent
destination. The question in the minds of the Navy and in my
mind is whether the fleet is going south."

"Singapore?" said several.

Roosevelt nodded. "Probably. That's the presumed objective if
they go south."

Knox interrupted excitedly. "Every indication is that they are
going south, Mr. President. That's the obvious direction."

Roosevelt cut in. "But it's not absolutely certain that they
wouldn't be going north. You haven't yet information that they're
not going north. You haven't got information with regard to direction."

"That's right, we haven't, but we must conclude that they are
going south. It's so unlikely that they would go north."

"Well," said the President, "there are the Aleutians. There are
fishing grounds. We do know there have been very large fishing
fleets in those waters in recent months, larger than usual."

Knox thought this was ridiculous. "That might be, but it's not
likely."

For some reason Roosevelt persisted as if he knew something
Knox did not. "They might be going north. There is no evidence
that they're not going north."

Knox was equally stubborn. "No, but I must draw the conclusion that they're going south. I don't think they're out just to maneuver. We in the Navy think they must be going to do something."

Roosevelt surveyed the group. "Now, I want to try an experiment. They are at sea. What shall we do? If they proceed toward Singapore, what's the problem of the United States? What should the United States do? I'd like every person here one by one to answer and say what he thinks we ought to do. I want to warn you that I'm asking this for information and a kind of an opinion, not advice in the usual sense, because we're not going to take any vote and I'm not going to be bound by any advice that you give. I'm just checking to see how your minds are operating. It is a terrible problem. I hope we won't have to act on it, or settle it, but we may have to. We may have to decide to do something. What do you think?"

When Mrs. Perkins declared that they should go to the relief of the British if Singapore were attacked, Roosevelt was surprised as though expecting her to go along with the minority who opposed this course. The Secretary of Labor left the room feeling that this had been a dreadful session. "I remember going back to my office and just sitting down kind of limp, trying to face the music myself, saying, 'Is it possible that this country will be involved in a war with Japan in the Pacific?' That had never crossed my mind, I'm free to say." It had been a very shattering day, yet there was still no sense of immediacy and nothing had been said that made it seem imperative to change her weekend plans. She would still go to the Cosmopolitan Club in New York City where she'd have peace enough to write a report.

In Honolulu the lone Navy spy, Yoshikawa, was informing Tokyo that three battleships had arrived in Pearl Harbor. that morning, and that the carrier *Lexington* had left port with five heavy cruisers.

6.

It was about 5 A.M., December 6, Washington time, as Colonel Bonner Fellers, an American observer in Egypt, walked into the

Royal Air Force Headquarters in Cairo. The air marshal in charge of the Middle East was at his desk. His first words were: "Bonner, you will be in the war in twenty-four hours. We have a secret signal Japan will strike the U.S. in twenty-four hours."

Fellers—described by George Marshall as "a very valuable observer"—couldn't believe it. He replied that the Japanese were having a free hand in the Orient and it would not be to their advantage to attack America. But the air marshal was confident the Japanese would strike and made no secret of his elation that the United States would finally be in the war.

Fellers toyed with the idea of sending a dispatch to Washington relaying the air marshal's statement. "Finally, I decided that if the British knew of the attack, we also knew of it. Also I reasoned that if the report were false I would be in quite a pickle."[15]

About that time London was cabling Air Chief Marshal Sir Robert Brooke-Popham, commander in chief in the Far East, that they had "now received assurance of American armed support" in case of Japanese attacks on Siam, Thailand or the Netherlands East Indies.

As the morning wore on in Washington, the bad news from the Far East increased and Stimson felt that "the atmosphere indicated that something was going to happen."

At the White House Harry Hopkins was reading a cable from Averell Harriman, who had come to London after completing a mission for Roosevelt in Moscow:

THE PRESIDENT SHOULD BE INFORMED OF CHURCHILL'S BELIEF THAT IN THE EVENT OF AGGRESSION BY THE JAPANESE IT WOULD BE THE POLICY OF THE BRITISH TO POSTPONE TAKING ANY ACTION—EVEN THOUGH THIS DELAY MIGHT INVOLVE SOME MILITARY SACRIFICE— UNTIL THE PRESIDENT HAS TAKEN SUCH ACTION AS, UNDER THE CIRCUMSTANCES, HE CONSIDERS BEST. THEN CHURCHILL WILL ACT "NOT WITHIN THE HOUR, BUT WITHIN THE MINUTE." I AM SEEING HIM AGAIN TOMORROW. LET ME KNOW IF THERE IS ANYTHING SPECIAL YOU WANT ME TO ASK.

[15] "Had I known what I later learned," Fellers wrote Kimmel in 1967, "I would have alerted Washington, Panama, Pearl Harbor, and the Philippines—come what may. I truly made a horrible mistake which I'll regret to the end."

During Knox's daily meeting with Stark, Turner, Noyes and other leading naval officers there was a long discussion on Japanese intentions. "Gentlemen," asked Knox, "are they going to hit *us*?"

"No, Mr. Secretary," said Admiral Turner, who was generally considered the spokesman for Stark. "They are going to attack the British. They are not ready for us yet."

A recently retired American diplomat, Ferdinand Mayer, walked into the Japanese Embassy on Massachusetts Avenue a little after 11 A.M. He had been given to understand that his old friend, Saburo Kurusu, would talk to him openly about the degenerating negotiations. The special envoy received Mayer warmly and talked with such amazing candor that it became increasingly evident to Mayer that he was trying to convey something of shocking import. Finally he openly declared that the situation was "one of extreme danger of war." Mayer was so impressed, he begged Kurusu to dine that evening at the home of Ferdinand Belin, former ambassador to Poland. Mayer felt he needed a witness "for this most extraordinary expression of view which, if understood by our government, must surely at least provide it with a most urgent reason to alert all possible military establishments in the Far East." Mayer wasted no time in telephoning James Dunn of the State Department of his extraordinary interview.

In the Navy Building, Mrs. Edgers was showing Chief Yeoman H. L. Bryant a partial translation of the message from Consul General Kita to Tokyo concerning the light signals from a house on Lanikai Beach. She said it read like a detective story and they both agreed it should be brought to Lieutenant Commander Kramer's attention.

Commander Laurance Safford knew nothing of this message. He was involved in composing a warning to Kimmel: "In view of imminence of war destroy all registered publications in Wake Island except this system and current editions of aircraft code and direction finder code." The message was typed out and sent to Admiral Noyes for approval but the chief of communications didn't see it until returning from the big meeting in Knox's office. Noyes had been so impressed by Turner's declaration that the Japs would not attack the United States, only the British, that Safford's proposed message made him furious. He summoned Safford. "What do you mean by a message like this," he railed, "telling the commander that war is imminent?"

"Admiral," said Safford as calmly as he could, "war is a matter of days if not hours."

"You may think there is going to be a war but I think the Japs are bluffing!"

Knowing Noyes's fear of taking responsibility, Safford said, "Wake Island has all the Pacific crypto systems that we have printed, and covering the period up to July 1942. If those systems fall in the hands of the Japanese it will go very hard with you and very hard with me, too. I want that message sent."

"Well, that makes a difference," blustered Noyes, and began to rewrite the message. Safford was appalled at the "mayhem" committed on his original dispatch, for Noyes had left out any mention of Wake Island or any warning of war.

> In view of the international situation and the exposed position of the outlying Pacific islands you may authorize the destruction by them of secret and confidential documents now or under later conditions of greater urgency. . . .

To make matters even worse, the message was sent deferred precedence, which meant delivery on Monday morning.

During this discussion, Captain Ranneft, the Dutch naval attaché, arrived at the office of O.N.I. where he found Wilkinson, McCollum and Kramer. After they told of the Japanese movements toward the Kra Peninsula, Ranneft asked about the two Japanese carriers heading eastward. "Where are those fellows?"

Someone put a finger on the wall chart four hundred miles or so north of Honolulu. "What the devil are they doing there?" asked the amazed Ranneft. Someone said vaguely that the Japanese were perhaps interested in "eventual American intentions." This made little sense to Ranneft but he said nothing. And no one mentioned anything about a possible attack on Pearl Harbor. "I myself do not think about it," Ranneft wrote in his official diary, "because I believe that everyone in Honolulu is 100% on the alert, just as everyone here at O.N.I. is."

Ranneft returned to his embassy, told Minister Loudon what he had heard, and then cabled his superiors in London.

At the Twelfth Naval District in San Francisco, Lieutenant Hosner and Seaman First Class Z had tracked *Kido Butai* to a position approximately four hundred miles north-northwest of Oahu. There was now no doubt at all. Pearl Harbor was going to be raided the next morning. After passing on their calculations to Captain McCollough the two men had a private celebration. Tomorrow the Japanese were going to get the surprise of their lives.

That morning Joseph C. Harsch of the *Christian Science Monitor* talked for half an hour with Kimmel. The admiral said that the Germans had just announced they were going into winter quarters in front of Moscow. "This means that they have given up the effort to capture Moscow this winter. This means that the Japanese will not attack us. They are too intelligent to fight a two-front war. If Moscow had fallen they could attack us without any danger of being attacked by the Russians in their rear."

Despite his reassuring words to Harsch, Kimmel was deeply disturbed. In the forenoon he summoned members of his staff to evaluate the latest reports of Japanese activity. There was still no sign of the missing carriers. He took the problem to lunch. In an attempt to slow down the killing pace Kimmel had set for himself the past months, Admiral Smith urged him to take siestas in such a tropic climate.

"Come, Smith," said Kimmel shortly, "let's get back to work."

"Well, there are times when your chief of staff would like one."

Kimmel proceeded without delay to the Planning Division office where Colonel Omar Pfeiffer, a Marine on his staff, was discussing the possible outbreak of war with Kimmel's operations officer, Captain Charles McMorris. The admiral expressed his anxiety about the Japanese intentions toward the Pacific Fleet and Pearl Harbor. He was so worried, he admitted, that it "affected his guts."

"Captain McMorris tried to allay the admiral's concern, if not premonitions," recalled Pfeiffer, "by saying that the Japanese could not possibly be able to proceed in force against Pearl Harbor when they had so much strength concentrated in the Asiatic operations. I was not a participant in the conversation but I sensed the deep feeling of concern and responsibility felt by the admiral."

Kimmel was so uneasy, he ordered Lieutenant Commander Layton to take the latest intelligence report on the concentration of Jap transport and naval transports off Indochina to Admiral Pye, commander of Combat Force, for his comments. Pye, aboard the battleship *California*, guessed that the Japanese were probably going to occupy a position in the Gulf of Siam from which to operate against the Burma Road. Layton didn't believe they would stop there. He felt their objectives were farther south, probably the oil of the East Indies since the United States had stopped its export of oil to Japan. Besides, the Japs would never leave their flanks exposed and would therefore attack the Philippines. "And we'd be at war."

"Oh, no," said Pye. "The Japanese won't attack us. We're too strong and powerful."

Layton brought these heartening words to Kimmel but he still fretted. Late in the afternoon he took his own operations officers, McMorris and DeLany, to his quarters for further discussion. Searching for solutions, Kimmel finally hit upon an idea that appealed to him: they would recall all liberty parties, put everyone on the alert, and take the entire fleet to sea after dark under silence. The other two argued that this would violate the specific orders of Admiral Stark that nothing be done to alarm the people of Honolulu. Reluctantly Kimmel agreed and it was decided what they had already done "was still good and we would stick to it."

At the Japanese Consulate in Honolulu Yoshikawa had been in touch with Tokyo all day. In one message he informed his superiors that there were still "no signs of barrage balloon equipment," that the battleships had no torpedo nets, and that there was "considerable opportunity left to take advantage for a surprise attack" against Pearl Harbor and the Army airfields. A second message was equally encouraging: "It appears that no air reconnaissance is being conducted by the fleet air arm." These messages were interrupted by the special U. S. Army monitoring station at Fort Shafter and airmailed as usual to Washington for decryption.

After his hectic day, Kimmel spent a few hours at a party but he went home early to get a good sleep. It was just another Saturday night to the citizens of Honolulu. Many were celebrating the 20–6 victory of the University of Hawaii over Willamette in the annual Shrine football classic.

7.

At the White House, dinner for thirty-four was served at eight-ten, followed by a "violin musical" by Arthur LeBlanc.

Kurusu had accepted the invitation to dine at Belin's estate in Georgetown. He repeated in substance what he had told Mayer that morning. Former Ambassador Belin was "astonished beyond measure" at the Japanese envoy's frankness. And Mayer was now more certain than ever that Kurusu was "trying in the most desperate fashion to warn us of a momentary attack somewhere."

At about 8:30 P.M. Kurusu was called to the telephone. He returned to inform the company that Roosevelt had just sent a personal appeal to the Emperor. This, remarked Kurusu, was "a clever move" since the Emperor could neither give a flat "no" or even "yes." It was sure to cause "headaches in Tokyo and more thinking."

After his dinner, Captain Ranneft was summoned to the home of Minister Loudon where he also found the military attaché, Weijerman. The minister told the two that he had just returned from the White House and that Roosevelt had told him he had sent a message to the Emperor. If there was no immediate answer, said the President, war would probably break out on Monday.

In the meantime, the first thirteen parts of the fourteen-part message to Ambassador Nomura had been decrypted. About 8:30 P.M. copies were turned over to Lieutenant Commander Kramer for delivery. He was unable to reach either Stark or Turner. The first was at the National Theater and Turner happened to be out walking one of his many Lhasa apso terriers. Kramer did manage to telephone Wilkinson and tell him "in cryptic terms" of the general sense of the thirteen parts. The Admiral instructed Kramer to take copies first to the White House, then to Knox and finally to the Wilkinson residence.

Using his wife as chauffeur, Kramer arrived at the White House shortly before nine-thirty and turned over a locked pouch to Lieutenant Lester Robert Schulz. The latter went directly to the Oval Office. The President was clipping stamps. "These are for the children at Warm Springs," he told Schulz, who had accompanied him on the recent trip to Georgia. A few minutes later Roosevelt remarked to Harry Hopkins, "This means war."

Kramer was already at the Wardman Park Hotel talking with Mrs. Knox and her guests, the O'Keiths, while the Secretary of the Navy was studying the thirteen parts. Knox was concerned enough by what he read and the ominous significance of the fourteenth part that was yet to come that he telephoned both Stimson and Hull to set up an emergency meeting of the trio at 10 A.M.

By this time Colonel Bratton had completed his deliveries. Then he drove home to Georgetown and telephoned Miles, who lived nearby. The general was not at home.

Miles was having dinner with Admiral Wilkinson and the two of them were reading the copy Kramer had recently delivered. Wilkinson thought it was just "a diplomatic paper . . . a justification of the position of Japan." Miles agreed that it had "little military significance," and there was "no reason for alerting or waking up the Chief of Staff."

Marshall was not asleep but at a dinner party a few minutes' drive from the White House. He was attending a reunion of World War veterans of the 1st Infantry Company, R.O.T.C.[16] The gathering at the University Club on 16th Street, N.W., included Brigadier General Joseph A. Atkins, commander of the unit; Dr. A. M. Langford, dean of Peddie School; and Representative William P. Cole, Jr., of Maryland. The honored guest, General Marshall, was given a rousing "vote of confidence."

General "Hap" Arnold was on his way to Hamilton Field, California, to oversee departure of thirteen B-17s which were to take off that night for Hawaii on the first leg of a flight to the Philippines. He arrived about midnight Washington time and warned

[16] The December 7, 1941, issue of the Washington *Times-Herald* reported on p. A-23 that Marshall had attended this reunion dinner at the University Club the previous evening. See Notes.

the crews of the Flying Fortresses that they would "probably run into trouble somewhere along the line." He had in mind the mandated islands in the vicinity of Truk.

Arnold also conferred with the commanding officer of Hamilton Field and his staff. "He brought word of the imminence of war with Japan and ordered the planes dispersed," read the official history of Sacramento Air Service Command. "He is reported to have expressed stern disapproval of their being huddled together." Since there were no revetments, the available pilots immediately began flying planes to other fields in the vicinity.

Army Air Corps planes on the island of Oahu were still huddled together, an approved Air Corps policy for protection from saboteurs.

In the Aleutians, PBY crews were almost exhausted from long daily reconnaissance patrols. Fortunately, recollected Captain James Bowers, a message had arrived that Saturday to "cease all activity which may be interpreted as hostile." By now all patrols had been recalled and the flight crews were involved in "a great drinking bout."

Chapter Fifteen

DATE OF INFAMY
"BUT THEY KNEW, THEY KNEW,
THEY KNEW"
DECEMBER 7–8, 1941

1.

Early Sunday morning, Tom Nichols, sixteen, was delivering the
Washington *Times-Herald*. One of his customers was the Japanese
naval attaché, who lived on the top floor of the Broadmoor, a large
apartment building at 3601 Connecticut Avenue. Upon rounding
the hall the newsboy was startled to see two American Marines
standing outside his customer's door.[1] One of the Marines took
the paper and young Nichols left wondering what was wrong.

Readers of the New York *Times* were set at ease by Secretary
Knox's state-of-the-Navy message on page 1: "I am proud to report
that the American people may feel fully confident in the Navy. In
my opinion the loyalty, morale and technical ability of the personnel are without superior. On any comparable basis, the United
States Navy is second to none."

At breakfast, Admiral Richardson observed to his wife, "We are
on the verge of war, which may break out any minute." Eight

---

[1] A review of the muster rolls of Marine units in Washington for December 1941
reveals that no such assignment had been routinely made. It must have been an
emergency special detail. Why?

years before, while a student at the War College, he had written a thesis on Japanese policy. After breakfast he dug it up and found one of its "lessons" was: "That should it appear to her advantage to do so, she will strike viciously, effectively and unexpectedly prior to any declaration of war."

Because of the emergency meeting Knox had set up Saturday night, Stimson telephoned his military aide, Major Eugene Harrison, to say that they would have to skip riding. "Come by and pick me up. We're going to the office." They arrived at the Munitions Building about nine-thirty. In the adjoining building Stark was already in his office and would soon finish reading the entire fourteen-part Japanese intercept.

Bratton had been frantically trying to locate Marshall for half an hour. For he had received not only the fourteenth part but another message instructing Nomura to deliver the entire message to Hull at 1 P.M. He was stunned. One P.M. Washington time would be about sunrise in Hawaii! The implication was staggering. He called Marshall's quarters in Fort Myer only to learn that he was out horseback riding. He then guardedly telephoned Miles at his home. The general was impressed by Bratton's tone and started off for the Munitions Building. As soon as Miles arrived he accompanied Bratton to Gerow's office. Miles urged that the Philippines, Hawaii, Panama and the West Coast be alerted. But nothing could be done until Marshall showed up.

At 10 A.M. Captain John Beardall, Roosevelt's naval aide, delivered to the President the fourteenth part. Still in bed, Roosevelt said, "It looks like the Japanese are going to break off negotiations." He didn't seem at all "perturbed" to Beardall. Roosevelt did nothing until noon except see Admiral McIntire, the nose and throat specialist, who treated his sinus condition. For a man who had thrived on action all his career, this was a curious reaction.

It took about an hour and a half for the one o'clock message to travel from the Munitions Building to the Navy Department, about the length of three blocks. This message alarmed Wilkinson, who wondered aloud if the Philippines and the Pacific Fleet should be alerted. "Why don't you pick up the telephone and call Kimmel?" he suggested to Stark at approximately ten forty-five. Stark lifted the receiver, then shook his head and said, in effect,

"No, I think I will call the President." But the White House switchboard operator reported that the President was busy. Stark put down the phone and did nothing.

At 11:25 A.M. Marshall finally reached his office. But it took almost another hour before his warning message was filed. Stark had offered to send it by the Navy system, which was fast under pressure, but Marshall said he could get it out quickly also. He could have used a telephone with a scrambler device but he feared some eavesdropper might have a descrambler. The warning was taken to the message center with orders to send it by the fastest safe means. Since the War Department radio was temporarily out of contact with Honolulu, the vital message was sent by teletype to the Washington office of Western Union.

Just as the Hull-Stimson-Knox emergency meeting ended at noon, the Secretary of State was informed that Nomura requested an appointment with him at 1 P.M. Hull fixed the time for one forty-five. Stimson did not proceed to the Munitions Building to check with Marshall on the crisis. He had himself driven to Woodley for lunch.

At the White House, the President was telling Dr. Hu Shih, the Chinese ambassador, that he had sent a message to the Emperor the evening before. "This is my last effort for peace. I am afraid it may fail."

The S.S. *Lurline*, thirty-two hours out of Honolulu on its return trip to California, was loaded with a passenger list of 784, including the president of the University of Hawaii and the "Petty girl" model. Church services were being conducted by Commodore Berndtson in the ship's lounge.

A thousand miles northeast of Honolulu, the 2,140-ton American freighter *Cynthia Olson* was carrying lumber to Honolulu. None of the twenty-five crew members was aware that the ship was being trailed by a Japanese submarine. The *I-26* had left Yokuska on November 19 as part of the advance expeditionary force with orders to destroy American commercial and military shipping once war broke out. She had spotted *Cynthia Olson* the previous morning and her skipper, Captain Minoru Yokota, was preparing to attack.

At about 7 A.M. Honolulu time a radio operator on the *Lurline* picked up an S.S.S. signal from the *Cynthia Olson*, meaning she was being attacked by a submarine. Leslie Grogan tried to raise Pearl Harbor and San Francisco but to no avail. Finally he reached the U. S. Coast Guard Radio Station at Point Bonita, California.[2]

At 7:55 A.M. two aircraft mechanics at Hickam Field sighted a formation of planes. As they began to peel off, Ted Conway said, "We're going to have an air show." His friend noticed something fall from the first plane and guessed it was a wheel. "Wheel, hell, they're Japs!"

Dive bombers were roaring down on Ford Island. A sailor on the deck of the nearby battleship *Arizona* thought they were Army fliers on maneuvers. He shook his fist at an oncoming plane. "You're going to catch hell!"

Karl "Buzz" Boyer, radioman at NPM, the Wailupe naval radio station six miles east of Pearl Harbor, was receiving a Morse code message from the Marine Air Base twenty miles northeast: "We're being bombed and strafed; we're under attack."

"Go to bed and sober up," signaled Boyer.

"This is no drill. This is for real," came the frantic response.

Boyer took the message to his chief, who was crowded at a window with the rest of the staff, looking down on Pearl Harbor. They all thought Army planes were on milk runs, until they saw smoke puffs from anti-aircraft guns. Ashen-faced, the chief read the Marine message. "Get on the line to Washington. Don't bother to code it."

At seven fifty-eight Boyer tapped out in the clear the signal heard around the world:

AIR RAID ON PEARL HARBOR. THIS IS NO DRILL.[3]

Secret Agent Takeo Yoshikawa had been eating breakfast when the windows started to rattle and several pictures dropped to the floor. He ran into his back yard. Above was a plane with Japanese

---

[2] It took *I-26* three or four hours to sink the lumber ship. There were no survivors. In an interview with Yokota in 1979, he maintained he had launched his attack at 8 A.M. Honolulu time. Both Commodore Berndtson and Chief Radio Operator Rudy Asplund stated it was 7 A.M., fifty-five minutes before the attack on Pearl Harbor. Grogan thought it was a little after eight but three other crew members agreed with Berndtson.

[3] At almost the same moment a similar message was being sent from NSM, the standby station at Pearl Harbor.

markings. They did it! he told himself. Perfect, with so many ships in the harbor! Clapping his hands, he rushed to the back door of Consul General Kita's official residence. "Kita—san!" he shouted. "They've done it!" Kita came out and said excitedly, "I just heard 'East wind, rain' on the short wave!⁴ There's no mistake." Dense black clouds were rising from Pearl Harbor. The two men, tears in their eyes, clasped hands. Finally Kita said, "They've done it at last."

Locking himself and a clerk in the code room, Yoshikawa set about burning code books in a washtub. But within ten minutes someone shouted, "Open the door!" The door caved in and Lieutenant Yoshio Hasegawa of the Honolulu police burst in with several men. They began stamping on the smoldering code books.

Admiral Halsey's task force, which included the carrier *Enterprise*, was on its way back to Pearl Harbor after ferrying a squadron of Marine fighters to Wake Island. Sixteen scout bombers from *Enterprise* were approaching Pearl Harbor. Lieutenant j.g. Earl Gallaher, pilot of the lead plane, coming in at 500 feet, saw planes at 4,000 feet with wheels down. He called over the intercom to his radioman in the rear, "What the hell is the Army doing out here on a Sunday morning? Did we miss something on the board?"

There was some smoke ahead but they were always burning cane fields. Gallaher touched down at the Marine field near Barber's Point. As he taxied up a Marine sergeant jumped on the wing and shouted, "Get the hell off the ground! Can't you see what's going on?" Now Gallaher noticed grounded planes burning all over the place. He took off fast and, once airborne, broadcast to *Enterprise*: "Pearl Harbor is being attacked by the Japanese and this is no shit!" He began orbiting off Barber's Point at low level followed by his wing plane and five other *Enterprise* planes that had joined up with him. Several times Japanese fighter planes came down for a look but never fired.

Gallaher reported that the Japanese were retiring on a northwesterly course from a rendezvous point about halfway between

⁴ This message was never intercepted by station MS-5 at Fort Shafter. Neither was another from Tokyo which might have been a similar execute. It had arrived at 3:20 A.M. and read: RELATIONS STRAINED BETWEEN JAPAN AND THE UNITED STATES AND BRITAIN.

Oahu and Kauai. They must be making a beeline for home since they were probably low on gas. He wanted to go after the enemy carriers and led the way toward Ford Island to refuel and load bombs.

Gallaher's message to *Enterprise* that the Japanese task force was to the northwest was not heeded. Other messages from Pearl Harbor gave conflicting reports. The Navy could not get a cross bearing and, when Layton reported that there was no way to tell whether the enemy was to the north or south, Kimmel was understandably irked. To make matters worse, a garbled message was received from a ship reporting two carriers south of Oahu. Orders were given to search south for what turned out to be two American cruisers.

Ironically Rear Admiral J. H. Newton's Task Force Twelve was not far from the Japanese at a point between Oahu and Midway. Signalman First Class Thomas Thalken, aboard the heavy cruiser *Astoria*, recalled that they began an immediate search for the Japanese, heading northeast by north at flank speed. This meant that they would approach *Kido Butai* in several hours. Scout planes were launched. Then came the report from Pearl Harbor that two enemy carriers were south of Oahu. But officers on the bridge of *Astoria* were convinced this was a false lead. Thalken was ordered to signal *Chicago*, Newton's flagship, "Ignore Pearl Harbor. They don't know what they're doing." But Task Force Twelve obeyed orders and turned south away from the Japanese.[5]

At Kaneohe Naval Air Station on the eastern (windward) side of Oahu, they were preparing to withstand a second strike, this one a landing to seize the entire island before the Americans could organize for defense. A group stood in the hangar area discussing what to do next when one man, turning pale, shouted, "Oh, my God—there they come!" He pointed northward toward the seaward entrance to Kaneohe Bay. "Then," recalled Lieutenant Murray Hanson, "we saw it, too: the foremast and conning tower of a Japanese battleship coming around the point heading straight for our station!"

[5] It was a fortunate mistake. The Japanese had only lost twenty-nine planes and probably would have dealt such grievous damage to the two American carriers and their planes that Spruance could not have challenged the Japanese six months later at Midway.

There was frozen terror a few seconds until someone said, "Oh, hell, that's Chinaman's Hat." A prominent landmark seen every clear day had become a battlewagon. Such group hysteria was common that day.

The area around Honolulu was still smoldering by the time an RCA[6] motorcycle messenger, Tadao Fuchikami, managed to get through roadblocks and wreckage to deliver a telegram addressed to the Commanding General, Fort Shafter. And it was seven hours after the attack started before Marshall's message was decoded. The department signal officer didn't have the stomach to deliver it. He asked Colonel R. J. Fleming, a close friend of Short's, to do so. "If he jumps on you, you're used to it." Fleming brought it to Short. He read it, threw it on the desk. "This is a hell of a note!" He was angry but didn't take it out on Fleming. A copy was immediately sent to Admiral Kimmel, who told the Army courier that it wasn't of any use to him, then crumpled the paper and threw it in the wastebasket.

2.

At 2:26 P.M. WOR interrupted its broadcast of the Giants-Dodgers football game with the first news flash. Much of America heard the news of Pearl Harbor a moment before the 3 P.M. CBS broadcast of the New York Philharmonic concert.

Ralph Briggs was on an extended four-day pass to Cleveland as a reward from Chief Radioman DW for having intercepted the "winds" execute. DW himself had received a large bouquet of roses from Captain Safford with a note expressing his personal appreciation for the splendid job done by the Station M team in intercepting the crucial message. Briggs's first reaction was, "Good, we've done our job. Now our Navy will get the bastards!"

Laurance Safford, exhausted after two months' worry and almost sleepless nights, had slept around the clock. He was in his bathrobe eating breakfast when a friend telephoned that the Japs were bombing Pearl Harbor. He was so angry that he felt tempted to take his .38 and shoot Noyes and Stark.

His fellow cryptanalyst, William Friedman, could only pace

---

6 Since Western Union had no direct link with Hawaii, the message had been transmitted to San Francisco where RCA radioed it to Honolulu.

back and forth and mutter to himself repeatedly, "But they knew, they knew, they knew."

Captain Paulus P. Powell, formerly in charge of the Japanese desk in Naval Intelligence, told his wife the radio report of the attack was a gigantic hoax. "Because knowing what he does about the situation, Admiral Kimmel would never have the fleet in port."

Tricycle, who had passed a detailed plan of the attack to the F.B.I., was triumphant upon learning the news on board a tramp steamer. "What a reception the Japanese must have had! I paced the deck, no, not paced it, I floated above it exultantly."

Another who had warned the United States, Kilsoo Haan, got a telephone call from Maxwell Hamilton of the State Department. He demanded that Haan's December 5 warning of a Pearl Harbor attack that weekend not be released to the press. "If you do," he warned, "I can put you away for the duration." Haan reluctantly promised to hold the report until the end of the war.

At their meeting that morning Stimson, Hull and Knox had all thought America must fight if the British responded to an attack on the Kra Peninsula. "But now," observed Stimson, "the Japs have solved the whole thing by attacking us directly in Hawaii." His first reaction was "relief that the indecision was over and that a crisis had come in a way which would unite all our people. This continued to be my dominant feeling in spite of the news of catastrophes which quickly developed. For I feel that this country united has practically nothing to fear while the apathy and divisions stirred up by unpatriotic men have been hitherto very discouraging." Later he told his military aide, Major Harrison, that they could "never have gotten the country to war without Pearl Harbor."

3.

That afternoon Knox noticed that the President was "white as a sheet, visibly shaken." Yet later in the day James Roosevelt found his father "sitting in a corner with no expression on his face, very calm and quiet. He had out his stamp collection he loved so much and was thumbing over some of the stamps when I came in. 'It's bad, it's pretty bad,' he said without looking up."

At about 6:40 P.M. Roosevelt telephoned Henry Morgenthau to tell him that there would be a Cabinet meeting at eight-thirty. Morgenthau reported that they were freezing all Japanese funds. "And we're putting people into all the Japanese banks and business houses tonight and we're not going to let the Japanese get in there at all."

"That's good."

The one with the keenest memory of the Cabinet meeting was Frances Perkins. She had just come down from New York in the same plane with Henry Wallace and Postmaster General Frank Walker. All three had been so involved with work that they didn't know of the Japanese attack until her chauffeur picked them up at the Washington airport. "That's impossible," all three said when told about Pearl Harbor.

The Oval Office was filled. The President, sitting at his desk, didn't notice the three newcomers. He was studying papers, cigarette holder in mouth. Everyone sat down about 9 P.M. Mrs. Perkins was surprised that he hadn't spoken to anyone. "He was living off in another area," she recalled in a taped interview. "He wasn't noticing what went on on the other side of his desk. He was very serious. His face and lips were pulled down, looking quite gray. His complexion didn't have that pink and white look that it had when he was himself. It had a queer, grave, drawn look."

She recalled that his face was never relaxed, not for a minute. "It remained tense and screwed up around the mouth. His upper lip was pulled down and his lower lip sort of pursed in, an expression that I've seen him have many, many times. . . . It was the sort of expression that he sometimes used when people were making recommendations to him and he was saying, 'Oh, yes, oh, yes, oh, yes,' without the slightest intention of doing anything about it. . . .

"In other words, there have been times when I associated that expression with a kind of evasiveness. The fact that he wore his expression all evening means nothing. It was an observation from which I cannot rid my memory. My picture memory keeps that expression on his face throughout the evening. He never relaxed that expression once, and none of us felt like making the kind of joke or sally that would sometimes relax his face when he had that expression on. It always had remained in my deep memory as being anything but an emotional disturbance as far as I was concerned, but a deep emotional experience, which I never would rely upon, and I don't think anybody should. Nevertheless, it is the strange emotional crises of human nature that give one some of one's insight, and they are part of the imaginative function of the brain, which Aristotle described."

She recalled that his pride in the Navy "was so terrific that he was having actual physical difficulty in getting out the words that put him on record that the Navy was caught unawares. . . . It was obvious to me that Roosevelt was having a dreadful time just accepting the idea." He could have been condemning himself for the men and warships lost—because Kimmel had not been warned the attack was coming.

Mrs. Perkins was obsessed by Roosevelt's strange reactions that night. "I had a deep emotional feeling that something was wrong, that this situation was not all it appeared to be. That stuck with me all that evening and all that night. So much so that when I went home to my apartment I couldn't rid myself of it. I sat down and wrote in lead pencil on some snatches of White House paper. . . . I described this look on the President's face, and the curious emotional disturbance that I had, which carried with it the impression that something was wrong. I don't know why I wrote it down, except perhaps to remind myself in the future—not for historical purposes, but for the purpose of helping me, or somebody else, to understand the situation. The necessity of reviewing it has never risen in my experience. So when I find these notes among my papers, I not only remember them clearly, but am also still somewhat put to it to know why I did it, why I wrote them down. At the moment they seemed important to me, as though I ought to put down, while it was clear in my mind, in case I should ever need to call upon it to help me explain something upon which I might have to act, or upon which others might have to act. . . .

"I don't know what disturbs me about the whole thing, but something was wrong. Obviously he had to play a role of some sort. I don't think that I ever in my own mind cleared it to the point of saying that he played a false role that day. His surprise was not as great as the surprise of the rest of us." In her book, *The*

Roosevelt I Knew, she would reveal none of these misgivings.

"I've been asked if it might not be possible that the President, recognizing that this thing had happened, felt a certain element and wave of relief that the long tension of wondering what would they do and when they would do it, and would we have to go to the defense of Singapore without an apparent attack upon ourselves, and should we go to the relief of Singapore, all these conflicts which had so harassed him for so many weeks or months, were ended. You didn't have to think about that any more. That very wave of relief might have produced in him that psychological atmosphere reflected in his facial expression of tenseness and calmness, and yet a sense that something was wrong, that there was slight evasion here."

As the meeting was breaking up Walker, who was very close to Roosevelt, said under his breath to her, "You know, I think the boss must have a great sense of relief that this has happened. This is a great load off his mind. I thought the load on his mind was just going to kill him, going to break him down. This must be a great sense of relief to him. At least we know what to do now."

"Yes," she said. "I think so."

Long into the night Roosevelt worked with Hull and Under Secretary of State Sumner Welles, who were trying to persuade him to use one of their proposed war messages. "The President was very patient with them," recalled Hopkins, "and I think in order to get them out of the room perhaps led them to believe he would give serious consideration to their draft." After chatting with Colonel William "Wild Bill" Donovan and Edward R. Murrow of CBS, they all had sandwiches and beer. Finally at 12:30 A.M. the President "cleared everybody out and said he was going to bed."

Across from the White House the benches in bleak Lafayette Square were deserted for the first night in weeks. On the other side of the square the Veterans Administration Building remained one of the few in Washington without lights burning. And the traffic along Pennsylvania Avenue on either side of the White House was jammed. "There is a slight deliberation in the movement of the cars," reported Jerry Greene of the *Time-Life-Fortune* News Bureau. "The driver, passengers in each turn their heads, stare with unmoving lips at the White House from the time they come within range until they are beyond." Hundreds were walking past the tall, iron picket fence protecting the White House grounds. "They move along quietly, talking if at all in whispers, subdued murmurs. Silence on the Avenue, despite the mob of cars, the mass of people, is apparent, deep enough to gnaw at the nerves." Everybody, it seemed, was "watching the White House quietly, without noise, waiting, hoping somehow to see a visible sign of retaliation."

In the White House, not far from the President's room, Mrs. Hamlin, the old friend of the Roosevelts, was trying to sleep. "I heard voices and steps far into the night."

At his home in Virginia, General George Marshall said nothing except that he was tired and was going to bed. "I sat there trying to think of something I could do or say that might help him," remembered Mrs. Marshall. "But words are futile at a time like that, so I passed his door and went into my room. I knew he would rather be alone."

The next morning Stimson told Major Harrison, "I think I'll go and see Old Knox." The two men walked across the bridge to the Navy Building and found panic. In Knox's outer office one admiral was pacing one direction while a second was pacing another as if they were on the deck of a sinking ship. Knox's naval aide told Harrison, "My God, what will the American people think of the Navy!"

At 12:29 P.M. President Roosevelt entered the House chamber in the Capitol on the arm of his son James. There was a resounding ovation as he grasped the rostrum. "Yesterday, December 7, 1941," he began in the voice that no one who heard it would ever forget, "—a date which will live in infamy—the United States of America was suddenly and deliberately attacked. . . ."

Chapter Sixteen

THE SUMMING UP

1.

It is not clear why the Navy and Army Departments deprived Kimmel and Short of vital messages from the summer of 1941 to late that November. It may have been because of Marshall's fear that the Japanese would discover that the United States had solved their Purple code; the natural tendency of intelligence officers to guard new information almost obsessively; or interservice and interdepartmental rivalries.

Although both Marshall and Stark felt it was necessary to wage war with Hitler and Mussolini, both had vigorously opposed inciting Japan to battle on the grounds that neither the Army nor the Navy was yet prepared for a two-front war. Up to the very last moment before the Hull ultimatum to the Japanese on November 27, Marshall and Stark had urged Roosevelt to respond temperately.

The President himself had been wavering until the final day despite persistent urging from Stimson, Ickes and other Japanophobes. Less than a week later Roosevelt was faced with the most momentous decision of his life when a number of reports to Washington indicated that the missing *Kido Butai* was heading eastward toward Hawaii. These included warnings from the *Lur-*

line;[1] from the Twelfth Naval District (Lieutenant Hosner and Seaman First Class Z); and from General Ter Poorten and Thorpe in Java. Finally there was the meeting of Captain Ranneft at O.N.I., authenticated by excerpts from Ranneft's official diary.[2]

Ten years after the war, General Ter Poorten asked General Thorpe, "Did you really send that message I gave you?" After Thorpe gave assurance he had, Ter Poorten revealed that he had not trusted Consul General Foote to send the entire message to Washington and had sent one himself—including the mention of attacks on Hawaii and the Philippines—to Colonel Weijerman, the Netherlands military attaché in Washington. Weijerman informed him that he had personally taken this message to Marshall a few days before Pearl Harbor; the Chief of Staff had said, in substance, "Can you take such reports seriously?"

Confirmation of Dutch foreknowledge of the Japanese attack also came from General Albert C. Wedemeyer. In 1980 he informed the author that during a meeting in 1943 Vice Admiral Conrad E. L. Helfrich of the Royal Netherlands Navy expressed wonder that the Americans had been surprised at Pearl Harbor. The Dutch, Helfrich said, had broken the code and knew that the Japanese were going to strike Pearl Harbor. "He seemed surprised

[1] Minutes after the *Lurline* docked in San Francisco at 3:37 A.M., December 10, Lieutenant Commander Preston Allen entered the radio room to request that the voyage log be turned over to him. Chief Operator Asplund insisted the log be taken to Commodore Berndtson, who handed it over to the naval officer with other notes on the period from November 30 to December 7. There is no record in the Navy files of these documents or the incidents that took place. The Matson Line gave the author free access to its records, which included Grogan's journal.

[2] Captain Ranneft remained as naval attaché in Washington throughout the war. In 1946 Admiral Nimitz personally presented him the Legion of Merit Degree of Commander. His citation read: ". . . Discharging his responsibilities with great skill and initiative, Rear Admiral Ranneft rendered invaluable assistance in prosecuting the war against our common enemy . . . his contributions to the development of Naval ordnance were of inestimable aid to ships of Allied Navies carrying out defensive and offensive measures against the enemy." See Notes.

About 1960 Admiral Ranneft casually mentioned to an old friend, Admiral Samuel Murray Robinson (former Chief of Procurement and Material, who had initiated the largest shipbuilding program in history), that he was amazed to keep reading that the Americans were taken by complete surprise at Pearl Harbor. How was this possible when O.N.I. officers had shown him on a chart that the Japanese task force was only some four hundred miles from Honolulu on December 6?

Robinson was stunned. He knew nothing about it and insisted Ranneft ask Admiral Stark how this was possible. Later in the afternoon Admiral Robinson called back with a terse message: it was not necessary for Ranneft to see Stark. Robinson himself had just telephoned Stark, who refused to comment on the matter.

that I did not know this," recalled Wedemeyer, "and when I explained that I doubted seriously that this information was known in Washington prior to the Pearl Harbor attack, Admiral Helfrich was skeptical because it was his clear recollection that his government had notified my government."

There were other indications of imminent war that were either ignored or suppressed, including the warnings of Major Clear, Tricycle, and Army and Navy Intelligence and Communications officers such as Bratton, Sadtler and Safford.

2.

"A Fool lies here who tried to hustle the East."
Rudyard Kipling

By December 4 Roosevelt and a small group of advisers, including Stimson, Knox and Marshall, were faced with three options. They could announce to Japan and the world word of the approaching *Kido Butai*; this would indubitably have forced the Japanese to turn back. Second, they could inform Kimmel and Short that Japanese carriers were northwest of Hawaii and order them to send every available long-range patrol plane to discover this force. An attack conceived in such secrecy would necessarily depend on complete surprise for success, and once discovered out of range of its target, *Kido Butai* would have turned back.

A month before the Hull ultimatum to Japan, Ickes had written in his diary: "For a long time I have believed that our best entrance into the war would be by way of Japan." The first bomb dropped on Oahu would have finally solved the problem of getting an America—half of whose people wanted peace—into the crusade against Hitler. And the third option would accomplish this: keep Kimmel and Short and all but a select few in ignorance so that the Japanese could continue to their launching point unaware of their discovery. This would insure that the Japanese would launch their attack. If Kimmel, Short and others had been privy to the secret, they might possibly have reacted in such a way as to reveal to the Japanese that their attack plan was known.

This course was a calculated risk but Roosevelt, like Churchill, could take a gamble. Nor did risk at that moment seem so great.

Recall the memorandum the President had received from Marshall in May 1941, describing Oahu as the strongest fortress in the world, with assurances that any enemy naval task force would be destroyed before it neared Pearl Harbor. Long a Navy man, Roosevelt believed in its power. Also he had been receiving reports on the low efficiency of Japanese pilots, whose planes were second rate.[3] Consequently the Pacific Fleet would not only stem any Japanese attack with little loss to U.S. shipping but deal a crushing blow to *Kido Butai* itself. One of the keenest admirals in the Navy, "Terrible" Turner, believing this, had told the Navy Court of Inquiry, "I knew our carriers were out, and with the warnings which had been given, I felt we would give them a pretty bad beating before they got home by our shore-based aircraft and by our carriers."

Such a defeat would have been catastrophic to the Japanese militarists and perhaps eliminated Japan as a menace in the Pacific with a single blow. Moreover, Kimmel's two available carriers would be out of Pearl Harbor and those warships left were in no real danger of being sunk. Aerial bombs were not that much of a threat and the waters of Pearl Harbor were too shallow for a torpedo attack.

Only such reasoning could account for the events in Washington on December 6 and 7. What novelist could persuade a reader to accept the incredible activities during those two days by America's military and civilian leaders? Was it to be believed that the heads of the Army and Navy could not be located on the night before Pearl Harbor? Or that they would later testify over and over that they couldn't remember where they were? Was it plausible that the Chief of Naval Operations, after finally being reminded that he talked to Roosevelt on the telephone that night, could not recall if they had discussed the thirteen-part message? Was it possible to imagine a President who remarked, "This means war," after reading the message, not instantly summoning to the White House his Army and Navy commanders as well as

[3] Roosevelt's feeling was shared by most Americans. Famed cartoonist J. N. "Ding" Darling expressed it all in a drawing of a small, bucktoothed, scowling Japanese soldier wearing horn-rimmed glasses. He is vainly attempting to blow up a huge balloon. Across the Pacific stands a supremely confident Uncle Sam wearing a Navy cap. He is hiding a slingshot behind his back while smiling slyly.

his Secretaries of War and Navy? One of Knox's close friends, James G. Stahlman, wrote Admiral Kemp Tolley in 1973 that Knox had revealed to him that he, Stimson and Marshall had spent most of the night before Pearl Harbor with Roosevelt, waiting for a declaration of war[4].

The incredulities continued the following morning with Marshall insisting he did not reach his office until eleven twenty-five. Yet Stimson's military aide, Major Harrison, recently revealed in an interview that he saw the Chief of Staff in the War Secretary's office around 10 A.M. "I saw and talked to General Marshall: and whoever said he was out riding horses lied, because I saw him and talked to him at that time." So had Commander McCollum and Lieutenant Colonel John R. Deane, one of Marshall's assistant secretaries.

And why had Stark, having seen the complete fourteen-point message by 9:15 A.M. and the 1 P.M. message an hour later, not followed the urging of subordinates to telephone an immediate warning to Kimmel? And why, after finally reading all the messages and agreeing that this meant immediate war, had Marshall composed an innocuous warning to Pearl Harbor and Manila indicating he didn't know "just what significance" the 1 P.M. delivery time meant but to "be on the alert accordingly"? And why, instead of accepting Stark's offer of the naval radio facilities or using his own scrambler phone, had the message gone by Western Union and RCA? Marshall's excuse for not using the telephone was that it might have revealed to the Japanese that the Purple code had been broken. Seven months earlier a dozen intercepted messages had revealed that the Japanese feared their top code had been broken by the United States. And immediately following the

---

[4] Almost the first question Knox asked Kimmel, upon arriving at Pearl Harbor on December 10, was: "Did you receive our dispatch the night before the attack?" When Kimmel replied he had not, Knox said he was sure they had sent one. This was later explained as a slip of the tongue; he was referring to the message sent by Marshall the following noon. Was it a Freudian slip when Knox wrote in his original report to Roosevelt, "The Army and Navy Commands had received a general war warning on November 27th, but a special war warning sent out by the War Department at *midnight* [author's italics] December 7th to the Army was not received until some hours after the attack on that date"? Had those meeting at the White House on the night of December 6, as reported by Stahlman, decided to send a warning to Hawaii at *midnight*—a warning which later was rescinded without Knox's knowledge?

attack, the telephone connections between Washington and Hawaii were in common use.

The comedy of errors on the sixth and seventh appears incredible. It only makes sense if it was a charade, and Roosevelt and the inner circle had known about the attack.

3.

A massive cover-up followed Pearl Harbor a few days later, according to an officer close to Marshall, when the Chief of Staff ordered a lid put on the affair. "Gentlemen," he told half a dozen officers, "this goes to the grave with us." The unnamed officer, who is still alive, had lunch on May 4, 1961, with Brigadier General Bonner Fellers and Dr. Charles C. Tansill. According to the former, the officer stated that on December 7 Marshall was obviously dragging his feet regarding the warning to Short. That was why the Chief of Staff had bound certain members of his staff not to disclose the truth; and why he himself later conveniently forgot where he was on the eve of Pearl Harbor.

The cover-up continued with Roosevelt's revision of Knox's original report of Pearl Harbor, and was carried a long step forward by the report of the Roberts Commission. One of the members, Admiral Standley, later called Justice Roberts' performance "as crooked as a snake." Standley's outspoken criticism earned him a Distinguished Service Medal and an assignment as ambassador to Moscow where he would be out of reach of indignant Republicans and suspicious reporters.

The cover-up persevered after the Army and Navy Boards reversed the conclusions of Roberts to find Marshall and Stark rather than Kimmel and Short primarily guilty of dereliction of duty. Then amendments by Stimson and Forrestal to the Army and Navy reports led much of the public to believe that Roberts had, in fact, been upheld. Too little attention has been paid to the efforts of important government, military and naval officials to reverse the findings of the Army Pearl Harbor Board and the Navy Court of Inquiry. One of the main thrusts was the attempt to prove there was no "winds" execute; and this was so successful that the majority report of the congressional hearings concluded there

had been no such message since Safford alone believed in its existence. This ignored the testimony of Admiral Ingersoll and Colonels Dusenbury, Pettigrew and Sadtler that they too had seen an
execute. Strong.proof of its existence lies in the taped interview of
Ralph Briggs by the Historian, Naval Security Group Command,
on January 13, 1977. A transcript of this tape was released in 1980
at the author's request by the National Security Agency and the
U. S. Navy, with a few security deletions. Briggs served forty-four
years in the Navy as an enlisted man, officer and civilian specialist
up to the grade of GS-13. In the postwar years he was the case
officer for counterintelligence and a security review analyst in the
office of the director of Naval Intelligence.

All "winds" execute messages apparently have been lost or destroyed.[5] According to A. A. Hoehling, a former Naval Intelligence
officer and author of *The Week Before Pearl Harbor*, panic gripped
the Second Deck of the Navy Department immediately after Pearl
Harbor. "One officer then in intelligence, now in a high post in the
Navy, told this writer that he went to his office safe one morning
to find that a number of the 'magic' dispatches were mysteriously
missing. He never retrieved them. ONI, in fact, had done such a
thorough housecleaning of its top-secret and secret as well as not-
so-secret files that, according to another officer on duty at that
time, not even a departmental organization chart of November and
December, 1941, could ever be found."

Although Captain Safford emerged from the hearings branded
by some as a liar and by others as a brilliant but erratic genius who
suffered hallucinations, he invented the Super ECM shortly before
leaving the service. The idea had come to him, he said, while walking his dog; it was the answer to a problem which "had eluded us
for 15 years." In 1958 President Eisenhower signed a bill to reward
Safford with $100,000 for some twenty cryptographic inventions
he developed. Until the day he died Safford did his utmost to con-

[5] It could be no coincidence that other vital messages and documents concerning
Pearl Harbor also disappeared. These include: the material confiscated by the U. S.
Navy in San Francisco from the *Lurline* on December 10; the Thorpe and Ter
Poorten messages; the questionnaire and other papers Tricycle delivered to the
F.B.I.; records of the tracking of *Kido Butai* by the Twelfth Naval District; records
of Grogan's original report to the Fourteenth Naval District on December 3, 1941;
and records of the illegal collection of names of all Japanese-American citizens by
the Census Bureau.

Perhaps further revelations of suppressed information will come from readers of
this book, for there is no cover-up today in the Army, Navy or F.B.I.

vince the world that there had been a "winds" execute. It was to
his credit that he never told anyone about Ralph Briggs, whose career in the Navy would have been endangered.

General V.,[6] an intimate of Marshall, and perhaps the living
person with the most significant knowledge of Pearl Harbor, made
this comment on the "winds" execute in a recent letter which is in
the archives of a presidential library: what proved that Roosevelt
and Marshall shared responsibility for the Pearl Harbor tragedy
was the message used to hide the truth.

The testimony of the Chief of Staff at the various investigations
does not stand up now that the prestige and glamor of his high
office have gone. It was a tragedy that a man in his high position
was forced to lie. So too his two trusted subordinates, Bedell Smith
and Gerow. Both had refused to pass on any warning to Hawaii on
December 5. So testified Sadtler before the Army Pearl Harbor
Board. He later changed his testimony to Clausen, who brought
with him the rank and prestige of Marshall. But later at the congressional hearings Sadtler did reverse himself again and declared
he *had* given the message to Gerow and Smith. In his letter
General V. also wrote that he did not know what Roosevelt did to
suppress the message and prevent action, but he *did* know that
Gerow lied and *why* he lied.

Why did Gerow and Smith, perhaps the two closest subordinates of Marshall, stonewall this December 5 message? It is
difficult to believe they would have acted without Marshall's orders. By this time the Chief of Staff and the Chief of Naval Operations, caught in the web, were acting as faithful servants of their
Commander in Chief, the President.

It was also a tragedy that men like Stimson, Hull, Knox and
Forrestal felt obliged to join in the cover-up and make scapegoats
of two innocent men, Kimmel and Short.[7] Open criticism of this

6 The identity of General V. will be revealed after his death. The letter is addressed
to a prominent general.

7 Short lived quietly in retirement. The *Saturday Evening Post* offered him a large
sum to co-author an anti-Roosevelt article but he refused. He died in El Paso on
September 3, 1949.

   Kimmel never gave up the battle to clear his record. "My principal occupation—
what's kept me alive—is to expose the entire Pearl Harbor affair," the indomitable
admiral told the Associated Press when he was eighty-four, two years before his
death. "I don't know whether the whole story will get out. All incriminating documents have been destroyed." But he predicted history would "eventually" clear him.
He received far more support from Navy colleagues than Short did from Army
officers. In 1957 Kimmel was elected alumni president by his classmates at Annapolis.

injustice from such prestigious naval officers as Admirals Yarnell, Richardson, King, Standley and Halsey indicated how deep were the resentment and disgust among leading Navy officers.

Despite shortcomings, Franklin Delano Roosevelt was a remarkable leader. Following the maxim of world leaders, he was convinced that the ends justified the means and so truth was suppressed.

The greater tragedy is that the war with Japan was one that need never have been fought. And so we must continue to mourn the victims; first the 2,403 who died on Oahu, then those whose careers were ruined—such as Kimmel, Short, Safford, Bratton and Sadtler. In a larger sense we must also mourn the millions of dead and mutilated in the unnecessary war in the Pacific: the soldiers and sailors on both sides and the innocent civilians of many countries, particularly those of Japan, who were savaged by fire bombings and atomic warfare. A final victim is the present state of the world. Imagine if there had been no war in the East. There would have been no Hiroshima and perhaps no threat of nuclear warfare. Nor would it have been necessary for America to have fought a grueling, unpopular war in Korea and a far more tragic one in Vietnam which weakened U.S. economy and brought bitter civil conflict.

The profit was the lesson learned by Japan and America through the consequences of their war. The former realized that her true allies were not the Axis, and the latter that only a strong, industrialized Nippon, working in concert with the democracies, could stabilize Asia and prevent domination by Japan's traditional enemy, Russia. But a small group of men, revered and held to be most honorable by millions, had convinced themselves it was necessary to act dishonorably for the good of their nation—and incited the war that Japan had tried to avoid. It was, to quote Nietzsche, "Human, all too human."

The mistakes and cruel acts of violence committed by both Japan and America must not be forgotten—only understood. Enemies in the past, and friends today, they must remain equal partners in the future.

Acknowledgments

I am grateful to the following archives, museums and libraries: the Alexander Library, Rutgers University (Irene Czarda); Columbia University, Oral History Research Office (Louis M. Starr, Elizabeth B. Mason); the Danbury, Connecticut, Public Library; the main branch of the New York Public Library; the Library of Congress; the Yale University Library (Judith Schiff, Mary C. LaFogg); the Seeley G. Mudd Manuscript Library, Princeton University (Nancy Bressler); the Franklin D. Roosevelt Library (William Emerson, Donald Schewe, Robert Parks); the Herbert Hoover Presidential Library (Thomas Thalken, Robert Wood, Dale Meyer, George Nash, Mrs. Mildred Mather); the Dwight D. Eisenhower Library (John E. Wickman); the Harry S. Truman Library; the Archive of Contemporary History, University of Wyoming (Gene M. Gressley, Emmett D. Chisum); Chief Records Office of the Netherlands Ministry of Defense (M. J. van Druten); the Historical Department Naval Staff, the Netherlands Ministry of Defense (Commander F. C. van Oosten); the Naval Historical Center, U. S. Navy (Dean C. Allard); the Hoover Institution (Dr. Agnes Peterson, Charles G. Palm); the University of Hawaii (Stuart Gerry Brown, David Kittelson, Frances Jackson, Mona Nakayama); the George C. Marshall Research Foundation (Dr. Fred Hadsel, John Jacob, Larry Bland, Michael Shoop); and the National Archives (Dr. Robert M. Warner, William Cunliffe, Timothy K. Nenninger, John E. Taylor, Geraldine Phillips, William Heimdahl, William Leary, James Trimble, Paul White and Barbara Burger).

Numerous agencies, organizations and individuals made substantial contributions to this book. Fellow historians and authors:

Walter Lord, Gwenfread Allen, Walter Henry Nelson, Terence Prittie, Arthur Schlesinger, Jr., Joseph D. Harrington, B. Mitchell Simpson III, Roy Stratton, A. A. Hoehling, Richard Hanser, Ladislas Farago, Bradley Smith, Dr. Warren Ober, Dr. Martin V. Melosi, Dr. Lloyd C. Gardner, Dr. Duane Schultz, Colonel Charles D. MacDonald, Dr. Eric Roman, Dr. Roger Jeans and Associate Professor Paul Hooper. Also Alfred Geddes; Lawrence J. Dugan; Fred Stocking; Francis A. Raven; Edward B. Hanify; the Matson Navigation Co. (Charles Regal, Fred Stindt); Walter D. Short; Mr. and Mrs. Robert Trumbull; Corney Downes; Mrs. Bonner Fellers; William Gunn; Captain Ben Ferguson; Doris Obata Kumpel; Carl E. Geiger; Ruth Harris; the Pearl Harbor Survivors Association (Ken Murray); Tom Masland, the Philadelphia *Inquirer*; Virginia Keefe Nolan; Mrs. Ralph Townsend; Mrs. Albert F. Betzel; Hugh Winston Lytle; Harry Albright; Colonel William F. Strobridge, Office of Chief of Military Service and the Center of Military History, U. S. Army; Buck Buchwach and George Chaplin, both of the Honolulu *Advertiser*; Bud Smyzer, of the Honolulu *Star Bulletin*; William A. Bernrieder; Anna C. Urband, Media Services Branch, Department of the Navy; Captain Wyman Packard, U.S.N.; Mrs. Stanley Coppel; William Cleveland; Karel Rink; Colonel Eugene Prince; Colonel William Moreland; Mrs. Elizabeth Meijer; James Moser of Doubleday & Company, Inc.; my typist, Helen Collischonn; and Mary R. Mitchell and Frances R. Furlow, who allowed me to quote from the unpublished memoirs of General Henry D. Russell.

Special mention should be made of those who contributed outstandingly to the book: Dr. Warren Kimball, Rutgers University, who loaned me a manuscript copy of his history of the Roosevelt-Churchill correspondence, recently published by the Princeton University Press; Admiral Kemp Tolley, who sent me material on Pearl Harbor which led to this book; Commander Charles C. Hiles, who spent years of his life assiduously researching Pearl Harbor and turned over all his material to me; Bruce R. Bartlett, author of *Cover-Up: The Politics of Pearl Harbor, 1941–1946*, who generously allowed me to ransack his files; Thomas and Edward Kimmel, who gave not only their time but their material; Percy L. Greaves, Jr., an invaluable living source of the various Pearl Harbor investigations, who, besides reviewing the entire manuscript, allowed me to interview him at length and then select material from his immense collection of documents, manuscripts, notes and books; and Kacy Tebbel, my copy editor, not only for correcting mistakes but for suggesting many improvements in style and content.

Finally, I would like to thank my two editors at Doubleday, Carolyn Blakemore and Ken McCormick, who continue to make the editing process not only painless but enjoyable.

Sources

A. INTERVIEWS AND CORRESPONDENCE
(partial list)

Ambassador Max Bishop (tape)
Bennett Boskey
Karl "Buzz" Boyer
Captain John C. Burrill, U.S.N.
Robert Clack
Rear Admiral David H. Clark
Brigadier General Carter Clarke
Captain Paul Crosley, U.S.N.
Captain and Mrs. Prescott Currier, U.S.N. (tape)
Curtis B. Dall
Vice Admiral Walter DeLany
Robert Diggs (tape)
Vice Admiral George C. Dyer
Judge Charles Fahy (tape)
Brigadier General Bonner Fellers
Dr. Henry Field
Brigadier General Kendall Fielder
Major General Robert J. Fleming, Jr.
Rear Admiral W. Earl Gallaher (tape)
Judge Gerhard Gesell
Percy L. Greaves, Jr. (tape)
Edward B. Hanify (tape)
Major General Eugene L. Harrison (tape)
Colonel William F. Heimlich
Commander Charles C. Hiles
Tyler Kent (tape)
Edward R. Kimmel (tape)
Captain Thomas K. Kimmel, U.S.N. (tape)
Mrs. Harold D. Krick (tape)
Captain George W. Linn, U.S.N.

Colonel Roy F. Lynd
John J. McCloy (tape)
Vice Admiral John McCrea (tape)
Rear Admiral William C. Mott (tape)
Ken Murray
C. Roger Nelson
Thomas Nichols (tape)
Mrs. Barnet Nover
Robert Odell
Stefan T. Possony
Rear Admiral Johan E. Meijer Ranneft (tape)
T. S. N. Ranneft (tape)
Major General P. L. Ransom
Francis Raven (tape)
Major General William O. Reeder (tape)
Mrs. William O. Reeder (tape)
George W. Renchard
David W. Richmond (tape)
Frank B. Rowlett
Rear Admiral L. R. Schulz (tape)
K. M. Steiner (tape)
Judge Edward Allen Tamm
William Thompson (tape)
Brigadier General Elliott Thorpe
Lieutenant General Louis W. Truman
Martin Vitousek (tape)
General Albert C. Wedemeyer (tape)
Vice Admiral Charles W. Wellborn (tape)
Frederic Woodrough (tape)
Seaman First Class Z (tape)

B. DOCUMENTS, DIARIES, RECORDS AND REPORTS

Archival Materials
Columbia University Oral History Project
   Interviews with Frances Perkins, Admirals Thomas Hart, Kent
   Hewitt, and Royal E. Ingersoll
Hoover Institution
   Papers of Delos C. Emmons, Tracy B. Kittredge, General Walter
   Short and Robert A. Theobald
   Memoirs of Ivan Yeaton and Joseph W. Ballantine
   Collection of Stanley K. Hornbeck
Herbert C. Hoover Presidential Library
   Papers of William Castle, Herbert C. Hoover, Frank B. Keefe,

Verne Marshall, Westbrook Pegler, Admiral John F. Shafroth, Charles C. Tansill, Walter Trohan and Ivan Yeaton
Library of Congress, Manuscript Division
Papers of Cordell Hull, Felix Frankfurter, Frank R. McCoy, Robert A. Taft
National Archives
Record Group 80, General Records of the Department of the Navy
Record Group 107, Records of the Office of the Secretary of War
Record Group 128, Records of the Joint Committees of Congress
Record Group 335, Records of the Office of the Secretary of the Army
Naval History Division
Central Security-Classified Files of the Office of the Chief of Naval Operations
Papers of Harold R. Stark, Harry E. Yarnell, Thomas C. Hart, Arthur McCollum
Princeton University Library
Papers of Philip G. Strong
Diaries and papers of James V. Forrestal
Franklin D. Roosevelt Library
Papers of Harry Hopkins, Franklin D. Roosevelt, Samuel I. Rosenman
Henry Morgenthau, Jr. Collection
Rutgers University Library
Prime Minister Winston S. Churchill Manuscripts: PREMIER 3 Files, Prime Minister's Operational Files: PREMIER 4 Files, Prime Minister's Confidential Files
Harry S. Truman Presidential Library
Papers of Harry S. Truman and Samuel I. Rosenman
University of Wyoming Library, the Archive of Contemporary History
Collections of Harry E. Barnes, Charles C. Hiles, Husband E. Kimmel, George Morgenstern, William L. Neumann, Laurance F. Safford
Pearl Harbor File
George C. Marshall Research Foundation
Papers of George C. Marshall
Yale University, Sterling Memorial Library, Manuscripts and Archives
Diaries and papers of Henry L. Stimson
Government Documents
U. S. Congress. *Congressional Records*, 77th–79th Congresses, 1941–46, 87–91.
U. S. Congress. *Pearl Harbor Attack: Hearings before the Joint Com-*

mittee on the Pearl Harbor Attack. 79th Congress, 1st Session. 39 vols., 1946.

U. S. Congress. *Report of the Joint Committee on the Investigation of the Pearl Harbor Attack.* 79th Congress, 2nd Session, 1946.

U. S. Department of Defense. *The "Magic" Background of Pearl Harbor,* 8 volumes. Washington, D.C.: U. S. Government Printing Office, 1980.

U. S. Department of State. *Papers Relating to the Foreign Relations of the United States: Japan, 1931–1941,* 2 volumes. Washington, D.C.: U. S. Government Printing Office, 1943.

Unpublished Works

Hanify, Edward. "Memorandum." A report of evidence in the congressional hearings. Toland Collection.

———. Speech on Pearl Harbor at Union Club, Boston, MA, on December 7, 1979. Toland Tape Collection.

Hiles, Charles C. *Pattern of Betrayal: The Benign Conspiracy.* Hiles Collection.

Kimmel, Husband E. "Events Leading to the Congressional Investigation of Pearl Harbor." A history of Pearl Harbor. Thomas Kimmel Collection.

Lavender, Robert A. *Pearl Harbor.* His notebook and papers. Mrs. Albert F. Betzel Collection.

Russell, Henry D. Memoirs. George Morgenstern Collection, University of Wyoming Library.

Safford, Laurance. *Rhapsody in Purple.* Hiles Collection.

———. *Victims of the Kita Message.* Hiles Collection.

C. MAGAZINES

Bartlett, Bruce B. "The Pearl Harbor Coverup," *Reason,* February 1976, pp. 24–27.

Beatty, Frank E. "Background of the Secret Report," *National Review,* December 13, 1966, pp. 1261–65.

Burtness, Paul S., and Ober, Warren U. "Research Methodology: Problem of Pearl Harbor Intelligence Reports." *Military Affairs,* Fall 1961, pp. 132–46.

Butow, Robert J. C. "The Hull-Nomura Conversations: A Fundamental Misconception," *American Historical Review,* July 1960, pp. 822–36.

Chamberlain, John. "The Man Who Pushed Pearl Harbor," *Life,* April 1, 1946.

Current, Richard N. "How Stimson Meant to 'Maneuver' the Japanese," *Mississippi Valley Historical Review,* March 1957, pp. 67–76.

Esthus, Raymond A. "President Roosevelt's Commitment to Britain to Intervene in a Pacific War," *Mississippi Valley Historical Review*, June 1963, pp. 28–38.

Greaves, Percy L., Jr. "FDR's Watergate: Pearl Harbor," *Reason*, February 1976, pp. 16–23.

————. "Pearl Harbor," *National Review*, December 13, 1966, pp. 1266–72.

Harrington, Daniel F. "A Careless Hope: American Air Power and Japan, 1941," *Pacific Historical Review*, May 1979, pp. 217–38.

Hiles, Charles C. "The Kita Message: Forever a Mystery?" Chicago *Tribune*, December 7, 1966.

Kimball, Warren F. "Churchill and Roosevelt: The Personal Equation," *Prologue: The Journal of the National Archives*, Fall 1974, pp. 169–82.

Kittredge, Captain T. B. "Muddle Before Pearl Harbor," *U. S. News and World Report*, December 3, 1954, pp. 52ff.

Miles, Sherman. "Pearl Harbor in Retrospect," *Atlantic Monthly*, July 1948, pp. 65–72.

Morison, Samuel Eliot. "Did Roosevelt Start the War: History Through a Beard," *Atlantic Monthly*, August 1948, pp. 91–97.

Puleston, Captain W. D. "Blunders of World War II," *U. S. News and World Report*, February 4, 1955, pp. 109–11.

Tolley, Kemp. "The Strange Assignment of the USS Lanikai," U. S. Naval *Proceedings*, September 1962, pp. 70–83.

————. "Admiral-Ambassador Standley," *Shipmate*, September 1977, pp. 27–29.

Truman, Harry S. "Our Armed Forces Must Be Unified," *Collier's*, August 26, 1944, pp. 16, 63–64.

Whalen, Richard. "The Strange Case of Tyler Kent," *Diplomat*, November 1965, pp. 16–19, 62–64.

D. BOOKS

Allen, Gwenfread. *Hawaii's War Years*. Honolulu: University of Hawaii Press, 1950.

Anthony, J. Garner. *Hawaii Under Army Rule*. Stanford, CA: Stanford University Press, 1955.

Arnold, H. H. *Global Mission*. New York: Harper and Brothers, 1949.

Bailey, Thomas A., and Ryan, Paul B. *Hitler vs Roosevelt*. New York: Macmillan, 1979.

Barnes, Harry Elmer. *Perpetual War for Perpetual Peace*. Caldwell, ID: Caxton Printers, 1953.

Bartlett, Bruce R. *Cover-Up: The Politics of Pearl Harbor, 1941–1946*. New Rochelle, NY: Arlington House, 1978.

Beard, Charles A. *President Roosevelt and the Coming of the War, 1941*. New Haven: Yale University Press, 1948.

Berle, Adolf A. *Navigating the Rapids, 1918–1971*. New York: Harcourt Brace Jovanovich, 1973.

Biddle, Francis. *In Brief Authority*. Garden City, NY: Doubleday & Co., Inc., 1962.

Blair, Clay, Jr. *Silent Victory*. Philadelphia, New York: Lippincott, 1975.

Blum, John Morton. *Years of Urgency, 1938–1941*. Boston: Houghton Mifflin, 1965.

Borg, Dorothy, and Okamoto, Shumpei, eds. *Pearl Harbor as History*. New York: Columbia University Press, 1973.

Brownlow, Donald Grey. *The Accused*. New York: Vantage Press, 1968.

Buell, Thomas B. *The Quiet Warrior*. Boston: Little, Brown, 1974.

Bullitt, Orville H., ed. *Correspondence between Franklin D. Roosevelt and William C. Bullitt*. Boston: Houghton Mifflin, 1972.

Burtness, Paul S., and Ober, Warren U. *The Puzzle of Pearl Harbor*. Evanston, IL: Row, Peterson, 1962.

Churchill, Winston. *The Second World War*. Boston: Houghton Mifflin, 1949–60. Vol. 3, *The Grand Alliance*.

Clark, Ronald. *The Man Who Broke Purple*. Boston: Little, Brown, 1977.

Cole, Wayne S. *America First*. Madison: University of Wisconsin Press, 1953.

Current, Richard N. *Secretary Stimson: a Study in Statecraft*. New Brunswick, NJ: Rutgers University Press, 1954.

Dallek, Robert. *Franklin D. Roosevelt and American Foreign Policy, 1932–1945*. New York: Oxford University Press, 1979.

Divine, Robert A. *The Illusion of Neutrality*. Chicago: Quadrangle Books, 1962.

Eggleston, George T. *Roosevelt, Churchill and the World War II Opposition*. Old Greenwich, CT: Devin-Adair, 1979.

Emmerson, John K. *The Japanese Thread*. New York: Holt, Rinehart and Winston, 1978.

Farago, Ladislas. *The Broken Seal*. New York: Random House, 1967; Bantam, 1968.

———. *The Tenth Fleet*. New York: Obolensky, 1962.

Farley, James A. *Jim Farley's Story*. New York: McGraw-Hill, 1948.

Field, Henry. *Trail Blazers*. Miami, FL: Field Research Projects, 1980.

Flynn, John T. *The Final Secret of Pearl Harbor*. New York: Privately printed, 1950.

Forrestal, James. *The Forrestal Diaries*. New York: Viking, 1951.

Gauvreau, Emile, and Cohen, Lester. *Billy Mitchell*. New York: Dutton, 1942.

Grew, Joseph, C. *Ten Years in Japan.* New York: Simon and Schuster, 1944.

———. *Turbulent Era,* Vol. II. Boston: Houghton Mifflin, 1952.

Halsey, Fleet Admiral William F., and Bryan, J. III. *Admiral Halsey's Story.* New York: McGraw-Hill, 1947.

Harrington, Joseph P. *Yankee Samurai.* Detroit: Pettigrew Enterprises, 1979.

Hoehling, A. A. *The Week Before Pearl Harbor.* New York: Norton, 1963.

———. *December 7, 1941: The Day the Admirals Slept Late.* (Paperback edition of above). New York: Kensington, 1978.

Holmes, W. J. *Double-Edged Secrets.* Annapolis: Naval Institute Press, 1979.

Hull, Cordell. *The Memoirs of Cordell Hull.* New York: Macmillan, 1948. 2 vols.

Hyde, H. Montgomery. *Room 3603.* New York: Farrar, Straus, 1963.

Ickes, Harold L. *The Secret Diary of Harold L. Ickes.* New York: Simon and Schuster, 1953–54. Vol. 3, *The Lowering Clouds, 1939–41.*

Kahn, David. *The Code Breakers.* New York: Macmillan, 1967.

Kimball, Warren F. *The Most Unsordid Act.* Baltimore: Johns Hopkins Press, 1969.

Kimball, Warren F., ed. *Franklin D. Roosevelt and the World Crisis, 1937–1945.* Lexington, MA: Heath, 1952.

Kimmel, Husband E. *Admiral Kimmel's Story.* Chicago: Regnery, 1955.

King, Ernest J., and Whitehill, Walter Muir. *Fleet Admiral King.* New York: Norton, 1952.

Kubek, Anthony. *How the Far East Was Lost.* Dallas: Teacher Publishing Company, 1962.

Langer, William L., and Gleason, S. Everett. *The Undeclared War.* New York: Harper and Brothers, 1953.

Lea, Homer. *The Valor of Ignorance.* New York: Harpers, 1909.

Lombard, Helen. *While They Fought.* New York: Scribners, 1947.

Lord, Walter. *Day of Infamy.* New York: Holt, 1957.

Manchester, William. *American Caesar.* New York: Dell, 1979.

Marshall, Katherine Tupper. *Together.* Atlanta: Tupper and Love, 1946.

Masterman, J. S. *The Double-Cross System.* New Haven: Yale University Press, 1972.

Melosi, Martin V. *The Shadow of Pearl Harbor.* College Station: Texas A. and M. University Press, 1977.

Morgenstern, George Edward. *Pearl Harbor.* New York: Devin-Adair, 1947.

Newcomb, Richard F. *Savo: The Incredible Naval Debacle off Guadal-canal*. New York: Holt, Rinehart and Winston, 1961.

O'Connor, Richard. *Pacific Destiny*. Boston: Little, Brown, 1969.

Perkins, Frances. *The Roosevelt I Knew*. New York: Viking, 1946.

Pogue, Forrest C. *George C. Marshall*. New York: Viking, 1968–73. Vol. 2, *Ordeal and Hope*; Vol. 3, *Organizer of Victory*.

Popov, Duskov. *Spy Counter-Spy*. New York: Grosset and Dunlap, 1974.

Porteus, Stanley D. *And Blow Not the Trumpet*. Palo Alto, CA: Pacific Books, 1947.

Potter, E. B. *Nimitz*. Annapolis: Naval Institute Press, 1976.

Powell, John B. *My Twenty-Five Years in Japan*. New York: Macmillan, 1945.

Richardson, Admiral J. O., as told to George C. Dyer. *On the Treadmill to Pearl Harbor*. Washington, D.C.: U. S. Government Printing Office, 1973.

Roosevelt, Eleanor. *This I Remember*. New York: Harper, 1949.

Rosenman, Samuel I. *Working with Roosevelt*. New York: Harper, 1952.

Russett, Bruce M. *No Clear and Present Danger*. New York: Harper and Row, 1972.

Sherwood, Robert E. *Roosevelt and Hopkins*. New York: Harper, 1948.

Snow, John Howland. *The Case of Tyler Kent*. New Canaan, CT: Long House, 1962.

Standley, Admiral William H., and Ageton, Arthur A. *Admiral Ambassador to Russia*. Chicago: Regnery, 1955.

Stevenson, William. *A Man Called Intrepid*. New York: Harcourt Brace Jovanovich, 1976.

Stimson, Henry L., and Bundy, McGeorge. *On Active Service in Peace and War*. New York: Harper, 1947.

Stratton, Roy. *The Army-Navy Game*. Falmouth, MA: Volta, 1977.

Sulzberger, C. L. *A Long Row of Candles*. New York: Macmillan, 1969.

Sweeny, Charles. *Pearl Harbor*. Murray, UT: Privately printed, 1946.

Tansill, Charles C. *Back Door to War*. Chicago: Regnery, 1952.

Theobald, Rear Admiral Robert A. *The Final Secret of Pearl Harbor*. Old Greenwich, CT: Devin-Adair, 1954.

Thorne, Christopher. *Allies of a Kind*. New York: Oxford University Press, 1978.

Thorpe, Brigadier General Elliott R. *East Wind Rain*. Boston: Gambit, 1969.

Toland, John. *But Not in Shame*. New York: Random House, 1961.

———. *The Rising Sun*. New York: Random House, 1970.

Tolley, Kemp. *Cruise of the Lanikai*. Annapolis: Naval Institute Press, 1973.

Tully, Grace. *F.D.R. My Boss*. New York: Scribners, 1949.

Van Der Rhoer, Edward. *Deadly Magic*. New York: Scribners, 1978.

Wayman, Dorothy G. *David I. Walsh, Citizen-Patriot*. Milwaukee: Bruce, 1952.

Wedemeyer, General Albert C. *Wedemeyer Reports*. New York: Holt, 1958.

Whalen, Richard J. *The Founding Father*. New York: New American Library, 1964.

Wheeler, Burton K., with Paul F. Healy. *Yankee from the West*. Garden City, NY: Doubleday & Co., Inc., 1962.

Wilson, Rose Page. *George Marshall Remembered*. Prentice-Hall: Englewood Cliffs, NJ, 1968.

Winant, John Gilbert. *Letter from Grosvenor Square*. Boston: Houghton Mifflin, 1947.

Wohlstetter, Roberta. *Pearl Harbor: Warning and Decision*. Stanford, CA: Stanford University Press, 1962.

NOTES

Abbreviations

CR	Congressional Record
CUOH	Columbia University, Oral History Research Office, New York, NY
FD	Forrestal Diary, Seely G. Mudd Manuscript Library, Princeton University, Princeton, NJ
FDR	Franklin Delano Roosevelt Presidential Library, Hyde Park, NY
GCM	George C. Marshall Research Foundation, Lexington, VA
HI	Hoover Institution, Stanford, CA
LC	Library of Congress, Manuscript Division, Washington, DC
NA	The National Archives, Washington, DC
NYT	New York *Times*
PHA	*Pearl Harbor Attack: Hearings before the Joint Committee on the Investigation of the Pearl Harbor Attack*, 79th Congress, 1st Session. 39 vols., 1946.
SD	Stimson Diary, Yale University Library, New Haven, CT
TKC	Thomas Kimmel Collection
UWACH	University of Wyoming, Archive of Contemporary History, Laramie, WY

Chapter One "HOW DID THEY CATCH US . . ."

pages 3–4   Edgers story. Interview with Woodrough.

pages 11–12   Kimmel reaction. Interviews with DeLany, Murray, Clark; Brownlow 133. *The Accused* by Donald Grey Brownlow contains much original material of high quality.

page 12   Roosevelt-Hopkins meeting. Sherwood 530–1.

page 12   Hull story. U. S. Department of State Bulletin, V: 461–64.

page 12   "Have you heard the news?" SD.

page 13   Kawakami story. K. C. Li, comp., *American Diplomacy in the Far East: 1941* (New York, 1942), 414.

page 13   "So sorry, we sank your fleet this morning." Sulzberger 176.

pages 13–14   "The President was deeply shaken." Biddle 206.
page 14   Morgenthau story. Morgenthau diary, FDR.
page 14   "But they knew, they knew, they knew." Clark 170.
page 14   Popov story. Popov 190–91.

Chapter Two   MR. KNOX GOES WEST

page 15   "The Sun Will Soon Be Setting . . ." Melosi 3.
page 16   White House reaction. Tully 258–89.
page 16   "and slept the sleep of the saved . . ." Churchill, *Grand Alliance*, 608.
pages 16–17   "Oh! that is the way we talked to her . . ." Arthur Bryant, *The Turn of the Tide*, 282.
page 17   Spruance story. Buell 97–98.
page 17   "If I were in charge in Washington . . ." Brownlow 139.
pages 17–18   Knox story. Melosi 20; Knox papers, LC; Admiral Beatty article in *National Review*, Dec. 13, 1966, 1261.
page 18   Stowe story. CR 9646.
page 19   Tobey story. CR 9656–62.
page 20   "Altogether much is brewing . . ." SD.
page 20   B-18 accident. Accident report, Norton Air Force Base, CA.
page 21   "He read them most carefully . . ." SD.
page 21   Knox report to Roosevelt. PHA 24:1749–56.
pages 21–22   Roosevelt meeting with Knox, Stimson, Hull, etc. Memorandum by Roosevelt, undated, President's File, FDR; Melosi 25.
page 22   "You could have heard a tiny pin drop . . ." William Bernreider letter to City Hall Press Corps, Dec. 16, 1941, Bernreider Collection.
page 22   "The United States services were not on the alert . . ." NYT, Dec. 16, 1941, 1 and 7.
page 22   "as fairly extensive and unvarnished." *Nation*, Dec. 20, 1941, 626.
page 22   "it was almost possible to hear . . ." NYT, Dec. 16, 1941, 26.
page 23   Stimson-McCloy meeting. SD; interview with McCloy.
page 23   Roosevelt–Mrs. Hamlin story. Hamlin diary, FDR.
page 24   "Most confidentially we are sending . . ." Stimson letter, Dec. 16, 1941, Yale University Library.
page 25   "You always wanted the Pacific Fleet." Potter 9–10.

Chapter Three   "SOME ADMIRAL OR SOME GENERAL . . ."

page 28   "How about that, Frank?" Current 170–71.
page 29   Hoover letter. Dec. 17, 1941, Herbert Hoover Presidential Library, West Branch, IA.
pages 29–30   Standley story. Standley 80 ff.; manuscript, "The Pearl Harbor Debacle," by Standley and Arthur A. Ageton, TKC.
page 31   Testimony, Dec. 23, 1941. PHA 22:31 ff.
page 31   Nimitz story. Potter 16–17.

page 32   "If the United States has been found . . ." CR, Dec. 26, 1941.

page 32   "Of course, you are not here in the capacity . . ." Kimmel 151–52.

page 33   "that he desired to offer no objection . . ." Kimmel 154.

page 33   "I felt that, with all the information available . . ." Standley 84.

page 33   Kimmel's frustration. Kimmel 147.

pages 33–34   Testimony, Jan. 2, 1942. PHA 23:1068 ff.

page 34   Murray story. Interview with Murray.

page 34   "opposed to any correction of the testimony . . ." Kimmel 157–58.

page 35   "But Mr. Roberts is only one member . . ." Kimmel 158.

page 35   "Words don't alter facts": Kimmel letter to Barnes, June 12, 1962, TKC.

page 35   Standley report to Knox. Standley 88.

page 36   "We sat up until twelve o'clock . . ." SD.

page 36   "apparently persisted long after we both . . ." Standley-Ageton manuscript, "The Pearl Harbor Debacle," TKC.

page 36   "it did not present the whole, true picture." Standley 87–88.

page 37   "Is there any reason why this report . . ." Roberts to Samuel I. Rosenman in *The Public Papers and Addresses of Franklin D. Roosevelt*, Rosenman X:565.

page 37   "It is an admirable report . . ." SD.

page 37   Report of the Roberts Commission, January 23, 1942. PHA 39:1–21.

pages 37–38   "comprehensive and admirable view of the facts . . ." Beard 222.

page 38   Taussig letter to Kimmel. Kimmel 177–78.

page 38   "Naturally it stirs many reflections . . ." Frankfurter to Roberts, Jan. 25, 1942, Frankfurter Papers, LC.

page 39   Short story. PHA 7:3133. Original letter at GCM.

page 40   "as I feared it might give the impression . . ." SD.

page 40   "It's high time we were getting rid . . ." SD.

page 41   Stimson letter to Roberts. PHA 7:3261.

page 41   "I think it is regrettable that the committee . . ." NYT, Jan. 30, 1942, 4.

page 41   "If you think it would be a good thing . . ." McCormack to Edwin M. Watson, Feb. 6, 1942, Roosevelt Papers, FDR.

page 42   "It seems to me that this committee . . ." Ernest J. King Collection, LC.

Chapter Four "SETTLE YOURSELF IN A QUIET NOOK . . ."

page 43   Kimmel's retirement. "Facts and Correspondence," an unpublished memorandum by Kimmel, TKC.

pages 43–44   "I showed the Secretary and the President . . ." Stark to Kimmel, Jan. 27, 1942, TKC.

page 44   "I desire my request for retirement . . ." "Facts and Correspondence," TKC.

page 44   "Wait about a week and then announce . . ." SD.

page 44   "I told him the way in which . . ." "Facts and Correspondence," TKC.

page 45   "I wish for you, amid the clouds . . ." Ibid.

page 45   "Pending something definite, there is no . . ." Ibid.

page 45   "I stand ready at any time . . ." Ibid.

page 45   "I do not have to tell you . . ." Ibid.

page 46   May speech. Brownlow 148.

pages 46–47   Mix letter. Kimmel 172.

page 48   Thomas Kimmel story. Interview with T. Kimmel.

pages 48–49   Edward Kimmel story. Interview with E. Kimmel.

pages 50–53   Kimmel story: "Events Leading to the Congressional Investigation of Pearl Harbor," an unpublished account by Admiral Kimmel, TKC; notebook and papers of Robert A. Lavender, Mrs. Albert F. Betzel Collection; interviews with Thomas and Edward Kimmel and Edward Hanify; Hanify speech on Pearl Harbor at Union Club, Boston, MA, Dec. 7, 1979, Toland Tape Collection.

Chapter Five   MUTINY ON THE SECOND DECK

pages 57–63   For background on the mutiny I am indebted to A. A. Hoehling and two restricted studies in the Hiles Collection at UWACH by Captain Laurance Safford: *Rhapsody in Purple* and *Victims of the Kita Message.*

Commander Hiles's collections, which include twelve years of voluminous correspondence with Safford, have been an invaluable contribution to this book.

pages 57–58   "I thoroughly appreciate that you would probably . . ." Kahn 25–26.

page 58   "That Noyes!" Hoehling, *Day*, 62.

page 61   "Both officers were good haters." Interview with Hiles.

page 62   "You put in the words 'war warning.'" Hoehling, *Day*, 72–74.

pages 63–66   Safford story of Cipher 3. His two unpublished studies cited above.

page 63   "You have been capsized . . ." Safford letter, May 25, 1964, to Eugene Gressley, UWACH.

page 65   "I further informed Friedman . . ." Safford letter to Hiles, Dec. 31, 1961, Hiles Private Collection.

page 66   "I realized I would be one of the important . . ." PHA 36:69.

page 67   "I realize that your reply . . ." PHA, 8:3698–99.

page 68   "My dear Kramer: When the proper time comes . . ." PHA 8:3702.

page 68   Safford letter to Kramer, Jan. 22, 1944. PHA 8:3700.

page 69   Safford visit to Kimmel: Safford letter to Hiles, May 24, 1965, UWACH.

Chapter Six THE HART INQUIRY

page 70   "I feel that I am entitled to a speedy . . ." Kimmel letter to Hart, TKC.

page 71   Turner testimony. PHA 26:273–75.

pages 71–72   Knox's press release, April 14, 1944. Record Group 125, NA.

page 72   "I presume you have noted the recent . . ." Kimmel letter to Manning M. Kimmel, Apr. 27, 1944, TKC.

pages 72–73   Hanify story. Interview with Hanify.

pages 73–74   Halsey testimony. PHA 6:325.

page 74   "I have just come from the front office . . ." PHA 29:2392.

pages 74–75   Safford testimony. PHA 26:392–95.

pages 75–76   "I happened to remark to him . . ." Hart taped memoirs, CUOH.

Chapter Seven THE ARMY AND NAVY CLUB

page 77   "Kimmel's waiver of its provisions . . ." Interview with Hanify; Hanify speech, Dec. 7, 1979.

pages 77–78   Rugg-Kimmel conversation. Interview with Hanify.

page 78   Hanify story. Interview with Hanify.

page 78   "I have wanted it since Pearl Harbor . . ." Kimmel letter to Senator Weeks, May 25, 1944, TKC.

page 79   "Mr. Chairman, why is it necessary . . ." CR 5340 ff.

pages 79–80   "It would be a splendid contribution . . ." CR 5402–15.

page 80   "Nothing short of an impartial . . ." Kimmel letter to Rugg, July 13, 1944, TKC.

pages 81–82   "I know pretty well the general . . ." Brownlow 153; Lavender notebook; Hanify speech, Dec. 7, 1979.

page 82   "I found the messages and many more." Lavender notebook.

pages 82–83   "It appeared that this assignment . . ." King 632.

page 83   "I'm not really very excited . . ." Interview with Richmond.

page 83   "I have never been able to understand . . ." Ernest J. King Collection, LC.

pages 83–84   Marshall testimony. PHA 27:11 ff.

page 85   "I have always considered Admiral Kimmel . . ." PHA 32:75.

pages 85–86   Kimmel testimony. PHA 32:120 ff.

page 87   Schuirmann testimony. PHA 33:731.

pages 87–88   Rugg-Kimmel questions. PHA 33:731 ff.

page 89   Pye-Kimmel conversation. Kimmel 131–32.

page 89   Kimmel-DeLany conversation. Interviews with DeLany and Hanify.

page 89   "That son of a bitch . . ." Interview with E. Kimmel.

page 90   Kimmel at Army Board. PHA 28:946–47.

page 90   "I will cooperate to the best . . ." Brownlow 159.

page 90   "Dicky, it won't do you a Goddamn bit of good . . ." Ibid.
154.

page 91   "Well, I never saw three officers . . ." Ibid. 157.

page 91   "Jesus Christ, we'll adjourn!" Interview with Hanify.

page 91   "Short, Marshall is your enemy." Brownlow 156.

page 92   "It was an alert apprehensiveness . . ." Interview with Hanify.

page 92   Stark testimony. PHA 32:532–33.

pages 92–93   "Perhaps I was tired." Thomas C. Hart Papers, Naval Historical Center, Washington, DC.

page 93   Marshall testimony. PHA 32:852 ff.

page 94   "To give you an honest answer . . ." Interview with Hanify.

page 94   Hanify-Kramer conversation. Interview with Hanify.

pages 94–95   Kramer testimony. PHA 33:871 ff.

page 96   Turner testimony. PHA 33:806 ff; Ibid. 32:619–20.

page 97   Noyes testimony. PHA 33:898.

page 97   "General Marshall came in in the last part . . ." SD.

pages 97–98   Stimson testimony. PHA 29:2064 ff.

page 98   "I was sorry to learn . . ." Stimson letter to Roosevelt, Sept.
26, 1944, Yale University Library.

pages 98–99   Marshall testimony. PHA 29:2312.

pages 99–100   Short testimony. Ibid. 2251 ff.

page 101   "this was no longer a case of diplomatic . . ." Charles A.
Willoughby and John Chamberlain, MacArthur: 1941–1951 (New York:
McGraw-Hill, 1954), 22–23.

page 101   Yeaton story. Yeaton papers, HI; correspondence with Heimlich.

pages 102–3   Safford testimony. PHA 29:2385 ff.

page 103   "It is my personal belief . . ." Russell's unpublished memoirs,
Morgenstern Collection, UWACH.

pages 103–4   Marshall testimony. PHA 29:2400 ff.

pages 104–5   Bratton testimony. Ibid. 2415 ff.

page 105   "Marshall and his close associates . . ." Russell's unpublished
memoirs.

page 105   Grunert story. Grunert letter to Deputy Chief of Staff, U. S.
Army, Oct. 30, 1944.

page 106   Sadtler testimony. PHA 29:2427 ff.

page 106   "We knew nothing of the reasons . . ." Russell's unpublished
memoirs.

page 107   Navy Court of Inquiry Report. PHA 39:297 ff.

page 107   "undermine such faith as the great masses . . ." Russell's unpublished memoirs.

pages 107–8   Top Secret Army Pearl Harbor Report. PHA 39:221 ff.

pages 108–9   Rugg telegram. TKC.

Chapter Eight   "YOU DO NOT HAVE TO CARRY THE TORCH . . ."

pages 110–18   Kent Case. Interviews and correspondence with Kent;
British Public Records Office, FO/371/38704, File No. 2405; Snow; The

Earl Jowett, *Some Are Spies* (London: Stodder and Houghton, 1940),
40 ff; transcript of Kent Trial at Central Criminal Court, Old Bailey;
Whalen article in *Diplomat,* Nov. 1965; Whalen 313 ff.; Henry Taylor
article in Washington *Daily News,* Sept. 5, 1944.

page 118   Kimmel letter to Truman, August 20, 1944. TKC.

pages 118–19   "Dreyfus was on Devil's Island . . ." Broadcast transcript, Aug. 30, 1944, TKC.

page 119   Remarks in Congress. CR 7573–76; 7648–51; 8110–12.

page 119   "About 72 hours before Pearl Harbor . . ." PHA 29:2252.

pages 119–20   "There will be lots of things like that . . ." Roosevelt
press conference, Sept. 22, 1944.

page 120   "The American People demand . . ." Preston Kaye letter to
Roosevelt, Sept. 11, 1944, Roosevelt Papers, FDR.

page 120   "fear there would be an adverse report . . ." SD.

pages 120–23   Marshall-Dewey story. "Statement for Record" by Brigadier General Carter Clarke, Record Group 457, NA.

page 123   Luce story. Eggleston 186.

page 123   Roosevelt's health. Ibid. 186.

page 124   "won't intimate in the papers . . ." *Facts on File Yearbook
1944,* 360.

pages 124–25   "We each told the other . . ." SD.

page 125   "Since trial by general court-martial . . ." PHA 39:343–45.

page 125   "by the grace of God . . ." SD.

pages 126–27   Stimson-Roosevelt conversation. Ibid.

pages 127–28   Stimson letter to Roosevelt, Nov. 22, 1944. Yale University Library.

page 128   "His wish for coordination . . ." SD.

page 129   "The exercise of hindsight . . ." FD.

page 129   "turning back to his old form . . ." SD.

page 129   "The departure of Mr. Hull . . ." Ibid.

page 129   "Now I feel as if I had a burden . . ." Ibid.

pages 130–31   Kimmel-King conversation. Kimmel memorandum, TKC.

page 132   Pettigrew affidavit. PHA 35:23.

page 132   Dusenbury affidavit. Ibid. 25.

page 134   "I told him that I felt . . ." FD.

page 134   MacArthur story. Interview and correspondence with Fellers;
Fellers letter to Kimmel, Feb. 1967, TKC.

pages 135–36   Safford-Sonnett meetings. PHA 18:3345.

page 136   Sonnett-Hewitt conversation with Safford. Ibid. 3346.

pages 136–37   Kramer testimony. PHA 36:81.

page 137   "*thought* that a 'Winds' message . . ." Ibid. 93.

page 138   "One of the reasons why he suggested . . ." Rugg memorandum, July 10, 1944, TKC.

page 138   "no message was intercepted . . ." PHA 36:575.

page 139   "Some time during 1943 . . ." PHA 33:86.

pages 139–40   Spalding testimony. Ibid. 90–92.

page 140   Bissell testimony. Ibid. 101–2.

page 140   Richmond-Marshall story. Interview with Richmond.

page 141   "If I had received such a message . . ." PHA 35:92–93.

page 141   "an exceptionally good officer . . ." Ransom letter to author, March 27, 1980.

pages 141–42   Bratton story. Correspondence with Heimlich; Yeaton memoirs, HI; PHA 35:97–98.

page 143   "Secretary Forrestal had some very set ideas . . ." Hewitt taped interview, CUOH.

page 144   "only added to and accentuated . . ." FD.

pages 144–45   Truman press conference, Aug. 29, 1945.

page 145   "As the stories were 'rigged' in Washington . . ." Russell unpublished memoirs.

pages 145–46   Truman press conference, Aug. 30, 1945.

page 146   "I wish Congress could forget about it . . ." Chicago *Tribune*, Sept. 6, 1945.

Chapter Nine   "IF I HAD KNOWN WHAT WAS TO HAPPEN . . ."

page 152   "I simply ask the right . . ." CR 10345.

page 153   "whole legions of stories . . ." CR 10446.

page 153   "I shall never grant permission . . ." CR 10433.

page 154   "It is very distressing to me . . ." Mitchell letter to Randolph Mason, Nov. 10, 1945.

page 155   Testimony, Nov. 16, 1945. PHA 1:33 ff.

page 155   "a sneak attack upon the grave . . ." Melosi 149.

page 155   "tactic of desperation by a party . . ." NYT, Nov. 18, 1945.

page 156   "it seems almost certain that they . . ." Ibid.

page 156   Richardson testimony. PHA 1:265–66.

page 157   "I have been greatly disturbed . . ." Mrs. Roosevelt to Hopkins, Nov. 20, 1945, Hopkins Papers, FDR.

page 157   "Since Senator Ferguson devoted more time . . ." Greaves unpublished manuscript.

pages 159–60   Hull testimony. PHA 2:614–15.

page 161   Kent story: Washington *Times-Herald*, Dec. 5, 1945; New York *Post*, Dec. 4, 1945; New York *World-Telegram*, Dec. 4, 1945.

page 161   "If I had more experience . . ." Interview with Kent.

page 162   "That phone call as we came in . . ." K. T. Marshall 282.

pages 162–64   Diggs on Marshall. Interview and correspondence with Diggs.

pages 163–64   Gerow testimony. PHA 3:1036–37.

page 164   Marshall testimony. Dec. 6, 1945, Ibid. 1049 ff.

page 165   Marshall testimony. Dec. 7, 1945, Ibid. 1105 ff.

page 165   Marshall testimony. Dec. 8, 1945, Ibid. 1165 ff.

page 167   Miles testimony. Ibid. 1554.

page 167   Lucas-Greaves incident. Ibid. 1372–73.

page 168   "It seems strange to me . . ." New York *Herald-Tribune*, Dec. 12, 1945; Washington *Times-Herald*, Dec. 12, 1945.

pages 168–70   Marshall testimony. PHA 3:1406 ff.

page 170   "Totally honest." Interview with Gesell.

page 170   "I felt that his performance . . ." Interview with Diggs.

page 170   "sit and take it." J. L. Homer letter to Forrest Pogue, July 22, 1960, GCM.

page 170   Ferguson story. Interview with Greaves.

page 171   Mitchell announcement to committee. PHA 4:1585–87.

page 171   Barkley and George comments. Ibid. 1587–90.

page 171   Afternoon session. Ibid. 1612 ff.

page 172   "What was indicated in his statement . . ." NYT, Dec. 16, 1945.

pages 172–73   Greaves incident. PHA 4:1719–22.

pages 173–76   Wilkinson testimony. Ibid. 1793 ff.

page 173   "If you ever need a counsel . . ." Interview with Greaves.

pages 176–77   "Now, yesterday I made the mistake . . ." PHA 4:1859–60.

page 177   Turner story: Interview with Mott.

page 178   Turner testimony. PHA 4:1975 ff.

page 178   "The Committee wishes the press and all others . . ." Ibid. 2063.

Chapter Ten   THEIR DAY IN COURT

page 180   "Counsel has not yet had nor requested . . ." Barnes 453–54.

page 180   Stark-Richmond story. Interview with Richmond.

page 181   Greaves letter. Greaves Collection.

page 181   Stark testimony. PHA 5:2291 ff.

page 182   "I want the truth to come out." Brownlow 164.

page 182   "It wouldn't take much for Stark . . ." Interview with Richmond.

page 182   "This was unquestionably done . . ." Kimmel memorandum, TKC.

pages 182–83   Kimmel testimony. Jan. 16, 1946, PHA 6:2555 ff.

page 183   Kimmel testimony. Jan. 18, 1946, Ibid. 2701 ff.

pages 183–84   "Now, Mr. Chairman, the gentleman . . ." Ibid. 2775.

page 184   "I appreciate as you do . . ." Ibid. 2825.

page 184   Kimmel testimony. Ibid. 2839 ff.

page 185   "It contained the first inkling . . ." Barnes 456.

page 185   Greaves letter to Flynn, Jan. 19, 1946. Greaves Collection.

page 185   The war plan mentioned on page 185, WPL-46, dated May 26, 1941, was based upon the report of the United States–British Staff Conversations, the Joint Canada–United States Defense Plan and the Joint Army and Navy Basic War Plan. Apparently these Anglo-American plans were approved by the Secretary of the Navy on May 28, 1941. (PHA 15:1425.) The President on June 7, 1941, returned the war plan to the Navy Department after familiarizing himself with it, saying "since the report of the United States British Staff Conversations had not been approved by the British Government, he would not approve the report at this time, neither would he now give approval to Joint Army and Navy Basic War Plan. . . . However, in case of war the papers would be returned to the President for his approval." (PHA 3:995.)

On June 11, 1941, Admiral Stark instructed top Navy officials that "the highest priority in the preparation of war plans is assigned to the plans required by WPL 46. It is directed that the preparation and distribution of these plans be accomplished with the least possible delay." (PHA 5:2478.) In any case, despite the Administration's denial of a prewar agreement with Britain, these plans based on British-American conversations were in effect prior to December 7, 1941.

They reveal that once war came Kimmel had certain offensive tasks, including raids on the Caroline and Marshall Islands. The Pacific Fleet was not ordered to deploy and patrol the Hawaiian coast. As Admiral Stark testified, "I do not think there is any place in the plan where it could tell him [Kimmel] what to do in connection with a defensive deployment." (PHA 5:2449.) The deployment was meant for the Asiatic Fleet in the Philippines. This fleet was the first addressee of the "war warning" message and the one primarily interested in the suspected Japanese expedition in Southeast Asia.

To Kimmel the war warning message meant he should ready his forces for raids on the Marshall and Caroline Islands, which meant that his fleet had to come into Pearl Harbor—to strip, fuel and make ready for possible action. That is exactly what the Pacific Fleet was doing on December 7, 1941.

page 185   "when everybody above him . . ." PHA 6:2858–59.

pages 185–86   "confident that the Navy . . ." Kimmel letter to Col. Manning Kimmel, Jan. 25, 1946, TKC.

page 186   Short testimony. PHA 6:2964.

pages 186–87   Short testimony. PHA 7:3133 ff.

pages 187–93   Roberts testimony. Ibid. 3272 ff.

Chapter Eleven SAFFORD AT BAY

page 194   "He entered the Naval Hospital under orders . . ." Associated Press, Nov. 13, 1945.

pages 195–98   Briggs story. U. S. Navy official taped interview, Jan. 13, 1977, NA; Safford papers, Hiles Collection, UWACH.

pages 199–200   Hanify story. Interviews with Hanify and Mrs. William Reeder.

pages 201–3   Safford testimony. PHA 8:3593 ff.

pages 203–4   "I was instructed by the Secretary of the Navy . . ." U.S. News, Feb. 15, 1946, 22.

page 203   "I was sitting right behind Safford . . ." Lavender letter to Kimmel, Spet. 21, 1962, TKC.

pages 204–10   Safford testimony: PHA 8:3673 ff.

page 211   "He was not a forensic type." Interview with Hanify.

page 211   "We haven't touched the real meat . . ." New York Herald Tribune, Feb. 5, 1946.

pages 212–14   Safford testimony. PHA 8:3741 ff.

pages 215–16   Safford testimony. PHA 8:3839–93.

page 216   Before he left the room, Safford was stopped by Richardson's wife. "Captain, you were simply wonderful! You did not let them bully you into changing your story." Realizing who she was, Safford felt that this was an "angel from heaven." Gordon Prange, *At Dawn We Slept* (New York: McGraw-Hill, 1981), 715.

page 217   Kramer testimony. Feb. 6, 1946, Ibid. 3893 ff.

pages 217–18   Kramer testimony. Feb. 7, 1946, PHA 9:3929 ff.

pages 218–20   Kramer testimony. Feb. 8, 1946, Ibid. 4009 ff.

pages 220–22   Kramer testimony. Feb. 9, 1946, Ibid. 4093 ff.

pages 222–223   Kramer testimony. Feb. 11, 1946, Ibid. 4157 ff.

page 224   "some medal of higher dignity than that which was given to Captain Safford." Commander Baecher reported to Forrestal that the majority was indignant at the award to Captain Safford, particularly following his recent allegations about his superiors. "The suggestion had now been seriously made to me that the Navy in order to straighten out the matter should award to Captain Kramer some medal of higher dignity than that which was given to Captain Safford . . . because the effect of his testimony was to support the integrity of the higher command in the Navy and your Findings and Conclusions." (Baecher memorandum to Forrestal, Feb. 13, 1946.)

In a second memorandum to Forrestal three days later, Baecher wrote: "Congressman Murphy stated to me privately that while he knew there were 'two camps in the Navy' yet he desired to know whether it was 'a coincidence' that the award was made immediately following the attempt by majority members of the Committee to demonstrate as unfounded Captain Safford's statements including one of his letters to Captain Kramer that 'nobody in OPNAV can be trusted.' I told him that he should consider the timing as unfortunate and as having been a mere coincidence.

"When there was delivered to Senator Lucas the opinion by the JAG [Judge Advocate General], which was to the effect that Captain Safford had seriously violated Navy Regulations in mailing the letters to Captain Kramer, Senator Lucas stated to me privately that the only comment he would be able to make when he would put the JAG's opinion in the record was that the award to Captain Safford of the Legion of Merit immediately following the publicity attending his letters to Captain Kramer showed that the 'Navy was cock-eyed.' He said he considered that the seriousness of the matter should have been apparent to anyone reading the newspapers, including those in the Navy responsible for the making and approving of awards."

Chapter Twelve   "TO THROW AS SOFT A LIGHT AS POSSIBLE . . ."

pages 225–26   Clausen testimony. PHA 9:4308, 4319, 4428, 4470, 4464.

pages 226–29   Bratton testimony. Ibid. 4509 ff.

pages 229–31   Sadtler testimony. PHA 10:4635 ff.

pages 231–34   Schulz testimony. Ibid. 4659 ff; interviews with Schulz and Greaves.

pages 234–35   "The committee had some differences . . ." Ibid. 5150–51.

page 235   "The Congressional Pearl Harbor investigation . . ." NYT, Feb. 24, 1946.

pages 235–36   Wilkinson death. "Findings of the Naval Board of Investigation" submitted by the Chief of Naval Personnel, Rear Admiral T. L. Sprague, to the Secretary of the Navy, March 20, 1946; Washington *Evening Star*, Feb. 22, 1946.

page 236   "Wilkinson was the only decent one in the lot . . ." Safford letter to Hiles, May 24, 1965, UWACH.

page 236   Baecher report to Forrestal, Mar. 28, 1946.

page 237   Stark testimony. PHA 11:5154.

page 237   "has ended as it began on a note . . ." NYT, May 25, 1946.

page 237   "Well, we know. We were with you . . ." Interview with Mrs. Krick.

pages 237–38   Stark-Krick testimony. PHA 11:5543 ff.

pages 240–43   Majority and minority reports, along with additional views of Keefe, *Investigations of the Pearl Harbor Attack: Report of the Joint Committee on the Investigation of the Pearl Harbor Attack*, July 20, 1946. 79th Congress, 2nd Session.

page 240   Flynn letter to Gearhart, July 15, 1946. Greaves Collection.

pages 240–41   Flynn letter to Keefe, July 16, 1946. Greaves Collection.

page 241   Keefe letter to Flynn, July 18, 1946. Greaves Collection.

page 242   "constitute an arraignment of the Roosevelt . . ." Beard 346–47.

pages 242–43   Flynn letter to Keefe, July 19, 1946. Greaves Collection.

page 242   "by committee rules which permitted . . ." Barnes 464.

page 243   "When two Republicans joined with . . ." P.M., July 22, 1946.

page 243   "and even the minority report . . ." New York *Herald Tribune*, July 22, 1946.

pages 243–44   "The most disgraceful feature of the whole . . ." Barnes 408.

pages 244–45   Safford-Friedman conversation. This account, dated Aug. 14, 1946, was written by Friedman on the back of a Safford article, "Statement Regarding Winds Message." Friedman Collection, GCM.

page 247   "The truth must be repeated again and again . . ." Goethe, *Lexikon* (Leipzig: Alfred Kröner Verlag, 1912), 113. The translation is by Bettina Greaves.

Chapter Thirteen   OPERATION Z

page 250   "The economic development of these countries . . ." George F. Kennan, *The Decision to Intervene* (Princeton: Princeton University Press, 1958), 221–22.

page 250   "to train the two Services in the joint operation . . ." Report from the Chief Umpires, Grand Joint Army and Navy Exercise No. 4, to the Adjutant General, U. S. Army, Feb. 18, 1932. Record Group 80, NA.

page 251   "In case the enemy's main fleet is berthed . . ." Borg 237–38.

page 251   "On our return to Washington I was quoted . . ." Arnold 193–94.

page 252   "any practicable way of placing torpedo . . ." Richardson letter to Stark, Jan. 4, 1941.

page 252   "If war eventuates with Japan . . ." Stark letter to Knox, Jan. 24, 1941.

page 252   Knox reply, Feb. 7, 1941.

page 252   "I think an attack on Hawaii . . ." Toland, *Rising Sun*, 150.

page 253   Bishop story. Interview with Bishop.

page 253   "There is a lot of talk around town . . ." Grew diary, Jan. 27, 1941.

page 253   "The Division of Naval Intelligence places . . ." Stark letter to Kimmel, Feb. 1, 1941.

page 254   "If we fail we had better give up . . ." Toland, *Rising Sun*, 152.

pages 254–55   "The defense of Oahu, due to its fortification . . ." PHA 3:1093.

page 255   "in a very difficult position . . ." Kimmel memorandum to Stark, May 26, 1941.

page 255   Ickes-Roosevelt conversation. President's Secretaries File, FDR.

pages 256–57   "Under such circumstances, we had better . . ." Toland, *Rising Sun*, 86.

page 256   "I had expressed the opinion . . ." PHA 2:604.

page 256   "When President Roosevelt told the Americans . . ." NYT, July 2, 1941.

page 257   "With each day we will get weaker . . ." Toland, *Rising Sun*, 118.

pages 257–58   "Related with my recent report . . ." Intelligence Report, Office of Chief of Naval Operations, June 18, 1941. Released to the author by Defense Intelligence Agency, Sept. 22, 1980.

page 258   British Secret Service translation of the complete German questionnaire:

Hawaii. Ammunition dumps and mine depots.

1. Details about naval ammunition and mine depot on the Isle of Kushu (Pearl Harbour). If possible sketch.

2. Naval ammunition depot Lualuelei. Exact position? Is there a railway line (junction)?

3. The total ammunition reserve of the army is supposed to be in the rock of the Crater Aliamanu. Position?

4. Is the Crater Punchbowl (Honolulu) being used as ammunition dump? If not, are there other military works?

Aerodromes.

1. Aerodrome Lukefield. Details (sketch if possible) regarding the situation of the hangars (number?), workshops, bomb depots, and petrol depots. Are there underground petrol installations? Exact position of the seaplane station? Occupation?

2. Naval air arm strong point Kaneohe. Exact report regarding position, number of hangars, depots and workshops. (Sketch.) Occupation?

3. Army aerodromes Hickam Field and Wheeler Field. Exact position? Reports regarding number of hangars, depots and workshops. Underground installations? (Sketch.)

4. Rodger's Airport. In case of war, will this place be taken over by the army or the navy? What preparations have been made? Number of hangars: Are there landing possibilities for seaplanes?

5. Airport of the Panamerican Airways. Exact position? (If possible sketch.) Is this airport possibly identical with Rodger's Airport or a part thereof? (A wireless station of the Panamerican Airways is on the Peninsula Mohapuu.)

Naval Strong Point Pearl Harbour.

1. Exact details and sketch about the situation of the state wharf, of the pier installations, workshops, petrol installations, situations of dry dock No. 1 and of the new dry dock which is being built.

2. Details about the submarine station (plan of situation). What land installations are in existence?

3. Where is the station for mine search formations (minensuchverbaende)? How far has the dredger work progressed at the entrance and in the east and southeast lock? Depths of water?

4. Number of anchorages (Liegeplaetze)?

5. Is there a floating dock in Pearl Harbour or is the transfer of such a dock to this place intended?

Special tasks.

Reports about torpedo protection nets newly introduced in the British and U.S.A. Navy. How far are they already in existence in the merchant and naval fleet?

pages 258–60   Popov story. Popov 148.

page 260   "It is therefore surely a fair deduction . . ." Masterman 80.

pages 260–61   Kilsoo Haan story. Kilsoo Haan documents, TKC; Sevareid correspondence.

page 261   Clear story. Clear letter to Kimmel, Feb. 4, 1967, TKC; Clear letter to Hiles, Nov. 3, 1967, UWACH; C. M. Horn letter to Kimmel, Dec. 9, 1966, TKC; Farrier letter to author, Feb. 29, 1980, and Apr. 4, 1980; Clear memorandum to Assistant Chief of Staff, G-2, War Department, Nov. 2, 1941.

page 262   "We face the delicate question . . ." SD.

pages 262–63   Tojo-Togo-Sugiyama story. Toland, *Rising Sun*, 123–31.

pages 263–65   Mistranslations of Japanese messages. Ibid. 132–36.

page 266   When Secretary of the Interior Ickes learned that Hull had considered offering the Japanese a three-month truce he was furious at the "appeasers" in the State Department. "If this negotiation with Japan had been consummated," he wrote in his diary on Nov. 30, "I would have promptly resigned from the cabinet with a ringing statement attacking the arrangement and raising hell generally with the State Department and its policy of appeasement. I have no doubt that the country would have reacted violently. As a matter of fact some of the newspapers indicated that they were uneasy and printed editorials deprecating any attempt at even a partial resumption of relationship with Japan. I believe that the President would have lost his country on this issue and that hell would have been to pay generally."

page 267   "I didn't tell you at the time . . ." Interview with General
Sato.
page 267   "about made up his mind . . ." SD.
page 267   "He fairly blew up—jumped up in the air . . ." SD.
pages 269–70   Field story. Field letter to author, Mar. 24, 1980.
page 269   Ingersoll, Noyes and Schuirmann testimony. PHA 33:751,
808; PHA 10:4757; PHA 32:551.

Chapter Fourteen THE TRACKING OF *Kido Butai*

pages 272–73   "might be proceeding to the Philippines . . ." Farago,
Broken Seal, 283.
page 273   Hull's conference. Berle 379.
page 273   "I handed the note to the Japs." SD.
page 273   Hornbeck memorandum. Emmerson 118.
page 273   ". . . I made the mistake of yielding . . ." Hornbeck unpublished autobiography, HI; Emmerson 116–17.
page 274   "McMorris, what is your idea . . ." PHA 6:2802.
page 275   Footnote. Interviews with Sato, Suzuki, Hoshino and Kaya.
page 276   Mathews story. Mathews letter to Pogue, Oct. 3, 1963, GCM.
pages 276–77   Roosevelt-Stimson meeting. SD.
page 277   War Cabinet meeting. SD.
page 278   "I read it over and it was a comprehensive . . ." SD.
page 278   "This was in the shape of a virtual . . ." SD.
pages 278–80   *Lurline* story. Grogan journal, Matson Navigation Company Collection; *Ships in Gray*, the story of Matson in World War II;
interviews with Charles Regal and Fred Stindt of Matson.
page 281   Seaman First Class Z story. Interviews with Seaman First
Class Z.
pages 281–82   Thorpe story. Correspondence with Thorpe; Thorpe memorandum; Thorpe 51–59; memorandum of Thorpe-Kimmel conversation,
Aug. 28, 1957, TKC.
pages 282–83   Ranneft story. Interview and correspondence with Ranneft; interview with T. S. N. Ranneft, his son; information and documents from Netherlands Department of Defense, Naval Historical Department, including official diary of Admiral Ranneft.
pages 283–84   Layton-Kimmel conversation. PHA 39:360.
page 284   Nelson-Roosevelt conversation. Donald M. Nelson, *Arsenal of
Democracy* 182–83.
page 284   "running around like a lot of wet hens . . ." Morgenthau
diary, FDR.
page 285   Grogan story. Grogan journal, Matson Collection.
pages 285–86   Burns story. John A. Burns Oral History Project, University of Hawaii, Department of American Studies. Interviews with Paul
Hooper and Stuart Gerry Brown.
page 285   "Dr. Conrad Taueber, director of the . . ." Field letter to author, May 1980.

page 285   "Apparently there is some misunderstanding . . ." James D. Lincoln letter to author, May 19, 1980.

page 285   "I'm sorry to tell you . . ." Miss Tully letter to author, Feb. 19, 1980.

page 286   Nover story. Telephone interview with Mrs. Nover; PHA 29:2244.

pages 286–87   Briggs story. Briggs official interview; Safford material, Greaves Collection. In 1960 Briggs became officer in charge of the U. S. Naval Security Group Detachment at the depository for all U. S. Navy World War II Communication Intelligence and Cryptographic Archives. This gave him the opportunity to search further for any logs or messages concerning the December 1941 intercept period. He sought diligently for anything connected with the first week before Pearl Harbor, but the only thing he discovered was an operators' sign-on and sign-off log sheet. It was dated December 2, 1941, reflecting Greenwich Mean Time (GMT) as kept at intercept Station M. (See picture section.)

This particular watch standers' log sheet was important since it confirmed the existence of the special "winds" execute intercept mission. The operator signs of the three watch standers on duty were RT (Briggs), RS and SE. The log revealed that RS had the evening watch on December 2, 1941, and at 0402 (GMT) had started this new log sheet. He was monitoring a frequency of 12,430 kilocycles at that time. At 0500 (GMT) he was relieved by Briggs, who tuned to a new frequency of 12,275 kilocycles and began copying a scheduled broadcast. His entry read: "COPY PRESS SKDS HR ON . . . SEE OTHER LOGS." This meant: "Copying press schedule from here on, see other log sheet(s) containing entire intercept." At 1300 (GMT) an entry appeared indicating that Briggs was relieved by SE. This would have been 0800 (EST).

Unable to find any confirming messages for this period of his watch, Briggs concluded that this log sheet may have covered the period of the "winds" execute intercept. Knowing it was unauthorized to make a copy of the log sheet itself, he wrote on the bottom:

"Below comments added on 12/5/60

I, R.T., now on duty at a NAVSECGAUDET [sic] as OinC [Officer-in-Charge], duly note that all transmissions intercepted by me between 0500 thru 1300 on the above date are missing from these files & that these intercepts contained the 'Winds message warning code.' My operation sign was 'RT.' "

It is possible that Briggs's earlier recollection of having intercepted the "winds" execute on December 4 is correct; and in view of no other evidence of intercepted material, the operators' log sheet of December 2 may not cover the period of this intercept. At the same time, if this log sheet does not cover the "winds" intercept, why is all the traffic intercepted from 0500 to 1300 (GMT) on 12,275 kilocycles missing from the archives today? It is interesting to note that late on the afternoon of December 2 (Tokyo Time), Admiral Yamamoto signaled the commander of the Pearl Harbor Striking Force: "Climb Mount Niitaka 1208." This meant: "Attack as planned on December 8." It thus appears very possible that a "winds" execute could have been transmitted at about the same time.

pages 287–88   Wheeler story. Wheeler 32–33.

pages 288–89   Wedemeyer story. Interview and correspondence with Wedemeyer.

page 288   "The primary aim of this deception . . ." Stevenson 298–99.

page 289   "Hell, yes, but they don't dare . . ." Mathews letter to Pogue, GCM.

pages 289–90   Kilsoo Haan story. Kilsoo Haan material, TKC.

pages 291–92   Three small vessels story. Tolley 264 ff.; Buaas letter to author, Feb. 9, 1981; Hanson Baldwin, *The Crucial Years 1939–1941*, 436.

page 292   "Go ahead. Tell them." SD.

page 293   "What would you think of an American . . ." Ibid.

page 293   Roosevelt letter to Willkie, Dec. 5, 1941.

pages 295–96   Fellers story. Interview with Fellers; Fellers letter to Kimmel, Mar. 6, 1967, TKC.

page 296   "The President should be informed . . ." Sherwood 424.

page 297   Knox-Turner conversation. *National Review*, Dec. 13, 1966, 1261.

page 297   Mayer story. Hoehling, *Day*, 132–33; Mayer letters to Hoehling, June 11 and 22, 1962, Hoehling Collection.

pages 297–98   Safford story. PHA 29:2399; Safford letters to. Hiles, Feb. 23, 1965, and Mar. 29, 1967, UWACH.

pages 298–99   Ranneft story. Interview with Ranneft; documents and material from the Netherlands Department of Defense, Department of Naval History.

page 299   "This means that they have given up . . ." Brownlow 126.

page 299   Kimmel-Smith comments. Ibid. 126.

page 299   Kimmel conference with Pfeiffer, etc. Ibid. 127.

page 300   Pye-Layton conversation. U. S. Navy Report, PAC, Chapter Twelve, Naval Historical Center.

page 300   "was still good and we would stick . . ." Brownlow 127; interview with DeLany.

page 301   Mayer-Belin story. Hoehling, *Day*, 179–80; Mayer letters to Hoehling, June 11 and 22, 1962, Hoehling Collection.

page 302   "These are for the children . . ." Interview with Schulz.

page 303   Bowers story. *Shipmate*, Dec. 1977; Robert Clack letters to author, Dec. 19 and 26, 1978.

page 304   Nichols story. Interview with Nichols.

pages 304–5   Richardson story. Richardson 451–52.

page 305   Harrison story. Interview with Harrison.

page 305   "It looks like the Japanese are going to break off . . ." Hoehling, *Day*, 205.

page 306   "This is my last effort . . ." Ibid. 218–19.

pages 306–7   *Lurline* story. Grogan journal; Frances Berndtson Coppel letter to author, Oct. 25, 1979; interview with Yokota; five articles by Alf Pratte in Honolulu *Star-Bulletin*, starting Dec. 4, 1966; account by Eddie Collins, Chief Officer of the *Lurline*, Matson Collection.

page 307   Conway story. Toland, *Shame*, 29.

page 307   Boyer story. Boyer letter to author, Dec. 12, 1978.

pages 307–8   Yoshikawa story. Interviews with Yoshikawa and Lawrence Nakatauka.

pages 308–9   Gallaher story. Interview and correspondence with Gallaher.

page 309   Thalken story. Interview and correspondence with Thalken; record of movements of Task Force Twelve on Dec. 7, 1941, Naval Historical Center.

pages 309–10   "Oh, my God—there they come!" *The Retired Officer*, Dec. 1979.

page 310   Fleming story. Interview with Fleming.

pages 310–11   Friedman story. Clark 170.

page 311   Powell story. Powell letter to Kimmel, Feb. 22, 1955, TKC.

page 311   "What a reception the Japanese must have had!" Popov 190–91.

page 311   "If you do, I can put you away . . ." Kilsoo Haan material, TKC.

page 311   "But now the Japs have solved . . ." SD.

page 311   "never have gotten the country to war . . ." Interview with Harrison.

page 311   "white as a sheet, visibly shaken." *Shipmate*, Sept. 1977, 28.

page 311   "sitting in a corner with no expression . . ." *Newsweek*, Dec. 12, 1966, 42.

page 312   "And we're putting people into all the . . ." Morgenthau diary, FDR.

pages 312–14   Mrs. Perkins story. Taped interview, CUOH.

page 314   "The President was very patient . . ." Sherwood 433–34.

page 314   "cleared everybody out and said he was going . . ." Murrow letter to Hoehling, Feb. 8, 1962, Hoehling Collection.

pages 314–15   "There is a slight deliberation . . ." Greene account, *Time-Life-Fortune* News Bureau, Dec. 7, 1941.

page 315   "I heard voices and steps . . ." Mrs. Hamlin diary, FDR.

page 315   "But words are futile at a time . . ." K. Marshall 99.

page 315   "I think I'll go and see Old Knox." Interview with Harrison.

Chapter Sixteen   THE SUMMING UP

page 317   Ter Poorten story. Correspondence with Thorpe; Thorpe memorandum.

pages 317–18   Wedemeyer story. Interview with Wedemeyer.

page 317   Ranneft citation. See picture section.

page 317   Robinson story. Interview and correspondence with Ranneft.

page 318   "For a long time I have believed . . ." Ickes diary, Oct. 18, 1941.

page 320   Stahlman letter to Tolley, Nov. 26, 1973. Tolley Collection.

page 320   "I saw and talked to General Marshall . . ." Interview with

Harrison; Fellers letter to Barnes, May 13, 1960, Barnes Collection, UWACH.

page 320   Knox-Kimmel meeting. PHA 24:1955.

page 321   "Gentlemen, this goes to the grave with us." Interview with Fellers.

page 322   "One officer then in intelligence . . ." Hoehling, *Day*, 244.

INDEX

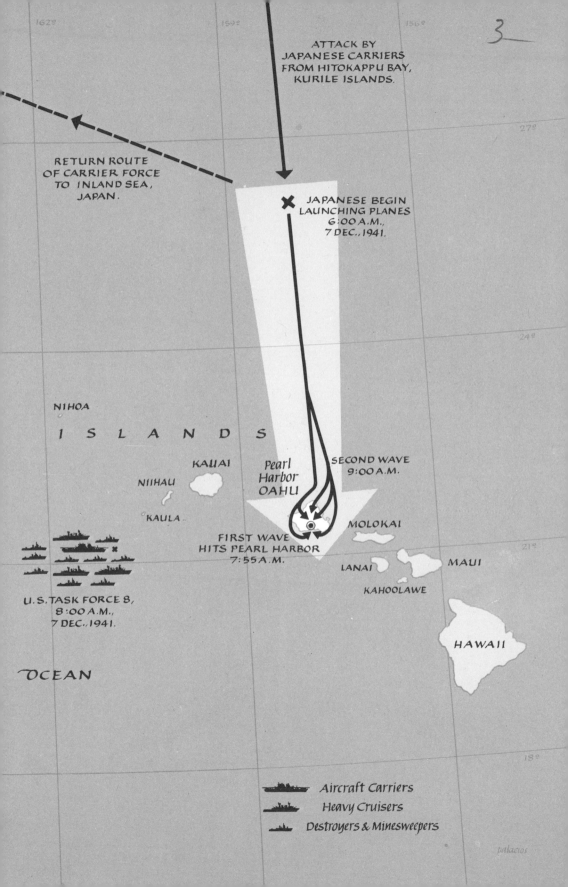

3

ATTACK BY
JAPANESE CARRIERS
FROM HITOKAPPU BAY,
KURILE ISLANDS.

RETURN ROUTE
OF CARRIER FORCE
TO INLAND SEA,
JAPAN.

✕ JAPANESE BEGIN
LAUNCHING PLANES
6:00 A.M.,
7 DEC., 1941.

NIHOA

I S L A N D S

KAUAI

Pearl
Harbor
OAHU

SECOND WAVE
9:00 A.M.

NIIHAU

KAULA

FIRST WAVE
HITS PEARL HARBOR
7:55 A.M.

MOLOKAI

LANAI

MAUI

KAHOOLAWE

U.S. TASK FORCE 8,
8:00 A.M.,
7 DEC., 1941.

HAWAII

OCEAN

Aircraft Carriers

Heavy Cruisers

Destroyers & Minesweepers

palacios